OBLIGING NEED

OBLIGING NEED

Rural Petty Industry in Mexican Capitalism

By Scott Cook and
Leigh Binford

 UNIVERSITY OF TEXAS PRESS, AUSTIN

First Edition, 1990

Requests for permission to reproduce material from this work
should be sent to Permissions, University of Texas Press, Box 7819,
Austin, Texas 78713-7819.

⊛ The paper used in this publication meets the minimum require-
ments of American National Standard for Information Sciences—
Permanence of Paper for Printed Library Materials, ANSI
Z39.48-1984.

Publication of this work was supported in part by the University of
Connecticut.

Library of Congress Cataloging-in-Publication Data
Cook, Scott, 1937–
    Obliging need : rural petty industry in Mexican capitalism / by
Scott Cook and Leigh Binford.—1st ed.
        p.   cm.
    Includes bibliographical references.
    ISBN 978-0-292-74068-6
    1. Home-based businesses—Mexico—Oaxaca Valley. 2. Small
business—Mexico—Oaxaca Valley. 3. Artisans—Mexico—Oa-
xaca Valley. 4. Peasantry—Mexico—Oaxaca Valley. 5. Oaxaca
Valley (Mexico)—Industries, Rural. I. Binford, Leigh, 1948–   .
II. Title.
HD2346.M42O183   1990
338.6'42'097274091734—dc20
                                                            89-49658
                                                            CIP
                                                            Rev.
First paperback printing, 2012

For Teodora Blanco, potter of Atzompa, whose life of creative toil and premature death symbolize the contradictory situation of rural Mexico's artisans

Contents

Tables

Preface

When I first set foot in the Oaxaca Valley in the summer of 1965, I had a premonition that my future career in anthropology might evolve in conjunction with field work there. Several reasons why this premonition was accurate can be best explained through a discussion that is essentially autobiographical. As a transplanted "yankee" growing up in South and Central Texas I became fascinated with Mexico, Mexicans, and the Mexican style of life—or at least with that variant of these which I encountered in San Antonio and Austin and on periodic trips with family or friends to the borderland from Eagle Pass/Piedras Negras to Brownsville/Matamoros and many of the places in between. From the time of my first trip to the border in 1946, and on each subsequent trip by car from San Antonio or Austin, I have experienced a powerful sense of excitement, which accelerates the closer I get to the border. The romance of Mexico, for me, became even more powerful on those occasions when I crossed the border and headed south toward Mexico City and Oaxaca.

Before encountering interior Mexico, I spent two and a half years in Puerto Rico where I discovered that my fascination with "things Mexican" was really with "things Latin American." As a graduate student at the University of Puerto Rico in 1961–62, I was exposed for the first time to the intellectual experience of being able to join two orders of reality: that which is imagined or understood theoretically and that which is understood empirically. Not only did I learn what underdevelopment, peasants, and rural proletarians were in the first sense, but also I was able to substantiate my abstract understanding with concrete experience and observation. Since then I have had a low tolerance for social science that fails to produce knowledge through a balanced combination of deductive and inductive methods.

By the time of my first trip to Oaxaca to participate in a summer field training program in 1965, I had already developed a systematic interest in economic anthropology, and shortly after my arrival, I recognized that the Oaxaca Valley presented a fertile ground for its pursuit. Whereas in Puerto Rico I had seen the moribund remnants of a once-vigorous rural proletariat and peasantry, in Oaxaca I was witnessing a fully viable, vibrant, diverse, and complex social economy in which peasants, artisans, rural proletarians, and other social groupings and classes were commingling. This was in a provincial region renowned for the size and diversity of its indigenous population, but which, in a perhaps underestimated sense, is also quintessentially Mexican. Tourists from all parts of Mexico are attracted to Oaxaca precisely to experience or renew their sense of a "world they have lost" or, at least, of *"another* Mexico," which complements *"their* Mexico." Just as the formation of the Mexican nation-state was profoundly influenced by two native sons of Oaxaca, Benito Juárez and Porfirio Díaz, so too is the contemporary sense of Mexican nationality (or *"mexicanidad"*) nurtured and reproduced through the continuing encounter of Mexicans with Oaxaca.

Unlike the work of many anthropologists, which accentuates the uniqueness of Oaxaca, especially with regard to its cultural history or its ethnic diversity, the principal thrust of my work has been to view Oaxaca in a broader comparative and world-historical framework. I have studied Oaxacans as exemplaries of types of socioeconomic conduct or as embodiments of particular social types, class relations, and class interests, not as bearers of particular variants of indigenous ethnicity or "traditional" culture. Although I am fascinated by many unique features of Oaxaca's sociocultural life, I do not dwell upon them. I think it is misguided in the late twentieth century to view the people of Oaxaca as a congeries of discrete ethnic groupings, as if somehow ethnicity operated to integrate them beyond the level of localities or as if their economic and political future within the Mexican and international capitalist system would be brighter if their ethnic diversity were reconstituted as an organizational or integrative mechanism for sociopolitical ends.

The Oaxacans I have known and studied over the years are, first and foremost, provincial Mexicans who happen to have been born and raised in Oaxaca. The most critical things to know about them as *Mexican* citizens (if one is genuinely concerned with understanding them or promoting their welfare) do not differ from those that must be known about people in other Mexican provinces. The fact that their ancestors were Zapotec, Mixtec, Cuicatec, Mixe, Chatino, and so on surely has less bearing on locating Oaxacans in present-day Mexican capitalism—and in understanding them socioeconomically—than do systematic data on such prosaic variables as birthplace, residence (including residential history), age, gender, household, literacy/schooling, occupation (including job history and position), income, land tenure status, instruments of agricultural, or craft production.

The project upon which this monograph is based is an outgrowth of my earlier work on the production and exchange of *metates* (querns) in four communities (and two separate districts) of the Oaxaca Valley. From its inception, this work was based on the assumption that research should be conducted in more than one locality to assure the broader applicability and representativeness of its results. I was privileged to experience the benefits of collaboration in research of a regional scope by conducting the second year (1967–68) of my field work on the metate industry through an affiliation with the Oaxaca Markets Study Project directed by the late Ralph Beals.

In the summer of 1977, I conducted an interdistrict survey of the incidence of petty industrial commodity production in the Oaxaca Valley and initiated case studies in one community, Tlacolula de Matamoros, a district head town (*cabecera*). This served as a basis for a major project (Proyecto de Estudios Socioeconómicos sobre las Pequeñas Industrias de Oaxaca, or *PESPIDEO*) between 1978 and 1981, which involved field work and data collection in twenty-three sites in three districts (Centro, Tlacolula, and Ocotlán; see Appendix).

It bears clarifying that "Valley of Oaxaca" is a geographical term traditionally applied to the upper drainage basin of the Río Atoyac (see the map in Chapter 2). With two exceptions, all the localities studied are located within the geographical limits of the Valley. The two exceptions, San Lorenzo Albarradas and Santo Domingo Albarradas, which are sites for palm and ixtle processing industries, are mountain villages located several miles outside the geographical Valley. Administratively, however, they both belong to the district headquartered in Tlacolula de Matamoros, located in the eastern arm of the Valley. Economically, their ties are stronger with the Valley than they are with the *sierra;* although, uncharacteristic of most Valley settlements, both San Lorenzo and Santo Domingo have significant economic ties with the Zapotec and Mixe Sierras. Also, Santo Domingo Albarradas has more in common with the Sierra Zapotec culture than with the Valley Zapotec culture.

As it turns out, the two Albarradas communities are the most distant and isolated from Oaxaca City (the state capital and dominant urban center, not only in the Valley but also in the state) of any included in the project. But even in their case, travel time by motor vehicle from the city was about one and a half hours to the nearer of

the two, San Lorenzo, and two and a quarter hours to Santo Domingo. All the villages in the study were linked by unpaved roads to
paved highways leading directly to the city and (with the one exception just cited) were accessible by motor vehicle in one and a half
hours or less driving time from the city; however, it would be mistaken to infer that distance or travel time to Oaxaca City necessarily
has important implications for local economy, society, and culture.
For example, one can find much closer to Oaxaca City poorer and
culturally more conservative communities than either of the Albarradas villages. This simply underlines the fact that locational factors are more often than not outweighed by any number of other factors in determining how a given locality measures up to others in a
district or region.

Of all the important topics not dealt with adequately in the 1978–
1981 project, perhaps the most important is the role of local, state,
and federal government in the economic life of the communities
studied. That role continues to be important, if lacking in continuity, commitment, and integrity. It involves everything from taxation
to credit and technical assistance, not to speak of the exercise of po-
lice powers and conscription. The project archives do contain data
on federal and state government programs in several communities,
especially with regard to artisans; nevertheless, due to the lack of
time, it was not possible to research the topic systematically during
the field work period, and due to the lack of space, it was not possible to treat the topic separately in this monograph. With specific
reference to the craft sector, the excellent study by Victoria Novelo,
Artesanías y capitalismo en México (1976), gives a comprehensive
overview of the role of the federal bureaucracy; however, the role of
government in peasant-artisan communities in Oaxaca is a topic for
a separate, and long overdue, study.

Another shortcoming that I regret is the lack of historical analysis. The project archives contain more systematic historical data, especially from the late nineteenth century to the present, than they
do data on the role of government. Again, time and space constraints
made it impossible to include a write-up of these data in this monograph. In this case, however, the gaps in the literature, while still
substantial, are not so pronounced. Comprehensive studies by Bill
Taylor (1971, 1972), Brian Hamnett (1971), and John Chance (1978,
1986) provide us with an excellent understanding of the colonial
period. Recent pioneering studies by Cassidy (1981) and Chassen
(1986) go a long way toward filling gaps in our understanding of the
development of Oaxaca Valley economy and society in the nineteenth and early twentieth centuries—especially from the Porfiriate

to the Revolution. Finally, the equally pioneering contribution of Helen Clemens (1987a, 1987b, 1988) begins to decipher the complexities of socioeconomic development at the village level in the Valley over the last one hundred years.

To conclude, I should say something about the origin and nature of the collaboration on this monograph. For several months during 1980, Leigh Binford, then a doctoral candidate in the Department of Anthropology at the University of Connecticut, worked for my project in the community of Santa Lucía del Camino, an important site of the brick industry. Among his accomplishments during this period was a detailed observational study of brickmaking, the results of which were incorporated into my book on the brick industry (Cook 1984a).

Following Binford's return to Connecticut in 1981, and during the period of his write-up of a project on agriculture in the Oaxaca Isthmus (district of Juchitán) for his dissertation, I learned of his skills in quantitative analysis and persuaded him to become the project's data analyst. At the time, neither he nor I was aware of the huge number of hours of drudgery and frustration that would be required to complete the analysis of the project's data set.

In short, what began as a professor/student and employer/employee relationship blossomed into a full collaboration between colleagues and friends (Binford completed his Ph.D. in 1983). Notwithstanding the difficulties encountered along the way, we have both enjoyed and profited from the intellectual give and take generated by the analysis. Our contributions to the monograph have been both complementary and joint, with Binford's skewed toward statistical analysis and mine toward ethnographic analysis but converging with regard to theoretical interpretation. Our separate contributions have been subjected to critical readings by the other, and their content has been mutually discussed and jointly approved. We hope that a majority of readers will share some of our satisfaction with the finished product.

Scott Cook

Acknowledgments

As mentioned in the preface, this monograph is based on the analysis of data collected between June 1977 and September 1981 by the Oaxaca Valley Small Industries Project (OVSIP). A pilot study during the summer of 1977 was made possible by a grant from the Social Science Research Council and additional funding from the University of Connecticut Research Foundation. The main project was initiated in September 1978 and operated continuously on location in Oaxaca until September 1981 with funding provided under a grant (No. BNS 78-13948) from the National Science Foundation. Supplementary funding for data processing, analysis, and write-up between 1981 and 1983 was provided by the National Science Foundation (grant No. BNS 81-20103) and by the University of Connecticut Research Foundation. The latter foundation also provided funding for field work in November 1985, as well as periodic supplementary funding for data analysis between 1984 and 1988.

OVSIP was originally sponsored in Mexico by the now defunct Dirección General de Artes Populares (DGAP), Alberto Beltrán, director. Following the demise of DGAP, sponsorship was obtained from the Dirección General de Culturas Populares (DGCP), Rodolfo Stavenhagen, director. DGCP generously provided the project with a full-time staff researcher, Ana Emma Jaillet, who worked as a research assistant with OVSIP from 1978 until 1980. Alejandro Guzmán was the liaison between DGAP and DGCP and the project. His assistance and interest were invaluable and are gratefully acknowledged. In Oaxaca, sponsorship was provided by the Dirección General de Desarrollo Económico within the state government, Ing. Fernando Ávila, director. Manuel Esparza of the Centro Regional de INAH, Pedro Arrieta of INI, Tito Cortés of FONART, Cecil Welte, and Arturo Solis provided assistance, hospitality, and friendship in Oaxaca.

Aside from myself as principal investigator, the 1977 pilot study involved Zoilo García, a doctoral candidate in anthropology at the University of Connecticut, and Fausto Díaz, a *licenciatura* candidate in sociology at the Centro de Sociología (now the Instituto de Investigaciones Sociológicas) at the Universidad Autónoma "Benito Juárez" de Oaxaca. Amelia Pacheco was the secretary/transcriber for the pilot project.

Alice Littlefield of the Department of Anthropology at Central Michigan University was a key contributor to OVSIP during 1978–79. She helped with the design of the principal survey instrument, designed another for use in a study of intermediaries and craft businesses in Oaxaca City, conducted interviews, and was responsible for sampling design and coding during the major household survey phase of the project. She served as acting field director during much of 1978–79. Rosa María Salgado, a social psychologist, also played an important role in the most intensive survey research phase of the project during 1978–79. She conducted interviews and also designed the code book for the principal household survey.

Leticia Rivermar and Javier Tellez, *licenciatura* candidates at the Escuela de Antropología (INAH) in Mexico City, worked for two years as research assistants on the project. They comprised an important component of the survey research team, conducting interviews and coding the results. They also conducted case studies of weaving and embroidery in the district of Ocotlán, completing a joint *licenciatura* thesis on the topic in 1984. Also participating in the household surveys during 1979 was Jim Schillinger, doctoral candidate in anthropology at the University of Connecticut; his contribution was especially noteworthy in the household survey and supplementary interviews conducted in Teotitlán del Valle. Luís García, a potter and son of Teodora Blanco of Atzompa to whom this monograph is dedicated, worked diligently and competently as an interviewer in 1978 and 1979. Amelia Pacheco worked continuously with the project from 1978 until 1981; her duties included general office work, interviewing, and transcribing tape-recorded interviews. Pierre Bernier, a doctoral candidate in anthropology at the University of Connecticut, participated in the household survey and initial brickyard study in Santa Lucía del Camino in 1980. Finally, Hilda Almenas Cook played an important role in household surveys and intensive interviewing during 1979–80. Her unique ability to generate instant rapport with informants helped considerably to improve the reliability of the interview data. Her contribution was especially important in the studies of brickmaking households in Santa Lucía del Camino, of the garment industry households of

Xaagá, and of the palm- and ixtle-working households of San Lorenzo and Santo Domingo Albarradas.

In addition to the yeoman service between 1982 and 1988 performed by Leigh Binford at the University of Connecticut Computer Center, which was acknowledged in the preface, I wish to also acknowledge the assistance of Peter Severance, who was responsible for entering the project's data into the computer and was the first to generate hard copies of preliminary results of the statistical analysis. Jeff Backstrand, doctoral candidate in the medical anthropology program at the University of Connecticut, has also provided periodic "trouble-shooting" services with regard to intractable programming problems.

Leigh Binford joins me in expressing gratitude to Jane Collins and Ray Bromley for their thorough and intelligent readings of the manuscript. Their constructive criticisms, corrections, and suggestions for revision were invaluable in the preparation of the final draft. Of course, we absolve them of any responsibility for the end product.

I would like to thank the editors of *Review of Radical Political Economics* and *Mexican Studies/Estudios Mexicanos* for allowing me to include in this work revised and expanded versions of articles I previously published in their journals.

Last but not least, I wish to gratefully acknowledge the tolerance, acceptance, patience, and cooperation of members of the 1,008 households sampled in the twenty-four survey communities, especially the nearly two hundred persons who agreed to in-depth interviews, household budget studies, and enterprise case studies during 1980 and 1981. I also wish to express my gratitude to the authorities in these communities who permitted us to work there and who, in several cases, offered extraordinary cooperation and hospitality.

Scott Cook

OBLIGING NEED

Chapter 1. Petty Production in Third World Capitalism Today

Introduction: Petty Production in Global Perspective

For centuries, throughout large portions of the globe, petty agri-culturalists and industrialists have set their physical and mental energies to work producing products for direct consumption and for exchange. Even if the instruments of labor employed in this process, like the products they helped to produce, were objects of market exchange, land and labor power were not. The mainstream view in political economy has been that the historic role of capitalist pro-duction is to extend the market exchange process to land and labor power by replacing (often forcibly) kinship- and community-based social relations with qualitatively new sets of social relations based upon private proprietorship of the means of production. This view also assumes that, once established, capitalist organization would inevitably invade all branches of production, subjecting each to a competition- and profit-driven process in which smaller labor-intensive forms of enterprise would be replaced by larger-scale capital-intensive forms. According to this scenario, autonomous petty production would be doomed as labor was drawn completely into capital's orbit both as a producer and as a consumer of capital-ist commodities (cf. Lewin 1985: esp. 114–115); and petty, labor-intensive forms of capitalist production—the putting-out system, workshops, and manufactories- –would give way to machinofacture and the factory form.

If capitalist development had followed this trajectory everywhere, then this book would be presenting the results of historiographic rather than ethnographic analysis. However, the tens of millions of small-scale commodity-producing enterprises in contemporary Asia, Africa, and Latin America, as well as millions more in indus-trialized capitalist economies, which employ unwaged household labor and/or wage labor, evidence the partial rather than complete spread of capitalist production. In rural areas, household-based enterprises usually combine some agricultural production for autoconsumption with commodity production. Additional income is frequently generated through some combination of wage labor and the provision of petty services (including trade), not to mention involvement in many forms of illegal activity, further supplemented by government transfer payments and/or remittances from absent members.

As the twentieth century draws to a close it is clear that small-scale commodity production thrives in the capitalist world economy, not only in the "periphery" but also in the "core." If in some branches of commodity production household-based and other forms of labor-intensive enterprises have all but disappeared, in other branches they have persisted and survived, while in still others they have proliferated.[1] The ubiquitousness of small-scale commodity production in rural and urban sectors of Third World economies suggests that it is not an "aberration from the 'normal' workings of the capitalist system or . . . a result of its imperfect penetration of subsistence economies but . . . an intrinsic aspect of its development, having different emphases at different historical moments and in different locations" (Redclift and Mingione 1985: 11).

The survival or growth of petty forms of production has taken place in the context of horizontal extension and vertical concentration and integration of capitalism, driven by a search for cheap labor and raw materials as well as new markets for realizing sales and investments. This contradictory set of developments, in which capitalist expansion is accompanied by a proliferation of noncapitalist economic activity, presents a real challenge to both modernization theory and orthodox Marxist theory. Neither Rostow's (1960) prediction of the Third World's inevitable take-off into sustained growth nor the classical Marxist claim that capitalist development would break down all precapitalist barriers (Warren 1980; Mandle 1980; cf. Shanin 1986) has proven capable of accounting for the multifaceted structure of the contemporary world economy.

Non-Marxists frequently view the evolution of global capitalism as further evidence for the development of interdependency among co-equal nations, each of which contributes to the common good according to its "natural" or "comparative" advantages (see Emmanuel 1972 for a critique of the classic Ricardian "comparative advantage" thesis). Marxists view these trends as simply the latest manifestations of the negative impact of capitalist exploitation and accumulation. The Marxist case is bolstered by the following observations: (a) while the GNP per capita may have risen for Third World nations as a whole over the course of the last two decades, the gap between the Third World and the First World is increasing; (b) there is a large group of Third World nations, variously referred to as "lesser developed countries" (LDCs) or "low-income developing countries," most of them located in Asia or Africa, whose gross GNP per capita in 1979 was U.S. $370 and below (Crow and Thomas 1983: 14) and has declined both absolutely and relatively in recent years; and (c) the income gap internal to Third World nations based upon the disparity between the incomes of those at the top and the remainder of the population is growing as well (Hoogvelt 1982: 34–45).[2]

In Third World countries like Mexico, there can be little disagreement that, as capitalist development has intensified and spread in industry and agriculture, the daily lives of workers and peasants alike have become more complicated and unpredictable. The absolute numbers, if not the proportion, of the economically active population with more or less stable wage employment have grown, but so has the peasantry as well as those who are nominally "self-employed" in the "informal" manufacturing and service sectors (Worsley 1984: 194–213).[3] Yet, empirical studies show that terms like "marginal" collapse a confusing potpourri of visible and invisible occupations. The term "marginal" crops up more and more frequently as a gloss for the poorest sectors of Third World populations (in the United States they are increasingly referred to as the "underclass"). Worsley (1984: 195) criticizes such formulations for their tendency to aggregate "different kinds of sub-populations which socially and culturally often share little in common beyond their poverty" and posits (1984: 196), instead, eleven occupational categories solely with reference to the Third World urban poor. Portes (1983: 154, 161) has estimated that direct subsistence production, simple commodity production and exchange, and what he calls "backward capitalist production" (which includes small enterprises employing unprotected wage labor and disguised wage workers hired by larger firms under subcontracting arrangements) currently account for 30 to 60 percent of urban employment in most Latin American countries.

In retrospect, mainstream developmentalist thinking (Roxborough 1979: Ch. 2) failed to understand the degree to which, under conditions of capitalist development in the Third World, the reproduction of labor-power would continue to involve household-based production for use and exchange. Capitalism may have reorganized, subverted, and indirectly incorporated noncapitalist production forms throughout the world system, but it has not brought about their disappearance. It may be, as Wallerstein (1983) suggests, more correct to link the *partial* rather than *complete* proletarianization of labor with historical capitalist interests since the reproduction cost of labor is invariably lower when the former condition prevails. This position is supported by the observed tendency for many of today's capitalist firms to, in effect, partially "deproletarianize" labor in order to reduce its cost by "informalizing" certain operations (e.g., avoiding minimum wages and fringe benefits through subcontracting household labor). Thus, in Western Europe in the last decade, "casualization of employment and a concomitant rise in homeworking have been among the most significant aspects of the industrial restructuring process" (Miller 1986: 37).[4] Ironically, this parallels (but does not replicate) a shift centuries ago in Europe of protocapitalist industry from urban centers, where guilds had driven up the cost of labor, to the countryside, where peasant household labor could be employed on an outwork basis for much lower wages (Medick 1981: 53).

Sectors and branches of industry in Mexico, as well as in other Latin American and Third World countries, are also experiencing restructuring processes. However, the linkage between these and labor casualization and, indeed, the possible linkages between large-, medium-, and small-scale enterprises, can only be determined a posteriori. Analysts of "self-employment" should proceed by analyzing enterprises according to specific forms of production and exchange, such as direct subsistence production, petty commodity production, petty commerce, petty industrial capitalist production, and their corresponding social relations. They should also carefully scrutinize the degree to which petty enterprises are, in fact, clandestine (or "informal") and specify the circumstances that make them so. Ideally, this should be done through field investigations of different branches of commodity production for local, regional, national, and international markets. The Oaxaca Valley, located in the central part of the southern Mexican state of the same name (see map in Chapter 2), provides a setting made to order for this kind of inquiry.

Petty Production in the Oaxaca Valley and the Scope of This Monograph

As will be outlined in Chapter 2 and analyzed in detail in the remainder of the book, economic life in the Oaxaca Valley, considered from the rural production side, involves a complex combination of household production for own-use and for exchange, together with petty forms of industrial and merchant capital. The particular combination of forms and the relative importance of each varies from one branch of commodity production to another and, perhaps, from one village to another as well. As practiced today in the Oaxaca Valley, petty industrial commodity production is often physically taxing. In the brick industry, for instance, a man's output reaches the maximum when he is in his early twenties and output falls off drastically after the age of thirty. While work in most craft industries involves considerable skill, often acquired through long periods of apprenticeship, it is also monotonous and demands concentration. Artistic creativity and expression are present to some degree even in the fabrication of the most prosaic commodities like bricks and metates, but the bottom line is that "mass production" and product standardization are necessary conditions of the typical industry's success (see Cook 1982: 199–200; cf. Herman 1956: 365 and Goody 1982: 16). Attesting to the disciplined and organized exertion of the weaver, the plaiter, the needleworker, the carver, the potter, and other artisans is the fact that many Oaxaca Valley artisan products are marketed through tourist and craft outlets around the world and occupy favored places in the wardrobes and on the walls and mantels in the homes of discriminating urbanites.

The strong regional, national, and international demand for artisan products from Oaxaca has not significantly affected the remuneration of the majority of direct producers, whose work is generally low paid. In the early 1980s, embroiderers were earning the equivalent of five cents (U.S.) hourly; treadle loom operators earned about $30 (U.S.) weekly, or seventy-five cents an hour; and the highest-paid producers in our survey, brick-producing households located in two periurban communities near Oaxaca City, earned $35–$70 (U.S.) weekly (but for the social labor of 2–5 household members).[5] With few exceptions these brickyard pieceworkers are landless and have to purchase out of wages all the goods and services they consume, a circumstance that must be taken into account when drawing comparisons between these and workers in other industries more involved in subsistence agriculture.

Because of the low levels of remuneration, a majority of household heads in most rural industries surveyed in the Oaxaca Valley found it expedient to supplement craft production with the small-scale cultivation of food staples (especially corn, beans, and squash) for domestic consumption—thus establishing the predominance of a household strategy that combines petty commodity production with production for own-use. As we will document in subsequent chapters, however, even when these two forms of production are combined with wage labor and petty commerce, the majority of households still have a meager standard of living.

To claim that poverty in the Oaxaca Valley is generalized does not imply that all households are poor or that all are poor in the same way. As in other parts of rural Mexico, unequal access to land and means of production serves as the basis for uneven income distribution and different levels of material well-being. There are differences among peasants and rural industrial commodity producers related to household size and composition, branch of production, position in the production process, access to markets, and so on. These factors affect the amount and value of total output as well as household potential for retaining a portion of its surplus product. Intermediaries, who may or may not have roles in production, are positioned to take a portion of the surplus value created by labor. The actual size of their value share depends upon the scale and location of their market operations (see Chapter 5). Finally, there are small-scale capitalists who regularly hire workers for a wage that is less than the value contributed by them to the commodities they produce for their employers. Assuming that the market price for these commodities exceeds their cost of production (including the wage bill), which of course is a condition of continued enterprise viability, these petty capitalists realize profits.

This monograph interprets the results of research conducted in Oaxaca between 1977 and 1985 on petty agricultural and industrial production in rural household enterprises (see Appendix). It shows how commodity production is organized and operates in different craft industries, as well as the ways in which it combines with other economic activities, such as household chores, agriculture, wage labor, and petty commerce at the local and regional levels. A main focus of our analysis is the potential of household commodity production in different branches to undergo transformation into petty capitalist production, and the identification of the circumstances or forces that promote or limit that potential.

We hope that our study will correct a series of interconnected fallacies about Oaxaca's rural economic life that have been nourished by a prominent ethnopopulist approach. This approach can best be characterized as a form of "ethnicized neopopulism," which combines the celebration of indigenous ethnic pluralism (through the use of the multipurpose, if cryptic, concept of *etnia*) with a genuinely romantic loathing of capitalism. It views capitalism in Oaxaca as an alien system imposed by an avaricious and corrupt *mestizo* bourgeoisie and state apparatus upon the "small domestic production" regime of the "indigenous peasantry." The latter are portrayed (Bartolomé and Barabas 1986: 54) as having "a characteristic specificity and a peculiar economic rationality, that imprints upon them not only their histories and particular languages but also their cultural norms and organizational and ascriptive systems, which they do not share with other nonindigenous peasants . . ."

Not surprisingly, these "indigenous peasants" are inserted into a kin-based communitarian household economy in which self-sufficiency is the goal and capital accumulation and a market orientation are precluded a priori (ibid., 54–56). Commodity production, even in the Oaxaca Valley, is viewed as being undertaken simply to complement agriculture "without the intervention of wage relations" (56). The indigenous "peasant economy" is posited as being in assymetric articulation with the external capitalist economy, and it is only in that separate arena where peasants participate in commodity and wage relations. In a subsequent section of this chapter, and in Chapters 2, 3, and 4, we will present a detailed refutation of Chayanovian dualism—the theoretical linchpin of the ethnopopulist approach outlined above—in its early-twentieth-century Russian, as well as in its latter-day Mexican and Oaxacan guises.

To conclude this section we enumerate and summarize the issues we shall address in this monograph as follows:

1. The relationship of rural industry to agriculture, which in the Oaxaca Valley entails forms of combination of petty industrial commodity production, subsistence agricultural production, and wage labor within household-based enterprises.

2. The internal dynamics of households involved in production for exchange and for own-use with particular focus on the relationship between household size, stage in the demographic cycle, and age/gender composition. We shall also examine the relative contributions of males and females, whether paid or unpaid, to the maintenance and reproduction of households and the ideologies associated with the gender division of labor.[6]

3. The dynamics of capital accumulation and the extraction of surplus value from nonwaged household labor, with special consideration of the potential for, and the conditions under which, wage labor supplements or replaces household labor to achieve petty capitalist accumulation.

4. The relationship of small-scale commodity production to merchant capital with a focus upon the role that the latter plays in promoting or inhibiting the metamorphosis from petty commodity production to petty capitalism.

This analysis will exercise special care in distinguishing between the various types of petty enterprise. In our judgment recent scholarly work (e.g., Benería and Roldán 1987) has been vitiated by failures in three areas: (a) it has not consistently separated commodity producers from service providers or intermediaries; (b) it has conflated independent or autonomous petty commodity producers with dependent outworker units usually located at the end of subcontracting chains; and (c) it has failed to clearly identify the nature of petty capitalist production and to specify its differences from petty commodity production.

Critically Rethinking the Concept of Petty Commodity Production

Much of the literature on petty commodity production exhibits a tendency to define the concept on the basis of the study of specific concrete cases. This often leads to conceptual schemes that are heuristically limited to situations similar to those from which the concept was inductively formulated. In order to avoid such a conceptual straitjacket, we propose the formulation of a broad generic concept, one informed by empirical study but derived, in the first instance, through deductive rather than inductive reasoning. What is required is a concept broad enough in scope to allow us to approach small-scale production in a variety of empirical circumstances.

Apart from the aforementioned issue, petty commodity production has become the object of competing theoretical claims. On the one side are those who maintain that petty commodity production should be theorized as a separate "mode of production," and on the other are those who view it as an economic form subordinate to discrete modes of production (Ennew et al. 1977; Cook 1977). A related problem concerns the conceptualization of the special relationship that exists between the concept of petty commodity production and that of capitalist production; both are forms of commodity production, with the former being simply an elementary or undeveloped form of the latter; although it can also be viewed as merely a heuristic construct valid only in the context of trying to understand capitalism as a mode of production (Cook 1976: 400; Ennew et al. 1977: 309).

Finally, there is debate regarding the relationship that exists between the concept of petty commodity production and that of peasants—with many of the ambiguities and disagreements associated with the latter concept being displaced to the former (e.g., see Ennew et al. 1977; Cook 1977: 382–385). Friedmann (1980), for instance, insists that the two concepts and their empirical referents should not be conflated and are, indeed, separate and distinct.

Many of these debates are unlikely to be resolved until there is more agreement about the definition of petty commodity production. Virtually all writers agree that petty commodity production involves production for market exchange, and most also hold (a) that petty commodity producers (typically equated with peasants) either directly produce some of their own subsistence requirements or produce for exchange in order to acquire their subsistence, and (b) that the means of production either are owned by or are under the control of the direct producers—and that production is undertaken by an unwaged domestic labor force drawn from household membership.

These conceptual points, though, have been subject to a series of qualifications and modifications. Gavin Smith (1985: 100–101) proposed (cf. Cook 1977: 384) that the domestic labor force rarely limits the total of nonwaged labor used in petty commodity production and that such labor is recruited from extrahousehold social relationships. In a more significant modification, Carol Smith (1984) and Joel Kahn (1975, 1978, 1980) contended that waged workers should be considered as generic to petty commodity production as long as petty enterprises do not "revolutionize" the forces of production over time.

Another frequently mentioned criterion of petty commodity production is the relative independence of production units from one another (MacEwen 1979: 110; Gerry 1979: 234). Nevertheless, Kahn (1978: 113–114) asserted that "social relations of equality" exist among producers, and Gavin Smith (1985: 100) included, as an internal feature of petty production, a series of mutually affirmative relationships that involve contributions of labor and money, without which access to the unpaid labor of the peasant community cannot be guaranteed.

Whether conceptualized as a mode of production (e.g., Bartra 1978: 75–90; Kahn 1978, 1980; Davies 1979; Chevalier 1982, 1983) or as a production form (LeBrun and Gerry 1975; Friedmann 1980), petty commodity production has been equated in urban research with the informal sector (Davies 1979: 89) so that the informal sector itself comes to represent "a subsidiary, peripheral and dependent mode of production" (cf. Lewin 1985: 108). More commonly, however, the informal sector is treated without reference to the variety of social relations of production present (e.g., Hart 1973), as noted by a number of writers on the topic: Breman (1977, 1985); Bromley (1978); MacEwen (1979); Portes (1983); Connolly (1985); Lewin (1985). This literature has, nevertheless, definitively demonstrated that petty commodity production is practiced extensively in Third World towns and cities. Curiously, few writers (e.g., Bernstein 1988) have systematically addressed the issues raised by the presence of petty commodity production in both rural and urban areas.

In the following sections we shall attempt to sort out the issues in this theoretical field by making a series of proposals pertaining to the conceptualization and analysis of petty commodity production. Then we shall indicate why our proposals, as opposed to alternative ones, provide a more fruitful basis for the conduct of empirical research. As a first step in this exercise we emphasize the importance of formulating a theoretically rigorous generic concept of petty commodity production without assuming any resemblance to observed conditions in any extant or extinct economy of record. This implies that petty commodity production, theorized generically as a possible form, may or may not be empirically realized in actual social formations.[7]

Our generic concept of petty commodity production contains the following four elements:

1. The regular and exclusive production of products for market exchange.

2. Small-scale private enterprise in which the means of production are privately controlled by direct producers and labor is nonwaged.

3. Mutual independence of production units, ruling out, therefore, the exchange of products within a larger enterprise, such as a factory. It likewise rules out situations in which apparently independent producers are subjected to tight control by merchants or by capitalist enterprises through subcontracting, the supply of raw materials and equipment through putting-out arrangements, and final product purchase.

4. The purpose or result of production may be simple reproduction but *never to the exclusion of capital accumulation or profit,* which may underwrite productivity increases up to the point at which labor must be hired to facilitate further increases.

Our concept of petty commodity production implies the presence of six historical preconditions that Keith Hart (1982: 40) refers to as stages in the "commoditization" of human labor: the embodiment of labor in an object external to the producer, the making of a product for other use (together these imply the presence of the commodity: Cook 1976: 396; cf. Marx 1967: I: 41, 180–181; Engels 1967: 897), the gender division of labor, reciprocal exchange, market exchange, and general purpose money.[8] These six preconditions are represented in political economic discourse by Marx's (1967: I: 146–166) deceptively simple C–M–C (commodity–money–commodity) scheme. It is notable, however, that the concept is not joined to household production. While petty commodity producers will be reproduced through membership in some sort of domestic group, the enterprise itself need not be isomorphic or coterminous with the household. The important point is that petty commodity production may be undertaken for a variety of motives and have a variety of results but its *raison d'être* is to engage labor power, raw materials, and instruments of labor to fabricate artifacts for market exchange. Nothing more, nothing less.

This set of theoretical statements is intended to clarify discourse and serve as a guide to research, but there is no mechanistic means by which it might be used to translate complex realities. For instance, the third element specifies that petty commodity-producing enterprises are "independent" and "relatively autonomous," determinations that require the investigator to examine, among other things, both the structure of the enterprise and its relationship to raw materials providers and the market. In short, identifying a petty commodity enterprise in concrete analysis requires attention to its relationship with, or form of insertion in, the wider economy.

The crucial point is that petty commodity-producing enterprises, like capitalist enterprises, must *regularly produce products for market exchange as a necessary condition of their reproduction;* their production of commodities is neither casual nor occasional but systematic and generalized. What distinguishes petty commodity enterprises from capitalist enterprises, aside from the scale of production, is the peculiar way in which labor is joined to capital. In petty commodity production the direct producer is also the owner-operator of the enterprise who employs nonwaged rather than waged labor. Capital accumulation, then, occurs through the extraction of surplus value from nonwaged labor, including that of the owner-operator (cf. Marx 1963: 407–408).

Given this affinity, if not identity, between petty commodity enterprises and capitalist enterprises, it is logical to assume that when petty commodity enterprises are inserted in a capitalist social formation the "absolute limits of their activity" are regulated by capitalist forms (Gibbon and Neocosmos 1985: 165). Thus, it is important to exclude units from the PCP category that are irregular or situational commodity producers; such units belong to non-commodity-producing modes (cf. Gibbon and Neocosmos 1985). Moreover, as element four in our generic concept of petty commodity production implies, it is equally important to exclude units that regularly produce commodities for profit with hired labor; such units, which still may be small in scale, derive their profits from the exploitation of wage labor and are, therefore, capitalist enterprises.

Petty Commodity Production and Peasant-Artisans within Capitalism

As soon as the term "peasant" enters discourse, it forces a confrontation with complex empirical reality and with two contradictory ideas: "commodity economy" and "natural economy." The term itself is loaded with many contradictory meanings derived from an array of extinct and extant empirical situations that may approximate but never completely meet either the commodity or natural economy models. These characteristics, taken together, make the term "peasant" analytically treacherous and guarantee that any effort to formulate a widely acceptable generic peasant concept will prove fruitless. Strangely enough, however, its usage persists and is widespread. We shall not attempt to explain why we think this may be so, except to observe that the answer probably lies in the perduring fascination of urban scholarship with the heterogeneous social category, the rural "other," to which the term obliquely refers. When we use the term "peasant" in something other than a specified emic sense (i.e., as a gloss for *campesino*), or as a statistical category, we will do so simply as a shorthand way of saying "rural–direct–producer–who–routinely–grows–crops–for–own-use–and/or–for–exchange." "Peasant-artisan," a term that will appear frequently in this study, refers to a peasant who, in addition to growing crops, routinely fabricates *nonagricultural* commodities.

Although peasants and peasant-artisans in capitalist economies cultivate the soil to supply a portion of household consumption needs, they must also obtain cash with which to purchase commodities that they do not produce. Rural direct producers may acquire cash through participation in any number of economic activities, such as sale of crops or the products of household industry, wage labor, or petty commerce. To the extent that peasants and peasant-artisans sell their crops or products in markets for cash, they are petty commodity producers. In other words, our generic definition is applicable to some but not all peasants.[9]

But peasants are also something else, namely, agriculturists who directly produce at least part of their own food supply and, therefore, directly reproduce a portion of their own labor. This notion of peasant evokes the images of "natural economy," autarchy, self-sufficient production, and "subsistence economy."

It can legitimately be said, then, that the peasant notion, aside from other associations that are more empirically or historically grounded (e.g., tribute, tax, or rent payment by a class of subalterns), evokes two contradictory ideas: (a) interdependence based upon commodity production, market exchange, and reciprocity; and (b) independence based upon production for own-use. The extent to which real flesh-and-blood peasants approximate (or have approximated) either of these ideal conditions (commodity economy or natural economy) is clearly a matter for empirical determination. Our own reading of the historical and ethnological record is that most peasants never completely approximate either ideal but live out their lives through some combination of both.

Although we will devote considerable attention to peasants in the course of this monograph, we will be more concerned empirically with peasant-artisans, or what we refer to as Peasant-Artisan Households (PAHs). Peasant-artisans, considered as subjects within a commodity economy (rather than as self-reproductive creatures of a natural economy), share a social condition in which their discrete households or domestic groups (as basic production-consumption units), are *in necessary articulation with other such units as a condition of their own reproduction.* Whereas the basic production-consumption unit among peasant-artisans is the discrete household unit, the basic social reproductive unit is the intercommunity region. Individual household enterprises, as product- and commodity-producing units, are necessarily enmeshed in social relations of production, exchange, and distribution with other such units in their own and in other communities in the outlying region (cf. Cook 1977: 384).

The regular production of products for own-use and for market exchange, without the relative proportions of the two types of production being fixed, is a necessary condition of the material reproduction of peasant-artisan production-consumption units. Production for profit is not a necessary condition but is a *possible* goal and result of peasant-artisan production. Peasant-artisan producers themselves dispose of their surplus product through reciprocity, barter, or market exchange. However, some portion of their surplus product is likely (a concession to the historical and ethnological record) to be appropriated by an extracommunity ruling class and/or the state. Another portion is likely to be redistributed within the local community of household units—often to provision underproducers or nonproducers (cf. Cook 1977: 383).[10]

In a capitalist social formation, the viability of discrete peasant-artisan households (PAHs) and their matrix settlements is achieved through participation in a wider commodity economy with a division of labor of regional, national, and international scope. Within capitalism, PAHs operate in a money economy in which land, labor, and products are either partially or completely commoditized. Consequently, PAHs must acquire cash to assure their reproduction. They can do so by selling agricultural and/or nonagricultural products and/or by selling their labor power for a wage. Also, depending upon their circumstances, they might sell or rent their own land or other means of production to others, lend money, or buy-up and re-sell commodities.

PAHs engage in these activities under a variety of conditions and through many relations over which they exercise little or no control. For example, the locus of control in the sale and purchase of many commodities by PAHs may reside in near or distant capitalist markets that have agents or representatives in the local community or region. Prices in these markets will be set by capitalists to the disadvantage of PAHs as buyers and sellers. This does not mean that PAHs have no space in which to maneuver in accord with their own agenda. It does mean, though, that to a significant extent they will maneuver within a structure and according to a dynamic over which they have little or no control. Their first priority is admittedly to achieve simple material reproduction; however, once this is assured, PAHs often seek to accumulate and invest money capital to expand the productive capacity of their enterprises.

It is also important to remember that PAHs retain the capacity to produce for their own-use. To the extent that they can do so, they diminish their dependency upon cash. However, production for own-use cannot obviate a need for some cash to purchase some means of consumption, tools, or raw materials, and to pay rent (e.g., if land or other means of production are rented), wages (i.e., if household labor is supplemented by hired labor), and interest (i.e., for money borrowed). As enterprises, PAHs within capitalism tend to pursue cash-raising opportunities when their objective circumstances permit.[11]

PAHs in capitalist formations are socioeconomically heterogeneous. Their heterogeneity reflects the impact of a decision-making process regarding choice of activities and allocation of resources in the home production process, choice of activities and job search (or worker recruitment) in the wage labor production process, disposition of the product between sale (marketing) and retention for home use, the formation of net income (sources of income), effective demand (disposition of net income), and so on (cf. Deere and de Janvry 1979: 603). The proposition that this broader approach opens to investigation, one that is central to understanding the dynamics of peasant-artisan life within capitalism, is the following: factors that increase PAHs' level of material reproduction may also augment their capacity for capital accumulation. Discourse surrounding this proposition has been controversial for reasons we will now examine.

The Chayanov Legacy, Dualistic Discourse, and the Nonaccumulation Fallacy

In the economic development/underdevelopment literature from the 1950s down to the present, it has been fashionable to consider household production in the rural Third World as persisting traditionalism and, therefore, anachronistic and inhibiting capitalist development. It has also been viewed as the playing out of a "subsistence first" (Scott 1976) or simple reproduction strategy geared toward household maintenance, or viability, with little or no accumulation potential. In short, petty production has been interpreted as a creature of poverty-driven logic that keeps its subjects/agents poor as long as they practice it. In our judgment these views distort understanding of the dynamics of livelihood and accumulation among contemporary Third World peasantries and preclude the possibility of explaining how rural change occurs and its socioeconomic and political implications.

Our contention is that a primary source of these flawed views lies in the controversial legacy of A. V. Chayanov. As the principal contributor to a neopopulist current of thought (identified as the "Organization and Production School") that enjoyed hegemony in Russian rural studies by 1920, Chayanov saw his views increasingly challenged by the emerging "Agrarian Marxist" current whose leading practitioner was L. N. Kritsman (Solomon 1977: Ch. 2; Cox 1986). The distinctiveness of neopopulist thought stemmed from the fact that its content was based on the study of the Russian family farm, a "commodity-producing economic unit that functioned without the benefit of hired labor" (Chayanov 1966: 273; Solomon 1977: 28), and that it focused on developing a microtheory of the internal dynamics of this production-consumption unit (Solomon 1977: 29).[12] The "Agrarian Marxists," on the other hand, were primarily interested in class differentiation among the peasantry. They "were concerned not with economic disparities as such, but with the relations of subordination and superordination that arose among peasants because of economic disparities in the possession of the necessary means of cultivation" (31).

The Chayanovian notion that lies at the core of the "moral economy" approach to the peasantry is that the limiting factor on household (i.e., "family labor farm") production is a culturally mediated predisposition of the producers to aim exclusively for simple reproduction without material gain, even when circumstances are such that capital accumulation and/or material gain would be feasible economic goals.[13]

Regardless of one's position on the uses, abuses, and limitations of Chayanov's work (see Harrison 1975, 1977; Durrenberger (ed.), 1984; Cook 1985b; Shanin 1986; Maclachlan 1987; Chibnik 1987), its resurrection in post-1966 peasant studies discourse has been accompanied by the revival of a debate over the past, present, and future of small-scale household-based production that was thrashed out during the early decades of this century. We refer, of course, to the "differentiation debate" (Lewin 1975: Chs. 2 & 3; Shanin 1972: Ch. 3; Solomon 1977; Worsley 1984: 108–116). Lenin (esp. 1963, 1972) and the "Agrarian Marxists" (Cox and Littlejohn 1984) were led, through the analysis of rural *zemstvo* census data, to argue that capitalism was developing from within the peasantry, one expression of which was its internal social differentiation. This analysis pitted Lenin and the "Agrarian Marxists" against various agricultural economists led by Chayanov of the "Organization and Production School," whose analyses of the same census data led to the view that the observed differentiation was demographic and circular, not socioeconomic and fostering class polarization.

Suffice it to note that Chayanov distanced himself from many radical populist positions and was by no means antagonistic to many Marxist views (Banaji 1976a; Cook 1985b; Cook and Binford 1986: 26), remaining, according to Shanin (1986: 17), the "nonparty Muscovite intellectual." He was unquestionably an advocate of peasant interests and an admirer of peasant logic and cooperativism. He even wrote, under the pseudonym Ivan Kremnev, a novel about a future peasant utopia in which large urban centers had all but disappeared and the countryside had become "a vast checkerboard cultivated by peasant families organized in cooperatives" (Kerblay 1986: xiv). His work has appealed to subsequent generations of rural specialists, especially in the United States, because of his advocacy of an unorthodox, relativistic approach to the study of noncapitalist economic phenomena, and also because his work presented the possibility of a nonmarxist approach that is systematic, empirical, and operationalizable (Cook 1985b). Not only is his legacy viewed favorably by contemporary scholars who are more or less consciously allied with peasant causes and movements (e.g., in Mexican peasant studies see Warman 1980; Esteva 1983; de Rouffignac 1985) but also his ideas, ironically, have found a following among some Marxists attracted by his views about the subsistence orientation of the family labor farm.[14]

Chayanov and the Marxists in Mexican Peasant Studies

In Mexico, beginning in the 1970s, discourse about the nature of rural economy and society split into two currents that Ernest Feder (1977) in a classic article labeled as the *campesinistas*, or "peasantists," and the *proletaristas*, or "proletarianists."[15] The first current, including such writers as Rodolfo Stavenhagen, Arturo Warman, Hector Díaz-Polanco, and Gustavo Esteva, defended the idea that Mexican capitalism was not capable of destroying peasant production forms for a variety of reasons ranging from capitalism's dependent character to the peasantry's capacity to resist and survive through community-based organizations and relations. The second, or proletarianist current, whose best-known contributor is Roger Bartra (1974, 1978, 1987), argued that the peasantry was disintegrating as its subjects were relentlessly drawn into capitalist markets for labor, land, products, and credit. The *proletaristas* found no "community mechanisms capable of detaining the rural proletarianization process" in modern Mexico (Foladori 1981: 155). By the end of the 1970s, the gap between the two approaches had become so wide that for the *proletaristas* the Mexican peasantry "was nothing more than a large group of inefficient producers being exploited by a retrograde faction of commercial capital," whereas for the *campesinistas* the peasantry was "a reservoir of cheap (in fact captive) household labor on which rested the profits, and therefore the growth, of a considerable part of the modern capitalist system" (Hewitt de Alcántara 1984: 152).[16] It should be noted that not all Marxist writers on rural Mexico in the 1970s were readily classifiable into one or the other of these camps; some, like Luisa Paré (1977) and Sergio de la Peña (1981), seemed to straddle them.[17]

Curiously, the key protagonists in both camps accepted the idea of a specific "peasant" economy, mode of production, or production form (e.g., de Appendini and Almeida 1976: 36–37; Stavenhagen 1978; Warman 1980; Bartra 1978: 75–90) distinguished from the capitalist economy by its undifferentiated and nonaccumulative character—even though admittedly inserted in, and surrounded by, capitalism. This strikes us as being a Marxian version of the oft-criticized neoclassical dual economy model that dominated underdevelopment discourse in the 1950s and 1960s: two economies or modes of production bifurcating one social totality, one capitalist and the other peasant, one dominating and the other dominated, linked mainly by market relationships. This approach has the added disadvantage of perpetuating a sterile brand of functionalism in which capitalism is viewed to benefit from the cheap food and labor of the peasant sector that it simultaneously props up and undermines (cf. Bartra 1974).

In a notable exception to the thesis of articulation of dual economies or modes (cf. Hewitt de Alcántara 1984: 143–146; Rello 1976; Wasserstrom 1976, 1983), Sergio de la Peña finds no evidence of any noncapitalist mode or sector in the four rural communities that he characterizes as integrated within the capitalist mode of production, although "noncapitalist productive processes and traits of past modes may persist" (1981: 62). Nevertheless, he continues to accept the notion of "refunctionalization" by capitalism of peasant elements—a process important in the articulationist approach (cf. Hewitt de Alcántara 1984: 148).

Another protagonist in the debate, Guillermo Foladori (1981: 159–161), rejects Bartra's (1978: 75–76) notion of a simple commodity mode of production that is secondary and subordinate to the capitalist mode in the Mexican social formation and conceives of one commodity economy with petty and capitalist spheres integrated by the same law of value. Through this conceptual innovation, with which we are in fundamental agreement, Foladori neatly circumvents the dualism of the articulation and refunctionalization theses.

Even when acknowledged by protagonists in the debate that the Mexican peasantry is socioeconomically differentiated (e.g., Paré (ed.), 1979: 7), the theoretical ramifications of this differentiation are ignored. It is either viewed statically (and as analytically unproblematic) or as an effect of externally imposed capitalism rather than of endogenous capitalist development. For example, Roger Bartra (1974: 61–66, 77–78, 147–150) reviews much of the data and interpretative schemes dealing with socioeconomic differentiation among the rural Mexican population and conceptualizes it as a "system of classes, not a simple sum or aggregate of social groups" (151). Without explicit reference to the Leninist literature on rural class analysis, Bartra proceeds to statically conceptualize the peasant class as encompassing two strata, the middle and the accommodated. He places the bulk of the small rural direct producers—who he calls "semi-proletarians" and "pauperized peasants"—outside the "peasant class" but inside the capitalist class structure (154–155). Bartra's justification for this innovation is that the peasantry is constituted as a single class by its mode of production, which, for him, is petty commodity production characterized by landed household production for use and for exchange, which may yield either subsistence without accumulation for the middle peasants or subsistence with accumulation for the accommodated peasants (72–79, 154).

With the two-in-one peasant class concept, the dynamic of rural social differentiation is explainable, for Bartra, only as "a creature of deformed capitalist development" (Bartra 1974: 155). Accordingly, peasant direct producers are socioeconomically inert within petty commodity production and only become upwardly or downwardly mobile through their involvement in capitalist relations (cf. Foladori 1981: 133; Bartra and Otero 1987). To Bartra's credit, despite the shortcomings of his handling of peasant differentiation, he does acknowledge that some peasant petty commodity producing units do accumulate capital that can be productively reinvested (1974: 78). With this exception, however, Warman's assertion that "the peasantry is the social segment which through a productive relationship with the land succeeds in subsisting without accumulating" (1974: 118; cf. 1980: 285) would seem to find no dissenters among other key protagonists in the debate. It is precisely here that the ghost of Chayanov haunts Mexican peasant studies.

In his critique of peasantist thinking, de Janvry (1981: 103) considers the Chayanovian principle of nonaccumulation as necessary to the viability of the dualistic model: "it is necessary to assume that peasants do not produce for profit in order to show that the peasant mode of production, with its single class, has internal laws of reproduction." Obviously if peasants are assumed to produce for profit, then random and unpredictable differences in the size and demographic composition of the household labor force, quality of the land, and so on would almost certainly lead to differences in agricultural and manufacturing output and would over time result in capital accumulation, investment, and expanded reproduction, on the one side, and proletarianization, on the other. If the dualistic approach revolving around a concept of a separate peasant economy is to be sustained, this heterogeneity of access to land and means of production can only be accounted for by assuming that external capitalist activities cause the impoverishment of those peasant households that for one reason or another have been unable to devise successful strategies of survival and resistance.[18]

One reason the Chayanov-inspired moral economy model of the self-sustaining peasant household production-consumption unit continues to thrive in the peasant studies literature is because rural Third World empirical reality appears to present us with living replicas of the ideal model. Like Chayanov's originals, these replicas are usually identified statistically in discourse about Latin America as comprising a "middle peasant" stratum in the rural social structure and occupy a space between the *minifundio* or subfamily farm and the capitalist farm (see de Janvry 1981: 109–116).

In rural Mexico and elsewhere in rural Latin America, however, the space for the Chayanovians' putatively self-sustaining "middle peasant" unit is increasingly squeezed by the commoditization of land, labor, and products associated with capitalist development (not to speak of demographic increase and continued fragmentation of landholdings through inheritance). Nevertheless, a non-self-reproducing version of the "middle peasant" cycle of reproduction does, indeed, persist in regions like the Oaxaca Valley. Whereas the ubiquitous insertion of "middle peasants" in external commodity and cash circuits is permanent, their degree of involvement in commodity production and monetized exchange is conjuncturally variable—a thesis that will be substantiated in Chapter 4.

The real issue for analysis, we argue, is not whether such units exist, but what they indicate about the dynamic of differentiation within the rural population. Obviously, the Chayanovian notion of self-reproducing peasant households is at odds with both the concept and the reality of peasant class differentiation that occurs hand-in-hand with involvement in petty commodity production. To the degree that rural populations are regularly involved as direct producers in commodity production, a market orientation sensitized to cost-benefit logic, capital accumulation, and class relations will develop among them in a natural way. In the words of Guillermo Foladori (1981: 30; cf. 18–19), one of the few contributors to the Mexican peasantry debate of the 1970s who recognized that social differentiation is a sui generis process of commodity economy: "Independently of capitalists who may arrive from the city, of the credit banker or of whatever type, commodity production itself engenders day to day, through competition in the market, social differentiation and capitalist relations."

Toward Untying the Gordian Knot of Dualism in the Neopopulist versus Agrarian Marxist Debate

The key question here is whether rural petty commodity producers integrated into capitalist markets are, as worker-owners, personifications of the contradictory relations within capitalism (cf. Gibbon and Neocosmos 1985; Bernstein 1988). If so, their differentiation into workers or capitalists must be understood to reflect (at least partly) the outcome of contradictory forces within petty commodity production itself. There would be no "either/or" question as to pauperization, simple reproduction, or capital accumulation since all three conditions would necessarily be present as possible for subjects in any commodity economy. Commodity economy, not petty commodity production or capitalism, then, would be the matrix of differentiation.

The Chayanov-influenced protagonists in the debate about the status of the Mexican peasantry—who posit a separate peasant economy (or petty commodity mode of production) and, thus, are committed to a dualistic conception of the Mexican economy—ended up in an explanatory impasse. They failed to produce explanations of three critical questions posed by their approach: (a) what is the nature of the distinct social relations of the peasant economy within another (i.e., the capitalist) economy? (b) how are the means of reproduction of the noncapitalist economy distinct from and yet articulated with the capitalist economy? and (c) how is simple reproduction a necessary outcome of the functioning of petty commodity (or peasant) relations of production? This explanatory failure exposes serious flaws in the theory that produced it.

There are some important differences between the idealized Chayanovian model—with its empirical referent exclusively targeted on a statistically homogeneous "middle peasantry"—and any actual population of rural petty commodity producers in a region like the Oaxaca Valley. First, according to the model, petty commodity producers (as "middle peasants") are *behaviorally inclined* toward simple reproduction, that is, they are not profit seeking or investment minded, but seek exclusively to provision their households at some acceptable level (based upon community standards) beyond physical subsistence. Against this Chayanovian view, we argue that simple reproduction within capitalist socioeconomic formations is better understood as a product of an objectively imposed set of structural conditions; it is an unintended, rather than an intended, outcome of peasant-artisan planning or behavior as we shall demonstrate in Chapter 3. As de Janvry (1981: 105) aptly observes with regard to Chayanovians: "they confuse the inability of peasants to capture profits with their presumed nondesire for profits" (de Janvry 1981: 105). The blunt fact is that, within capitalism, some peasants make profits and most peasants desire them.

Second, rural peasant-artisan households are not undifferentiated, except for size and age/sex composition of their membership, as the Chayanovians claim. Rather, they are differentiated by the scale of their enterprises, by the value of their productive and nonproductive assets, by the magnitude and value of their output, and, most important, by the relations of production that operate between their house-holds. As we will show in Chapter 4, this socioeconomic differentia-tion within a peasant-artisan population may be partly attributable to demographics, and, for want of valid indicators, it may or may not be directly indicative of class relations. Nevertheless, the Chayano-vian assumption of an equilibrative or homeostatic "invisible hand" that propels peasant-artisan households toward a state of budgetary balance between production (or income) and consumption (or ex-penditures)—and, thus, qualifies them as middle peasants—is very much at odds with socioeconomic inequality and, most important, inequality in access to land and means of production.

In sum, commodity economy, even when conceived wholly in ag-ricultural terms, generates diversity among rural direct producers. When industrial branches of the division of labor are also consid-ered—they must be to understand a rural economy of the Oaxaca Valley type—the diversity multiplies. These statements must not be read as an anthropological retreat to the sanctuary of empirical com-plexity but, rather, as a call for a reconstituted theory of the peasan-try that is attuned to the real world of rural direct producers and petty enterprisers within neocolonial capitalism.

Autonomy versus Dependency: Petty Commodity Production or Disguised Exploitation?

Rather than pose the question of whether the growth and develop-ment of small enterprise is possible, we agree with Hubert Schmitz (1982: 6) that it is analytically more fruitful to inquire "under what conditions" it might occur. The pursuit of an answer to this ques-tion obliges us to examine the economic and political environments in which small enterprises are embedded. It reorients fieldwork and analysis away from an exclusive focus upon the internal characteris-tics of the enterprises themselves toward the ways in which the in-ternal features (both objective and subjective) interact with and are shaped by the wider economy. In the underdeveloped areas of the Third World, the wider economy will be capitalist; but this does not mean that the degree of capitalist control or development is uniform throughout a given national economy, or that the processes and forms through which capital subordinates labor are invariant from one branch of enterprise to another. On the contrary, the empirical record in both urban and rural studies shows the extraordinary com-plexity not only of relationships between commodity-producing en-terprises and labor but also among the enterprises.

Among the issues to consider when studying the prospects for small enterprise development that are raised by the unevenness of capitalism are control over the production process and independence from other enterprises and merchants. Another related issue concerns the potential for petty commodity producing enterprises to pass the threshold of petty capitalism through a process of "endo-familial accumulation," that is, capital accumulation based upon the unpaid labor of household members and thus conditioned by the size and demographic makeup of the household as well as by its access to economic resources (Cook 1984a: 199–200; 1984c: 27–30).

Regarding the first of these issues, Schmitz (1982: 21) notes that "one needs to know to what extent the small producers are independent or simply an extension of the production network of large firms, a sort of disguised wage labor." Equally critical, however, but overlooked by Schmitz is the possibility that exploitative relations may develop between households in the same branch (i.e., of agriculture or industry). This issue was first identified and examined by members of the Kritsman group in Russia in the 1920s, who suggested that very few households conducted farming completely independently and "thereby raised doubts about the concept of a middle peasant as a self-sufficient independent farmer with different interests from the rich and poor peasants" (Cox 1984: 58). Enterprise independence, therefore, is a double-sided issue involving vertical (subordination to large firms) and/or horizontal (dependence upon other household producers for access to capital, markets, raw materials, and so on) linkages.

The important distinction between these two kinds of enterprise independence is partially clarified by the application of Marx's (1977) discussion of the "formal" as opposed to the "real" subordination of capital (Foladori 1981: 143–154; Chevalier 1983). In the case of formal subordination, capital (either merchant or industrial) leaves the means of production in the hands of the direct producers and "subsumes the labor process as it finds it, that is to say, it takes over an *existing labor process* developed by different and more archaic modes of production" so that "these changes do not affect the character of the actual labor process, the actual mode of working" (Marx 1977: 1021). Thus, the labor process is subordinated to capital and the conditions of production confront the producer "as alien property," conditions most likely to occur where rural and urban property, previously oriented toward the satisfaction of the needs of the household "are transformed into autonomous branches of capitalist industry" (1026–1027). Because formal subsumption does not affect the forces of production or the character of the labor process, surplus value extraction can only occur through the intensification of labor or the prolongation of the working day (absolute surplus value). In fact, capital is accumulated in small-scale capitalist workshops and manufactories in precisely this way.

To the formal subsumption process Marx (1977) counterposed real subsumption by capital. Here labor is fully proletarianized and the forces of production undergo a constant revolution, making it possible to raise the level of surplus value by altering the proportion of surplus labor to necessary labor (relative surplus value), for example, by raising labor productivity through mechanization or by cheapening the cost of wage goods and, hence, of wage bills.

It is reasonable to assume that Marx viewed the structural change from formal to real subsumption as both progressive and inevitable (1967: I: 134–138) once "free" labor comes into being. Although his assumption of the progressiveness of this change remains moot, and his assumption of its inevitability wrong, Marx's distinction between formal and real subsumption reminds us that capitalism embraces a wide range of capital/labor relationships. While his discussion of formal subsumption is not particularly helpful in explaining how small-scale capital develops in the first place, it does provide a corrective for many urban researchers who have treated the informal sector of the economy as the site where small-scale independent industrial and commercial enterprises combine enterpreneurial drive with a level of remuneration commensurate with the "formal" capitalist sector (Hart 1973).[19]

Independence from capital, in both urban and rural petty enterprise, requires three conditions: (a) juridical ownership of the means of production; (b) direct appropriation of the profits of the enterprise; and (c) control over the decision-making process associated with production (MacEwen 1979: 107). These conditions—and the independence based upon them—are usually matters of degree. A main point is that the more subordinated a household-based enterprise, the less its opportunity to retain the surplus value that its workers generate and, therefore, the less its potential for accumulation and enterprise expansion/transformation. Judgments about independence cannot be based upon just the examination of employment status but must involve the investigation of both enterprise structure and the organization of the branch of production in which the enterprises under consideration operate (Schmitz 1982: 3, 193). Scrutinized this way, many of the formally independent petty enterprises in the urban informal sector invariably turn out to be so thoroughly subordinated to capital that petty producers dissolve into wage workers "even though a pretense of autonomy is kept up on both sides" (Gerry 1979: 246). Cook (1984a: 124–130, 194–200) has pointed out how the piece-wage system is a particularly effective mechanism for integrating direct producers into capitalist enterprises while cloaking their exploitation behind a façade of quasi independence.

For instance, Schmitz (1982: 81–122) provides us with a cogent analysis of the hammock industry in northeast Brazil (Fortaleza) in which numerous workshops and even more homeworkers are little more than extensions of the production networks of bigger firms, dependent upon them for raw materials (cotton yarn) and semifinished work (cf. Littlefield 1978). Even if the petty producers become independent, Schmitz notes, they are unlikely to earn more than two or three times the minimum wage (or little more than what is earned by a wage worker in a hammock factory). A similar situation was reported in the textile/garment industry and the henequen tapestry industry in Michoacán, Mexico, which were examined in a pioneering study by Novelo (1976: 210–227). Roldán (1985), also attentive to the issue of control, studied 140 female outworkers in Mexico City in the branches of joinery, plastics finishing, textiles, the confection of garments, electrical component assembling, metal sorting, and a wide range of miscellaneous activities drawn together by the fact that they represented a single stage in the creation of a final product for the market. Seemingly proletarianized, these women retained control over a portion of the production process, but to the benefit of capital, which no longer had to assume the total cost of maintaining and reproducing labor power. Nevertheless, their involvement in subcontracted homework is not totally negative. As noted by Benería and Roldán (1987: 169): "According to the homeworkers, their wages, no matter how low, can be used as a lever to secure a minimum space of autonomous control; as a mechanism to pursue goals of household well-being; and to ameliorate the damage to self-image caused by economic dependency on their husbands." This issue of "independence" takes on additional dimensions when examined from the perspective of intrahousehold gender relations (see Chapters 3 and 5 for a discussion of these dimensions in the rural Oaxaca Valley context).

Even in the case of highly dependent household industry, capital accumulation and enterprise expansion are sometimes possible at the lower or household level of subcontracting chains as evidenced in the work of Jorge Alonso (1983). He studied the garment industry in one area of Mexico City (Neza), which is full of clandestine, home-based workshops of "semi-independent producers" who assemble and sew (*maquilar*) precut cloth put out by clothing enterprises located in the downtown area. These enterprises have reorganized themselves from congregated manufactories to dispersed household workshops as a way of surviving competitively without incurring the costs of modernization and capital intensification. Alonso is critical of these enterprises for "superexploiting the unorganized labor force" and for contributing "to the stagnation of the Mexican clothing industry and not to its development and modernization" (171).

In an earlier study of the same industry in another area of Mexico City (Ajusco) Alonso determined that what appeared at first to be small and medium-sized capitalist workshops (in which the facilities, machinery, and other means of production were privately owned by an individual who employed several pieceworkers) turned out to be a dependent production unit (maquilero) within a larger matrix enterprise (taller matriz) (Alonso (ed.), 1980: 193–194). The latter, through its control of the design and cutting process, the raw material supply (factory made cloth), and the market, was able to capture the lion's share of the surplus value generated in the dependent unit, thus relegating the proprietor of the latter to little more than a disguised proletarian status (197). However, it is clear from the data presented that, in this particular case, the subordinate assembly unit had a prior history of capital accumulation based upon exclusive reliance on household labor, which, combined with other sources of capital, facilitated the expansion of the enterprise (including the purchase of twenty-four industrial sewing machines and an enlarged locale) (195). How and why the enterprise ceased to accumulate capital—since presumably prior accumulation also occurred as a maquilero within the matrix enterprise—is not clear.

Significantly, in a later study, Alonso notes that the seamstresses "dream of having their own workshop, their own small business that will grow with the years" (1983: 171). To some extent such dreams are apparently being realized (though Alonso does not admit this) when what he calls "unipersonal" workshops become "multipersonal" as more household members or hired employees are absorbed into the production unit (163–164). Possibly, this last stage would involve the passage from petty commodity production to petty capitalism (as it did in the case of the Ajusco maquilero), with the multipersonal workshop still subordinated to downtown industries and always threatened with the loss of its raw materials supply (especially in the face of a major market downturn), but until that time extracting surplus value from its small wage labor force.

The preceding discussion shows that, like the "peasant economy," the "informal sector" is characterized by heterogeneity. Indeed, much of the criticism we made regarding the peasant concept is also applicable to the informal sector concept. In our opinion, neither term should be used as anything other than a general empirical marker. To formally conceptualize these terms as representing separate spaces in the capitalist economy is to invite the reification of petty production by obscuring in abstractions its empirical complexity as well as the relations that condition the performance of petty enterprises.

Household Production, Capitalism, and the Articulation Problem

The trajectory of household production in a capitalist social economy—especially regarding the involvement of households in capitalist relations—is a complicated issue that provokes controversy in both academic and political circles. Many scholars ignore the relational character of household production and view its dynamics as internally generated. Others treat its dynamics as an outgrowth of the interaction between household enterprises and extrahousehold conditions. Both of these approaches suffer from paradoxical thinking, at once one-sided and dualistic, in which household production (for use and exchange) is either conceived as self-determining or as determined by capitalist production. Contrary to the two prevailing approaches, we insist that the total field of investigation be conceptualized as a single commodity economy containing multiple forms, relations, and processes whose interaction is guided by multiple, or at least mutual, causation. In Mexican rural studies, as we have seen, petty producers are regularly portrayed as bearers of their own economy or mode of production. Confronted with our data on Oaxaca Valley households, this paradoxical notion of a separate but subsumed peasant economy, or petty commodity mode of production, dissolves. In its place emerges a concept of a single, complex, regionally and locally segmented commodity economy encompassing a variety of domestic units, including those of producers for own-use as well as petty commodity producers in various socioeconomic circumstances, of capitalists, and of wage laborers (usually paid by piece rate). It is obvious that all of these subjects act within the same economy. It is also obvious that there are differences in their modes of involvement in that economy, as well as in the aims and the material results of their participation. We are convinced that there is little empirical or theoretical basis for interpreting such differences as reflective of participation in an economy within an economy (Cook 1988: 73).

Within this unitary structure, simple reproduction without capital accumulation will characterize the situation of many petty producer units for a variety of reasons over which they have no control (e.g., prices of producers' and consumers' goods, prices of the labor power or products they sell). It is important to emphasize that this is a condition that these households would rather not experience; it is not a condition that embodies their expectations, their goals, or their aspirations. On the contrary, most of them seek to emulate the successful capitalist enterprises in their industries regardless of how petty these may be. This reinforces the theoretical notion that peasants and peasant-artisans, as joint owners/workers in household-based commodity-producing enterprises, combine characteristics of capitalists and wage laborers in a single contradictory social location (Gibbon and Neocosmos 1985; Bernstein 1986, 1988).

If there is any other approach that has produced as much misunderstanding in Third World rural studies as that which considers peasant behavior to be explainable exclusively within the bounds of "peasant economy," it is the approach that reduces peasants to dependents of external capitalism.

The idea that rural direct producers, more often than not, respond to what external capitalists do (or somehow serve the interests of capitalist enterprise or capital accumulation beyond the peasant sector) has been widely accepted since Eric Wolf's (1955) classic article conceptualized the fluctuating impact of the world capitalist market upon varieties of Latin American peasantry. Even Roseberry's (1983: 208) recent characterization of peasantries as "'precipitates' of the uneven development of capitalism and of forms of accommodation to particular directions that development may take"—notwithstanding his reservations about the "precipitate" metaphor (206–207) and his careful critique of the Marxist literature—is still burdened with the one-sidedness of Wolf's earlier thesis.

The same one-sidedness is evidenced in Novelo's (1976) pioneering study of craft production and capitalism in Mexico. Although she recognized the presence of a petty capitalist form of production of "artisan commodities," which was developmentally linked to a household form, she tended to view this development or expansion of petty production as responding entirely to stimuli from the dominant capitalist sector. More specifically, petty forms of craft commodity production—whether of the household or manufactory type—exist in an economy dominated by capitalist factory production only because a specific demand for handicrafts, especially derived from tourism, cannot be met by factory production (222). This approach ignores factors which influence petty production from the supply side.

A more extreme example of a one-sided approach is an otherwise incisive contribution to the macrosociological literature (Cockcroft, 1983) where peasants, petty traders, and petty industrialists are indiscriminately lumped together as "proletarians." Household production for own-use is seen as a fund of surplus value for big capitalist enterprises. Self-employed petty commodity producers and petty capitalist employers are unmasked as proletarians because the surplus value their enterprises generate allegedly flows into the coffers of big capitalists. The employees of petty industrial employers are accused of suffering from false consciousness if they view their own employers as exploiters instead of the big national and transnational capitalists. The "penny capitalist" (Tax 1953) ideology of the Mexican countryside is branded as a creature of big national and transnational capitalist accumulation. In short, Mexican capitalism is reduced to the status of a puppet on the string of big capitalist puppeteers who are the masters of the international capitalist arena. Its laws of motion are identified as indistinguishable from those of the "mainstream of capitalist development/underdevelopment" that operate exclusively to assure a flow of profits for big capital and to generate immiseration or, at best, simple reproduction for the masses of direct producers, petty traders, and petty industrialists (Cockcroft 1983: 89, 97–98; cf. Cook 1984b: 77).

In the same vein, peasants are portrayed as inert, lacking initiative, and completely reactive to external capitalist-induced stimuli in most of the Mexican rural studies literature. They are seen to participate in capitalism only as buyers of capitalist products or sellers of their products and/or labor to capitalists, but always as exploited, losers of economic value, never as exploiters or accumulators. The situation is so one-sided that, in the words of Stavenhagen, "the peasantry transfers [to the capitalist sector] . . . not only its economic surplus but . . . a part of its income needed for survival." Therefore, "the peasant economy not only fails to embark upon a process of capital accumulation, but is generally to be found involved in a process of progressive decapitalization" (1978: 33). It is not surprising that, according to Stavenhagen, "the maintenance and even the constant re-creation of the peasant economy is functional for the capitalist system" (35). Its functions include staying on the land and out of the overcrowded cities, serving as a sanctuary for temporary members of the proletariat, reproducing labor for capitalists at a low cost, and serving as a reserve of cheap labor. Clearly, there is no room in this approach for capital accumulation by rural direct producers.

This same capital-centric functionalist scenario is more or less implicit in Bartra's characterization of Mexican peasants as pawns in a subsumed process of "permanent primitive accumulation" (1974: 23).

Although Warman's writings contain important insights into the nature and development of the peasantry, little in our reading makes us disagree with Foladori's contention (1981: 27–28) that Warman's work is flawed by notions of a "different, alien capitalism, that comes from the exterior toward peasant communities" and that it is "foreign capital that tends to transform peasants." It is doubtful that one could find any two scholars more firmly entrenched on opposite sides of the *campesinista-descampesinista* split in Mexican rural studies than Warman and de la Peña, yet curiously, Foladori's critique of Warman on the issue of capitalism is equally applicable to de la Peña. It goes without saying that not one trace of the capitalism that de la Peña (1981) finds in his four rural communities is, according to his analysis, seen as having any roots whatsoever in indigenous or local commodity production; rather, it is viewed as penetrating those communities exclusively from the national or international economy.

It is, of course, erroneous to fail to recognize the existence of petty rural capitalism in Mexico or that petty rural enterprises can become regular employers of wage labor. As Gavin Smith's (1979: 307) work in Peru demonstrates, though, even such a recognition does not suffice to overcome dual economy thinking according to which rural petty producers are relegated to a subsumed economy with the "ineluctable tendency of accumulation and expansion . . . firmly located in the specifically (large-scale) capitalist mode of production." The case of Novelo (1976) is also illustrative. In her search for the "meaning that small family or independent production acquires when it takes place in a capitalist system of production" she finds that, "not only does a dual economic system following different roads (capitalist–non-capitalist) not appear but there is a unity in that the first makes use of the second to assure its reproduction and the second produces for the first and consumes its products, to survive by picking up the crumbs that the first offers it" (232–233). Thus, in the space of a few sentences dualism is rejected rhetorically but reinforced discursively.

We argue for a complete rejection of dualistic thinking and for the acceptance of a unitarian commodity economy concept. Once this is done, analysis can then proceed to address issues of enterprise dynamics, differentiation, and relations without explaining one category of enterprises (e.g., petty or peasant) in terms of another (e.g., big or capitalist). In short, under conditions of commodity economy, capital accumulation occurs through the actions of petty commodity producers and capitalists of all types and scales in various branches and regions of the economy. Their concern is not with the interests of capital accumulation in general (or of the capitalist system) but with the interests of their particular enterprises. In pursuing those interests, they may compete, cooperate, or be mutually indifferent, and the relationships between them may be assymetrical and will, in any case, affect performances and outcomes—so that persistence, disappearance, or proliferation of enterprise forms may ultimately be at stake in this dance of commodity production. Capital accumulation may be a stimulant in this dance, but it operates as such among all commodity-producing forms, not just among those that are highly capitalized.

As we have argued above, only one Mexican commodity economy exists; this means that analysis must proceed without assuming that different rationalities or logics operate for special sets of actors within exceptional spaces. Rather, the assumption should be that individual and unit performance in the commodity economy is market driven and rational but will be affected by the different material circumstances in which these actors are located. Clearly, the differentiation of enterprises, which is manifested empirically through different scales and types of organization within a heterogeneous and variegated commodity economy, requires explanation. One such explanation may have to do with issues like economies of scale, which make larger units competitively more viable than smaller units. This kind of process will occur throughout the entire economy, however, not just in rural or urban sectors, or in big enterprise and small enterprise sectors, and so on. The expansion of enterprise scale and commodity-producing capacity and the movement of enterprises from conditions of viability to nonviability occur ubiquitously, if selectively, in the economy. Today's capitalist may be yesterday's petty commodity producer, just as tomorrow's petty commodity producer may be today's capitalist. In commodity economies these processes occur in the city as well as in the countryside and in agriculture or industry. It so happens that petty commodity production, which is indigenous to provinces like Oaxaca, in addition to contributing to the subsistence of direct producers and providing surplus value to capital (merchant, industrial, commercial, and financial) also generates capital to fund its own expansion. Over time, this process may transform petty commodity enterprises into petty capitalist enterprises. This is merely an example of the many processes that are neither visible nor explainable from a dualistic perspective. The fact that these processes do occur and can be documented empirically simply proves the bankruptcy of that perspective.

Petty Commodity Production and the Law of Value

As with the problem of peasant differentiation, it is unlikely that a scholarly consensus will ever be reached about the significance and applicability of the labor theory of value. Our position is that, despite the never-ending controversy about the transformation problem, the labor theory of value is a sine qua non of Marxist analysis and, as such, must be addressed in any Marxist economic study. However, given space limitations, all that we intend to do here is briefly summarize the recent history of a specific debate about the applicability of the labor theory in Mexican rural studies and outline our own position.

The labor theory of value or, more precisely in the case before us, the question of whether or not peasant household labor should be accounted for in terms of wage equivalents has been approached from two perspectives, the neopopulist and the Marxist. The neopopulist position developed through the ICAD (Inter-American Committee for Agricultural Development) studies begun in 1965 (see Hewitt de Alcántara 1984: 123–128, 137–139). Its most significant publication, which appeared in 1974 (Reyes Osorio et al.), held that, since peasant producers did not calculate the value of household labor in terms of the going wage for agricultural labor, labor cost should not be included in the comparative cost-benefit analysis of peasant and capitalist enterprises. In other words, labor was treated as an abundant and unpaid factor. The result of this treatment, as might be predicted, was that, "once the cost of labor was excluded from input/output matrices, it could be shown that small family holdings utilized available physical resources far more efficiently than large capitalist ones" (Hewitt de Alcántara 1984: 138).

The Marxist critique of the neopopulist position, associated principally with Roger Bartra's work (1974; 1975), rejected the ICAD group's rationale for not imputing a wage, and argued that peasants' failure to valorize their own labor represented ultimately a net transfer of value to the capitalist sector, not an appropriation of surplus value (which could occur only if peasants were exploited as wage laborers) but an outright gift or donation. Bartra reworked the ICAD group's input/output ratios for peasant (i.e., petty), medium, and large enterprises, assigning the value of the prevailing rural wage for peasant household labor. This resulted in reversing the efficiency rankings of the ICAD study. Peasant units went from the most to the least efficient. Indeed, according to Bartra's calculations, they regularly operated at a loss since they did not even recoup the equivalent of their wages (1974: 74). Capitalist units went from the least efficient to the most efficient. These results supported the classic Marxist posture that favored capital-intensive over labor-intensive agriculture and envisioned the inevitable demise of the peasantry as the capitalization of agriculture proceeded (Kautsky 1974: 107–152; Banaji 1976b). In turn, Bartra's results provided fuel for the neo-populist image of Marxist contempt for the peasantry (cf. Hewitt de Alcántara 1984: 133–141).

Both theoretically and empirically, Roger Bartra's careful reworking of the ICAD input/output study (by imputing the going wage equivalent for household labor expended in peasant agriculture) was justified. He is vulnerable to criticism, however, for failing to properly and consistently conceptualize peasants as producers within a commodity economy and to recognize that, as such, a certain proportion of them—as successful family farmers or petty capitalist farmers—were already performing makeshift cost-benefit analyses of their agricultural enterprises' operations. They were doing so simply because they were in the same competitive struggle for viability as their more highly capitalized commodity-producing cousins. Given their social differentiation, it is misleading to reduce earnings among all peasant commodity producers to "nothing more than a self-remunerated wage" (Bartra 1974: 75).

Moreover, with the proviso that agriculture is a special case, given the peculiarities of state intervention and the direct competition between production units of diverse scales in the same markets, Bartra's analysis minimizes the extent to which peasant agricultural commodity production may either bypass or occur on the margins of the capitalist market. To the extent that it does this, the Marxist law of value operates so that commodities exchange at rates much closer to their embodied labor ratios than they do in pure, unfettered capitalist markets, where they tend to exchange at rates closer to their prices of production (i.e., labor and other costs of production + average profit). This is, for example, precisely the kind of situation that is not uncommon in provinces like Oaxaca—especially in the production of nontourist craft commodities like metates (Cook 1976; 1982: Chs. 6 & 7). In markets for these types of commodities, prices are negotiated between buyer and seller. While buyers-up definitely have an important, sometimes determinant role in setting commodity prices in such markets, the fact remains that prices are negotiable and fluctuate. In other words, Bartra's blanket assertion that "the peasant simple commodity economy does not contribute to the determination of product prices: these are determined by the capitalist market" (1974: 75) is, we think, still far from being true in many of the far-flung markets and hinterlands of provincial Mexico (cf. Reinhardt 1988: 41). Having said this, we now turn in more detail to our analysis of commodity production and exchange in an important region of provincial Mexico—the Oaxaca Valley.

Chapter 2. Agriculture and Craft Production: An Expedient Relationship

The Oaxaca Valley Today and Yesterday: Continuity or Discontinuity?

Oaxaca—a large and diverse southern Mexican state bordered by Veracruz and Puebla to the north, Guerrero to the west, Chiapas to the east, and the Pacific ocean to the south—is synonymous in the minds of Mexicanists with underdevelopment. It invariably evokes images of traditionalism, peasants, Indians, rusticity, and poverty and is widely viewed as one of Mexico's poorest and least developed provinces. In 1970, Oaxaca had the lowest per capita income in the country (764 pesos), only about one-sixth of the per capita income of the highest income area, the Federal District (4,461 pesos) (Hernández and Córdoba 1982: 25). The minimum wage in Oaxaca in 1977 was 77.5 pesos per day, tying it with Guerrero and Chiapas as the lowest in Mexico (40). A recent comparison (Bartolomé and Barabas 1986) of 1970 and 1980 census data notes that the state's gross domestic product had declined in the national rankings to twentieth place (out of 31 states plus the Federal District), which leads its authors to generalize that, with a few exceptions, Oaxaca's productive structure is entropic, or "in a permanent and progressive retrocession" (47). Associated with this relative poverty is the fact that Oaxaca exported more labor than any other Mexican state toward centers of capital-intensive agriculture; it accounted for 10.63 percent of the national total, with most of the laborers going to the cane harvests in Veracruz and the coffee harvest in Chiapas (Paré 1977: 110–121; Cook 1982: 395, 1984a: 9). While Oaxaca does have some areas of large-scale, capital-intensive agriculture (see Boege (ed.) 1977), a recent analysis of official agrarian statistics (Schejtman 1983) shows that 90 percent of its agricultural production units are of the "peasant" type, which control 70 percent of the potential arable and 70 percent of the capital and account for 80 percent of the

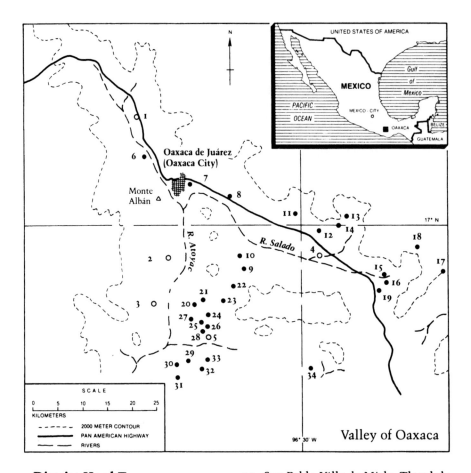

Valley of Oaxaca

District Head Towns

1. San Pedro y San Pablo Etla
2. Zaachila
3. Zimatlán de Alvarez
4. Tlacolula de Matamoros
5. Ocotlán de Morelos

Villages by District

6. Santa María Atzompa, Centro
7. Santa Lucía del Camino, Centro
8. Santa María del Tule, Centro
9. San Juan Teitipac, Tlacolula
10. San Sebastian Teitipac, Tlacolula
11. Teotitlán del Valle, Tlacolula
12. Santa Ana del Valle, Tlacolula
13. San Miguel del Valle, Tlacolula
14. Díaz Ordaz, Tlacolula
15. San Pablo Villa de Mitla, Tlacolula
16. Xaagá, Tlacolula
17. San Lorenzo Albarradas, Tlacolula
18. Santo Domingo Albarradas, Tlacolula
19. Santiago Matatlán, Tlacolula
20. San Martín Tilcajete, Ocotlán
21. San Pedro Guegorexe, Ocotlán
22. Santa Cecilia Jalieza, Ocotlán
23. Santo Domingo Jalieza, Ocotlán
24. Santo Tomás Jalieza, Ocotlán
25. San Jacinto Chilateca, Ocotlán
26. San Juan Chilateca, Ocotlán
27. San Isidro Zegache, Ocotlán
28. San Antonio Castillo Velasco, Ocotlán
29. San Pedro Mártir, Ocotlán
30. San Pedro Apóstol, Ocotlán
31. Magdalena Ocotlán, Ocotlán
32. Santa Lucía Ocotlán, Ocotlán
33. San Dionisio Ocotlán, Ocotlán
34. San Baltazar Chichicapan, Ocotlán

workdays and 60 percent of the value of agricultural output (176). In the focal area of this study, the Oaxaca Valley (located some 350 miles south of Mexico City in the central highlands), urban and rural populations are sharply set apart by official census measures of employment and levels of living: peasant agriculturists are glaringly poor in comparison with urban dwellers (Clarke 1986: 22, 28–29).

If we follow Kitching (1982) in defining populism and neopopulism as ideologies that "oppose industrialization and large-scale produc- tion in the name of small-scale individual enterprise" (21), then the Oaxaca Valley may approximate the ideal of a "small is beautiful" populist utopia. Not only is the Valley's agriculture representative of the preponderance of peasant *minifundia* throughout the state, but also the rapid growth of Oaxaca City (Oaxaca de Juárez) to a popula- tion of around 250,000 by the mid-1980s (roughly 40 percent of the Valley's total population) has not been accompanied by significant industrialization. Machinofacture is represented by one plywood factory with some three hundred employees, three soft-drink bot- tling plants with thirty employees each, and a moribund thread fac- tory (Clarke 1986: 29). Industry, or "transforming employment" (Clarke 1986), in the Oaxaca Valley more often than not means petty workshop manufacturing of the labor-intensive, minimally capi- talized, informal sector variety and is more likely to have a rural than an urban location (cf. Clarke 1986: 23).

Since prehispanic times, the Oaxaca Valley has had an intercom- munity division of labor and specialization with widespread in- dustrial commodity production (Blanton et al. 1981; Blanton and Kowalewski 1981; Kowalewski and Finsten 1983; Feinman 1986). Indeed, some communities continue to produce commodities first produced in the prehispanic or colonial periods, though, of course, the conditions and dynamics of their production have been trans- formed in proportion to their direct producers' increasing involve- ment in capitalist circuits. In other communities, however, the in- dustrial specialization currently practiced is of postcolonial origin. By contrast, Oaxaca City can probably be said to have experienced a significant deindustrialization since the colonial heyday of *gremios* and *obrajes* (Semo 1973: 161–187; Chance 1978), and perhaps even since 1875 (at least in a proportional sense) when the occupational census included some two thousand individuals in manufacturing or artisan occupations (Esparza 1983: III–V). With few exceptions, Val- ley settlements other than Oaxaca City—including those with craft industries—are substantially involved in agriculture on lands com- munally or privately possessed, although private ownership is pre- dominant over other forms of tenure (cf. Clarke 1986: 22). In other words, not only is Oaxaca Valley industry predominantly small scale and labor intensive, but it also continues to be wedded to agriculture.

We are still very far from having a comprehensive understanding of the historical sequencing of the growth of the commodity economy and the expansion of the market in the villages and towns of the Oaxaca Valley. It is likely that household products were commoditized to a significant degree before land or labor were—if only because the periodic marketing system and the intercommunity structure of production and exchange upon which it was based were functioning throughout the colonial period (Taylor 1971). However, even prior to the passage of the Ley Lerdo in 1856, which forced their privatization, communal lands had all but disappeared, and village lands were already privatized (Cassidy 1981: 211–217, 262). After 1850, the privatization process accelerated in estate lands burdened by mortgages. These lands were parceled and sold to peasants, some of whom apparently enlarged their arable holdings to provide for the growing population (Cassidy 1981: 69).[1] Documentary evidence, including wages among Mexico's lowest, points to a buyers' market for labor power in the rural Oaxaca Valley during the nineteenth century. This was probably a reflection of population growth and an increasing need for cash within the peasantry (Cassidy 1981: 174, 197). In the years immediately prior to the 1910 Revolution, there was an incipient proletariat in mining, construction, electrical power, transportation, textiles, and shoe manufacture. The percentage of full-time wage laborers in the economically active population of Oaxaca was a low 1.54 percent compared to fifteen percent nationwide (Chassen 1986: 240). Despite the low percentage of full-time wage laborers, however, by 1910 the Oaxaca Valley social economy had its share of capitalists with interests in commercial agriculture, commerce, mining, small manufacturing, and finance juxtaposed with an increasing presence of agricultural wage labor within a differentiated peasantry (Chassen 1986: 217–218, 245–247).

It would be mistaken to interpret the long record of commodity production as indicative of persistence or continuity rather than of transformative change and discontinuity in the Oaxaca economy (see Kowalewski and Finsten 1983). Commodities that were produced and circulated prior to the development of monetized market exchange—not to mention of money capital, wage labor, and industrial capital—clearly had different implications for material and social production and reproduction than do commodities produced and circulated after these developments reshaped the meaning and organization of the labor process and its wider economic, sociocultural, and political superstructure. In other words, from the perspective of political economy, the penetration and transformation of the indigenous Oaxaca commodity economy by Spanish colonialism in the sixteenth century and subsequently by the development of capitalism, despite its uneven trajectory over the centuries, represents a major break with the prehispanic (and precapitalist) period (cf. Cook 1983). This is not to deny the fact that the complementarity of agricultural and industrial production within local and regional divisions of labor originated in that period.

The "On Again/Off Again" Treatment of Industry in Rural Studies

The classical Marxist literature on the rural economy, including the studies by Kautsky (1974) and Lenin (1964), as well as the neopopulist classics like Chayanov's (1966), recognized the complementarity of agriculture and industry at the interior of the peasant household. Regrettably, their incisive observations about that complementarity have been largely ignored in the literature since World War II due to an agrarian bias that has led investigators to focus on agriculture to the exclusion of industry in the rural social economy. In effect, there has been a tendency to compartmentalize underdeveloped countries into rural and urban sectors, assigning the former exclusively to agriculture and the latter to industry (cf. Cook 1984a: 5–15).

Such compartmentalization has led many writers to overlook the close association of rural agriculture and rural industry, and the implications of that association for household economic strategies. Nothing prevents peasants, in their role as agriculturalists, from producing industrial commodities. Indeed, peasant producers of industrial commodities, whom we choose to call peasant-artisans, are in a better position than either full-time peasants or full-time artisans to alter their production strategies when agricultural markets collapse or raw materials rise in price, adversely affecting household income. Peasant-artisans have the capacity to shift domestic labor and resources into or out of subsistence (or cash crop) agriculture, and, more generally, to alter the balance between industrial and agricultural production. In Mexico's contemporary crisis economy the availability of a variety of strategies can play an important role in the household's effort to maintain a given standard of living and perhaps even its capacity to remain intact without having to send members on a migratory quest for additional cash with which to meet household expenses, as more and more households are obliged to do (Binford 1989; Grindle 1987).

After a brief examination of the demographic characteristics of our sample, this chapter will discuss in detail the results of our data analysis that pertains to agriculture and industrial production. Our principal goal is to show that while rural industrial commodity production accounts for a substantial proportion of the aggregate income in many rural communities in the Oaxaca Valley—and represents a realm of activity separate from agriculture—rural industrial households tend to till the soil if their circumstances permit. This tendency reflects neither an unthinking adherence to persisting peasant traditions nor some mystical peasant economic logic, but a considered, practical response to material conditions nurtured in rural Oaxaca by the fluctuating forces of the wider capitalist economy.

Demographic Preliminaries

During the course of the project we interviewed representatives from 1,008 households in twenty-four localities, which included twenty-one villages and two district *cabeceras* (head towns)—the market centers of Tlacolula de Matamoros and Ocotlán de Morelos—along with selected interviews in Oaxaca City (see Appendix). Random sampling methods were employed in twenty of the villages, accounting for 952 rural households. This information is the basis for the demographic analysis made here. Table 1 summarizes the age and sex distribution for the 5,503 persons in our household sample.

The mean household size is 5.9 persons, and the mean age is 23.6 years. A young population is indicated by the fact that 44 percent of the individuals sampled were under the age of 15 years and more than half (53.9 percent) less than 20. The overall distribution of males and females approaches 50 percent (2,769 males to 2,734 females) but there are substantial male/female differences when the sample is disaggregated into five-year cohorts and contributions by sex to these cohorts are compared. Whereas the distribution by sex is almost even from birth to age 19, a substantial drop-off of females relative to males occurs in the cluster between ages 20 and 24.

Information was not gathered with respect to migration (although the survey did inquire as to presence or absence and amount of funds remitted to households by absent members), but studies from other areas of Mexico (e.g., Arizpe 1978; Kemper and Foster 1975; Grindle 1987), from other parts of Oaxaca (Méndez y Mercado 1985; Young 1976; Ortíz Gabriel 1980; Binford 1989), and from communities in the Oaxaca Valley (Ornelas López 1980; Vázquez Hernández 1980; Barabas and Bartolomé 1986: 75; Larmer 1988) suggest that high

Table 1. *Age and Gender Distribution of 952 Oaxaca Valley Households*

Age	Males	% M	Females	% F	Total	% Sample
0–4	385	50.0	385	50.0	770	14.0
5–9	443	49.7	449	50.3	892	16.2
10–14	372	50.4	366	49.6	738	13.4
15–19	272	48.1	293	51.9	565	10.3
20–24	221	54.2	187	45.8	408	7.4
25–29	145	47.2	162	52.8	307	5.6
30–34	139	47.6	153	52.4	292	5.3
35–39	149	48.5	158	51.5	307	5.6
40–44	139	50.7	135	49.3	274	5.0
45–49	138	55.0	113	45.0	251	4.6
50–54	86	50.3	85	49.7	171	3.1
55–59	98	51.6	92	48.4	190	3.4
60–64	64	53.8	55	46.2	119	2.2
65–69	41	57.8	30	42.2	71	1.2
70–74	42	57.5	31	42.5	73	1.3
75–79	25	53.2	22	46.8	47	.9
> 79	10	35.7	18	64.3	28	.5
Total	2,769	50.3	2,734	49.7	5,503	100.0

rates of out-migration best explain the current demographic structure. There are fewer males in the 20–24 years cluster than among those 15–19 years (a difference of 51), but the largest difference occurs from 20–24 years to 25–29 years (221 to 145 or a difference of 76), suggesting that 25–29 years represents the age when the majority of migrating males first leave the community.

The fact that there are nearly 2.5 times as many males in the 10–14 age group as in the 25–29 group simply cannot be accounted for by increases in fertility and declines in mortality rates alone. As will be documented below, sampled communities in the districts of Tlacolula and Ocotlán, despite some differences in their landholdings (amount of land and land type), are overwhelmingly relegated to small infrasubsistence holdings of fewer than 3 hectares. The small area of these *minifundio* lands and the fact that 90 percent of them are rain fed (only 10 percent irrigated) and, therefore, susceptible to unpredictable rainfall, means that most middle-aged and elderly males have little in the way of patrimony to be inherited by their sons; consequently, their sons have little material incentive (at least in inheritance terms) to remain in the community. It would not be in any potential heir's interest if the father were to divide his *minifundio* to provide some land to each of his offspring, since each heir would have even less possibility than the father of sustaining an independent household by tilling the soil. Partible inheritance of infrasubsistence parcels merely leads, *ceteris paribus,* to the proliferation of rural poverty—a fact that is well understood among the Oaxaca Valley peasantry where estates are regularly apportioned among heirs without extreme parcelization (cf. Quinn 1964; Cook 1969: 95; Downing 1971; Beals 1975: 270).

The Incidence of Rural Industrial Commodity Production

In an effort to assess the incidence of rural industrial commodity production and its relationship to agriculture, the 1,008 households surveyed were grouped into the following four mutually exclusive categories:

1. *Peasant* (N = 191, or 19 percent)—households whose members are currently working land and are not involved in craft production.
2. *Artisan* (N = 191, or 19 percent)—households whose members do not cultivate the soil and that contain at least some members who work full-time in craft industries.
3. *Peasant-Artisan* (N = 574, or 57 percent)—households that both cultivate the soil and contain some members who work full- or part-time, permanently or seasonally in craft industries.
4. *Other* (N = 52, or 5 percent)—households whose economically active members are involved in occupations other than agriculture or craft production. They are often employees in the public or the private sector. The rural proletariat is included here.

Aggregating the artisan and peasant-artisan categories indicates that slightly over three-quarters (76 percent) of the 1,008 households in the sample have at least some craft involvement (and an equal percentage, based on an aggregation of peasant and peasant-artisan categories, some agricultural involvement). To be sure, this figure would have been lower if villages from the districts of Etla and Zimatlán, which have extensive areas of irrigation agriculture and a lower incidence of craft production, had been included. It also would have been lower if the selection of villages from the districts of Centro, Tlacolula, and Ocotlán had been random. With the exception of a small sample of artisan workshops in Oaxaca City, however, and the inclusion of nonrandomly selected cases from the important market towns of Ocotlán de Morelos and Tlacolula de Matamoros, villages were targeted for study because of a high incidence of craft involvement, as determined largely on the basis of a preliminary survey (Cook 1978). Within these villages, the incidence of craft involvement among households varied substantially, from a high of nearly 100 percent in the palm weaving villages of San Lorenzo Albarradas and Santo Domingo Albarradas to a low of 25 percent in the treadle loom weaving village of Xaagá. Thus, non-craft households can be found even within villages in which crafts assume an important economic role.

The reasons for differential participation in craft production between households, villages, or industries in the Oaxaca Valley are complex. At the regional level, there is generally a low incidence of village specialization in craft production in districts, such as Etla and Zimatlán, with relatively extensive areas of irrigation agriculture. At the community level, the local availability of natural resources transformable into raw materials for particular industries and their relative degree of communalization are potentially significant determinants of the degree of industrialization—although industrial commodity production can and does occur in their absence (e.g., by importing raw materials). Finally, at the household level, poverty in the agricultural means of production, as well as the size and sex/age composition of the household, bears significantly upon the incidence, rate, and level of participation in craft production but, as will be demonstrated below, not always in anticipated directions.

Crafts, Land, and Household Types

The fact that a majority (57 percent) of the sample households are classified as joint peasant-artisan underlines the fact that agriculture and craft production should be regarded as complementary rather than competing economic activities in many areas of the rural Oaxaca Valley. The overall land situation in the Valley provides a rationale for this complementarity. In many areas of Mexico, land is bimodally distributed into a few large, private capitalist farms and a large number of *minifundios* held as private property or in private usufruct (CEPAL 1982).

In the Oaxaca Valley, however, generally sparse and unpredictable rainfall and a paucity of irrigated land, together with a pattern of dispersed tenure, parcelized land, and a generalized unwillingness to sell land to outsiders, have considerably hindered the development of large-scale capitalist farms. Rather, rapid population growth, the

Table 2. *Distribution of Land and Agricultural Means of Production in 1,008 Rural Households in the Oaxaca Valley*

Land Category	N	%	% w/ oxteam	% w/ oxcart	% w/ both
Landless	243	24.1	4.9	1.2	.8
Landed < 1 ha	274	27.2	18.6	5.1	4.7
1–3 ha	331	32.8	45.6	14.8	11.4
3–5 ha	103	10.2	61.1	33.0	28.2
> 5 ha	57	5.7	66.7	52.0	45.6
Total					
All cases	1,008	100.0	31.2	12.9	10.7
Landed only	765	100.0	39.6	16.6	13.8

lack of new land to cultivate, and the active land markets within corporate communities, have combined to create a degree of generalized *minifundismo* unusual even for rural Mexico. Of the 958 households for which we have detailed information regarding landholdings, 24 percent are landless and an additional 60 percent cultivate 3 hectares or less of seasonal land units.[2] Furthermore, cultivated land is rainfall dependent, or seasonal (*temporal*), in a ratio of 10 to 1 to irrigated land. Those who do have land often lack other resources necessary to practice agriculture on an independent basis: an oxteam for plowing and an oxcart for hauling fertilizers and other inputs to the fields and crops from the fields after harvest.[3]

Yet, as Table 2 makes clear, less than 40 percent of the 765 landed households reported owning an oxteam, and only 16.6 percent reported owning a cart. Most significantly, a mere 13.8 percent held land together with the principal means of production required to work it (oxteam + cart). Overall 462 households are without an oxteam, and of the 303 that do have an oxteam, 197 have no cart.[4] Those peasants without oxteams rent them for cash or a labor equivalent, but usually they are not able to do so until the owners finish planting their fields. As a result, renters and borrowers often plant later and under less favorable soil and climatic conditions. It is not surprising that households lacking oxteams frequently seek to develop share (*a medias*) or reciprocity arrangements (*guelaguetzas*) with owners in order to gain timely access to them (Diskin 1986: 267–268, 278–280; cf. Martínez Ríos 1965; Cook 1982: 67).

Even within the generalized *minifundio* situation, then, resources are unequally distributed, a point seldom noted in the peasant studies literature. For instance, a strong relationship exists between the ownership of an oxteam and/or oxcart and the amount of land cultivated. Of the households with 1 hectare or less of seasonal land units, fewer than 20 percent possess oxteams and only 5 percent have an oxcart. These percentages increase as we survey progressively larger land categories.[5] Oxteams and oxcarts are particularly concentrated among those households with 3 or more hectares of seasonal land units, which account for 21 percent of all landed households but concentrate one-third of the oxteams and 56 percent of the oxcarts. In our top land category, those with more than 5 hectares of land, two-thirds of the households have an oxteam, half of them have an oxcart, and 46 percent have all the essential means of production. Not only are these households in the best position to get the most out of their land, but also at least some of them can rent out instruments of production to raise cash or exchange for labor, in some cases appropriating surplus value from resource-poor peasants (cf. Kritsman 1984). These households are exceptional since the vast majority of peasants and peasant-artisans do not control the resources required to plan the production cycle in a manner consistent with their knowledge of agriculture, their work capacity, and their aspirations.

In our initial analysis of project data, we designated households that combined an oxteam and 3 or more hectares of seasonal land units as "self-sufficient" in corn production.[6] Further analysis has indicated that this was an overly optimistic assessment. Even the households best endowed with land and means of production (those with >5 hectares, an oxteam and oxcart, of which $N = 26$) produced a median of only 1,000 kilos of corn in 1979 and met a median of only 49 percent of their annual corn need. About half of these households claimed that they bought corn for five or more months during the preceding year. Even among this group, then, the satisfaction of their annual corn requirement was achieved only through substantial market dependence. Much worse off were the 223 households that cultivated between .1 and 1.0 hectare and lacked both oxteam and oxcart. These households, which comprised the largest single category in our survey, produced a median of only 100 kilos of corn in 1979 and fulfilled a median of only 7 percent of their annual corn requirements. Almost 70 percent of them depended upon market purchase of corn for seven or more months after their paltry harvest was exhausted. Thus, it would seem that agriculture is a viable full-time option for only a small proportion of the households in the villages surveyed, a conclusion supported by the fact that a mere 19 percent of the 1,008 households in the sample satisfied the criteria

Table 3. *Agricultural Resources and Performance of 765 Landed Households in the Oaxaca Valley*

	ha(s)	All Landed N	All Landed (%)	Peasants N	Peasants (%)	Peasant-Artisans N	Peasant-Artisans (%)
Seasonal Land							
Units/	.1–1.0	274	(35.8)	62	(32.4)	212	(36.9)
Household							
Land	1.1–3.0	331	(43.2)	85	(45.1)	246	(43.2)
Worked	3.1–5.0	103	(13.5)	28	(14.7)	75	(13.1)
	>5.0	57	(7.4)	16	(7.9)	41	(6.8)
Total		765	(99.9)	191	(100.1)	574	(100.0)
Ownership of Means of Production							
Oxteam		303	(39.6)	85	(44.5)	218	(38.0)
Oxcart		127	(16.6)	50	(26.2)	77	(13.4)
Oxteam and oxcart		106	(13.8)	41	(21.5)	65	(11.3)
Agricultural Production, 1979							
Corn harvest (kg)							
Mean		477		598		435	
Median		250		250		250	
Prop. corn needs							
Median		.16		.17		.14	
Buy corn (months)							
Median		6		5		7	
Oxteam							
No				106	(55.5)	356	(62.0)
Yes				85	(44.5)	218	(38.0)

of our peasant classification. It follows that some additional cash-earning activities are necessary to the survival of most rural Oaxaca Valley households.

The local agricultural wage labor market, which provides a necessary income supplement for land-poor households in many other parts of Mexico, is limited in the Oaxaca Valley by the highly fragmented character of land holdings and the low development of capitalist relations of production in agriculture. Consequently, less than one-fifth of the income of peasant households derives from participation in agricultural wage labor. Thus, one can better appreciate why in many villages in the districts of Ocotlán, Tlacolula, and Centro the major complement to agriculture is household production of pottery, mats, baskets, bricks, wooden utensils, embroidered garments, weavings, and other craft products. Whereas agriculture and craft production may in some instances present competing demands upon available household labor, they are best understood as complementary types of productive activity, which together facilitate household reproduction (and, in some cases, serve as a basis for capital accumulation).

One might expect that there would be an inverse relationship between access to land (and agricultural means of production) and craft production, that is, that as access to land increased, the likelihood that a household would be involved in craft production would decrease. Such a straightforward relationship does not, in fact, exist. Table 3 compares peasants and peasant-artisans regarding the variables relevant to this proposition. There is little overall difference in access to land between the two groups, nor does the difference increase greatly when land under cultivation is recalculated on a per capita basis to take into account differences in household size; peasant households have a mean of .62 and a median of .32 seasonal land units per person, while peasant-artisan households have a mean of .40 and a median of .28 seasonal land units per person. Peasants are slightly more likely than peasant-artisans to have oxteams (44.5 percent to 38.0 percent) but even that difference is small. Whereas land poverty, a prevalent condition in the Oaxaca Valley, provides an incentive for household participation in craft production, other factors are clearly at work.

Household Demographics, Craft Involvement, and Agriculture

The common assumption that producers tend to cease direct participation in agricultural production for own-use when specialized commodity production increases is what is usually meant by the development of the social division of labor (e.g., Goody 1982: 4). This thesis appears to need qualification in light of Oaxaca Valley data, which show that intensive market involvement by craft producers is often associated with their continued involvement in agricultural production. As we have seen, access to land and agricultural means of production helps to explain the pervasiveness of craft production in some areas of the Oaxaca Valley, but differences in access do not help us understand precisely why some households combine agriculture and craft production while others practice agriculture exclusively.

As it turns out, a whole series of what are commonly referred to as "demographic factors" (i.e., those relating to household size and the age and sex distribution of the members) may be involved in furthering our understanding of this question. Though generally treated as independent biological invariants by Chayanov and contemporary scholars inspired by him (e.g., Sahlins 1972), household size and structure obviously develop within a context of economic constraints and social ideologies, and their relationship to economic activity is complex and reciprocal rather than simple and determinant (cf. de Teresa and Rees 1989).[7] We will examine such relationships in more detail in Chapter 4, where we address the question of demographics and social stratification. Here we limit ourselves to a consideration of the relationships between household composition and rural occupational structure.

Household size and composition determine the amount of income (in money or kind) required to maintain the household at a given level of subsistence. The capacity to produce this subsistence input depends upon, among other things, the household's access to land and means of production (agricultural and nonagricultural). It also depends upon the household's labor supply that is a function of household size, composition, and stage in the life cycle. The pioneering attempt to theorize the relationship among these variables was by A. V. Chayanov (1966) who formulated the consumer/worker ratio to measure the effect of household size and composition upon peasant production.

For Chayanov, the life of peasant households encompassed a biological cycle that determines the changing ratio between the number of consumers and the number of workers. The ratio in a newly formed domestic unit (husband and wife) is 1.00, the lowest possible (each consumer is also a worker), but it proceeds to increase with the birth of each successive child. As the number of consumers rises, the available workers must progressively intensify their labor in order for the household to attain culturally prescribed levels of consumption. Eventually the older children begin to mature and assume some of the labor burden. Work, then, is spread among more and more workers, resulting in a general decline in labor intensity (at least such a decline becomes feasible). As older children leave the household to begin their own families, the ratio of consumers to workers may rise again, although it is unlikely that the ratio will attain its previous high point (Chayanov 1966: 54–60, 76–79).

Chayanov assumed that the level of household consumption was fixed—an assumption that we shall critique in Chapter 4—and thought that peasant households with favorable (low) consumer/worker ratios would prefer to trade off enterprise expansion and the possibility of capital accumulation for the additional leisure that a decline in work intensity makes possible. For these and other reasons, Chayanov (1966: 75) maintained that *"in the labor farm, rates of labor intensity are considerably lower than if labor were fully utilized."*

Ironically, students of the agrarian question and the peasantry in Mexico (e.g., Bartra 1975; Hewitt de Alcántara 1984: 85–88, 135–136; Warman 1976: ch. 6) have adopted many of Chayanov's ideas, but they have not, for the most part, followed him either in recognizing that the "family labor farm" incorporates a series of diverse economic activities—among which agriculture is usually (but not always) the most important (1966: 106–110)—or in treating income from crafts and trading as integral components of the total income of the peasant family (1966: 102).[8] Chayanov sought to account for the balance between agriculture, crafts, and trade in several different ways. Most prominent among these was the claim that the importance of crafts and trading activity tended to be in inverse proportion to the amount of land held:

> when, in a particular year, the farm does not have the land or capital needed to develop an agricultural undertaking optimal as to relationship between farm and family size it is obliged to make its volume of agricultural activity conform with these means of production in minimum supply. The volume is not established automatically by being arithmetically derived from the minimum element, but is set by a complex process of the influence of deteriorating conditions for agricultural production on the basic equilibrium of the economic factors. Moreover, the family throws its unutilized labor into crafts, trades, and other extra-agricultural livelihoods. The whole of its summed agricultural, crafts, and trades income is counterposed to its demands, and the drudgery of acquiring it leads to an equilibrium with the degree of satisfaction of these personal demands. (Chayanov 1966: 100–101)

Such an explanation has, as we have seen, general validity for large areas of the Oaxaca Valley with its extreme *minifundismo* and unpredictable corn yields.[9] On the other hand, the inverse relationship between crafts and agriculture does not appear to apply, given the land poverty experienced by most rural households.

Chayanov (1966: 106–110) posited two other reasons for the predominance of crafts. First, he noted that, because much agricultural work is seasonal, producers frequently find themselves with a great amount of leisure time during a period of the year. Off-season craft or trading activity may be taken up with the object of "easing the load of summer agricultural work" (1966: 107) by spreading the work load over the entire year. He also maintained that peasants may, regardless of their access to land, substitute craft for agricultural labor when the reward to labor is higher in crafts than in agriculture. Under such circumstances "the peasant family behaves with its labor just like a capitalist distributing his capital, so that it gives him the highest net income" (108).

While these points are plausible, their highly abstract formulation reduces their potential application to specific cases. Chayanov's comments on relative rates of reward in crafts and agriculture, in particular, treat crafts generically when rural industrial commodity production—in Mexico today as in early twentieth-century Russia—exhibits large variations in capital-labor intensiveness; also, rural craft products are directed toward a variety of local, regional, national, and international markets resulting in substantial differences in reward to labor. We shall examine some of its diverse forms in the following chapters.

In retrospect, it is surprising that Chayanov's remarks on crafts and trades did not address some of the same variables related to household size and composition that proved so fruitful in his analysis of agriculture. Assuming that the lack of land at least partly accounts for the existence of full-time craft households, we would like to take a closer look at household structure and composition for possible insights into the occupational bifurcation between peasants and peasant-artisans. Chayanov's emphasis on demographic (as opposed to social) differentiation need not be accepted in order to accept the thesis that "the family life cycle may be an important explanation of household choice of activity" (Deere and de Janvry 1981: 255).

Murphy and Selby (1981: 255), apparently inspired by Chayanov (cf. Chayanov 1966: 56), have developed a typology that permits each of the households in our sample to be assigned to one of five discrete stages of a developmental cycle:

Stage I.   All young single individuals and young married couples without children.

Stage II. Married couples with at least one child under the age of five. They refer to these as households with incomplete fertility.

Stage III. All children living in the home are over the age of five; these are households with completed fertility.

Stage IV. Households in which all children are at least fifteen years old and have thus reached the age of economic maturity.

Stage V. Older individuals and couples living without their children in the household.

Because the Murphy-Selby stages describe phases in the family life cycle, they bear a predictable relationship to the consumer/worker ratio which generally increases from the first to the second stage, after which it declines until the fifth stage. Tables 4 and 5 summarize data on household maturity and the consumer/worker ratio.[10]

In Table 4, two sets of percentages have been calculated for each cell. Those to the right of the numbers indicate the percentage of the particular stage accounted for by each of the four occupational groupings (they should be read vertically). The percentages below the numbers specify the proportion of each stage accounted for by the occupational grouping to the left (they should be read horizontally). Hence, the 350 peasant-artisan households in which all children are less than five years old account for 63.4 percent of all households in which children are less than five years old, and account as well for 61.4 percent of all peasant-artisan households.

If there was no systematic relationship between the demographic cycle and occupational specialization, we would expect to find each of the four occupational categories represented in the same proportion in *each* of the stages as it is in the sample as a whole. This is, in fact, the case with artisan and "other" households. Peasants and peasant-artisans, however, radically depart from the expected pattern. Discounting the "young, single/married" category due to the small number of cases, we note that the percentage of peasant households increases and that of peasant-artisan households decreases as one passes from less mature to more mature stages in the household development cycle. Peasant households account for only 15.4 percent of the households with "all children under 5," but 30.4 percent of those consisting of "adults over 30"; peasant-artisan households, on the other hand, decline in representation from a high of 63.4 percent in the "all children under 5" category to 53.6 percent (all children 5 or more), 46.4 percent ("all children over 15"), and 38.0 percent (adults over 30). As we pass from less mature to more mature biosocial stages the likelihood of a household being exclusively agricultural (i.e., peasant) increases and the likelihood of its being peasant-artisan declines. The categories of "other" and "artisan" suggest no clear pattern.

Table 4. Stage in Household Developmental Cycle by Occupational Category

	I Young Single/Married	II All Children < 5 Yr	III Children > 5	IV Children > 15	V Adult > 30	Total
Peasant	0 (0.0)	85 (15.4)	55 (20.9)	23 (27.4)	28 (30.4)	191
(%)	(0.0)	(44.5)	(28.8)	(12.0)	(14.7)	(100.0)
Artisan	6 (50.0)	93 (16.8)	48 (18.2)	20 (23.8)	21 (22.8)	188
(%)	(3.2)	(49.5)	(25.5)	(10.6)	(11.2)	(100.0)
Peasant-Artisan	5 (41.7)	350 (63.4)	141 (53.6)	39 (46.4)	35 (38.0)	570
(%)	(0.9)	(61.4)	(24.7)	(6.8)	(6.1)	(100.0)
Other	1 (8.3)	24 (4.4)	19 (7.2)	2 (2.4)	8 (8.7)	54
(%)	(1.8)	(44.4)	(35.2)	(3.7)	(14.8)	(100.0)
Total	12 (100.0)	552 (100.0)	263 (100.0)	84 (100.0)	92 (100.0)	1,003

Note: Not coded N = 5.

The distribution, though static, suggests that it is possible for landed Oaxaca Valley households to circulate between the status of peasant and peasant-artisan, whereas artisan households, being landless, have fewer options. The pattern of occupational categories observable at any particular time is, therefore, to a degree, the product of household economic strategies responding to conjunctural factors like the weather, raw material supply, market prices and/or household consumption requirements, and labor availability change. Landed households in craft-producing villages make adjustments in the way they purchase raw materials and means of production and in their allocation of domestic labor. If such adjustments lead peasant households to take up craft production, or peasant-artisan households to dedicate themselves full-time to agriculture, a change in occupational categorization results.

An analysis of Table 5, which summarizes socioeconomic characteristics of households that have pursued different production strategies, suggests that household size and the total number of household workers may play important roles in choice of household economic activity.[11] Where households are large with many small children, there is a positive reward for those able to supply the labor and capital to undertake craft production alongside agriculture. The households best able to accomplish this are those that are characterized by greater labor strength. Thus, Stage II peasant-artisan households have an average of one more worker than do the Stage II households which remain committed solely to agriculture, thus replicating in Oaxaca an observation made by Deere and de Janvry (1981: 359) in Cajamarca, northern Peru. For succeeding stages (III, IV, V) the pressure on income is reduced as household size (and with it minimum consumption requirements) declines. Even considering the fragmented character of landholdings, low levels of capital investment, and low yields, more or less exclusive involvement in agriculture is selected by an increasing proportion of the landed households in our sample as they move through the life cycle.

Still, one must not lose sight of the fact that, even in Stage V (adults over 30), the stage category with the highest percentage of peasant households (30.4 percent) and the lowest percentage of peasant-artisan households (38.0 percent), the latter represents a plurality of all households and a solid majority (35 of 63, or 55.6 percent) of the landed ones. The reason is not difficult to discover. Peasant-artisan households have a median per capita yearly net income of 1,825 pesos, almost two and a half times the 753 pesos registered for peasant households, of which 61 percent is derived from

Table 5. Employment Variables for 991 Households by Occupational Categories and Stage

	N	Paid Jobs M	Paid Jobs Md	Unpaid Jobs M	Unpaid Jobs Md	Total Jobs M	Total Jobs Md	C M	W Md	Ratio M	Ratio Md	Family Size M
Stage II: Child <5												
Peasant	85	1.5	1.0	0.5	0.0	1.9	2.0	4.4	4.0	1.7	1.7	7.3
Artisan	93	1.7	1.0	1.0	1.0	2.7	2.0	2.7	2.5	1.9	1.9	6.3
Peasant-Artisan	350	2.1	2.0	1.0	1.0	3.1	3.0	2.6	2.3	1.8	1.7	6.9
Other	24	1.4	1.0	0.2	0.0	1.5	1.0	4.6	5.0	1.9	1.8	6.9
Subtotal	552											
Stage III: Child >5												
Peasant	55	1.6	1.0	0.4	0.0	2.0	2.0	3.5	2.5	1.4	1.3	5.5
Artisan	48	1.7	1.5	1.4	1.0	3.0	3.0	2.5	2.0	1.4	1.3	5.8
Peasant-Artisan	141	2.0	2.0	1.2	1.0	3.2	3.0	2.0	1.8	1.4	1.3	5.6
Other	19	1.5	1.0	0.0	0.0	1.5	1.0	4.6	4.5	1.4	1.4	5.7
Subtotal	263											

Stage IV: Child >15

Peasant	23	1.6	2.0	0.6	0.0	2.1	2.0	2.4	2.0	1.1	1.1	4.2
Artisan	20	1.8	2.0	0.8	0.5	2.6	2.0	1.4	1.4	1.3	1.1	3.2
Peasant-Artisan	39	2.2	2.0	1.2	1.0	3.3	3.0	1.2	1.0	1.1	1.1	3.9
Other	2	1.5	1.5	.0	.0	1.5	1.5	2.5	2.5	1.0	1.0	4.0
Subtotal	84											

Stage V: Adult >30

Peasant	28	1.1	1.0	0.0	0.0	1.0	1.0	1.6	2.0	1.4	1.2	1.9
Artisan	21	1.4	1.0	0.2	0.0	1.6	1.0	1.3	1.0	1.4	1.3	1.9
Peasant-Artisan	35	1.5	1.0	0.4	0.0	2.0	2.0	1.3	1.0	1.3	1.0	2.4
Other	8	1.2	1.0	0.0	0.0	0.9	1.0	1.1	1.0	1.5	1.3	1.8
Subtotal	92											

| Total | 991 | | | | | | | | | | | |

M = mean; Md = median; C = consumer; W = worker.

rural craft activities and only 23 percent from agriculture (median figures). These figures reveal the importance of craft production in the survival of a land poor population.

Artisans with Land or Peasants with Crafts?

Given the heuristic character of the distinction we have drawn between "peasant" and "artisan" households, it would be a mistake to maintain that we advocate the study of the agriculture/craft production relationship from an either/or perspective, which holds that as craft production increases among a given rural population a necessary decrease in agricultural production occurs. It would be equally mistaken to construe this heuristic separation as favoring the separate study of agriculture and industry in the rural economy in lieu of the study of their forms of combination (cf. Lenin 1964: 378–380). Rather, our analyses support the view that these two branches of production are mutually stimulating and interdependent at the level of household enterprises with respect to their viability, productivity, and growth. They also support the view that the relationship, or the mix between them, in any given enterprise is conjunctural and, therefore, subject to variation over time—with the direction of change (i.e., toward complete disappearance of one or the other) being indeterminate.

Preliminary research findings (Cook 1978: 301) found instances in which successful peasant-artisan domestic units leased, rented, or sharecropped their privately held land—resulting in reductions of their direct agricultural involvement—to enable them to devote more of their available labor and capital to craft production, which was perceived to be more profitable.[12] This pattern was further documented by subsequent research. Evidence from Xaagá treadle loom weaving households indicated that the most successful enterprises were perhaps permanently distancing themselves from direct involvement in agriculture as their expanding businesses became wholly capitalized through profits. This process suggested an "embryonic trend toward the separation of agriculture and industry in the regional division of labor as a consequence of capitalist development" (Cook 1986: 63).

Follow-up interviews with the same weavers in 1985, however, proved these generalizations premature. They were derived from observations that, in fact, pointed to short-term conjunctural movements, rather than long-term structural trends. More specifically, as will be discussed at length in Chapter 7, the most devastating local manifestation of the post-1982 Mexican economic crisis was across the board, recurrent, and severe price increases for producers' and wage goods. This forced weavers' (and other artisans') production costs up and profits down (given constraints limiting their ability to make compensatory increases in their own selling prices). In response to these crisis conditions, weavers became more involved in agriculture and expanded their production of subsistence and cash crops. Earnings from the sale of cash crops were used to capitalize their weaving enterprises (especially to buy thread and to pay wages).

Even in those cases where petty capitalist enterprises have emerged from the ranks of peasant-artisan enterprises and the separation of industry from agriculture appears to be underway, agriculture becomes indispensable to the petty industrialist as a source of subsistence or cash when living and business conditions worsen. It is fitting that in the next chapter we turn our attention to peasant-artisan households whose material reproduction strategy negates the forces that would rupture the symbiosis between industry and agriculture.

Chapter 3. Obliging Need: Craft Production and Simple Reproduction

"Obliging Need" and the Peasant-Artisan Dilemma

In the popular culture of rural Oaxaca there is no better expression of the situation of the hyphenated countryfolk called "peasant-artisans" than the oft-repeated maxim *"la necesidad obliga"* or, in a literal translation, "need obliges."[1] This adage is regularly elicited when one asks a peasant-artisan, for example, why he or she practices a particular craft (*oficio*). Cook first heard it in 1965 during his initial fieldwork session with the *metate* makers of the Teitipac villages and has heard it countless times since from peasant-artisan informants representing the entire gamut of craft occupations. The phrase is succinctly expressive of the recognition that work is not so much a matter of free, individual choice as it is of material need and, ultimately, of survival. It is a shorthand way of saying that artisans work not because they like to (although that also may be the case) but because they have to. In effect, this aphorism from the cultural repertory of Oaxaca's peasant-artisans, by poetically alluding to their daily struggle for subsistence, belies the sappy, nostalgic, tourist promoters' view of backward yet contented, skilled yet unsophisticated, unambitious yet resourceful practitioners of "traditional" native crafts.

As a starting point toward the correction of contradictory urbanite views about peasant-artisans, and to underline the active and creative role of peasant-artisan labor, the "obliging need" adage can have real merit. Insofar as it may be construed to mean that peasant-artisans are stoic, unenterprising creatures of circumstance who persist in traditional and unrewarding work for want of innovativeness, however, it is deceptive. In actuality, many peasant-artisans innovate to make their work more rewarding and persistently seek alternatives to unrewarding work; if their efforts in these directions fail, it is not for want of trying or of desire for change. In some cases failure may be a function of the low productivity and limited capacity for surplus production of a particular rural industry or it may be that surplus value is appropriated by intermediaries who control the raw materials market, the final products market, or both.

Despite these limits on accumulation by direct producers, it is demonstrable that in the contemporary Oaxaca Valley, as in eighteenth-century England (Dobb 1963), late-nineteenth- and early-twentieth-century Russia (Harrison 1977; Lenin 1964), and contemporary Brazil (Schmitz 1982), among others, some households in some rural (and urban) industries do accumulate and invest surplus to enlarge their means of production and stock of raw materials. It is also demonstrable that, in particular circumstances, this process of expansion may be accompanied by the hiring of labor power additional to or substituting for unpaid domestic labor, and that this may propel household enterprises beyond the threshold of petty commodity production and into the ranks of petty capitalism.[2]

Our primary focus in this chapter will be upon peasant-artisan households (PAHs) that make and earn their living by combining agricultural and craft production for own-use and for exchange. Although such household enterprises, which comprise a majority of those in our survey, participate in wage labor and capital accumulation, many of them do not seem to be headed toward either full-proletarian status or petty capitalist status. But neither are they under the influence of some mysterious cultural calculus or logic that locks them into a cycle of simple reproduction without accumulation.

For purposes of analysis it is preferable to group PAHs according to the branch of craft activity in which they are involved (cf. Schmitz 1982: 47). Different branches of production are characterized by different technologies, markets, sources of raw materials, and divisions of labor by gender and/or age, which condition the deployment of land, labor, and capital by their constituent household enterprises. Since specific branches of production in the Oaxaca Valley division of labor have been traditionally pursued by residents of particular settlements, division by branch coheres, with a few exceptions, to division by settlement.

In this study we focus especially upon embroidery, treadle loom weaving, backstrap loom weaving, palm plaiting (and its associated broom making), wood carving, ropemaking, and brickmaking. However, these are but a few among the total of thirty-nine artisan occupations represented among the sampled households, which also include carpenters, fireworks makers, blacksmiths, sandal makers, candlemakers, adobe makers, bakers, masons, lime makers, and basket makers. These are common occupations found in rural Oaxaca Valley communities that either supply the needs of the local population or meet a social demand originating in the wider regional population or beyond (see Cook 1982: 56–64 for a more comprehensive discussion of the "levels" of the division of labor in the Oaxaca Valley). The industries that we have selected for analysis account for more than 80 percent of the total of 933 craftspeople (in 765 artisan or peasant-artisan households) for which systematic information was collected and coded.[3] Moreover, just three craft industries—embroidery with 256 cases, weaving (backstrap and treadle loom combined) with 274 cases, and palm plaiting with 103 cases—account for 68 percent of the artisans sampled and reveal the important role that these occupations play as a source of employment in the Ocotlán and Tlacolula districts where they are practiced.

Tables 6, 7, and 8 contain statistical summaries of selected demographic, employment, income, and agricultural variables for 525 peasant-artisan and artisan households and 145 artisan households in five different branches of industrial commodity production, and one mixed-craft category.[4] The mixed-craft settlements contain multiple crafts and thus defy simple categorization, although embroidery is the predominant activity. By our definition all of the peasant-artisan households have access to land and are engaged in agricultural production although, as Chapter 2 clarified, most of this land consists of infrasubsistence-sized holdings and provides only a portion of yearly corn requirements.

One of the most significant variables in these tables is annual income per household member (Table 8), the calculation of which is based upon the estimated net value (gross income less production costs) of all cash and noncash income sources—including agricultural and animal production, own-account (*por su cuenta*) craft production, and wage labor—over the course of the year prior to the interview. Cases where information on major variables was missing or deemed unreliable (as when income from craft production was coded negative or zero) were eliminated for purposes of income calculation. A per capita figure was calculated for each household in order to facilitate relevant income comparisons among households of different sizes. Because the distributions in each branch were skewed toward the lower end of the range (with a few very high figures contributing to a disproportionate rise in the means), medians (in parentheses) as well as means were relied upon to estimate central tendency.[5]

Significantly, brickmaking and treadle loom weaving are characterized by mean and median incomes (Table 8) that are 2–3 times higher than those in other branches of rural industry. It is no coincidence, then, that these two branches are the most active arenas of capital accumulation and of the development of petty capitalist enterprises.

By contrast, the low median incomes (Table 8) in embroidery, palm/ixtle weaving, backstrap loom weaving, and mixed crafts determine that saving to expand production is difficult and that craft production is most likely to supplement agricultural production for the vast majority of these households.[6] This category of producers pursues a deliberate strategy of mixed participation in crafts and agriculture because neither form of production alone suffices to provide the cash and noncash basis for simple reproduction. As shown in Tables 6 and 7, it is precisely among these households where wage labor participation (especially through migration) is most important. Capital accumulation, when it occurs in these branches, is restricted to intermediary operations and occasionally becomes the basis for organizing production through piecework.

The data presented in Table 6 testify to the higher incidence of combined peasant-artisan production than to craft specialization without agriculture: peasant-artisan households outnumber artisans by a ratio of almost 4 to 1. This reflects the complementarity of agriculture and craft production discussed in the previous chapter and, from the perspective of rural household reproduction, highlights the desirability of combining these two basic types of productive activity. It is noteworthy that in Table 8 per capita artisan incomes average 25 to 50 percent higher than those of peasant-artisans. This suggests the possibility that there may be a material incentive operating to shift households away from peasant-artisan production and toward artisan production. In the short run there may be such a tendency. In the long run, however, most households with access to land and available labor tend to allocate a portion of their labor supply to the cultivation of staple crops like corn, beans, and squash (which have the dual advantage of being directly consumable or marketable for cash) or to the production of cash crops. This provides households with a greater degree of direct control over their subsistence but also makes it possible for them to respond to market fluctuations or to raise cash more readily as the need arises. It is precisely this versatility that provides artisans with a material incentive to acquire land for cultivation, and dampens any tendency toward the separation of agriculture and industry in the Oaxaca Valley.

The 1979 corn crop (Table 7) appears to have been subnormal with the mean and median harvest per household of 398 kg and 250 kg, respectively, adequate enough to provide only 5–6 months' con-

Table 6. Selected Demographic and Employment Variables for 525 Peasant-Artisan and 145 Artisan Households in 21 Oaxaca Valley Communities

	N	Family Size	Head of Household		Family Type (percentage)			Employment Data					Position in Occupation (percentage)		
			Age	Years School	Nucl.	Extd.	Single Par./Per.	Paid Jobs	Unpaid Jobs	Total Jobs	Craft Jobs	CW Ratio	Self-Empl.	Em-ployee	Em-ployer
Peasant-Artisans															
Embroidery	59	6.4	43.7	2.3 (2.0)	66.1	15.3	5.1	2.1 (2.0)	.9 (1.0)	3.0 (3.0)	1.8 (2.0)	2.4 (2.2)	56.3	40.6	3.1
Mixed crafts	209	6.2	44.4	2.0 (2.0)	56.9	22.9	2.4	2.4 (2.0)	.7 (0.0)	3.1 (3.0)	2.2 (2.2)	2.2 (2.0)	87.0	12.0	1.0
Palm/ixtle	94	5.4	46.6	2.2 (2.0)	64.9	13.8	7.5	1.9 (2.0)	1.2 (1.0)	3.1 (3.0)	2.0 (2.0)	1.9 (1.7)	100.0	00.0	00.0
Backstrap loom	30	6.8	47.7	2.5 (3.0)	50.0	16.6	6.7	1.9 (2.0)	1.7 (1.0)	3.5 (3.0)	2.4 (2.0)	2.0 (2.0)	100.0	00.0	00.0
Treadle loom	111	5.8	43.7	3.2 (3.0)	65.8	23.4	3.6	1.4 (1.0)	1.4 (1.0)	2.9 (2.0)	2.5 (2.0)	2.2 (2.0)	85.1	3.2	11.7
Brickmaking	22	7.4	45.2	3.9 (3.5)	77.3	9.1	9.1	1.9 (1.0)	.9 (0.0)	2.7 (2.0)	ND	4.3 (3.5)	50.0	00.0	50.0
All peasant-artisans	525	6.1	45.0	2.4 (2.0)	61.7	19.6	4.4	2.0 (2.0)	1.1 (1.0)	3.1 (3.0)	2.2 (2.0)	2.2 (2.0)	86.2	8.5	5.3

Artisans

Embroidery	18	6.3	38.0	2.2 (2.0)	66.7	0.0	5.6	2.2 (2.0)	.6 (0.0)	2.8 (2.0)	1.8 (1.5)	2.4 (2.5)	60.0	40.0	00.0
Mixed crafts	23	4.5	47.1	1.0 (0.0)	52.2	8.7	8.6	2.0 (2.0)	.1 (0.0)	2.2 (2.0)	1.6 (1.0)	2.4 (2.0)	46.7	40.0	13.3
Palm/ixtle	11	4.4	50.9	2.0 (2.0)	27.3	27.3	27.3	2.2 (2.0)	.4 (0.0)	2.6 (2.0)	2.2 (2.0)	1.8 (1.3)	100.0	00.0	00.0
Backstrap loom	14	5.8	44.6	2.2 (2.0)	50.0	7.1	21.4	1.6 (1.5)	1.0 (1.0)	2.6 (2.0)	1.9 (2.0)	2.4 (1.8)	100.0	00.0	00.0
Treadle loom	66	4.8	43.8	2.5 (2.0)	60.6	12.1	9.0	1.4 (1.0)	1.2 (1.0)	2.6 (2.0)	2.5 (2.0)	2.1 (1.7)	86.4	11.9	1.7
Brickmaking	13	6.9	35.4	3.2 (3.0)	69.2	7.7	7.7	1.5 (1.0)	2.2 (2.0)	3.8 (4.0)	ND	2.2 (1.8)	50.0	00.0	50.0
All artisans	145	5.3	44.7	2.2 (2.0)	57.2	10.4	11.0	1.6 (1.0)	1.0 (1.0)	2.6 (2.0)	2.1 (2.0)	2.3 (2.0)	79.4	16.7	3.9

Table 7. Selected Agricultural Variables for 525 Peasant-Artisan and 145 Artisan Households in 21 Oaxaca Valley Communities

	N	Land (Hectares)		Corn Production and Purchase		Instruments of Production			Agricultural Wage Labor		Value of Animals (Pesos)
		per House	per Capita	1979 (kg)	Months Bought	Value Owned	Value Rented	% with Oxteam	Days Hired	Days Worked	
Peasant-Artisans											
Embroidery	59	2.4	.44	303	5.9	3,387	730	31.1	17.0	12.7	5,280
		(1.6)	(.25)	(200)	(6.0)	(0)	(535)		(0.0)	(0.0)	(2,400)
Mixed crafts	209	2.2	.40	341	7.1	4,970	533	47.4	6.2	10.6	6,610
		(1.8)	(.30)	(250)	(8.0)	(2,500)	(130)		(0.0)	(0.0)	(4,150)
Palm/ixtle	94	2.2	.46	ND	4.7	11,210	80	42.6	9.3	17.6	10,726
		(1.5)	(.28)		(5.0)	(7,350)	(0)		(0.0)	(0.0)	(5,300)
Backstrap loom	30	2.6	.37	366	6.2	7,763	480	43.3	28.5	0.0	7,253
		(2.0)	(.30)	(300)	(6.0)	(1,850)	(190)		(1.0)	(0.0)	(4,000)
Treadle loom	111	1.8	.32	672	6.8	4,349	962	22.5	3.8	11.3	3,147
		(1.3)	(.26)	(250)	(7.5)	(0)	(650)		(0.0)	(0.0)	(1,450)
Brickmaking	22	ND	ND	ND	ND	5,255	2,345	10.0	0.6	3.3	4,968
						(0)	(1,900)		(0.0)	(0.0)	(3,550)
All peasant-artisans	525	2.1	.39	404	6.4	6,001	635	37.3	9.3	11.5	6,297
		(1.5)	(.28)	(250)	(7.0)	(200)	(200)		(0.0)	(0.0)	(3,000)

Artisans

Embroidery	18	—	42 (0)	10.9 (12.0)	0 (0)	0 (0)	0.0	0.0 (0.0)	17.3 (0.0)	2,422 (800)
Mixed crafts	23	—	45 (0)	9.5 (12.0)	1,668 (0)	17 (0)	17.4	0.0 (0.0)	29.4 (0.0)	1,109 (200)
Palm/ixtle	11	—	ND	7.4 (8.0)	3,022 (0)	3 (0)	33.3	2.0 (0.0)	10.9 (0.0)	8,200 (3,400)
Backstrap loom	14	—	78 (0)	9.4 (12.0)	729 (0)	0 (0)	7.1	1.7 (0)	ND	2,921 (1,500)
Treadle loom	66	—	0 (0)	11.2 (12.0)	159 (0)	0 (0)	1.6	0.6 (0.0)	26.5 (0.0)	1,231 (100)
Brickmaking	13	—	ND	9.6 (12.0)	0 (0)	0 (0)	0.0	0.0 (0.0)	0.0 (0.0)	2,238 (0)
All artisans	145	—	20 (0)	9.2 (12.0)	498 (0)	2 (0)	5.1	0.4 (0.0)	18.4 (0.0)	1,858 (300)

Table 8. Selected Income Variables for 328 Peasant-Artisan and 86 Artisan Households in 21 Oaxaca Valley Communities

	N	Income Measures (pesos)			Division of Income (proportion)			
		Annual per Cap	Weekly House	Living Conditions Index	Field Labor	Agri-culture	Animals	Artisan Product
Peasant-Artisans								
Embroidery	48	2,075 (863)	278 (94)	4.2 (3.5)	.12 (.00)	.42 (.39)	.05 (.00)	.42 (.36)
Mixed crafts	148	2,138 (1,372)	203 (153)	3.1 (3.0)	.08 (.00)	.30 (.20)	.03 (.00)	.59 (.68)
Palm/ixtle	62	4,136 (1,188)	299 (188)	3.3 (3.0)	.09 (.00)	.43 (.41)	.01 (.00)	.47 (.41)
Backstrap loom	2	691 (691)	140 (140)	4.0 (4.0)	.00 (.00)	.17 (.17)	.00 (.00)	.82 (.82)
Treadle loom	68	5,174 (4,126)	534 (433)	2.6 (3.0)	.07 (.00)	.22 (.08)	.03 (.00)	.66 (.86)
Brickmaking	0	ND	ND	ND	ND	ND	ND	ND
All peasant-artisans	328	3,127 (1,672)	300 (672)	3.2 (3.0)	.08 (.00)	.33 (.21)	.03 (.00)	.56 (.64)

Artisans

Embroidery	14	375 (238)	50 (33)	3.8 (4.2)	.12 (.00)	.04 (.00)	.09 (.00)	.78 (1.00)
Mixed crafts	15	1,181 (456)	102 (35)	2.4 (3.0)	.25 (.00)	.28 (.00)	.02 (.00)	.72 (1.00)
Palm/ixtle	7	5,274 (1,141)	419 (87)	2.8 (3.0)	.00 (.00)	.60 (.44)	.00 (.00)	1.00 (1.00)
Backstrap loom	0	ND	ND	ND	ND	ND	ND	ND
Treadle loom	50	6,023 (3,650)	497 (364)	1.2 (0.0)	.11 (.00)	.00 (.00)	.00 (.00)	.88 (1.00)
Brickmaking	0	ND	ND	ND	ND	ND	ND	ND
All artisans	86	4,198 (2,499)	349 (237)	2.0 (1.8)	.13 (.00)	.11 (.00)	.02 (.00)	.85 (1.00)

sumption. Insofar as our "living conditions index" (Table 8) is consistently higher for peasant-artisans than for artisans, either a poor harvest year or underreporting is probable. This index, which rates households according to house size (number of rooms), type of house construction, and tenure of house and house lot, as well as ownership of a television set, provides a rough measure of some of the factors that determine "standard of living," or "level of material reproduction." As such it represents aggregate economic performance over the medium to the long term and might be less susceptible to short-term fluctuations.

As Table 6 indicates, peasant-artisan households tend to be larger than artisan households (means of 6.1 to 5.2 members). They are *more likely* to be extended either viri- or uxori-locally but *less likely* to contain a single person or a single parent. These statistics suggest that demographic factors influence economic strategy. Some households are restricted to craft work because there are not enough workers to pursue both agriculture and craft production at the same time, or because the labor force has the wrong configuration, that is, there is only one adult or there are no adult males. Such households may divest themselves of landholdings and concentrate upon the (generally) more remunerative craft production and accept (for lack of alternatives) the risks that attend such commitment to commodity production in a market economy.

According to Table 7, most peasant-artisans are "dependent" agriculturists, that is, two-thirds of them lack ownership of an oxteam and must rent this crucial means of production from others in order to plow their fields or to transport the harvested crop from field to residence lot. Peasant-artisans are obliged to rent oxteams in the treadle loom and brickmaking communities where there is a particular shortage. Since average peasant-artisan incomes in such communities tend to be high, relative to those in embroidery, mixed-craft, and other communities, the lack of investment in oxteams may indicate that investment in craft production rather than in agriculture provides a generally higher return on labor time invested. In the case of brickmaking, land is the source of clay for making bricks and provides the soil for growing corn and other crops. In Santa Lucía del Camino, many hectares of agricultural land have been rendered useless for growing corn due to the intensification of clay excavation over time. Brick production is abandoned when the clay pits approach the water table (5 to 10 meters beneath the surface), at which point the land is often returned to agricultural production via the cultivation of alfalfa (Cook 1984a: 60).

Among the various peasant-artisan households are some rather significant differences with respect to a number of demographic and employment-related variables (Table 6). Some of the variations are easily explained. It seems logical, for instance, to attribute the higher average number of craftworkers in treadle loom and backstrap loom households to their greater dependence (relative to other branches) upon craft production as opposed to agriculture (70–80 percent of net income comes from craft production as compared to 40–60 percent for embroidery, mixed-crafts, and palm/ixtle households). Other variations are more difficult to explain, for example, those relating to mean household size in the different branches. Many elements—climatic, geographic, cultural, economic, political, and ideological—contribute to the structure and functioning of households, villages, and branches of industry. Since many of these elements are interactive it is difficult to discern the influence of any one without investigating the entire field. It is instructive to examine some of the major variables relating to the organization of production for own-use and for sale by peasant-artisans and to analyze the implications of various demographic configurations and economic resource bases in different rural industries.

Case Studies: The "Mixed-Craft" Villages and Their Industries.

The villages in this group combine involvement in embroidery with one or more additional craft industry. Table 9 presents the distribution of occupations by sex in six villages. As will be pointed out in Chapter 5, these figures often hide real cooperation between the sexes under an appearance of rigid gender division. Nevertheless, for purposes of discussion in this chapter, we will assume that the gender division is as decisive, without "sex-line crossing" (Shashahani 1986: 118), as it appears from the tabulated data.

Embroidery is the most widely diffused occupation, followed by basketry, backstrap loom weaving, and broom making. One of the peculiarities of the regional division of labor is that even though a village may have several craft occupations it tends to be identified (in the minds of the regional population at large) with only one commodity-producing specialization, which typically is the occupation its residents have practiced the longest but may not necessarily be the most widely practiced. For example, Santa Cecilia Jalieza is primarily identified with wood carving (but also has embroidery, weaving, and basketry) and San Pedro Guegorexe is identified with lime processing (but also has embroidery, wood carving, weaving,

Table 9. Distribution of Occupations in the 6 Mixed-Craft Villages by Gender

					Occupations						
Village	Embroidery	Basketry	Thread Spinning	Wood Carving	Weaving	Mescal	Lime	Firewood	Brooms	Metates	Total
Santa Cecilia Jalieza (N = 29)											
Males	6	3	0	36	5	0	0	0	0	0	50
Females	62	0	0	0	1	0	0	0	0	0	63
Santo Domingo Jalieza (N = 62)											
Males	2	12	0	0	37	0	0	22	10	0	83
Females	100	0	0	0	4	0	0	1	0	0	105

San Pedro Guegorexe (N = 25)											
Males	1	0	0	1	0	0	9	0	7	0	18
Females	31	0	0	0	10	0	0	0	0	0	41
Magdalena Ocotlán (N = 19)											
Males	0	0	0	0	0	0	0	0	0	3	3
Females	34	0	0	0	0	0	0	0	0	0	34
San Pedro Mártir (N = 27)											
Males	1	14	0	0	0	0	0	0	0	0	15
Females	29	2	0	0	0	0	0	0	0	0	31
San Baltazar Chichicapán (N = 48)											
Males	0	0	1	0	0	8	0	0	0	0	9
Females	44	0	57	0	0	0	0	0	0	0	101
Total	310	31	58	37	57	8	9	23	17	3	553

and broom making). Likewise, Magdalena Ocotlán has many more embroiderers than *metate* makers, yet its regional economic identity revolves around the *metate* industry. There are also cases of multiple identity as illustrated by San Baltazar Chichicapan. Ask at random any villager from the Ocotlán district how the people of Chichicapan make their living and the response will invariably include thread spinning and/or mescal distilling (although respondents are also apt to make reference to its alleged role in the marijuana trade).

Perhaps the key determinant of a village's public economic identity derives from its most visible role in the periodic marketplace or *plaza* system that has traditionally been the principal integrative mechanism of the regional peasant-artisan economy (Malinowski and de la Fuente 1982; Beals 1975; Cook and Diskin 1976). In short, villages are identified regionally with traditional commodities like pottery, serapes, wooden spoons and stirrers, *metates*, mats, baskets, and mescal, which are regularly sold in the *plaza* and/or in extra-plaza, intervillage trade. Ironically, this popular identity may be at variance with economic reality as villagers take up new occupations or diversify their product lines and their marketing patterns in traditional occupations. Many of the commodities produced under these new conditions are not marketed through traditional channels.

Embroidery

The type case of a new occupation in many villages is embroidery. Although embroidery by piece rate is today the most widely practiced craft occupation in the mixed-craft villages (except for San Baltazar where it is outstripped by thread spinning), for the most part it has been introduced or conceivably reintroduced after a long hiatus only during the last decade by regional putting-out merchants and their commission agents (see Waterbury 1989). This explains why in Table 10 embroiderers are the youngest (mean age of 33) and the least experienced (mean of 3.7 years) among the occupations listed. Embroidery products, if made in previous generations in these villages, probably did not circulate as commodities either locally or regionally. Today embroidered goods are destined exclusively for the tourist trade in Oaxaca City (or elsewhere in Mexico) or for export. This is precisely the same destination as the products of backstrap loom weaving, an occupation that has also been recently introduced (mean experience of 6 years per weaver) in several mixed-craft villages from Santo Tomás Jalieza. In short, what appear prima facie to be ancestral industries producing "traditional" products often turn

Table 10. *Selected Data on Occupations in Mixed-Craft Villages*

Variable	Occupations				
	Embroidery	Basketry	Thread Spinning	Wood Carving	Weaving
Age of producer	33	37	40	37	36
Sex of producer					
Male	10	29	1	37	42
Female	300	2	57	0	15
Years in craft	3.7	8.1	17.7	17.5	6.0
No. of family workers	.6	.3	.3	.3	.7
No. of employees	0	0	0	0	0
Sells when (intervals in days)	30.0	11.5	8.0	8.0	15.0
Sells in plaza	No (98.2%)	No (88.9%)	No (100%)	No (53.3%)	No (96.7%)
Sells to whom	Resellers (100%)	Resellers (84%)	Resellers (45%)	Resellers (69%)	Resellers (93%)
Length of prod. cycle (days)	30	15	15	8	15
Sales value per cycle	121	581	133	367	323
Total cost per prod. cycle	0	50	50	20	60
Income per prod. cycle	90	380	70	280	155
Yearly net income	1,095	9,247	1,825	12,775	3,650

Note: Quantitative variables are means or medians, whichever is most valid. Monetary values are in pesos.

out on further inquiry to be recently introduced and producing new products or modified versions of "traditional" ones.

Basketry

Baskets of a utilitarian type used primarily for harvesting corn (made with a bamboolike reed called *carrizo*) have been produced seasonally for sale locally and in the Ocotlán marketplace by a few households in San Pedro Mártir for generations. However, in the last decade or so the occupation has grown in San Pedro and in Santo Domingo Jalieza through the activity of buying-up merchants from Oaxaca City and elsewhere (and their local commission agents, or *comisionistas*) who export specialty baskets (e.g., clothes hampers and fruit baskets) or sell domestically to businesses in the tourist trade. Consequently, most of the basket makers in our survey, who average only 8 years in the industry, took up the craft during this recent period of growth and sell exclusively to buyers-up who come to their village (or have a resident commission agent) without ever selling baskets in the marketplace (see Druijven 1988).

Metates *and* Manos *in Magdalena Ocotlán*

In a few industries in the mixed-craft villages, traditional peasant-artisan production persists relatively unchanged. This is illustrated in Magdalena Ocotlán where the women have been drawn into the new putting-out system in embroidery, but several men continue to produce *metates, manos,* and mortars and pestles for sale in the Friday market in the district head town, or *cabecera.* Probably no other commodities still produced in the Oaxaca Valley embody more material and ideological elements representative of traditional peasant-artisan village life than do the products of this lapidary industry.

As utilitarian artifacts, the *metate* and *mano* emerged historically together with maize-based village agriculture as milling tools necessary for realizing the full-food potential of shelled maize (i.e., to grind into dough for tortillas). They continue to be manufactured and sold to satisfy a persisting social demand even though their food processing role has been greatly diminished by the introduction of mechanical grinding mills (*molinos de nixtamal*) into most rural Oaxaca villages, not to speak of tortilla factories in cities and towns. Many rural housewives, however, find that without further processing mill-ground maize dough (*masa*) is not suited for making tortillas and that the proper consistency can only be achieved by re-grinding and kneading the dough with a *metate* and *mano.*

Another reason for these ancient artifacts' persistence has to do with their symbolic content. The artifact set, *metate* and *mano,* in effect symbolizes the conjugal relationship, the gender division of labor, and, more particularly, the role of the peasant housewife as mistress of the hearth and provisioner of the food staple—tortillas. It is this symbolism that is ritually reinforced in Valley Zapotec villages during the *fandango* when the godfather of the bride (or his representative) dances with a *metate* on his back as it is presented to the bride as a wedding gift. This same symbolism is openly expressed by Zapotec peasant women of all ages, married or unmarried, in their responses to the question as to why they use *metates*. According to them, to be a woman is to use a *metate* and *mano* to grind maize into dough for making tortillas.

Yet, even in the case of the production of ancient artifacts like *metates* and *manos* appearances are deceiving because Magdalenans are also relative newcomers, by Oaxaca Valley standards, to the *metate* craft. Oral tradition traces the origin of the Magdalena branch of the *metate* industry to a *metate* maker (*metatero*) from San Juan Teitipac (where the craft probably had a prehispanic origin—see Cook 1982: 181–184) who married a Magdalena woman, took up residence there around 1900, and began to practice his craft and to teach it to others. That he was successful is clear from an official 1920 Agrarian Department delegate's report, corresponding to the village's petition for an *ejido*, which states that "whereas it is certain that the men of Magdalena are dedicated to the industry of the fabrication of *metates*, they do so in a rudimentary way and merely as a means to increase in part their meager resources" (*Archivo de la Secretaría de Reforma Agraria, Expediente 14, Documento 15*). Although the industry was introduced and caught hold in the pre-ejido years when most of the Magdalenans were landless peons and sharecroppers on a large hacienda that owned most of the land in the region, it was obviously maintained as an important supplement to agriculture after the ejido grant ended their landlessness.

Wood Carving in Santa Cecilia

In the case of Santa Cecilia Jalieza, historical sources and oral tradition confirm that its families have practiced wood carving—particularly of wooden spoons and beverage stirrers (*acahuetes*)—for many generations, at least since the colonial period and, perhaps, even earlier (Taylor, 1972: 103). In and of itself, the longevity of this craft tradition is equaled or excelled by other Oaxaca Valley populations, but what makes Santa Cecilia noteworthy is its small size (346 inhabitants in 1978 according to the official local census compared to 200 inhabitants in a 1923 census) and its history of troubled relations with larger neighboring populations. Indeed, in several occasions from the seventeenth century into the twentieth century the Santa Cecilians have been forced to relocate or vacate their settlement. According to oral tradition, survival during these periods of turmoil was made possible by the refuge provided to women and children by relatives or friends in other communities while the men went off to distant mountainous districts with ample wood resources to practice their craft and sell their products in Oaxaca City.[7]

Today, Santa Cecilia Jalieza has the highest rate of household participation in craft production among the six mixed-craft villages—of 34 households surveyed only 3 had no craft producers. It also has the highest average number of artisans per household—2.9 compared to an average of 1.8 in the other villages. This difference is not surprising since of the twenty villages surveyed Santa Cecilia has by far the highest percentage of extended family households (38 percent) and the second-largest average household size (7.4)—both figures being well above the mean for the other villages in the "mixed-craft" group (18.8 percent and 5.5, respectively).

Embroidery, with 31 participating households, is the most widely practiced craft, followed by wood carving with 25 participating households. As Table 11 shows, embroidery is almost exclusively practiced by females, whereas carving is practiced by males (with field observations indicating that women occasionally help to finish carved products by sanding). Wood carving, which has been practiced in Santa Cecilia for centuries (in contrast to embroidery, which was introduced in 1970), is more evenly distributed among male age groups than is embroidery among female age groups.

The typical Santa Cecilia household includes a male head who tills the soil and carves, his wife who embroiders in addition to her household duties, and one additional member who either embroiders or carves. All of the craft households in our Santa Cecilia sample are landed, with a median of 2.0 hectares per household (.27 hectares per household member). The high degree of landedness is attributable to Santa Cecilia's status as an ejidal community with a limited zone of private parcels.

The carving industry involves the manufacture of various utensils from wood, which, until recently, was cut by the carvers themselves from communal woodlands. Boundary disputes with the contiguous settlement of San Juan Teitipac, together with depletion of the favored types of trees, have forced the Santa Cecilians in recent years to buy most of their wood in the Ocotlán marketplace from wood cutters residing in other district villages. This loss of self-sufficiency with regard to their principal raw material may ultimately contribute to the demise of the wood carving industry in Santa Cecilia. Interviews conducted there in 1985, however, show that adequate supplies of wood have been forthcoming in the market and that the cost has been partially compensated for in selling prices. Theoretically, this change in wood procurement could result in increased output since it frees carvers of the obligation of spending one day a week in

Table 11. *Distribution by Age and Gender of Embroidery and Wood Carving among 30 Households in Santa Cecilia Jalieza*

Age	Embroi-dery	Wood Carving	Total
Males			
0–09	0	0	0
10–19	2	2	4
20–29	2	11	13
30–39	0	10	10
40–49	2	8	10
50–59	0	2	2
60+	0	3	3
Subtotal	6	36	42
Females			
0–09	2	0	2
10–19	24	0	24
20–29	15	0	15
30–39	13	0	13
40–49	4	0	4
50–59	4	0	4
60+	0	0	0
Subtotal	62	0	62
Total	68	36	104

the hills obtaining their wood supply—giving them an additional day each week to carve.

Santa Cecilia products have traditionally been sold in the Ocotlán and Oaxaca City marketplaces; however, in recent decades they have diversified their marketing patterns (or, as one informant phrased it, "looking for a way to earn a little more money"), as well as their products, to cater to the tourist trade in Oaxaca City. Indeed, the largest-selling product is an ingenious adaptation of the traditional chocolate beverage stirrer (*acahuete*—see Parsons 1936: 36–37); the rectangular shaft and squared end of the stirrer have been curved and pointed to convert it into a letter opener. The handle retains its original configuration but now includes a wider variety of animal figures. A few of the most skilled and enterprising carvers also began to make wooden combs (modeled after products made in a Oaxaca City workshop), which are popular with tourists. These letter openers and combs, as well as small spoons, are aggressively marketed by the wood carvers and other members of their households on the streets of Oaxaca City, but the wood carvers prefer to sell wholesale—and on an advance order basis—to dealers.

In recent years, the city government has periodically enforced a policy of discouraging street sales by itinerant craft peddlers. Despite this obstacle the Santa Cecilians have persisted in their efforts to make street sales to tourists and, in fact, seem to have expanded such sales. They also remain committed to direct sales to souvenir shops and dealers (which have included government agencies like FONART and INI). These sales strategies seem to have succeeded since in 1979–1980 they enjoyed the highest yearly net income per household (12,775 pesos, or 568 dollars) of the five occupations listed in Table 10.[8]

Case Studies: The Palm and Ixtle Industries

The palm- and ixtle-processing industries[9] in the Albarradas villages of San Lorenzo and Santo Domingo are located in the eastern mountain hinterland of the Oaxaca Valley above Mitla. These two industries have prehispanic and colonial roots as well as other hallmarks of "traditional" peasant-artisan industries but, paradoxically, are well on their way to persisting into the twenty-first century.

Both industries' products are fabricated by a simple technology that has changed little over the centuries. Their raw materials are locally produced from indigenous plants, fan palm and maguey, with only the latter being cultivated. A variety of mats, baskets, and rope products are made in household-based production units with non-waged or reciprocal labor and are marketed through haggling in local and regional marketplaces; the sellers are either the producers or petty buyers-up, whereas the buyers are mostly rural householders from other communities of the region.

The two Albarradas villages have the highest household participation rate in craft production of all the villages surveyed: in San Lorenzo, 95 percent of the 77 households surveyed had members actively engaged in either palm plaiting or broom making, whereas in Santo Domingo, 98 percent of the survey households had palm plaiters and 30 percent had either ixtle makers or rope twiners. Table 12 shows the distribution of occupations among these two populations by age and sex.

These data suggest that the division of labor by gender in these villages is more rigidly structured than the age division: palm plaiting is overwhelmingly a female occupation (as is palm product reselling), whereas broom making, ixtle fabrication, and rope twining

Table 12. *Distribution of Craft Occupations by Age and Gender in the Albarradas Villages*

Age	San Lorenzo (n = 77)			Santo Domingo (n = 39)		
	Palm Plaiting	Reseller	Brooms	Palm Plaiting	Ixtle	Rope
Males						
0–9	0	0	0	0	0	0
10–19	0	0	1	0	2	2
20–29	1	0	4	0	2	1
30–39	1	0	5	0	1	1
40–49	2	0	7	0	2	1
50–59	1	0	2	0	3	3
60+	0	0	5	0	1	2
Subtotal	5	0	24	0	11	10
Females						
0–9	1	0	0	0	0	0
10–19	24	0	0	21	0	0
20–29	24	0	0	10	0	0
30–39	24	1	0	14	0	0
40–49	10	1	0	9	0	0
50–59	17	1	0	7	0	0
60+	10	0	0	5	0	0
Subtotal	110	3	0	66	0	0
Total	115	3	24	66	11	10

Note: Tabulations include all household members. The 74 households surveyed in San Lorenzo had a total of 388 members, with an average household size of 5.2; the 38 survey households in Santo Domingo had a total of 200 members, with an average size of 5.3.

are exclusively male occupations. It is also significant that females in the 10–19 age range comprise a much larger proportion of the labor force in the predominantly female industries than do males in that age range in the male industries. Among other factors, this reflects the assignment to males in this age group of tasks in agriculture that require them to be in the fields or elsewhere in the countryside away from the village residence area. By contrast, females, with some exceptions (e.g., crop planting or harvest, gathering cut fronds during the palm harvest), are mostly allocated tasks that can be performed in the village proper and, especially, within the confines of the household residence lot. Field observations confirmed that females do not participate in cutting palm (though a few do help in collecting and sorting cut palm).

Cultural differences may explain the fact that a handful of men in San Lorenzo engage in palm plaiting while none do in Santo Domingo. The latter community is Zapotec whereas San Lorenzo is mestizo and exclusively Spanish speaking (see Cook 1983b). In Santo Domingo the gender division in the palm industry is encompassed within a general ideology that rationalizes the separation of female and male domestic provisioning responsibilities in the ideal household. Men are expected to provide corn for tortillas while women, aside from the responsibility of preparing tortillas, are expected to provide basic kitchen provisions like tomatoes, chile peppers, salt, sugar, soap, lard, coffee, and chocolate. It is expected that women will meet this obligation by plaiting baskets and mats or helping to twine rope.

An analysis of income data shows that almost two-thirds of palm industry households earn gross cash incomes of less than 100 pesos ($4.44) weekly from plaiting mats or making brooms (dry season only). By contrast, all households participating in ixtle production and rope twining reported gross weekly incomes (dry season only) ranging from 100 to 500 pesos weekly. It is not surprising, then, that palm plaiters said that they plaited palm *"por la necesidad"* (out of need), since it is the only occupation available to them, and admitted that they would prefer an alternative occupation because palm plaiting was physically punishing, low paying, and deprived them of the opportunity to accumulate capital or improve their standard of living.

The Palm Plaiting Industry

The mountainous terrain of the municipality of San Lorenzo Albarradas is generously endowed with stands of native palm that serve as the principal resource for the plaiting industry and for traders who supply palm fronds to several surrounding communities, including Santo Domingo. The stands are located mostly on ejidal and communal land and their exploitation is closely regulated by the two village authorities (i.e., those of the *ayuntamiento municipal* and those of the *comisariado ejidal*). Annually, during a six-week period between December and February, the San Lorenzo authorities sponsor two consecutive, carefully administered palm cuttings (called *"destajo de la palma"*) in which households are assigned cutting rights over designated stands containing roughly the same number of trees and potential frond yields.

Once household palm allotments are demarcated, the fronds are cut, sorted, and tied into bundles (manojos) of 100 fronds each. Before the palm can be hauled out of the cutting area back to the village for drying and eventual use, the bundles must be counted by a municipal official who then collects a fee of 2 pesos per bundle from the responsible villager.

The respective treasurers of each village authority (i.e., municipal and ejidal), using a list of eligible taxpayers, keep complete records of every annual palm cutting. These records for the season, which ran from December 1978 to February 1979, show that a total of 10,698 bundles (1,069,800 fronds) were cut on the public lands controlled by the two authorities (an additional 300 bundles were estimated to have been cut on privately owned parcels). This averaged out to 7.7 bundles per comunero (645 persons on the communal list) and 9.1 bundles per ejidatario (629 names on the ejido list). However, this average varies considerably: the range of palm purchased from the communal land in 1979 was from 1 to 87 bundles per person listed (compared to 1.5 to 92 bundles in 1978), and the range for palm from the ejidal land was 3 to 57 bundles per person listed.

A comparison of the 1978 and 1979 lists for palm cut on communal lands shows that 645 persons cut and purchased palm in 1978, whereas only 540 were on the 1979 list (8.2 bundles per person average vs. 7.7 bundles per person average in 1978). In other words, there is interannual variation in the number of persons participating in the palm harvest. Not everyone qualified actually gets a palm allotment for such reasons as illness, shortage of household labor, or because of a decision to forgo cutting palm, with the result that they must buy palm later in the year from other households. Many households that are entitled to allotments from both communal and ejidal lands will take only one of them. Unclaimed allotments are reassigned, often to members of the respective authorities (incidentally, in both 1978 and 1979 the largest number of bundles cut on the communal land went to the municipal president, 92 and 87 bundles, respectively). Also, in any given year, it is difficult from the lists to calculate how much palm is cut annually per household since persons other than household heads may appear on the list, either as representing a particular household head or as a taxpayer who is not a household head.

One result of the variable distribution of palm is that households with a surplus sell to deficit households or to intermediaries who in turn sell palm to plaiters in neighboring villages that have little or no native palm. One of two principal palm traders estimated that he sold 800 bundles annually, mostly to customers in Santo Domingo.

At the time he was interviewed in the spring of 1980, this trader was buying palm for 20 pesos per bundle ($.90) and reselling it for an average price of 30–35 pesos (ca. $1.35). Informants agreed that the price of palm is pegged to the price of mats—the most widely produced product. As with most peasant-artisan products produced for regional sale, the supply, demand, and prices of mats (and, by implication, of palm) increase in the postharvest, dry season period from October to March and shift downward during the rainy season from April to September when the fields are planted, plants are tended, and cash is scarce (cf. Cook 1982: Ch. 7).

After newly cut palm fronds are sorted into bundles and hauled back to village residence lots, the bundles are untied and the fronds are spread out on the ground or on tile roofs of houses where they remain for 6–8 weeks until they desiccate. Next, the fronds are re-sorted (by length, color, and quality); those that are unsuitable for plaiting mats (*petates*) or baskets (*tenates*) are used to make griddle brushes (*limpiacomales*), fans (*sopladores*), brooms (*escobas*), roofing material, or fuel. In short, all of the palm that is harvested is put to productive use. Several hours before use, fronds of plaiting quality are dampened with water to soften them, then the separate leaves are cut into strips and plaiting begins.

The most commonly produced products are mats, which are widely used in peasant households for a variety of purposes ranging from sleeping to covering or bundling merchandise. They are produced in a variety of standardized square or oblong sizes (and qualities), which are customarily measured by hand lengths (roughly 16 cms), counted in tens, and referred to as *pares* (pairs) or *cuartos* (quarters). The smallest standard-size mat is 20 hand lengths (roughly 100 cm, or 6 average hand lengths, by 68 cm, or roughly 4 hand lengths) and is used primarily as a sleeping mat for infants. The 30 and 40 hand-length sizes are used mostly as *tapacargas* (cover for merchandise loaded into large reed baskets). The most demanded size is the 60 hand-length size (used as a double-bed-sized sleeping mat), but mats measuring as large as 100 or 150 hand lengths are also made, usually on a special order basis. One bundle of palm yields, on the average, three size-20 mats and two size-60 mats.

Given the variability of daily worktime allocated to plaiting by various female members of a household, the variable incidence of working alone or in tandem (two persons often work jointly on mats size 60 or larger), and other factors such as the differential labor supplies between households and the variety of products plaited, it is difficult to measure productivity in the palm industry. Table 13 presents estimates derived from field observations and from an analysis of the eight best cases from the household survey. Among other things, this table shows that the more than 20.5 hours labor required to fabricate a standard size-60 mat are highly cooperative, involving both males and females as well as individuals working with one or more partners.

Half of 100 reporting households in both villages indicated that their last sale of palm mats had been not more than a week prior to the interview (for an average gross return ranging between 50 and 199 pesos), with the rest indicating that longer intervals had elapsed since their last sale. Eighteen percent had last sold at intervals longer than one month (for an average gross return exceeding 250 pesos). Thirty-eight percent of the responding households reported that they regularly sold palm mats at intervals of one week or less. More than half of the households sell regularly in the village to intermediaries (all women), referred to locally as *empleadoras,* who customarily provide credit to the direct producers, either in the form of cash or on account in small stores they own and operate. The rest sell to clients in external marketplaces (especially in Tlacolula, the district head town), which they regularly attend.

The female resellers, most of whom also plait palm themselves, comprise roughly 15 percent of the women surveyed in both villages. Most of them operate on a relatively small scale, buying for resale less than six mats weekly (for an average profit ranging from 10 to 25 percent of the purchase price). One woman was observed to bring one dozen size-60 mats, which she purchased for 60 pesos ($2.65) each, to the Tlacolula marketplace where she resold them for 85 and 90 pesos ($3.75) each. Her gross profit on that particular market day (9 mats sold) was 255 pesos ($11.30), which was substantially above her estimated weekly profits of 120 pesos ($5.30). It is only through the operations of a few larger volume resellers, who combine mat reselling with store keeping, that the volume of transactions is of sufficient scale to permit significant levels of capital accumulation.

The Ixtle Twining Industry

Ixtle fiber production in Santo Domingo Albarradas, a dry season activity, depends upon a locally cultivated supply of maguey. Ixtle-producing households, which may or may not twine rope, grow their own supply of maguey, purchase it from other households, or gain access to maguey through a share arrangement.

A typical arrangement is for the owner of maguey plants, who is not an ixtle producer, to cut the maguey; next the ixtle producer will

Table 13. The Labor Process of Palm Mat Production

	Cutting & Sorting Palm	Preparation of Palm for Plaiting		Plaiting Mats
Nature and Order of Operations	1. Cut, gather, sort, bundle, and haul fronds to village	2. Green fronds are unbundled, laid out to dry, resorted and rebundled	3. Dried fronds are softened by dampening overnight and then cut into strips	4. Moisture-softened palm strips are plaited on one end first, followed by body and two sides and, finally, by other end; protruding ends of strips are cut to finish mat
Required Means of Production	long-handled pruning knife, machete, burro	None	Small knife	Deer bone awl (Santo Domingo only), small knife
Stage in Material Transformation	From green fronds on trees to 100-frond bundles (*manojos*)	From sorted green fronds to resorted and rebundled dried fronds	From dried, sorted fronds to softened palm strips	From palm strips to finished mats
Work	Two males or 1 male	One worker (usually)	One or 2 female	Two females working

Organization	cutting and 1 female gathering/sorting	workers	together or 1 female
Duration of Operation[a]	405 minutes × 2 = 810 minutes (for 15 sorted bundles of 100 fronds each) = 54 minutes/bundle	1 hour per bundle 3 hours (1 bundle)	1 female × 18 hours or 2 females × 9 hours = 18 hours
Amount of Work in Hours of Cooperative Labor Time[b]	.45 hours × 2 = .90 hours/bundle (two workers)	1.00 hours + 3.00 hours = 4.00 hours (1 bundle)	18 hours × 2 = 36 hours of individual and cooperative labor time embodied in plaiting two size 60 mats

.90 + 4.00 + 36.00 = 40.90 hours of cooperative labor time to produce a weekly household average of two size-60 mats.[c]

[a] Figures based on field observations.
[b] Calculation based on an average bundle yield of two size-60 mats.
[c] Average derived from 8 best cases; figures in columns 2, 3, & 4 are computed for a standard size-60 mat.

scorch and partially roast the maguey leaves over a smoldering fire in crudely improvised firing areas (*hornos*) located near the fields, crush the partially roasted maguey leaves with a wooden maul, and then bundle and haul them to the "factory" (*fábrica*), an area on communal terrain near the village where a stream feeds a series of pools sunk in bedrock. The leaves are soaked in water, crushed for a second time with wooden mauls, shredded, cleaned, bundled and, finally, hauled to the village for drying. The users of the communal ixtle processing area pay a nominal surcharge (assessed according to output) to the village government. A typical production cycle begins with the cutting of four maguey plants (*matas*), requires an average of fifteen workdays (8 hours each plus 8 days' soaking time) and yields 4 *arrobas* (1 *arroba* = 25 pounds, or 11.5 kilos) of fiber worth 300 pesos ($13.30) per *arroba*.

One Santo Domingo household with a father-son team produces an average of 7–8 *arrobas* of fiber monthly during three dry-season months each year (usually January, February, and March). Of each month's fiber output, perhaps 2–3 *arrobas* will be used for rope production and the remainder will be sold to other village rope-producing households. Two household members working for approximately two and one-half days can transform an *arroba* of ixtle into a quantity of rope that in May 1980 was worth about 500 pesos ($22.20).

In one case on record, the members of a household worked 22.5 hours (a 54-year-old man and his 18-year-old son with 1.5 hours assistance from the man's wife) to produce (from 1 *arroba* of their own ixtle) one dozen lengths (8 *brazadas*, or arm lengths, each roughly equivalent to 1 meter) of half-inch-thick rope with a market value of 600 pesos ($26.65). In another case a father and his 12-year-old daughter worked 4 days to twine 8 dozen lengths of rope with a market value of 120 pesos per dozen (960 pesos, or $42.65, for 8 dozen) from 2.5 *arrobas* of ixtle. Since in this case the ixtle was purchased for 750 pesos, they earned a profit of only 210 pesos ($9.35, or a daily per capita return to labor of roughly $2.00 dollars). By contrast, in San Lorenzo a young husband and wife, who produce rope from ixtle imported from other Mexican states, purchased 6 *arrobas* monthly (175 pesos, or $7.75, each) for an estimated net daily earnings per month average of 100–115 pesos (ca. $4.50).

Despite variable productivity and cash returns among households engaged in ixtle production, the latter mostly supplements agricultural production for own-use and does not promote capital accumulation or enterprise development. A handful of intermediaries who are also direct producers of rope, however, do earn returns significantly higher than the majority of nonintermediary households.

Case Studies: Treadle Loom Weaving

Treadle loom weaving was introduced into the Oaxaca Valley by the Spanish in the sixteenth century. Although the region's principal city, Antequera (to be renamed Oaxaca de Juárez in 1872 immediately following the death of its most illustrious resident Benito Juárez—Nolasco 1981: 186), did have a few small-scale textile sweatshops by the end of the eighteenth century, the weaving industry was mostly located in Indian communities (Chance 1978: 111). According to a recent comprehensive study of the weaving industry in Mexico from 1539 to 1840 there is no evidence that Oaxaca had *obrajes* (i.e., weaving manufactories) but that it had "the putting-out system in cottons: small masters financed by merchant clothiers, looms maintained in dwellings, and little or no integration of production" (Salvucci 1987: 55). There is, however, substantial evidence to indicate that by the end of the eighteenth century the clothing and textile industries "were by far the most important economic activities in the city, employing by 1792 over a quarter of the male non-Indian work force" (Chance 1978: 148).

Although the scale and type of enterprises in the urban weaving industry remain unclear, treadle loom weaving retained its importance in the city's economy until the end of the nineteenth century when it suffered a decline that continued through the early decades of the twentieth century. Starting around 1940, the industry experienced a minor rejuvenation, which lasted for nearly three decades until it entered another decline, which has not abated to this day. The rejuvenation of the industry was apparently based on the importation by local entrepreneurs of specialized looms from Puebla that produced a cloth known as *cambaya*, a coarse cotton cloth of the type more widely known as *manta*, woven in different colors with designs and used primarily in the manufacture of clothing. With these looms, and apparently by recruiting weavers from the ranks of petty producers who wove shawls, sashes, and wraparound skirts for local and regional markets, the cloth industry (*industria mantelera*) was reborn in Oaxaca City—producing multicolored tablecloths, napkins, towels, and bedspreads with "traditional Mexican" borders and designs (e.g., a precolumbian figure in the center). The principal raw material was cotton thread produced in Puebla factories and dyed in the Oaxaca City workshops.

The industry flourished during the 1940s, enjoying export sales in addition to sales in local, regional, and national markets, but began to experience difficulties in the post-Korean War period, because of foreign competition and the Mexican government's imposition of new fiscal obligations (e.g., social security) on manufacturers. The withdrawal of capital from the cloth industry began in response to these conditions by 1970 and, today, with a few exceptions, the industry survives through petty household and workshop production located in peripheral urban zones of Oaxaca City, in Mitla, and in Ocotlán de Morelos (Rivermar and Tellez 1984: 94–104). Symptomatic of the relocation of treadle loom weaving to the countryside is that several of the looms in use in Xaagá today were purchased secondhand at liquidation sales in Oaxaca City *mantelerías*.[10]

In the remainder of this section we will examine treadle loom weaving in three communities located in the district of Tlacolula: Teotitlán del Valle, the pioneering and most important community of rural treadle loom weavers in the Oaxaca Valley; the neighboring community of Santa Ana del Valle (essentially a weaving satellite of Teotitlán); and the village of Xaagá, a weaving and garment producing satellite of Mitla, an important commercial and tourist center renowned for its precolumbian ruins.

These three communities represent the two basic branches of Valley treadle loom weaving. The woolen products branch, represented by Teotitlán and Santa Ana, produces mainly serapes, blankets, and tapestries. The cotton products branch has two sectors: one of these is the *mantelería* branch described above, and the other, represented by Xaagá, produces mainly shawls, shirts, blouses, and dresses. It should be cautioned, however, that this differentiation according to raw material and product type is not absolute since weavers in all three communities also weave with acrylic yarn and overlap in the weaving of products like handbags and vests. Even though the two branches share a treadle loom centered labor process, a crucial difference between them needs to be underlined. The loom operator in the Teotitlán–Santa Ana branch produces, for the most part, finished products (woolen blankets or tapestries), whereas the loom operator in the Xaagá branch produces a raw material, bolt cloth, that must be further transformed to obtain a finished product (e.g., a shawl that has been hand knotted, or a shirt that has been hand cut and machine sewn). In other words, in Xaagá we are dealing with a garment industry rather than a weaving industry per se. This difference should be kept in mind as we compare the division of labor in these branches.

The Woolen Products Branch in Teotitlán and Santa Ana

This branch provides a good illustration of how the prevailing relations of production and exchange in petty industry are shaped by
the nature of the labor supply and by the conditions surrounding
the supply of raw materials and other means of production. It also
provides an excellent case study of how relations of dependency
and subordination may develop between different settlements in one
branch of production.[11]

Treadle loom weaving begins with making or acquiring yarn
(which in the case of wool yarn may include cleaning and washing
the wool, carding the wool, and spinning the yarn), continues with
bleaching or dyeing the yarn and setting up the loom, and culmi-
nates with the loom operation. In Teotitlán more factory-made yarn,
especially the 80- percent wool content variety but also 100 percent
acrylic, is used than hand-spun yarn; this yarn is purchased in stores
and shops in the village, often on credit (*fiado*). Although some
weavers buy their supply of hand-spun yarn, most weavers use it
only when it is produced at home. Typically, women take two to
three weeks to spin a sufficient quantity of yarn for a week or so of
weaving (usually a quantity targeted to weaving a particular piece or
pieces).

The Teotitlán weavers do more dyeing, do a better job of dyeing
with synthetic dyestuffs, and also use more homemade vegetable or
cochineal dyes than their Santa Ana counterparts. The same pattern
carries over into product design. The Teotitlán weavers have a larger
repertory of designs as well as more sophistication in designing than
do the Santa Ana weavers. In Santa Ana, almost the entire output
consists of such standard commercial designs as simple precolumbian figures, whereas the Teotitlán weavers, in addition to these designs, are justifiably famed for more complicated patterns.

The overall quality of weaving in Teotitlán is superior to that in
Santa Ana for two reasons. First, the Teotitlán weavers have more
experience; they come from a village with a longer tradition of weaving. Innovations in product design from a utilitarian style to an artistic or ornamental style were made in Teotitlán. Second, and more
important, at least 40 percent (and perhaps more) of the Santa Ana
weavers receive yarn on credit (*recibir hilo fiado*) from local intermediaries who also buy-up their finished woven products. When
the yarn is supplied to the weavers, the intermediaries specify the
type of product and design that they want to buy. These Santa Ana
buyers-up, in turn, sell the products to merchants in Teotitlán and

Mitla for a small profit. For this reason the prices paid to Santa Ana
weavers for their work are lower than those paid to Teotitlán weavers
for products of comparable quality. Undoubtedly, the weavers of
Santa Ana are capable of weaving better-quality products, but they
find themselves compelled by relations of production and exchange
to continue to weave lower-quality, utilitarian, and highly commer-
cialized products.[12]

During the spring of 1979, 121 households were interviewed by
random sample in these two villages in order to gather more systematic data on these issues. As it turned out, 85 percent (104) of the
households had at least one male or female weaver; there were 166
weavers (153 males, 13 females), or an average of 1.6 weavers per
household. In addition to weaving (tejido), two other types of work
related to weaving were widespread in these villages: thread spinning (hilado) and dyeing (teñido). With the exception of 3 households with members who spin thread to sell, thread spinning and
dyeing are unpaid jobs. An important difference between the two
groups of weavers emerges at this point, that is, a much higher percentage of Teotitlán households engaged in all three wool-working
activities: spinning, dyeing, and weaving. Of the 62 households in
which more than one person wove, 76 percent engaged in all three
activities (compared to 20 percent in Santa Ana).

Furthermore, 68 percent of the households interviewed in Teotitlán
spun thread, compared to only 21 percent in Santa Ana. Accordingly,
the proportion of Santa Ana weavers using factory-made yarn (either
acrylic or 80 percent wool content) in their products is higher than it
is in Teotitlán, although Teotitlán weavers also mix factory-made
and hand-spun yarn.

In addition to weaving, spinning, and dyeing, another widespread
task practiced in this branch is winding yarn onto small spools (llenar
canillas) for the weavers. This task normally occupies from 15 to 30
minutes daily when there are persons weaving that same day. Table
14 presents the distribution of these tasks in Teotitlán and Santa
Ana by age and gender. This table shows clearly the division of labor
by gender that exists within this branch: there are more than ten
male weavers for every female weaver, and only one male is involved
in spinning, yarn winding, or dyeing for every five females. It is interesting to note, however, that crossover occurs in every instance,
which suggests that the division may be subject to conjunctural
change. This possibility is somewhat dampened by the fact that
twenty-four of the males who participate in these other tasks are
principally weavers, which indicates that males simply assist women
when necessary. Although the table does not show it, there were

Table 14. *Distribution of Tasks by Age and Gender in Treadle Loom Weaving in 2 Tlacolula Villages (Teotitlán del Valle and Santa Ana del Valle)*

Age	Weaving	Spinning	Bobbins	Dyeing
Males				
0–9	0	0	0	0
10–19	37	1	6	2
20–29	32	1	7	12
30–39	22	0	2	3
40–49	25	4	0	6
50–59	24	4	7	11
60+	12	0	0	1
Subtotal	152	10	22	35
Females				
0–9	0	0	0	1
10–19	2	19	24	14
20–29	8	12	26	16
30–39	0	22	28	27
40–49	2	16	18	14
50–59	1	12	13	12
60+	0	6	2	2
Subtotal	13	87	111	86
Total	165	97	133	121

proportionately twice as many female weavers in Santa Ana as in Teotitlán. Relevant considerations here are that many fewer women spin in Santa Ana than in Teotitlán and that product prices are at a lower level in Santa Ana; lower product earnings, therefore, place more pressure on Santa Ana women to earn income through weaving.

A household survey conducted in Teotitlán del Valle during the summer of 1978 (about six months prior to our own survey) found that the category of "self-employed," or "independent," weavers included an undetermined but significant number of outworkers who were paid by piece rate, that is to say, they were supplied with yarn to weave on their own looms, and when the product was finished, they received an undefined payment from the putter-out (Silva 1980: 25–26). The results of our survey and fieldwork dispute this interpretation. We found three types of direct producers in Teotitlán weaving: (a) independent or own-account weavers who buy their yarn and sell their products as they wish, but some of whom will take yarn on credit (*hilo fiado*) when pressed for cash; (b) employees who weave

Table 15. Distribution of Position in Weaving among Weavers in Teotitlán del Valle and Santa Ana del Valle, District of Tlacolula, for 28 Households

Position	Number of Weavers			Percentage[a]		
	Teotitlán	Santa Ana	Total	Teotitlán	Santa Ana	Total
Own-account (cash)	34	21	55	65.4	37.5	34.2
Own-account (credit)	8	0	8	15.4	0.0	5.0
Own-account cash and credit	10	13	23	19.2	23.2	14.3
Subtotal	52	34	86	49.5	60.7	53.4
Employee	9	0	9	37.5	0.0	5.6
Employee + Own-account (cash)	6	1	7	25.0	1.8	4.3
Employee + Own-account (credit)	6	0	6	25.0	0.0	3.7
Employee + family (unpaid)	3	0	3	12.5	0.0	1.9
Subtotal	24	1	25	22.9	1.8	15.5
Family weaver (unpaid)	27	21	48	93.1	100.0	29.8
Family weaver + Own-account (credit)	2	0	2	6.9	0.0	1.2
Subtotal	29	21	50	27.6	37.5	31.1
Subtotal (all weavers)	105	56	161	54.4	67.5	58.3
Family workers (unpaid nonweavers)	88	27	115	45.6	32.5	41.7
Total	193	83	276	—	—	—

[a] Row percentages within the categories of own-account, employees, and family weavers are of the subtotals within each separate category; the percentages for subtotals (except family workers who are nonweavers) are of the subtotal for all weavers (excluding nonweaving family workers); the percentages for family workers (unpaid nonweavers) are of the Total for all workers (weavers + nonweaving household workers).

for an employer, either in their own homes on their own looms but with their employer's yarn or in the employer's workshop with the employer's looms and yarn; and (c) unpaid household workers who perform various tasks in weaving (including loom work) as a family service or duty. Table 15 shows the results of our survey in Teotitlán and Santa Ana regarding various direct producer conditions in weaving.

As Table 15 indicates, there are several important differences between Teotitlán and Santa Ana. First, a substantially higher percentage of weavers in Santa Ana are "self-employed" (60.7 percent of all weavers) than is the case in Teotitlán (49.5 percent). Indeed, our Santa Ana sample yielded only one piece-rate shop weaver, although Plattner (1965: 27) reported a higher frequency in an earlier survey. This leads us to the second important difference: Teotitlán has a much higher proportion of piece-rate shop weavers (22.9 percent), although nearly two-thirds of them also weave on their own account or as unpaid household weavers. The situation of one Teotitlán informant who said that he spent half of each month weaving as an employee and the other half weaving on his own account with yarn taken on credit is typical of this latter group. In any case, this figure indicates a significant degree of piece-wage labor and capitalist enterprise development within the Teotitlán industry in 1979 (cf. Silva 1980: 24).

Still another contrast is the markedly different situation of the "own-account + credit" (fiado) weavers in the two villages. Weavers in both villages buy yarn independently for cash and sell their products as they wish. But at times even the most independent weavers are short of cash and must get yarn on credit. This situation, as will be explained below, has quite different ramifications in Santa Ana than it does in Teotitlán.

Finally, we wish to note that although Santa Ana has a higher percentage of unpaid household weavers than does Teotitlán—given the higher proportion of female weavers in Santa Ana—it has a much lower ratio of nonweaving household workers to weavers than does Teotitlán, a difference that reflects Teotitlán's fabrication of higher-quality products containing handspun yarn and yarn colored with natural, homemade dyestuffs. The processing of these raw materials demands a greater commitment of household labor, especially children and females (see Table 14). Precisely because of greater participation of unpaid household labor in Teotitlán weaving, in combination with the greater availability of household weavers and the highly skilled nature of weaving labor itself, enterprises in this community are the principal foci of capital accumulation in the woolen products branch of the industry.[13]

As mentioned earlier, in Santa Ana the suppliers of yarn on credit are also the buyers of finished products; they are putters-out. These Santa Ana putters-out specify to their outweavers the type of design, colors, and other characteristics desired in the product to be woven. When the finished product is "sold" by the outweaver to the putter-out, the cost of the yarn is discounted from the selling price of the finished product. If sufficient cash remains (or is available from other sources), the Santa Ana weaver will pay cash for yarn; if not, which is usually the case, yarn will again be taken on credit and the cycle continues. Many informants told us that, if they did not sell their products in Santa Ana, it was very difficult for them to buy yarn there. For that reason, if a Santa Ana weaver sold his or her products in Teotitlán, it was likely that he or she would buy yarn there as well. Consequently, most Santa Ana weavers buy yarn and sell their products in Santa Ana.[14]

In 1979, five intermediaries (putters-out) in Santa Ana sold yarn and bought-up finished products. Informants in Santa Ana and Teotitlán disclosed that most of the products bought by these intermediaries were resold in Teotitlán. This explains why these intermediaries would not sell yarn to weavers who did not sell products to them. To keep their businesses solvent, the intermediaries probably need to profit as sellers of factory-made thread and as resellers of weavers' products. This "double dealing" by intermediaries, as agents of factory capital, on the one hand, and as buyers-up and resellers of peasant-artisan commodities, on the other, will be examined more comprehensively in Chapter 6.

The Cotton Products Branch: Xaagá

The asymmetry that exists in the relationship between Teotitlán and Santa Ana is even more pronounced in the Mitla/Xaagá relationship. Located 5 kilometers east of Mitla in the district of Tlacolula, Xaagá is an ex-hacienda ejidal community with an entirely mestizo population.[15] Oral tradition in Xaagá indicates that weaving was practiced there for the first time around 1950 when several looms were set up in a contiguous ex-hacienda property (a walled compound including ruins of the big house) by the brother of the owner, a weaver who had been forced to close his Oaxaca City workshop due to a labor dispute. With the support of Xaagá authorities, this weaver, who was born in a remote mountain village and had arrived in Oaxaca City via Tlacolula where he learned to weave as a boy, recruited five apprentices from Xaagá to work with him in the ex-hacienda weaving shop. The undertaking was short-lived, however, partly owing to disputes over compensation, and none of the Xaagá apprentices continued to work as weavers afterward.

In 1953, this master weaver was invited to relocate his looms to the famous Hotel Sorpresa in Mitla by its owner, E. R. Frissell, an American expatriate and devotee of traditional Oaxaca culture, for the purpose of establishing a weaving school on the premises. This undertaking was more successful; all of the original weaving entrepreneurs in Mitla, many of whom remained prominent figures in the industry in 1979, were trained as apprentices in this school. Moreover, the hallmark product of Mitla treadle loom weaving, the fine, white woolen shawl (which tourists believe is an authentic artifact of traditional Mitla Zapotec culture) was designed and first woven by this master weaver. In the 1960s, the Mitla apprentices trained in the "Sorpresa School" became the principal entrepreneurs in a 100-loom industry (Beals 1975: 258). Ironically, these Mitla weaving workshops—the largest of which employed as many as twelve loom operators—served as a training ground for a new generation of weavers from Xaagá, many of whose elder relatives had been participants in the failed ex-hacienda experiment. Some of these Xaagá weavers subsequently quit their jobs in Mitla, acquired looms, and started weaving at home. In this way, the Xaagá weaving industry was born. Several of these ex-Mitla *operarios* (piece-rate weavers) are today employing *operarios* to operate looms in their own workshops. When the 70-year-old maestro was located and interviewed in 1981, he was, ironically, employed in Oaxaca City as a pieceworker in a decrepit one-room sweatshop, which is among the last of the downtown *mantelerías*.

Three principal jobs are found in the Xaagá clothing industry: weaving, machine sewing, and shawl knotting (i.e., of the loose ends). Most weaving households also have some members who participate in sewing or shawl knotting. Two of forty-four craft households surveyed participated exclusively in sewing, which is indicative of the extent to which it is linked to weaving in the household enterprise. By contrast, 60.9 percent of the households with shawl finishers had no other artisans, a result of the prominence of shawl knotting by women as a cash-earning outwork supplement to domestic chores. Table 16 shows the distribution of these three principal jobs in Xaagá by age and sex for the forty-four artisan households surveyed.

A perusal of the data in this table shows that the division of labor by gender is stricter in Xaagá than it is in the Teotitlán–Santa Ana woolen products branch. Not a single female works as a loom operator, or a single male as a machine sewer, and only one male works (part-time to help his wife) in shawl finishing. Although there is

Table 16. *Distribution of Weaving, Machine Sewing, and Shawl Knotting for 44 Artisan Households by Age and Gender in Xaagá, District of Tlacolula*

Age	Weaving	Machine Sewing	Shawl Knotting
Males			
0–9	0	0	0
10–19	9	0	0
20–29	12	0	0
30–39	9	0	1
40–49	3	0	0
50–59	1	0	0
60+	0	0	0
Subtotal	34	0	1
Females			
0–9	0	0	2
10–19	0	8	6
20–29	0	6	10
30–39	0	7	5
40–49	0	3	4
50–59	0	0	4
60+	0	0	1
Subtotal	0	24	32
Total	34	24	33

an apparent basis for seeking an ethnocultural explanation for the higher rate of gender crossover in Teotitlán and Santa Ana, which are Zapotec-speaking communities, than in Xaagá, which is an exclusively Spanish-speaking community, it is probably best explained in terms of economic logic, without excluding the possibility that ideological processes linked to the sociocultural construction of gender identity may also be involved (see Chapter 5).

In these terms, two questions require answers: (a) why is there significant crossover by females into loom operation in Teotitlán and Santa Ana, while no such crossover occurs in Xaagá and (b) why is there no crossover by males (with one exception) into machine sewing and shawl knotting in Xaagá? In Teotitlán and Santa Ana, available household labor power (regardless of gender) in households that do not specialize in high-priced, luxury products tends to be allocated to loom work simply because it is the most labor-intensive and value-creating (i.e., in monetary terms) activity available. Expressed differently, the allocation of available labor power to loom work is the best means available to many households to cope with the "simple reproduction squeeze" (Bernstein 1979: 427) or to realize their aspirations for petty capital accumulation. Households that do specialize in high-priced output in the Teotitlán–Santa Ana branch, however, have a dual demand for labor: in loom operations and in yarn spinning and dyeing. Here optimum value realization is dependent upon the performance within the household enterprise of all three jobs. A luxury tapestry cannot be produced without hand-spun and home-dyed yarn.

The successful household enterprise in the Xaagá clothing industry is one that combines weaving with machine sewing. Males, again by customary patterns of enculturation, are led into weaving, whereas females are led into machine sewing and shawl knotting. In value-added terms, machine sewing takes preference over shawl knotting in allocating available household labor. Therefore, an extrahousehold labor pool comprised of females in nonweaving households is tapped through a piece-rate system of outwork to finish shawls. This explains why shawl knotting alone, among all the jobs in the Xaagá clothing industry, has a high rate of occurrence as the only artisan activity practiced in some households (31.8 percent of 44 households surveyed, compared with 9.1 percent in weaving, and only 4.5 percent in machine sewing).

A comparison of Table 17 with Table 15 shows that the distribution of job positions in Xaagá weaving is somewhat less complicated than it is in Teotitlán–Santa Ana. Xaagá weavers tend not to purchase thread on credit and do not receive thread from buyers-up. Consequently, no dependency relations exist between direct producers in Xaagá and thread suppliers; the Xaagá weavers buy their thread in cash transactions either in Mitla stores or from distributors in Oaxaca City. Xaagá weavers, however, regardless of the scale of their enterprises, are almost entirely dependent on Mitla buyers for their sales since they are unable to gain direct access to the heavy Mitla tourist trade (attracted principally by Mitla's well-known archaeological site). It is the regular cash purchase of Xaagá's garment output by highly capitalized Mitla merchants (for resale in Mitla and elsewhere) that sustains Xaagá weaving.

A comparison of Table 17 and Table 15 also shows that the proportion of employees is higher in Xaagá than in Teotitlán; one in five Xaagá weavers regularly employ loom operators on a piece-rate basis. Although some Xaagá weavers continue to work in Mitla shops or

Table 17. *Distribution of Jobs by Job Position in the Xaagá Garment Industry for 44 Households*

Job and Position	No. of Artisans	Per- centage
Weaving		
Own-account (nonemployer)	14	38.9
Own-account (employer)	7	19.4
Employee (*operario*)	10	27.8
Family (unpaid)	5	13.9
Subtotal	36	100.0
Sewing		
Own-account (nonemployer)	4	16.7
Own-account (employer)	1	4.2
Own-account + family	2	8.3
Employee	3	12.5
Family (unpaid)	14	58.3
Subtotal	24	100.0
Shawl Finishing		
Employee	22	68.8
Family (unpaid)	10	31.2
Subtotal	32	100.0
Total	92	

for Mitla employers on an outwork basis (one weaver in our sample weaves at home for a Mitla employer on his employer's loom), most work in Xaagá in their employers' shops.

Machine sewing shows a greater range of variation with regard to the position of the direct producer than does weaving. The fact that 58.3 percent of the seamstresses are unpaid household workers reinforces our earlier discussion regarding the strong linkage between weavers/looms and seamstresses/sewing machines within the household enterprise in the Xaagá garment industry. Most of the sewing machines are owned by households that also own at least one loom; in 1979, three households had two machines. It was precisely in these households that seamstresses without their own machines were employed. Some households without looms have at least one sewing machine operated by a female household member who is employed as a piece-rate "out seamstress" by one or more weaving households. In households with looms, the principal seamstress (typically the wife of the weaver) is in charge of the garment-making process; this entails working on the machine herself, in addition to supervising the work of her daughter on a second machine and contracting additional work with "own-account" seamstresses.

The Xaagá weavers produce two types of cotton cloth: a loose weave called *tela deshilada* and a tight weave called *tela tupida.* Both types of cloth are used to make dresses, shawls, and short-sleeved, pullover-type shirts. Some weavers produce and sell only cloth, but most prefer to make garments from the cloth and sell them. They either design, cut, and sew cloth into garments in the home weaving shop or put-out precut garments to seamstresses in other households who sew on a piecework basis (2 pesos per shirt in 1979). The weavers who turn out cloth for shawls either have shawl finishers in their households or put-out shawls to women in other households, again on a piecework basis (4–7 pesos per shawl in 1979). The typical production unit in Xaagá combines at least one weaver with a loom and one seamstress with a sewing machine. The most successful units incorporate multiples of these complementary pairs, usually through a combination of in-house and hired labor.

The process of producing shirts from loose-weave cloth begins with the acquisition and bleaching or dyeing of the thread, continues with setting up the loom (during which the preparation of the warp requires the cooperation of 3–4 workers) and weaving the cloth (1 weaver averages from 2.5 to 3.0 meters of cloth per hour), and ends with measuring and cutting the cloth, sewing the shirts, and folding them. The results of a labor time analysis of several cases (using as a base line an 8-kilo, or 40-skein, quantity of thread) showed that the socially average amount of labor required to perform all the necessary steps just outlined was 117.5 hours. This yielded 127.5 meters of cloth, which were made into 85 shirts (worth 25 pesos each in 1979, or 2,125 pesos). In terms of hours of individual labor, this factored out to 1.32 hours per shirt at a rate of 18 pesos ($.80) per hour (2,125/117.5). How this translates into wages and profits is addressed in the next chapter.

Petty Commodity Production and Consumption

The artisan activities examined in this chapter are characterized by low productivity and low levels of remuneration for expended labor. The activities take place in communities where a high proportion of the households are also involved in agriculture, and the incomes earned generally supplement the food and money procured from agriculture in order to complete the household budget. It bears reiterating that this combination of agricultural and craft production provides the basis for the survival of thousands of rural Oaxaca Valley households but, with a few exceptions, generates little capital accumulation and investment in productive, as distinct from mercantile, activities. Most of these households are geared to simple reproduction while capitalist production and accumulation are most common in brickmaking and treadle loom weaving.

Before proceeding, it is necessary to clarify the meaning of "simple reproduction" or, more specifically, what is implied when we refer to a peasant-artisan household as "simple reproducing," or as achieving a "level of simple reproduction." In the most general sense, the concept implies subsistence or survival; that is, a necessary prerequisite of the viability of a peasant-artisan household is that the productive activities of its members provide the means of consumption—the food, the clothing, the shelter, and so on—that enable them to live in accordance with their cultural background and training. This is what Beals (1975: 88–89) called the "subsistence budget," but it by no means exhausts the meaning of simple reproduction, which also implies provision or replacement of the material means (e.g., seeds, raw materials, tools, equipment) used in production. This second component of simple reproduction—which, incidentally, encompasses production for own-use as well as commodity production—was called the "operational budget" by Beals (1976: 95–96) and the "replacement fund" by Eric Wolf (1966: 6). Together, these two components of simple reproduction, namely, subsistence and replacement, are often referred to as constituting the "necessary labor product" or "necessary consumption," which implies an amount necessary to maintain an existing level of production (Kay 1975: 15).

In the case of peasant-artisan households, however, viability (or the maintenance of their productive operations) also depends upon paying taxes and/or rent to gain access to land or the necessary agricultural means of production (like draft animals and carts). Furthermore, as Beals (1975: 96) correctly observed: "In addition to the expenditures for household subsistence and for maintaining productive operations, all but the most poverty-stricken Oaxaca peasant households make expenditures for other goods and services." Beals subsumed those expenditures under the rubric "public and festive budget," Wolf's (1966: 7–9) "ceremonial fund." In Oaxaca these expenditures are engendered through participation in the civil-religious hierarchy, or cargo system, in the celebration of saint's cult festivals (mayordomías), weddings (fandangos), or birthdays, and in meeting reciprocity (guelaguetza) obligations. As necessary prerequisites for complying with the duties of membership in a Oaxaca Valley community, therefore, we include a minimal level of ceremonial expenditures in our concept of simple reproduction. What the concept precludes is capital accumulation for purposes of productive investment—an activity that is associated with *expanded* rather than *simple* reproduction.

That weavers, wood carvers, rope twiners, embroiderers, seamstresses, and other artisans and peasant-artisans have low incomes that leave little potential for saving and investment tells us nothing, however, about their consumption strategies. It should not be assumed that all poor households are poor in the same way. The concept of poverty as a homogeneous state obfuscates more than it explains. First, it overlooks the fact that, where commodity relations predominate within a capitalist economic system, social and economic stratification will be generated even in the absence of capitalist accumulation and, thus, even among "the poor."[16] Second, it ignores the variation in household composition (sex, age, marital status) and the manner in which such variations influence consumption strategies. Third, it denigrates rural Third World peoples by viewing their subjective consumption decisions as the product of determinant economic situations alone and thus denies them an active role in shaping their own lives. The following budget study carried out among seven households in Santo Tomás Jalieza, a backstrap loom weaving village located in the district of Ocotlán, suggests a surprising degree of variation among low-income rural Oaxaca Valley households in one community.

Household heads were paid (at the end of the study period) to keep a daily record in a notebook provided by the investigators of every cash transaction (sales and purchases). Five of the households kept accurate records for periods ranging between three and four weeks. These records, summarized in Table 18, form the basis for our analysis of consumption patterns of simple reproducing, peasant-artisan households.

At least one backstrap loom weaver in each of the five households is involved in rural industrial commodity production. As Table 18 indicates, however, there is substantial variation in household size and composition, as well as involvement in noncraft activities. Two of the households are landless and lack animals while two more raise corn and have small numbers of animals, mainly goats. The fifth is landless but does have a small goat herd. Income and expenditures are widely discrepant in two of the five cases, possibly because the budgets were recorded between periods of commercialization of household-produced commodities. It is assumed that total

Table 18. Analysis of Five Cases of Income/Expenditure from Santo Tomás Jalieza

			Household Number		
Craft Occupation	I Weaver	II Weaver/ Bricklayer	III Weaver	IV Weaver	V Weaver
Basic Occupational, Demographic, and Economic Information					
Family size	5	7	7	6	10
Age children	11, 7, 5	ND	15, 12, 9, 4, 1	13, 8	17, 14, 10, 8, 6, 4, 1
C/W ratio	2.5	ND	1.4	2.0	3.3
Land (has.)	0	0	1.25	4.0	0
1979 corn prod.	0	0	3 fanegas	6 fanegas	0
Months corn bought	12	12	8	4	12
Animals	0	ND	15 goats, 1 pig	3 goats a medias	12 goats
Survey duration (days)	21	28	28	28	28
Total income	1,870.0	2,500.0	14,706.5	940.0	4,880.0
Total expenditures	3,430.3	2,871.1	14,222.9	2,873.9	4,516.0
Income less expenditures	−1,560.3	−371.0	484.6	−1,933.9	364.0
Purchases					
(1) Craft raw materials	1,229.0	0.0	10,330.5	315.0	906.0
(2) Agricultural raw materials	0	0.0	317.5	0.0	25.0
(3) 1 + 2	1,229.3	0.0	10,648.0	315.0	931.0
(4) Household reproduction	2,201.3	2,871.1	3,574.9	2,558.9	3,585.0

Per Capita per Week Expenditures and Distribution

Food	65.0	72.1	73.5	82.7	53.7
(%)	(44.3)	(70.3)	(57.5)	(77.6)	(59.5)
Household	35.6	3.2	29.2	4.5	30.1
(%)	(24.3)	(3.1)	(22.9)	(4.2)	(33.6)
Health	7.5	0.0	6.1	0.0	0.8
(%)	(5.1)	(0.0)	(4.8)	(0.0)	(0.9)
School	0.0	25.8	14.7	10.4	0.0
(%)	(0.0)	(25.2)	(11.5)	(9.8)	(0.0)
Transport	4.0	0.6	4.2	9.0	0.0
(%)	(2.1)	(0.6)	(3.3)	(8.4)	(0.0)
Taxes	0	0.9	0.0	0.0	5.0
(%)	(0.0)	(0.9)	(0.0)	(0.0)	(5.6)
Animal feed	24.7	0.0	0.0	0.0	0.0
(%)	(16.8)	(0.0)	(0.0)	(0.0)	(0.0)
Other	10.0	0.0	0.0	0.0	0.0
(%)	(6.8)	(0.0)	(0.0)	(0.0)	(0.0)
Total	146.7	102.5	127.7	106.6	89.6
(%)	(100)	(100)	(100)	(100)	(100)
Food					
Expenditures (%)	44.3	70.3	57.5	77.6	59.9
Weekly expenditures	325.0	504.8	514.2	496.4	536.8
Weekly per capita	65.0	72.1	73.5	82.7	53.7
Number different items	40	34	34	ND	28

expenditures approximate total income. Net income is calculable by subtracting from total expenditures the cost of purchased raw materials worked up by weavers (mainly thread and dyes) or used in agricultural production (e.g., fertilizer, seed). The remaining nonproduction expenditures are those dedicated to the maintenance of the household and reproduction of the labor force, both its daily biological reproduction and generational reproduction (Bernstein and Thomas 1983). Though low, overall average weekly per capita nonproduction expenditures varied considerably—from 89.6 pesos ($3.98) to 146.7 pesos ($6.52).

Table 18 divides expenditures into eight categories. It is not surprising, given the low incomes and priority of physical maintenance, that food purchases occupy first place and usually account for over 50 percent of all expenditures (in one case almost 80 percent!) in monetary terms. What is surprising, however, is that a substantial variation in per capita weekly food expenditure does not follow directly from variations in total per capita expenditure and/or access to land and domestically produced food items, such as corn. Thus, there seem to be significant differences in the domestic strategies adopted with respect to what and how much to purchase, although a longer survey period might have revealed greater convergence. Household IV, for instance, spent 82.7 pesos per capita per week on food, 77.6 percent of the 106.6 pesos available, while household I, with much larger per capita expenditures (146.7 pesos per week), dedicated only 65 of these pesos (44.3 percent) to food purchases. Last, we might note that all of the households for which we have data purchased a large variety of different food items (28 to 40) during the 3–4 week period of the survey, indicating that assumptions that rural southern Mexican diets invariably involve the monotonous repetition of corn, beans, rice, and chili, spiced with the occasional egg or chicken, may be overdrawn. Nevertheless, a large percentage of cash purchases of food, often exceeding 80 percent, pertain solely to eight or 10 items, although these are not the same for all households (again indicative of variations in consumer preference). Household items and school expenses require periodic infusions of cash, more so in some cases than in others; however, such expenditures must not be allowed to infringe upon the household's daily subsistence requirements.

Too much can be made of variations in expenditure. Whatever the petty luxuries and minor variations in taste enjoyed by petty commodity producers in many communities, one is struck by the pervading sense of necessity and the low degree of waste that inform their behavior as consumers. Objective conditions do not dictate market behavior in an absolute sense, but they place certain limits upon the development and expression of individual taste.

It is notable that, whereas three of the households did make health-related purchases during the period of the survey, none was subject to a major health crisis that might have required the intervention of a physician or hospitalization. Where 45–75 percent of income goes to buy food, little remains (once household and school expenses have been subtracted) to cover such crises. These are the cases in which households are compelled to sell their animals (semi-liquid savings) or take out loans with friends, relatives (real or fictive), or local usurers. In cases where the funds cannot be located, any major crisis—illness, harvest failure, prolonged hyperinflation, decline or disappearance of the market for cash-generating, household-produced commodities—that drastically elevates costs (of production or reproduction) or reduces income may provoke partial or full entry into wage labor. As Harrison (1977: 149) observed: "One of the fundamental characteristics of peasant agriculture [and the same might be said of peasant-artisan production] is its vulnerability to the accidental." In the socioeconomic context of the rural areas of the Oaxaca Valley, where capitalism exhibits, despite its overall dominance, only a low level of development, the search for wage labor opportunities often entails emigration (temporary or permanent) on the part of some, if not all, of the members of the household to major urban zones or the United States (cf. Ornelas López 1980; Vásquez Hernández 1980). Nonetheless, Oaxaca Valley peasant-artisans are far from being passive victims. As we shall show in Chapter 7, they have improvised a range of active compensatory strategies in order to defend their meager standards of living from the ravages of the post-1982 Mexican economic crisis.

Why Is Peasant-Artisan Simple Reproduction Not So Simple?

The following set of generalizations about peasant-artisan industries in the Oaxaca Valley made by two investigators (Alba and Cristerna 1949: 495–496) who conducted field work in the early 1940s is a fitting way to begin to answer this question.

> The fact that some of the industries studied may be capable of providing those who practice them with sufficient returns to satisfy their needs has not taken from them their status as agriculturists, since directly or indirectly (availing themselves of sharecropping) they continue to till the soil. The study has made manifest that most of the existing small industries are insuffi-

cient for meeting the household and even the individual budgetary needs of those who dedicate themselves to them, so their role within the economic framework is that of a merely accessory activity which, together with the principal one, agriculture, realizes the ends of providing them extra, complementary earnings for the household budget.

These statements underline the continuities in petty industrial commodity production over the decades in the Oaxaca Valley economy. As we have seen, it is still true that, for the most part, craft-producing households also practice agriculture; but crafts typically complement agriculture rather than vice-versa. Likewise, it is true that there are two broad categories of peasant-artisan industries: those, constituting a minority, that provide, at least, a "living" household income and others, a majority, that provide only a portion of the income requirement for household maintenance.

Two important issues overlooked in the above statement are (a) the impact upon peasant-artisans of their participation in capitalist markets, and (b) the development of petty capitalism from within peasant-artisan production. Although we have already argued that peasant-artisans in Oaxaca today must be viewed as integral components of the Mexican capitalist economy, we will take up this issue again in the concluding section and also in more detail in subsequent chapters. At this juncture, however, it is incumbent upon us to identify a series of factors at the interior of the rural economy that operate (together with exogenous factors) to limit many peasant-artisan households to simple reproduction without capital accumulation. Six factors, three objective and three subjective, can be isolated. The three objective factors are (a) location within the regional division of labor and specialization, (b) land tenure status or access to arable land, and (c) household reproductive performance (fertility) and household composition. Finally, the three subjective factors are (a) scheduling performance, that is, how household labor is allocated among competing production possibilities; (b) knowledge, skill, and intensity of household labor; and (c) managerial skill, risk-taking posture, and readiness to experiment.

A household's chances to regularly produce a surplus product, above and beyond the level of simple reproduction, are heavily influenced by its matrix community's location within the intercommunity division of labor and specialization. That location itself reflects not only the community's natural resource endowment but also its technological repertoire as well as the population's skill and dedication, over the centuries, in making productive use of it (cf.

Cook 1982: 35). Many occupations practiced by twentieth-century Oaxaca villagers involve labor processes transmitted from as far back as the prehispanic epoch. Enculturation inclines villagers to enter agricultural and craft occupations that follow lines mediated through their families of orientation—with regard not only to sex and age requirements but also to standards and limits of performance. Thus, a male born into a *metate* making household in Magdalena Ocotlán will, if he remains in the village into adulthood and pursues a craft, more than likely pursue *metate* making rather than wood carving, weaving, or some other craft not practiced in his village. The same can be said of a male born into a wood carving household in Santa Cecilia Jalieza, a female born into a palm weaving household in San Lorenzo Albarradas or into a backstrap loom weaving household in Santo Tomás Jalieza, and so on. In other words, individual occupational participation is greatly influenced by village occupational structure.

Moreover, if the industry in which a household participates has low capital accumulation potential, the household can do little to overcome the simple reproduction barrier. As a general rule, the industries in this category are those that produce utilitarian commodities like grindstones, mats, baskets, or wooden utensils primarily for use in rural households. This is not to preclude the possibility that some household enterprises in such industries may successfully accumulate, nor is it to imply that all household enterprises in higher accumulation potential industries (e.g., treadle loom weaving) will necessarily do so. It simply means that the probability that a household enterprise will accumulate capital is determined by the accumulation potential of the industry in which it participates. In other words, if the market (among other things) is not "right," a peasant-artisan industry is apt to provide a "marginal subsistence occupation" (Herman 1957: 374). Under these circumstances the industry will generate little or no surplus value (cf. Spengler 1957: 372).

Without question, the most important factor (over which a household has a modicum of control) that impinges upon the capacity to produce through self-employment below, at, or beyond the level of simple reproduction is its arable land tenure status (how much and what kind of land it has access to for agricultural purposes). As Beals (1975: 68) pointed out with regard to the rural Oaxaca social economy: "The landless family, lacking special skills or control of some handicraft, occupies the most precarious economic position in the village." This is indisputable. The landless or land-poor craft-producing household, however, while perhaps in less precarious circumstances, is nevertheless most likely to engage in a constant struggle to achieve simple reproduction. One hope for households in such circumstances is to obtain land through inheritance; barring that occurrence, in some villages there is the possibility of acquiring access to communal or ejidal land for agricultural purposes. If that route is also closed, the remaining possibilities are to gain access to arable through sharecropping, rental, or purchase. Even if a household succeeds in gaining access to arable by one of these means, however, it still may not be able to effectively work the land for lack of the necessary means of production (e.g., oxteam, plow) or, if the land is of poor quality or lacks irrigation, it may not make a significant contribution toward the household's maintenance. Finally, a landed craft-producing household that makes poor production decisions or suffers bad luck may be in as destitute a condition at any given time as a landless or land-poor craft-producing household.

The scheduling of available household labor among competing productive activities, the first of the subjective factors listed, can have a significant influence on productivity—although its influence is closely intertwined with the second subjective factor, namely, the knowledge, skill, and intensity behind the exercise of household labor. To some extent scheduling is culturally programmed. For example, given the predominance of rain-fed agriculture, the agricultural cycle is seasonal, with craft production being most feasible during the postharvest dry season when the demand for agricultural labor is relatively low. Also, the gender division of labor simplifies household scheduling by culturally circumscribing male and female activities in separate domains: "men's work" versus "women's work." Yet many occasions remain during the year when decisions must be made about the allocation of available labor power between agricultural work on the household's own fields, agricultural wage labor, craft production or craft marketing, and, perhaps, some other cash-earning or subsistence-producing activities.

Even during crucial periods of the agricultural cycle, it is feasible that a household may decide to plant less and to make and sell more craft products; this depends upon factors like market perceptions and the outcome of the last agricultural cycle. Regarding working-age dependents, decisions must be made about whether to allocate their available work time to household tasks, to tasks in craft production, or to other cash-earning activities (e.g., domestic service in the city). In short, scheduling is a constant ingredient in peasant-artisan householding—and discounting the luck factor, which has a random impact on performance—it is not easy to determine if, in the last analysis, *harder* work or *smarter* work has a more consistent impact on household productivity. It is probably safe to conclude that the most successful households are those that combine both (cf. Beals 1975: 67–77).

It is difficult to prove that households that are short on managerial skills (e.g., record keeping, planning, organizing, and directing productive activity), conservative regarding risk-taking, or hostile to experimentation (e.g., planting new crops, adopting new techniques, adopting new product designs, seeking new markets) are the most likely to be engaged in a perpetual struggle to achieve simple reproduction without capital accumulation. However, it is reasonable to consider this set of subjective factors as being much more influential in determining which household enterprises achieve the status of successful capital accumulators than it is in determining those which do not. Objective factors weigh more heavily in determining which households fail to achieve success in capital accumulation—a goal we consider to be shared by the great majority of peasant-artisan households. Deficiencies in the basic skills of petty wealth mobilization and handling (e.g., fattening animals as a form of savings, knowing when and how to buy and sell crops and other commodities, knowing how to invest petty cash surpluses when they are generated) are likely to determine the extent to which a given peasant-artisan household is condemned to constantly struggle to achieve simple reproduction without sustaining capital accumulation.[17]

Any notion that factors internal to the local or regional social economy somehow magically operate to prevent capital accumulation or social differentiation, or operate to eliminate these if they do somehow occur, must be rejected. Petty commodity producers are, to use Polly Hill's words (1986: 71), "highly competitive people" and, in rural commodity economies, "every householder is basically concerned with bettering his household's economic situation by legitimate means . . . without regard to the effect that this has on other households." Within socially differentiated populations, however, the real problem is not how "individuals" respond to constraints and opportunities but how such constraints and opportunities are structured around the performance of the more accommodated socioeconomic strata or class locations.

Villages in the Oaxaca Valley, for example, vary according to how households are conditioned to meet social or ceremonial obligations that entail economic expenditure. Few communities make individual sponsorship of *mayordomías* obligatory, although the patron saint's *mayordomía* is now subsidized in many communities through a surcharge levied on each head of household. Individual sponsorship, however, continues in all communities under the banner of voluntarism and according to ability to pay. As one informant expressed it: "It is voluntary, according to what one's circumstances are. Those who can afford it, do it, and those who can't afford it, don't do it." That is to say, prestige points are not necessarily meted out according to the scale of the sponsored *mayordomía* but rather, for example, a relatively poor pieceworker, who volunteers to sponsor a *mayordomía* for a lesser saint at a cost of two or three dollars a week for flowers and a candle for a year (and an expenditure on the saint's day perhaps amounting to an equivalent of several days' salary) will gain as much social approval as his employer who spends several thousand pesos in the sponsorship of a major *mayordomía.* The point is that the custom reinforces and legitimizes the existing class hierarchy.

Ideologically, some resistance is found at all socioeconomic levels to expenditures of time and money associated with service in the civil-religious hierarchy. But there is no evidence that nonparticipation in the *mayordomía* or *cargo* system is associated with secular capital accumulation. Rather, the data suggest that money saved from *mayordomías* may be spent on other fiestas (e.g., weddings, birthdays), other forms of recreation, or other categories of nonproductive consumption. To complement Waldemar Smith's (1977: 14) argument against the thesis that social/ceremonial expenditures operated effectively as economic levelers given the lack of evidence for the redistribution of productive capital within the Guatemalan highland villages he studied, it should be noted that, as a general rule, a household enterprise's fund of productive capital does not necessarily grow in direct proportion to a reduction in social/ceremonial expenditures since the latter tends to be offset by nonproductive expenditures in other categories.[18]

In conclusion, the impact of many of these social/ceremonial obligations clearly motivates households to intensify productivity, reduce costs, and economize in anticipation of meeting those obligations (Smith 1977: 14)—efforts that, if directed into commodity-money channels, would undoubtedly increase capital accumulation within the household enterprise. However, nonmarket exchanges, community service, festive sponsorship, and other forms of conspicuous consumption in honor of saints or household members continue to be the stuff of sociocultural life in Oaxaca and as such they are highly motivating reasons for people to work (and to live).

Peasant-Artisans, Wage Labor, and Simple Reproduction

The "peasant-artisan" category, as noted earlier, disguises the significance of wage labor for household maintenance. This was demonstrated clearly in the section on the treadle loom weaving industry. The degree of wage labor participation by rural direct producers, measured by the number of participants and the extent to which wage earnings contribute to household reproduction, remains a key indicator of capitalist development.

Craft producers were classified as employers, employees, or "independent" producers (see Table 6) based upon responses to questions about their employment of nonhousehold workers, position in their principal occupation (i.e., employer, employee, own-account worker, household worker), and payment form (i.e., direct sale for cash, wage or salary, piece rate, cash advances, payment in kind, unpaid). For the 888 artisan and peasant-artisan producers in 670 craft-producing households for whom we have information, representing six branches of rural industry (embroidery, mixed crafts, treadle loom weaving, backstrap loom weaving, palm plaiting and brickmaking), 80 percent claimed to produce and sell commodities on their own-account for cash payment (another 4 percent claimed to be self-employed but received cash advances for their wares). Only 10 percent claimed "employee" status, almost all of whom were paid by piece rate. As shown in the case of embroidery, however, an analysis of data disaggregated by branch often yields a much higher percentage of employee self-identification. Nonetheless, these self-reports undoubtedly underestimate the true magnitude of rural industrial wage labor in the Oaxaca Valley. For instance, a majority of embroiderers identify themselves as "own-account" workers yet are supplied with cloth and thread by the very same merchants to whom they sell embroidered garments for a price that discounts the cost of the supplied raw materials. In other words, these embroiderers are by no means working on their own-account but are outworkers on the merchants' accounts. Brickmaking pieceworkers frequently identify themselves as self-employed, despite receiving piece-rate payments from their employers, in order to befuddle government inspectors, whose efforts to tax brickyard enterprises are generally perceived to be threatening to owner and worker alike (Cook 1984a: 173–186).

Whereas quantitative data are lacking on labor migration, it should be noted that many peasant-artisan households depend on cash remittances from absent household members who are working for wages in Oaxaca City, elsewhere in Mexico (e.g., Mexico City), or perhaps as far away as the United States. Some 99 (11 percent) of 907 households for which information was available claimed to have received remittances over the course of the year prior to the interview. The mean amount reported was 9,688 pesos ($430), although the median of 5,000 pesos ($222) is probably a better measure of the cen-

tral tendency. Sons and daughters of the household head accounted
for 86 percent of the remitters. This figure accords well with our assumption that the demographic profile of the villages surveyed is
best understood in terms of systematic out-migration. The number
of households receiving remittances and the amount received, however, are probably greater than what was recorded by the survey due
to underreporting by respondents.

A more detailed analysis of remittances according to the employment status of the remittee household head indicates that, overall,
employer households—whether of agricultural or artisan labor—
were somewhat more likely to receive remittances than were nonemployers, and the amount they received was likely to be larger.
Employers of agricultural labor stand out in this regard—30 percent
received a mean of more than 12,000 pesos ($533 dollars) during the
year preceding the interview. Undoubtedly, some of these remittee
households operate petty capitalist agricultural enterprises, and the
remittances from their sons and daughters are contributing to enterprise capitalization (e.g., purchase of fertilizer, oxteams, rental of
tractors, payment of wages). In terms of the census data, craft industry employers do not seem to differ much from nonemployers in
terms of the likelihood of receiving remittances and the amount
remitted.

Despite the limitations of these survey data on wage labor, they
do indicate both the presence and the limits of wage labor and capitalist development in rural industry in the Oaxaca Valley. Appearances to the contrary, rural industrial wage laborers and petty merchant and industrial capitalists are concealed behind the residence
lots (solares) of the region's villages, enclosed by walls of adobe,
organ cactus, and thorn branches. The smallness in scale of capitalist enterprises, as indicated by low ratios of employees to employers, combined with low levels of capitalization, helps to explain why
many visitors to the Valley treat its rural zones as bastions of subsistence and petty commodity production and as lacking capitalist development. We will turn to a more detailed analysis of the nature
and extent of this development in the next chapter.

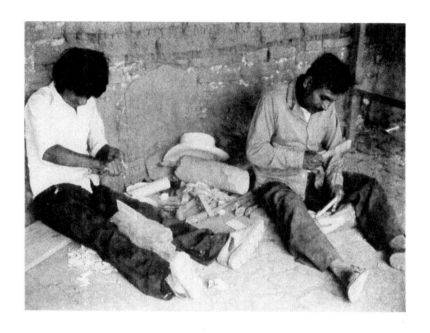

Father and son carving wooden utensils in Santa Cecilia Jalieza.

The palm products harvest in San Lorenzo Albarradas.

Palm plaiting in Santo Domingo Albarradas.

Cooperative family labor: mothers and daughters plaiting palm mats in Santo Domingo Albarradas.

Broom maker at work in San Lorenzo Albarradas.

Palm products from San Lorenzo Albarradas being sold in the Tlacolula marketplace.

Piece rate weaver at treadle loom in a Xaagá workshop.

Xaagá seamstress at work in her home.

Self-employed treadle loom weaver in Xaagá.

Employee winding spools in a Xaagá weaving workshop.

Brothers and their employees preparing a treadle loom warp in a Xaagá weaving workshop.

Xaagá outworker knotting shawls for a weaver in her village.

Milero molds bricks as his son observes and a peasant plows in the background.

Sun-dried bricks being loaded by pieceworkers from the *patio* onto their boss's flat-bed truck for transport to his kiln.

Milero, his wife, and their three-year-old daughter perform complementary brickyard tasks.

Chapter 4. Beyond Simple Reproduction: The Dynamics of Peasant-Artisan Differentiation

Introduction: Commodity Production and Social Differentiation

Under conditions of privatized rural commodity economy in which land and other agricultural means of production are readily bought and sold by household enterprises, it is generally agreed that there will be inequality in wealth distribution.[1] Major disagreements, however, persist among scholars regarding the causes and significance of this inequality. As discussed in Chapter 1, a fundamental cleavage exists between followers of Chayanov, who attribute rural inequality to household demographics and life-cycle stages and deny that it is part and parcel of a process of wider capitalist development, and followers of the "Agrarian Marxist" tradition, who view differential ownership of land and other means of production as indicative of class formation and capitalist development.[2]

Significantly, the same life cycle and demographic factors that Chayanov and his followers interpret as assuring peasant simple reproduction and nondifferentiation will be shown to selectively operate in commodity economy to promote (rather than discourage) expanded reproduction and class differentiation. It might seem that to demonstrate this through empirical analysis effects a synthesis between Chayanovian and Marxist approaches (e.g., Deere and de Janvry 1981); however, the mutually contradictory methods and ideas, not to mention antagonistic politics, advocated by both Marxists and Chayanovians preclude the possibility of any genuine reconciliation between them (see Walicki 1969; Shanin 1972; Solomon 1977; Deere and de Janvry 1981: 333; Goodman and Redclift 1982).

Despite the possibility of understanding some of Chayanov's arguments and ideas as broadly within Marxist discourse (e.g., Banaji

1976a; Cook 1985b] or, in places, as openly supportive of it, the mainstream of Chayanovian discourse has evolved in tandem with neoclassical economic and "moral economy" (Scott 1976) approaches that are at odds with Marxism. Whatever this process reflects in the dimensions of theory and method (or intellectual history), it has now developed to a point where students of rural economy and society are confronted with an either/or choice between the Leninist approach and the Chayanovian approach.[3]

Many scholars have neglected the constantly changing diversity of capitalist forms and relations. As proponents of an abstract, technicist, and teleological concept of capital formulated in the image of the advanced factory form of industrial capital, such scholars are ill-equipped to understand phenomena like incipient or petty capitalist enterprises and to distinguish these from either peasant-artisan household enterprises or full-blown capitalist enterprises. From their perspective, all capital must exhibit a tendency to become (or to behave like) "Big Capital"; consequently, reinvestment, expansion, and development of the means of production—linked to the evolution and functioning of "Western" industrial forms—are taken as minimal criteria for identifying capitalism.[4]

The thesis that the types and conditions of capital are necessarily as variegated and changing as are the types and conditions of labor that capital exploits counteracts the tendency to mechanistically identify capitalism with any single condition, such as complete proletarianization or constant technological innovation (see Wallerstein 1983). This thesis also serves as a reminder that empirically grounded analysis of capitalism must address issues at the level of branches of production and specific enterprises within those branches; such an analysis proceeds skeptically with regard to abstract laws of motion, invariant logic, or universal conditions that presumably apply uniformly to all capitalist activity.

It seems unlikely that empirical data on economic scale and performance will suffice to definitively prove or disprove the presence or absence of capitalist forms of enterprise and social relations in the countryside. This appears to be one of the messages of the continuing differentiation debates, for example, in Russian peasant studies (e.g., Shanin 1972, 1980; Harrison 1975; Solomon 1977; Kingston-Mann 1980; Cox and Littlejohn 1984; Cox 1986) and Indian peasant studies (e.g., Patnaik 1971a and b, 1972, 1979; Chattopadhyay 1972; Herring 1984; Shanin 1980: 86–88; Athreya et al. 1987). No matter how sophisticated the methodology or how complete the data, it seems that the problem of differentiating between noncapitalist and capitalist forms of small-scale production, as well as the issue of the social and ideological effects of commodity production, will remain controversial.

One way to overcome this impasse is to rely on the comparative method, that is, to compare (within a given regional social economy) the organization and performance of enterprises in different branches of commodity production and, in some cases, to make comparisons between enterprises in different local industrial units (within specific branches of production). Such comparisons—combining cross-sectional census data with case studies of selected enterprises—will provide a solid basis for clarifying the nature and extent of capitalist relations of production.

To anticipate an argument that will be substantiated analytically in this chapter, the movement of peasant-artisan household enterprises from conditions of petty commodity production to those of petty capitalism is significantly affected by household demographics through their impact on productive capacity, capital accumulation, and material wealth (e.g., as measured by landholdings, means of production, and type of housing). This argument, despite having been influenced by the detailed analysis of household demographics, does not imply acceptance of Chayanov's labor-consumer balance theory of the peasant family economy with its emphasis on simple reproduction. A principal finding of our analysis is that household labor contributes critically to the accumulation of capital and material assets in most household units that experience this movement. By no means, however, do all petty commodity-producing households in our sample that experience such "endofamilial accumulation" (Cook 1984a) cross the threshold into petty capitalist production. Those that do represent exceptions to the Chayanovian emphasis on peasant-artisan "self-exploitation" to secure the simple reproduction of the household unit. To the extent that wage labor comes to replace or permanently supplement household labor in particular household enterprises, these households illustrate Lenin's (1963: 374) thesis that "family cooperation" is the "foundation of capitalist cooperation" (cf. Cook 1984c: 7).

It bears reiterating that we do not regard the class polarization of rural household enterprises within a commodity economy to be inevitable. Rather, our position is that, apart from household demography and life cycle, a series of material and ideological conditions in the wider commodity economy will either stimulate or constrain the process of class differentiation. In other words, demographic or life-cycle factors only become relevant to the analysis of class differentiation to the extent that they operate together with extrahousehold factors.

Class Differentiation in the Oaxaca Valley: Which Approach?

It should be clear that we accept the role of household demography only as a gross limiting factor. Likewise, we deny the existence of any specifically "peasant consciousness" that systematically operates to restrict or prevent capital accumulation and the enterprising use of capital. Furthermore, it is our contention that the detailed analysis of the relationship between economic factors and household size, composition, and life cycle strengthens the Leninist approach without compromising its focus upon the dynamics of social differentiation and class relations. In contrast to the thesis of its "undifferentiating" and "unexpanding" nature, our findings suggest that petty industrial commodity production may stimulate class differentiation and capital accumulation, leading to investment to expand enterprise scale (if not to underwrite "technological innovation"). In short, we find that rural petty commodity production—especially in local industries linked to wider capitalist circuits (particularly as buyers of raw materials and wage goods or as sellers of commodities)—may, under certain conditions, operate as a seedbed for capitalist development.

In order to substantiate the above theses, we analyzed socioeconomic differentiation along three axes: the total sample of households surveyed ($N = 1,008$) was placed along the first axis; along the second axis the household sample was disaggregated into four mutually exclusive categories—"peasants" (agriculture exclusive), "artisans" (craft exclusive), "peasant-artisans" (agriculture and craft production), and "other" (neither agriculture nor craft production);[5] finally, along the third axis, the data were disaggregated and analyzed for craft-producing households classified into one of seven mutually exclusive craft-industry categories—embroidery, treadle loom weaving, mixed artisan, town artisan, palm-ixtle, backstrap loom weaving, and brick fabrication.[6]

Along each of these axes, analysis of socioeconomic differentiation revolved around the following eight variables: (a) number of resident household members; (b) number of workers in household, paid and unpaid, (c) number of nonworkers in household (a minus b), (d) consumer/worker ratio, (e) annual income per household, (f) annual income per household worker, (g) annual income per household member, and (h) the five stages in the household developmental cycle. These eight variables, which are included in Tables 19–21, are labeled as follows: (1) FAMSIZE; (2) NUMFAM; (3) FAMDEPS; (4) CWRATIO and RATIO (depending upon method of calculation); (5) INCOME; (6) WORKINC; (7) CASH; and (8) STAGE.

The CASH variable represents an effort to quantify all sources of household income taking into consideration production costs. It was computed separately for each of four RURALJOB classifications: "Peasants," "Artisans," "Peasant-Artisans" (which combines the strategies employed in income calculations for peasants and artisans), and "Other." Sources of income include agricultural products (corn, beans, goats, pigs, etc.) whether sold or directly consumed— in either case they were valued at the going market price; rural industrial products (embroidered blouses, woven blankets, mats, etc.), and wages. Costs include hiring of agricultural labor and means of production (e.g., oxen); cost of raw materials or labor in artisan production, as well as transport costs and taxes for those who sell in marketplaces. For households in each RURALJOB category, gross income over the course of the last production cycle (or pay period in the case of waged and salaried employees) was computed; expenses were then subtracted and a net income figure was arrived at. It was assumed that the last production cycle or pay period was an average one and could be used to estimate yearly income by factoring in the number of production cycles completed in a year based upon the length of the last cycle. The variable INCOME thus derived provided an estimate of the household's net yearly income. INCOME could be divided by 52 to estimate WEEKINC (household's estimated weekly income) or by FAMSIZE (number of members in the household) to provide an estimate of net income per member per year, making comparisons with households of different sizes possible. The latter computation yielded values for the CASH variable. The variable WORKINC, or annual income per household worker, is computed by dividing INCOME by NUMFAM.

Table 19 presents information on the central tendency of these variables for the 639 cases (of the total of 1,008 cases) for which sufficient data was available to calculate household income. Oaxaca, as already noted, is one of the poorest states in the Mexican federation, with an average per capita income among the lowest in the country. As Table 19 indicates, mean and median per capita income figures in selected outlying areas of the Oaxaca Valley accord well with state and national trends. Median income per household member is only $74.00, while income per household worker is $487.20 and the total income per household a mere $873.70 dollars.[7]

Two correlations are relevant for an initial encounter between the Oaxaca Valley data and Chayanovian analysis. Both the number of nonworkers in the household and the consumer/worker ratio are negatively related ($-.29$ and $-.23$, respectively) to annual income per household worker with a significance level ($N = 639$) in each

Table 19. *Some Basic Values for 7 Key Variables for 639 Oaxaca Valley Rural Households*

Variable	N	Median	Mean	SD
FAMSIZE	639	6.00	5.76	2.45
NUMFAM	639	2.00	2.59	1.36
FAMDEPS	639	3.00	3.18	2.19
CWRATIO	639	2.00	2.69	1.75
RATIO	594	1.54	1.59	.42
INCOME[a]	639	379.6	873.7	3,419.7
WORKINC[a]	639	155.6	487.2	3,300.8
CASH[a]	639	74.0	160.2	359.1

[a] All monetary values converted to U.S. dollars at the 1979 exchange rate of 22.50 pesos to 1 U.S. dollar.

case of .0001.[8] For Chayanov, the consumer/worker (c/w) ratio was important because it determined the intensity with which available labor power would have to work in order to satisfy peasant household needs. As the c/w ratio rises due to the birth of new members of the household, Chayanov predicted that labor intensity would also rise.[9] With further development—younger children maturing and entering the household work force—he predicted a corresponding decline in labor intensity because of the smaller ratio between productive and nonproductive workers (lower c/w ratio). From this heuristic, marginalist perspective, ultimately predicated on an attributed psychology of pan-historical dimensions, the level of material reproduction was assumed to be fixed.

If the level of material reproduction is fixed, however, there should be no correlation at all between the c/w ratio and annual income per household member. The latter variable would be constant, and higher work intensity would compensate for higher c/w ratios and vice-versa. That is not the case in the Oaxaca Valley, where annual income per household member is inversely related to the c/w ratio. This growing income per household worker in the context of declining c/w ratios gives rise, as shall be discussed, to a potential for capital accumulation based on the employment of unwaged household labor (i.e., endofamilial accumulation).

Table 20 summarizes data on some basic demographic and income variables aggregated by stages in the household developmental cycle. Changes in the c/w ratio parallel changes in household size and, therefore, conform to Chayanovian expectations in their relationship to the household demographic cycle. Median annual income

Table 20. Demographic and Income Variables by Stage in the Household Developmental Cycle (income variables in U.S. dollars)

Stage	(f)	FAMSIZE	NUM-FAM	FAMDEP	C/W	RATIO	INCOME	WORK-INC	CASH	SUBSIST	HOUSE-SCALE
I	8	2.2	2.0	0	1.0	1.0	607	249	249	12.5	1.2
II	360	6.7	2.0	4.0	2.5	1.8	388	141	60	28.9	3.0
III	160	5.7	3.0	3.0	2.0	1.3	438	171	79	31.2	3.0
IV	56	3.9	3.0	1.0	1.4	1.1	382	159	105	42.8	3.5
V	52	2.0	1.0	0	1.0	1.2	233	176	126	19.2	3.0
No data	3	—	—	—	—	—	—	—	—	—	—

Note: The variable labels are defined above. The values for FAMSIZE are means; values for SUBSIST are percentages; values for all other variables are medians. INCOME and WORKINC are in dollars. Stages I–V in the household developmental cycle are as follows: I, Single/married; II, all children less than 5 years old; III, all children 5 years or older; IV, all children 15 years or older; V, all household members over 30 years old. The variable (f) is the frequency of number of cases.

per household worker (value produced per worker per year) is relatively stable, but annual per capita household income rises steadily as the c/w ratio declines. Thus, analysis of the sample disaggregated by household demographic stages confirms the sample-wide trends noted above.

Those households having access to at least three hectares of non-irrigated land, or its equivalent, as well as an oxteam and oxcart, are considered to have sufficient means (excluding labor) to approximate a subsistence level of food production (this is designated by the SUBSIST variable in Table 20). By stages, households with this subsistence potential increase from 28.9 percent of all households in the "all children less than 5 years old" category, to 31.2 percent in the "all children 5 years or older" category, and then to 42.8 percent where all children are over 15 years old, subsequently declining to 19.2 percent of the cases for adults more than 30 years old. It is noteworthy that the largest jump in subsistence-producing capacity parallels the largest jump in median annual per capita household income (from $79 to $105), a rise of over 30 percent. Households with a median income of $105 per capita also have the highest value for the "housescale index" (designed to approximate the level of material comfort achieved by the households surveyed).[10] The correspondence of these three measures (i.e., median annual income per household member, approximation of subsistence level of food production, and level of material comfort) at their highest values (Stage IV households) is supportive of the proposition that, as household productive capacity increases, so does production, income, and standard of living.

Collectively, these results dispute the Chayanovian claim that labor intensity and duration is positively correlated with consumer/worker ratios (declining when c/w ratios decline and rising when they rise) so as to generate a more or less constant annual income per household member. On the contrary, Table 20 indicates that annual income per household member rises from $61 per person per year in households where all children are less than 5 years old, to $105 per person per year in those households with all children more than 15 years old. This variable continues to rise—to a median of $126—in households composed of adults over 30 years old even though annual income per household worker has declined. This rise was possible only because annual income per household worker declines *less* on average than the decline in the c/w ratio. At the very least, these results confirm the *possibility* that many industrial commodity-producing household enterprises may accumulate capital.

Table 21 presents data on per capita income, household size, land-

Table 21. Annual per Capita Household Income and Other Variables According to Occupational Grouping

	N Cases	% in Group	FAMSIZE (mean)	Has. per cap[a]	Cash (md) ($)	Days Worked (mean)	Days Worked (md)	% Increase Agricultural Labor (mean)	% Increase Agricultural Labor (md)
Peasant w/ Agricultural labor	34	25.7	5.7	.26	62.5	68	>98	64.2	73.5
Peasant w/o Agricultural labor	103	74.3	5.8	.40	18.7				
All peasants	137	100.0	5.8	.33	33.3				
Artisan w/ Agricultural labor	35	27.8	5.2	.00	160.4	66	78	33.5	26.0
Artisan w/o Agricultural labor	79	72.2	5.6	.00	118.1				
All artisans	114	100.0	5.5	.00	136.0				
Peasant-artisan w/ Agricultural labor	91	25.5	5.6	.25	94.4	47	36	33.3	23.0
Peasant-artisan w/o Agricultural labor	268	74.5	6.0	.32	66.2				
All peasant-artisans	359	100.0	5.9	.30	81.1				
Other w/ Agricultural labor	11	29.0	6.2	.00	138.4	90	>98	40.0	32.0
Other w/o Agricultural labor	18	71.0	4.7	.00	319.7				
All others	29	100.0	5.3	.00	202.2				

[a] Hectares per capita per household member (median).

holding, and agricultural wage labor for each of the occupational categories.[11] Because of the significant contribution that agricultural wage labor makes to total household income for a substantial proportion of the households, the data has been disaggregated to allow examination of the influence of this factor that is so important to Leninist analysis.

Agricultural wage labor makes a substantial contribution to the total household income of between 25 and 30 percent of the households in each occupational category, although it is the principal source of income for only one group: the agriculturally employed peasants. Indeed, petty commodity production aside, this material provides strong evidence for the presence of an agricultural rural proletariat and semiproletariat in the craft-producing towns of the Oaxaca Valley. Moreover, with the exception of the "other" category, those households participating in agricultural wage labor, regardless of occupational type, have higher incomes than those that do not. This is particularly true in the case of the landed peasantry but for artisans and peasant-artisans also. The peasant-artisans work the least number of days in agricultural wage labor, no doubt because their multiple economic activities leave little additional time. Even so, it is significant that such wage labor contributes 20 to 30 percent of the income for one quarter of all peasant-artisan households.

The highest incomes are found in the "other" grouping, which is a heterogenous mix including professionals, wage laborers, and other employees—the latter includes everything from poorly paid and unskilled labor to better-paid skilled jobs with various fringe benefits. Among the remaining categories, the artisans have the highest per capita annual income. The overall median income for the artisans is more than three and a half times as large as that of peasants and one and a half times that of the aggregated peasant-artisan group.

All of the artisans' income is in cash; therefore, they are totally market dependent. The peasants and the peasant-artisans, a portion of whose income is in products for home consumption, may sell or consume these according to market conditions and household economic strategy. Thus, vis-à-vis the other two groups, artisans have fewer economic options.

These data highlight certain important features of social differentiation in contemporary rural Mexico. Normally, we expect social differentiation to be accompanied by increasing occupational specialization as direct producers are divorced from their means of production and assigned by the social division of labor to specialized roles in industry or agriculture. But where such a process is underway, its early stages are not so clear-cut. In the Oaxaca Valley, both households and individuals pursue multiple occupations with the hope that the aggregate income will provide a minimal standard of living since it cannot be sustained from any single source. The peasant-artisan households that also participate in wage labor represent the extreme of this tendency; they produce commodities for market sale, directly produce a portion of their food requirements, *and* hire themselves out to others for wages.

The development of a labor market signals a concomitant development of capital. Indeed, one of the most interesting features of the Oaxaca Valley division of labor is the development of capitalist relations of production within particular local craft industries where noncapitalist relations of production used to predominate. The remainder of this chapter will revolve around a detailed examination of this process in two such industries: treadle loom weaving and brickmaking.

Household Composition, Labor Processes, and Social Differentiation: A Further Look at Treadle Loom Weaving

In Chapter 3, quite different circumstances were documented for treadle loom weaving in Teotitlán del Valle, Santa Ana del Valle, and Xaagá. The Santa Ana industry is essentially a satellite of Teotitlán. A handful of Santa Ana weaver intermediaries supply yarn to weavers on credit, buy-up products at prices lowered to cover the cost of the yarn, and resell these products at higher prices (primarily to Teotitlán businesses). By virtue of their control over the supply of yarn, the Santa Ana intermediaries are able to dictate the type, design, colors, and yarn quality of the products woven by the households they supply. This has the effect of making the bulk of Santa Ana production conform to standards that are lower than those of many Teotitlán weavers who specialize in high-quality, high-priced products for the elite segment of the tourist and export market. Thus, despite the fact that most Santa Ana weavers identify themselves as "independent" (*por su cuenta*) producers, their dependent position within the industry leads us to classify them as disguised wage workers for the buyers-up.

The Xaagá weavers, on the other hand, specialize for the most part in the production of loose-weave cotton cloth (*tela deshilada*) for further elaboration into garments in a production process that combines weaving with the work of design, cutting, and sewing (or in the case of shawls, finishing by knotting). Return on invested capital and expended labor is maximized when household enterprises are able to combine weaver/loom units with seamstress/sewing machine units. The Xaagá enterprises' dependency upon larger Mitla enterprises derives from the control that the Mitleños exercise over the large craft market located at the town's famous archaeological site. Xaagá weavers also buy most of their thread in Mitla in stores that, unlike the Santa Ana merchant outlets, are not necessarily involved in the garment industry or tourist market, although some weavers do occasionally receive thread from Mitla intermediaries in exchange for discounted products.

In short, there are three very different situations in this branch of production, despite the fact that treadle loom weaving figures prominently in all of them. Because intervillage differences may have significant consequences for the study of social differentiation, the data have been disaggregated so that the analysis may be conducted village by village. We will focus upon the relationship between household size, number of weavers, number of nonweaving household workers, number of instruments of labor, and economic performance of the production unit as measured by the output and income of weaving households.

Santa Ana del Valle

Information is available for 33 weaving households in Santa Ana, 31 of which are either one-loom/one-weaver ($N = 15$) or two-loom/two-weaver ($N = 16$) units. Somewhat surprisingly, the median cash income of the one-weaver households ($N = 13$) is more than twice that of the two-weaver households ($N = 8$). On the other hand, the two-weaver households have more land (median of 1.0 to .7 hectares of seasonal land units) and produce more corn (320 to 100 kilos, 1979 harvest, median figures) than the one-weaver units; furthermore, 50 percent of the former own oxteams compared to only 20 percent of the latter. This indicates a more diversified production and investment strategy, associated with greater access to land and, as will be shown below, a larger labor supply.

The fact that 14 of the 15 one-weaver households have unpaid, nonweaving household workers, compared to 10 of the 16 two-weaver households is evidence of a greater concentration on weaving in the former than in the latter. It is likely that weavers in two-weaver households without household workers will individually spend less time weaving than weavers in one-weaver households with nonweaving household workers, since, in the latter situation, the weavers will also have to perform the preparatory tasks.

Whether households are able to add looms or to intensify the output of a single loom is probably a function of household size and sex ratios in the context of the gender division of labor. Since men have customarily been preferred as weavers and women preferred as unpaid, nonweaving household workers, it makes sense for households to add looms where there are more male offspring and to intensify loom work by the male household head where female offspring predominate. These factors also help to explain why two-loom households diversify into agriculture (they have the requisite male labor power), as well as why one-loom households are more likely to intensify weaving activity rather than farming (they have female labor available to help with spinning and dyeing as well as with loom work).

We relate the lack of employees in Santa Ana weaving to the tight control exercised by the buyers-up in Teotitlán who dominate the regional market in the woolen products branch. This control structure leaves direct producers with little potential to expand production beyond the limit of the household labor supply (the supply of both yarn and wage labor presents formidable obstacles) and is a strong material disincentive for the Santa Ana buyers-up to establish workshops with on-site piecework loom operators. Through their control of the yarn supply and access to the tourist market in Teotitlán and Oaxaca City, the rate of profit enjoyed by local intermediaries is probably higher than it would be if they invested capital in looms and a workshop facility. Even in Teotitlán the organization of treadle loom weaving tends toward dispersal in household units rather than toward nucleation in manufactories, suggesting that the high degree of labor intensity and individual artistry required to produce high-quality woolen blankets and tapestries is another factor that inhibits the development of more-rationalized forms of production.

Teotitlán del Valle

The random sample for Teotitlán includes 69 weaving households distributed according to the number of weavers as follows: 36 have one weaver, 27 have two, 5 have three, and 1 has four—a distribution comparable to that of Santa Ana. Of these households, 63 claimed nonemployer status and only 3 admitted to having employees. Unfortunately, none of the employer households is included among the 47 for which we have per capita income figures.

Table 22, which divides these households according to the number of resident weavers, shows a strong positive relationship between household size and the total number of weavers and household

Table 22. Weaving Households in Teotitlán del Valle Classified by Number of Weavers and Other Social and Occupational Variables

No. of Weavers	N	Family Size	No. of Family Weavers	No. of Non- weaving Fam- ily Workers	No. of Looms	Cash in Pesos
1	36	4.5	0	1.4	1.2	4,279
			(0)	(1.0)	(1.0)	(3,550)
2	27	5.85	.8	1.2	1.9	7,204
			(1.0)	(1.0)	(2.0)	(4,666)
3	5	6.6	1.8	1.6	2.8	6,841
			(2.0)	(2.0)	(3.0)	(2,871)
4	1	8.0	3.0	2.0	4.0	12,044
			(3.0)	(2.0)	(4.0)	(12,044)

Note: Figures for means are on the top and median figures are below.

weavers. The expected positive relationship between total number of weavers and the number of nonweaving household workers fails to occur only in the move from one-weaver to two-weaver households, where the number of nonweavers declines. We might predict that the gross value of output per loom would be lower because weavers ostensibly have to dedicate a portion of their potential weaving time to tasks like spinning, bleaching or dyeing, and designing. It is also possible, however, that factory yarn and synthetic dyes could be used in lieu of the homemade variety, which would reduce the demand for nonweaving labor time (at the risk of jeopardizing product quality, though given the *caveat emptor* rule of the market, the actual difference in quality may or may not translate into price differences). Our data do not permit us to estimate the frequency with which this substitution strategy is employed in multiple weaver/multiple loom enterprises.

Even though the average number of nonweaving household workers falls from one- to two-weaver households, per capita income rises substantially, and with it the potential for capital accumulation on an endofamilial basis. It is clear from the presence of three-weaver/three-loom households that some enterprises continue to expand the productive capacity up to the limit of their supply of available household weavers.[12]

Peasant Industrial Capitalism: Clothing and Brickmaking

Enterprising Weaving and Piecework in Mitla's Backyard: Xaagá

As we explained in Chapter 3, the garment industry in Xaagá has been an arena for the development of petty capitalist workshops that integrate the activities of cloth weaving, cutting and design, and machine sewing. Although a perusal of the data presented in Table 23 discloses that the five weaving units in our subsample are smaller in scale than, for example, units studied by Carol Smith (1984) in Tontonicapán, Guatemala—averaging, for example, only 3 regular employees per unit versus 8 per unit in her sample—we are prepared to argue, on the basis of case study data, that these five units have crossed the dividing line between petty commodity and petty capitalist production (which runs counter to the interpretation Smith made of her larger Guatemalan units that she insists had not crossed the divide).

How is petty capitalist production to be recognized empirically? From our operational point of view, a commodity-producing unit (or

Table 23. Production Data, 12 Cases, Brickmaking and Treadle Loom Weaving Industries, Oaxaca Valley (all values in U.S. dollars)

(1) Case No.	(2) family	(3) No. of workers hired	(4) Means of Production (MP)	(5) Raw Materials	(6) Wages (W)	(7) Value of Output	(8) Profit (P)	(9) P/W	(10) P/ (MP+W)
Weaving (N=5)									
1.	0	3	387	64	42	156	50	1.19	.15
2.	1	2	265	177	124	368	67	.54	.17
3.	2	5	1,184	193	147	578	238	1.62	.18
4.	1	3	1,100	237	142	512	133	.94	.11
5.	1	3	1,117	171	118	533	244	2.07	.20
Subtotal	5	16	4,053	842	573	2,147	732		
Mean	1	3.2	811	168	115	429	146	1.27	.16
MD	1	3	1,100	177	124	512	133	1.19	.17

Brickmaking (N=7)

6.	0	3	1,778	45	311	933	577	1.86	.28
7.	0	2	2,700	67	244	667	356	1.46	.12
8.	0	3	1,138	53	336	667	278	.83	.19
9.	0	2	1,302	69	293	756	394	1.35	.25
10.	0	2	4,000	67	304	547	176	.58	.04
11.	0	1	1,405	53	371	889	465	1.25	.26
12.	1	3	4,264	84	444	889	361	.81	.08
Subtotal	1	16	16,587	438	2,303	5,348	2,607		
Mean	.14	2.3	2,370	63	329	764	372	1.17	.17
MD	0	2	1,778	67	311	756	361	1.25	.19
Total	6	32	20,640	1,280	2,876	7,495	3,339		
Mean	.5	2.67	1,720	106.7	239.7	624.6	278.2	1.21	.17
MD	0	3	1,243	68.0	268.5	622.5	261.0	1.22	.18

Note: Values in Columns 5–10 have been computed for periods of one month.

enterprise) can be identified as "petty capitalist" when the following conditions are met: (a) the means of production are privately owned or controlled; (b) wage labor is regularly employed either in lieu of or to supplement household or reciprocal labor to the degree that it produces more than half of the value of unit output per turnover period; (c) the purpose of production for each turnover period is to generate a net cash return (profit) in excess of input costs; (d) the individual proprietor spends at least as much time in management and marketing as participating directly in production; and (e) over time, in response to market conditions (e.g., as they affect the cost and availability of labor and other means of production, product pricing, etc.) and profitability, the unit will expand or contract its productive capacity by altering its investment in labor or other means of production.[13]

It is possible, in any given situation, that the dividing line between noncapitalist and capitalist production can be crossed at the enterprise level without being associated with a permanently polarized structuration of social classes at the community, industry, or regional levels. The dividing line, however, may be crossed at the industry-wide level, for example, even though only a minority (say, 10 percent) of the enterprises regularly employ wage labor (and meet the other criteria of capitalist performance) intergenerationally, provided that the value of their aggregate output accounts for more than half of the value of the total output of their industry. This may or may not be accompanied by a structural tendency toward such polarization, which would be expressed in the status or social location of individual households at any given time.

Among the 55 households randomly surveyed (of 191 households) in Xaagá, 84 percent participated in craft production. The craft occupation with the highest number of participants was shawl finishing (by patterned tying of loose ends of woven shawls), which was practiced in 36 percent of the households; 32 percent of the households had weavers, and 20 percent had sewing machine operators (i.e., seamstresses). About 90 percent of the seamstresses resided in weaving households (a fact that will be discussed below). Of 28 weaving households surveyed in Xaagá, 10 had self-employed weavers who do not employ pieceworkers, 9 had self-employed weavers who regularly employ pieceworkers (from which 5 cases have been selected as the subsample in Table 23), and 9 had weavers who were full-time pieceworkers (operarios) in other shops. The average weekly income of the piecework weavers was much higher than that of the seamstresses or the shawl finishers. Most shawl finishers (young girls or old women) earned less than $2.20 weekly, while seamstresses earned from $3 to $12 weekly. Weaving pieceworkers, by contrast, earned $12 to $20 weekly, whereas the average weekly net income for self-employed weavers (including both employers and nonemployers) was $30.

A relative devaluation of female, as opposed to male, labor power is operative here. Male weavers were paid 3 pesos ($.13) per meter for the standard type of cotton cloth and wove an average of 3 meters per hour (24 meters in an 8-hour day); seamstresses were paid 2 pesos ($.09) per shirt and sewed an average of 4 shirts per hour (most work only 4-hour days because of the need to perform domestic tasks). The average weaver's wage then was 9 pesos ($.40) per hour, or 72 pesos ($3.20) per 8-hour day, compared to the average wage for a seamstress of 8 pesos ($.35) per hour, or 32 pesos ($1.42) per 4-hour day. Shawl finishers, on the other hand, earned only 4–7 pesos per shawl (2 hours' work), equivalent to an hourly wage of 3 pesos ($.13). The issue of the devaluation of female labor power does not end here. An important contributory factor to the viability of the weaving enterprise is not *low* wages but *no* wages; the male-run household enterprise appropriates value from unwaged female labor power, which is ideologically construed as "helping out" (*ayuda*) rather than "work" (*trabajo*) (Cook 1984a: 169; cf. Deere and León de Leal 1981: 349).

Almost 90 percent (24 of 27) of the weaving households in Xaagá had only one weaver; only one of these had unpaid weavers, but 29 percent had nonweaving household workers who performed accessory tasks in weaving (e.g., bleaching and dyeing thread, winding thread), and the same percentage had shawl finishers. Fifty percent of the one-weaver households, however, had at least one seamstress and one sewing machine and were therefore fully capable of producing finished garments; an additional 13 percent had sewing machines but had to hire seamstresses to produce finished garments. Only one single-weaver household specialized in shawl production; it had no sewing machine but did have a shawl finisher. In the remaining households, the single weaver was either an employee or specialized in producing and selling bolt cloth.

The 1.2 looms per one-weaver household average obscures a considerable disparity in the distribution of looms. Four of these households had no looms, which means that the weaver in these cases was an employee, either in his employer's shop or in his own home operating a loom that belonged to his employer. At the other pole was one five-loom household, which, at the time, was the largest employer unit in the village (case no. 3, in Table 23). The remaining six households had either two or three looms each, with all but one of them also being employer units. These units either expanded beyond the limits of available household labor or suffered attrition in the household work force.

The male proprietors of the employer units (see Table 23) were young (average age 30 years), had recently achieved their employer status (average of 2.4 years prior to the interview), and had long prior experience (average of 9 years) as weaving pieceworkers in the workshops of Mitla. Mixed incentives underlay their transitions from pieceworkers to independent operators. Two explained their decisions to become independent in terms of the inconvenience of the daily commute to Mitla (either on foot or bicycle). Another cited disagreements with his last Mitla employer. Still another expressed his rationale as seeking to make more money by selling his own products. Two of these individuals, prior to establishing their own workshops, had temporarily withdrawn from the craft citing various physical ailments and exhaustion from long hours spent on the loom. One of them, who worked as a goat trader for more than a year, admitted to "having in mind the idea of getting my own loom, but I couldn't figure out how to get the money."

In three cases the initial capital required to purchase a complete loom outfit was accumulated by savings from pieceworker earnings. In other cases, money was obtained through goat trading, a wife's inheritance, or a loan. Following this initial investment, subsequent purchases of additional looms, sewing machines, and other equipment were made, in most cases, with saved earnings. In one case a sewing machine was already owned by the household prior to the purchase of its first loom, and in another a sewing machine was purchased simultaneously with the first loom. In all other cases, sewing machines were purchased after looms had been in operation for a year or longer.

The expansion of home workshops by these independent weaver-employers was steady and rapid. For example, case no. 3 (Table 23) in 1977, was a one-loom/no sewing machine/no employee operation that by 1979 had evolved into a five-loom/two-sewing machine/four-employee operation; in 1980 this proprietor purchased a used pickup truck for $2,200, again from saved earnings. In doing so, he became the first weaver in Xaagá to acquire a motor vehicle, thus following a path already traversed by many Mitla weaver-merchants who serve as role models for the Xaagá weavers. Without exception, the other employer units in Xaagá have experienced comparable (if less dramatic in some cases) success in capital accumulation over the same period.

The following case history of one Xaagá weaver, Enrique, will illustrate the process of enterprise development in this industry:

By the time he was eight years old, Enrique was tending cattle and flocks of sheep and goats for his father and others in the village. He did this for four years (being compensated with food by some of the animal owners). At the age of twelve, Enrique started helping his father in agricultural tasks (clearing fields, planting, harvesting) and also in cutting firewood and making charcoal, which they hauled by burro to sell in Mitla. At the age of fifteen, Enrique began to cut and sell firewood on his own account and continued working as a *leñero* until he was seventeen. This was his first cash-earning job and it yielded him a few pesos daily. For the following six years, he worked as a day laborer in Mitla for a coffee merchant (loading and unloading trucks) and also in a mescal distillery; during this period, he also worked on road construction crews and in agriculture in the Isthmus. His wage during this period varied from 8 to 12 pesos daily.

While working in Mitla, he learned that there were weaving workshops where one could become an apprentice and earn according to what he wove. In his words: "I began to learn by winding thread and preparing the loom, then I began practicing on the loom, and I was paid according to what I did. I had a real desire to learn, and in two weeks I learned everything." He was paid 1 peso for each shawl-length piece of cloth (1 meter) and, by working extra-hours, took home 200 pesos weekly. As he explained: "I worked from 8:00 A.M. until 5:00 P.M., then I left for a while, and in the evening would begin again at 7:00 P.M. until 10:00 or 11:00 P.M." Enrique was an *operario* in this workshop for nine years; he quit because the employer refused to raise the piece rate beyond 2 pesos per meter, which translated into 40 pesos per day (since Enrique wove an average of 20 meters of cloth daily)—a wage that was, more or less, the same as the going day wage for agricultural labor. He then went to the Isthmus to work in a cement block factory, but in three months was back in Mitla where he was a loom operator successively in two different workshops until 1976 when he was able to acquire a loom and began to work at home in Xaagá.

Why did he go independent? He explained that he had observed over the years of work in Mitla that the loom operators from Mitla would work for a while in a workshop and then leave, buy a loom, and start working for themselves. "I saw," he said, "that they had progressed and lived better." Also, the loom work was beginning to take its toll on him physically. He asked his employer for a week off to recuperate from kidney problems that had been flaring up periodically as a result of long hours at the loom. The employer granted the leave, but when he returned to the shop he found another weaver at his loom and a replacement weaver waiting on the sidelines. In other words, the workshop had clearly become a classic sweatshop. In his words: "I made that decision to help myself because in Mitla I suffered. At least I would be at home and eating at regular hours."

How did he manage this change in status given his precarious financial situation? He explained that he had saved enough from his prior earnings for a down payment on a used loom that a friend of his from Mitla (who was closing his workshop to expand a ranching operation) sold him at a good price on easy-payment terms. He had to borrow 300 pesos from his father-in-law to make his initial purchase of thread, but within six months his fledgling enterprise was successful, and, at the end of the first year, he was able to buy a second loom and hire a loom operator. He attributed this success to joint effort with his wife: "I worked hard and my wife helped a lot also. Between the two of us we worked hard. I wove and she wound thread, or I wound thread and she sewed on the machine. Within six months we were able to pay off the loom and our debt to my father-in-law. After that I was able to buy my own thread. And we have both worked that way until now."

The subsequent expansion of Enrique's enterprise (which in 1979 had four looms, two sewing machines, several employees, including in-house loom operators and sewing/shawl-knotting outworkers, a new brick and cement building, and a motor vehicle) has been financed principally from saved earnings.

Enterprise histories such as these provide strong backing for our interpretation of synchronic data and our view that, given appropriate conditions, rural petty industrial commodity-producing units are fully capable of developing (by no means irreversibly) into petty capitalist enterprises.

Why did units like those in the subsample succeed in recruiting and regularly employing wage labor when many other proprietor units did not? One likely explanation lies in the division of labor by gender and household demographics or, more specifically, the composition of the in-house workforce. As already emphasized, in Xaagá a rigid gender division of labor channeled females, without exception, away from weaving into sewing and shawl finishing and channeled males away from sewing and shawl finishing into weaving. Consequently, households with a shortage of working-age males are more likely to employ piecework weavers than those without such a shortage. As it turns out, all five of the households in our subsample of petty capitalist enterprises lacked sufficient personnel to expand weaving operations without hired labor. Since they are all relatively young households, it is possible that as underage members mature they will displace hired workers; however, it is equally plausible— and, indeed, had already occurred in case no. 3—that new entrants into the household labor force will lead to additional hiring (e.g., a daughter is trained as a seamstress to work alongside her mother and a hired seamstress, giving the enterprise more sewing capacity, which, in turn, facilitates the acquisition of an additional loom and the hiring of an additional weaver) and, thus, further expansion of productive capacity.

Before examining more closely the dynamics of the expansionist units, it is instructive to briefly consider the issue of nonexpansion. More specifically, why do some self-employed weaver units with the objective capabilities to expand fail to do so? In some cases, the units in question were recently established and had not had time to expand (e.g., five units were one year old or younger at the time of the study). In other cases, weaving was looked upon by the weaver-proprietor, who was also a peasant cultivator, strictly as a part-time, seasonal occupation. In still others, the weaver-proprietors were un-usually skilled and opted to increase earnings by weaving high-quality products exclusively with household labor and felt that quality would be sacrificed if workers were hired. Finally, one weaver-proprietor explained his decision not to purchase an additional loom and hire an employee in terms of his dislike for spending time look-ing for new customers, buying materials and, in effect, managing a business rather than working at a craft. Consequently, subjective fac-tors do condition the behavior of particular enterprises and can act as impediments to capital accumulation and enterprise transformation, but, as we have shown, such factors cannot be regarded as absolute barriers to enterprise growth, expansion, and metamorphosis.

A comparison of ten self-employed weaving units in Xaagá, which have no employees, with the five-employer units shows that the nonemployee units average 2.3 household workers each, compared to only 1.0 for the employer units. This deficit in household workers is offset by an average investment in means of production by the em-ployer units that is more than double that of the nonemployer units. Combined with the employment of wage labor, additional means of production result in a monthly production value for the employer units that is 2.3 times greater than for the nonemployee units. While these figures do not shed any light on the means or the reasons for the expansion of petty commodity-producing enterprises, they do suggest that the results of such expansion bring substantial material benefits.

A comparison of the employer and nonemployer weaving units with respect to agriculture yields mixed results. Employer units were better off than nonemployers in terms of the amount of land worked, amount of shelled corn harvested, and the number of months during the year when corn was purchased, though it is not certain whether this is a cause or a consequence of success in weaving. Interviews with Xaagá weavers point to a bifurcation between an agrarian and a craft ideology; among a majority of employers this is coupled with a bias against the practice of agriculture. Two of our five successful employers, each with more than eleven years of experience as weavers, expressed the peasant-artisan ideology that considers dual involvement as complementary and necessary for survival—though one of them qualified this by saying, "We lose our work in the fields but not in weaving" (alluding to the risk element in rainfall-dependent agriculture). A third employer argued the same point but summed up his view by observing, "We were born in the countryside and don't dare to abandon agriculture." Nevertheless, he admitted that when he inherits his father's land as anticipated, he planned to sell his oxteam and work the land with hired hands.

The two remaining employers were less ambivalent in expressing negative views about agriculture, as well as about peasants who are part-time weavers. Their views suggested the possibility of an emerging antiagrarian ideology among the most successful weaving entrepreneurs, a development that in turn would reinforce the thesis that, as capitalist development takes root in rural industry, it may drive a wedge between agriculture and industry in the regional division of labor. There seemed to be an undercurrent of resentment among the full-time weavers against peasant interlopers in weaving whose cardinal sin was deemed to be an alleged tendency to recklessly underprice their products.

Here the full-time weavers were impaled on a contradiction. Their own long experience as exploited pieceworkers in Mitla sweatshops taught them the value of labor power and the nature of exploitation. It also taught them that taking up weaving independently by acquiring a loom was the preferred route to progress. But the viability of their own operations, in a market controlled by Mitla buyers-up, hinged significantly upon their ability to produce with unwaged household labor—especially that of their seamstress wives and daughters—in combination with hired workers.

Piecework and Profits in the Brickyards of Santa Lucía

The data presented in Table 23 demonstrate clearly that the typical brickmaking enterprise is significantly more productive and profitable than is the typical weaving enterprise. Another difference between the brick and weaving industries resides in the fact that in the community studied, Santa Lucía del Camino, brickmaking has been practiced continuously at least since the nineteenth century. Over the decades it has evolved from a seasonal peasant-artisan occupation practiced by a relatively few households to a year-round peasant capitalist industry practiced by many households clearly differentiated, though not completely polarized, into a class of proprietor-employers and a class of propertyless pieceworkers.[14]

Located in communities near to Oaxaca City, the brick industry has grown markedly over the last several decades, more or less in response to the growth of the city's population from 31,000 inhabitants in 1940 to 200,000 in 1980 (cf. Aguilar Medina 1980: 53–57; Nolasco Armas 1981: 191–196). By 1940, brick transport had been motorized, with flatbed trucks replacing oxcarts. Brick production increased (in terms of the number of brickyards and of output per brickyard) to meet the growing demand for bricks by the urban builders, who are the brick producers' principal clients (see Cook 1984a: esp. 14–37).

The units listed in Table 23 (all employers) represent only the top stratum of six strata comprising the socioeconomic hierarchy in the industry. At the bottom is the brickmaking pieceworker, known as the *milero* or *destajista,* who is paid by piece rate for each 1,000 unfired and stacked bricks produced. The brickyard pieceworkers either have migrated to the brickyard zone from other districts or regions of Oaxaca and reside with their families in the brickyards in shanties provided rent free by their employers or are natives of the brick-producing villages who live there and walk to the brickyards daily.

At the apex are the most highly capitalized employer units, which combine the ownership of multiple brickyards, kilns, and trucks and whose business includes selling bricks produced in their own brickyards as well as reselling bricks produced by other units (Cook 1984a: 38–45). An examination of the work histories of several brickyard operators discloses a career trajectory through which direct producers who entered the industry as *mileros* eventually became self-employed clay buyers, then renters or lessees, and, later, achieved the status of private proprietors of brickyards (and, more than likely, employers of *mileros*). This career trajectory is still operative today, but our impression is that the proportion of *mileros* who actually experience it is small and diminishing due to the increasing concentration of capital in the industry and the rising cost of entering as a fully independent producer (owner of the necessary tool kit, the brickyard, and a kiln). It is important to note that self-employed nonproprietors, like the first-stage private proprietors, lack control over kilns. Consequently, they tend to sell unfired bricks, since if they wish to sell fired bricks they must rent kilns, which raises their production costs.

Considering that most of the brickyard employers interviewed were born and raised in Santa Lucía, it is surprising that only two came into the occupation—and the land on which their brickyards are currently operating—by inheritance. Most of the others grew up in landed peasant households with full-time agriculturist fathers. (The same is also true of one-third of the workers.) The employers had spent an average of twelve consecutive adult years in the brick industry (vs. 9.7 for the employed workers), and their mean age was a relatively high 48 years. In essence, the picture that emerges is one of diverse occupational histories with shifting fortunes but shows a trend toward increasing affluence and material success after brickmaking becomes their principal source of livelihood.

In some cases, an early experience in the brickyards was interrupted by a series of other occupational experiences both within and beyond the bounds of the village division of labor. In others, current involvement in the brick industry reflects either a progressive, though prolonged, passage through a series of stages in the development of the domestic enterprise or an abrupt, opportunistic entry into the industry at a fairly high level of commitment of time and capital.

The typical pattern of development may be represented in the cases of Porfirio and Máximo.

Porfirio

The case of Porfirio spans a seventeen-year period and passes through all the principal stages in the developmental cycle. Porfirio was born and raised in a traditional Zapotec agricultural village located a few miles to the southeast of Santa Lucía in the district of Tlacolula. His father, a landless agricultural proletarian, died when Porfirio was nine, and his destitute mother placed him in the care of a better-off peasant household. He earned his keep by tending animals and later, in his teens, by working as a field hand.

At the age of 19 Porfirio left the employ of his village *patrón* and got work on a highway construction crew where he earned five times the daily wage that he had been paid in the village. He worked on highway construction for about a year and then returned to his mother's house in the village where he took up basket making. This occupation was thriving under the influence of an American expatriate who had established an export business specializing in reed baskets produced by hundreds of peasant households throughout the Oaxaca Valley. Porfirio married a local woman and worked on a piece-rate basis for this American merchant for the next fifteen years. In his words: "I made all kinds of baskets. I made baskets for the United States. I even made baskets for dogs to sleep in."

During those years, Porfirio also acquired a second occupation as a butcher. Then in 1960, as a result of political factionalism and violence in his village (which is endemic in that section of the Valley), he accepted an invitation from his *comadre* (ritual co-parent) to move to Santa Lucía. He worked at his two trades, basketry and butchering, in his adopted village, but his sons soon started to work in the brickyards and they convinced him to try it out.

Porfirio worked with his sons as a *milero* in a Santa Lucía brickyard for five years but then decided to pay the owner of a clay pit (*barranca*) for the clay extracted per 1,000 bricks—an arrangement known as *comprar tierra*. He rented a kiln, fired the bricks, and sold them directly to clients. Porfirio worked on this basis for three years. Next, he leased an abandoned clay pit from the widow of a deceased brickmaker, put it back into operation, built his own kiln on the leased property, and became a de facto brickyard operator. At the end of his three-year lease term, he was presented with an opportunity to buy a parcel of land suitable for establishing a brickyard; he bought it outright for 25,000 pesos he obtained by making a secured loan at a Oaxaca City bank through the good offices of his exemployer, the American basket merchant. With hired hands and his remaining sons (his oldest sons had migrated to Mexico City), Porfirio dug a clay pit, constructed a kiln, and began operating his own brickyard. He repaid his bank loan in two years and immediately applied for another, this time for 50,000 pesos, to enable him to buy a used flatbed truck for hauling bricks.

Porfirio still makes an effort to grow subsistence crops on a small parcel (.5 ha.) of arable land and admits to liking agricultural work, especially because it helps to cut down food and fodder expenses. Nevertheless, he considers brickmaking to be a less risky and more profitable occupation. He emphasized that bricks that are not sold one day can be sold the next and noted that "working as a peasant

. . . a bad season comes along with no harvest and one loses the money invested."

Máximo

Máximo, the second case to be considered, was born and raised in Santa Lucía in a peasant household. He had only sporadic experience in the brickyards until around 1970 (three years after marrying) when he decided to enter the industry by buying clay. Like Porfirio, he fired his bricks in a rented kiln. Máximo explained his decision to become a brickmaker as follows: "We couldn't get by on agricultural work. I began to make bricks to help meet household expenses."

The "clay buying" arrangement worked as follows: "They sold clay to me by the thousand. From my earnings I had to pay for the clay, for hauling the bricks to the kiln, for the firewood, and for the kiln. I had to save up, and I had to do the work myself in order to make ends meet. I began to work little by little. It took me two or three months to make enough bricks for a firing. I saved money by doing everything myself. I took out a little to live on but saved the rest. The corn that I always had in the house helped too."

As this statement indicates, Máximo took up brickmaking as a supplement to agriculture; the viability of his brickmaking operation, at first, depended upon the success of his agricultural activities. Within three years after entering the brick industry, he had accumulated sufficient savings from brick earnings and animal sales to enable him to buy a piece of land suitable for establishing a brickyard. He subsequently built his own kiln. Máximo's children were too young to be of much help in the brickyard or in agriculture, so he often employed hired help.

As these cases illustrate, in the brick industry the statuses of self-employed and of owner-employer have been achieved, in a majority of cases, through hard work and experience in the industry from the ground up. For the most part, today's owners and employers were yesterday's pieceworkers. In several cases, as natives of Santa Lucía del Camino, they had been around the brickyards since childhood. It must be kept in mind, however, that most successful brickyard operators have had a variety of work experiences outside the brick industry and that several of them either came to it relatively late or returned to it after substantial experiences in other lines of work.

Whereas no single, sequential line of development has been followed by these units, most of them have evolved through a stepwise process: first, the acquisition of private ownership or use rights over the land (or a brickyard); next, the construction of a kiln; and last, the acquisition of a flatbed truck. The combination of brickyard, kiln, and flatbed truck is the most productive and profitable type of enterprise in the industry. Of course, not all units achieve this level of integration. Such achievement requires the presence of several conditions (assuming motivation, health, and luck to be equal), including inputs from agriculture to household subsistence or capital accumulation, labor inputs from nuclear or extended family, and the willingness and ability to obtain outside financing (e.g., loans from credit institutions).

Most of the employer units in brickmaking do not own instruments of agricultural production and, consequently, must rent these to undertake agriculture. The amount of land cultivated, even by Oaxaca Valley standards, is small, with only three of these units cultivating more than one hectare or reporting shelled corn yields of one metric ton or greater—a fact that is not surprising given the high ratio of population to arable land in Santa Lucía. On the other hand, in five cases, the sale of animals, crops, or arable land was the source of the money capital used to purchase brickyards. Rather than expressing an antiagrarian ideology, most of the employers stated that, while they considered brickmaking to be a much less risky enterprise than agriculture, they also felt that agriculture was a helpful supplement to brickmaking for domestic provisioning. Those who still pursue agriculture do so mostly by raising animals and by growing alfalfa (and some corn) on irrigated land (or in abandoned brickyards, which, due to years of excavating, approach the water table) and not by planting corn, beans, and squash according to the traditional peasant dry-farming method.

Most of the brickyard proprietors interviewed did not perform manual work in brickmaking, though they had done so earlier in their careers. Two of them could be marginally classified as "worker-owners," whereas the rest spent much of their time away from the brickyards attending to agriculture or other business. The majority employ *mileros* who reside with their families in the brickyard area. One real advantage to employer and *milero* alike from this arrangement is that the *milero's* productivity is enhanced by the assistance of his wife and offspring (especially teen-age sons, the production leaders in brick molding), who become sort of "captive" workers performing various tasks that either reduce the *milero's* work load (making it possible for him to raise his daily brick output) or directly contribute to productivity (by molding bricks themselves). In short, the Saturday wage that is paid by the *patrón* to the *milero* is a payment for labor performed by the *milero's* entire household.

Competition among brickyard employers for skilled, reliable pieceworkers results in some employers jacking up piece rates or extending generous cash loans to lure *mileros* away from competitors. As this implies, there is no formal association of either brick industry employers or pieceworkers, but a great deal of informal discussion among members of both groups about wages and prices takes place. Information about these matters travels quickly from brickyard to brickyard, with truckers and their helpers often being the messengers. Piece-rate hikes demanded or granted quickly become common knowledge and provide new ammunition for *mileros* in the bargaining process with employers.

When the prices of consumer goods rise, *mileros* almost immediately demand compensatory hikes in piece rates. In 1980, for instance, the Mexican government increased the price of sugar and other staples triggering demands by *mileros* for employers to raise piece rates. As one employer explained at the time with some resentment: "My *mileros* are telling me that they can't live on what I'm paying them. They're pestering me with demands for a fifty peso [per 1,000 bricks] increase because sugar is now more expensive!" Our impression is that demands for piece-rate increases are usually taken seriously by employers and conceded to only because, as one employer put it, "If we don't grant them a raise they'll leave and find another employer who'll pay them more."

Summary

Employer status in Xaagá treadle loom weaving and Santa Lucía brickmaking has a dual relationship with labor. First, employers more often than not begin their careers as direct producers and learn the craft through that experience. Second, and without exception, the existence and viability of employer units in both industries depends upon the availability of a pool of labor power that can be engaged for a low or inferior wage, or for no wage at all. The brickyard proletariat is paid a wage that approximates the cost of its reproduction (i.e., necessary labor)—a wage that approximates that cost only because of the regular contribution of unwaged household labor to the production process. The surplus labor/necessary labor ratio in this industry, therefore, hovers around the survival minimum and would fall below this minimum without the unwaged labor of the *milero's* dependents.

There appears to be little opportunity for today's brickyard proletariat to achieve the status of independent producers through endofamilial accumulation as did some of their counterparts in past
decades. For one thing, the level of capital required to acquire a
brickyard and kiln now generally exceeds the limits of endofamilial
accumulation. For another, control over the production and marketing of bricks is increasingly concentrated in several capitalist enterprises so that fledgling household enterprises increasingly find themselves confronted with a choice between producing unfired bricks
for the larger brickyard operators or being squeezed competitively by
them. Though it is still possible for the petty household enterprises
to survive this competition, it appears that the brick industry is becoming "a refuge in which people with few resources crowd for their
subsistence" (Schmitz 1982: 163) rather than a space where pieceworker households can develop into viable independent enterprises.

In the Xaagá garment industry, by contrast, even though most of
today's employers were yesterday's pieceworkers, it is still possible
for independent producers without employees to become successful
employers and for pieceworkers to initiate independent production.
In other words, both the past and present trajectories of garment-
producing enterprises reflect the possibility of upward mobility and
the absence of insurmountable entry barriers (e.g., start-up capital
costs beyond the limits of endofamilial accumulation). In this industry, the achievement of employer status, as well as the viability of
the enterprises, continues to hinge significantly upon the use of
nonwaged household labor; however, nonwaged labor in the brick
industry is a necessary means to raise the income of the pieceworker
household unit to an acceptable level of subsistence. Or, expressed
differently, nonwaged household labor is the link that binds self-
exploitation, within the household, to the exploitation of pieceworking brickmakers by brickyard capitalists.

Differentiation, Class Relations, and Social
Consciousness: Weaving and Brickmaking

In his study of Teotitlán del Valle, Silva (1980: 24) makes the following statement, which succinctly expresses the relationship between
craft activity and class relations in the Oaxaca Valley: "In reality artisan activity is what defines the community in terms of social
classes, as much for the relations that exist inside the commodity
production process as for the relations between producers and intermediaries or, on the other hand, the relations that exist between
producers who own capital and wage workers." If Silva's thesis is

correct (and we think it is), no better testing ground can be found in the rural Oaxaca Valley than the two branches of production that have been the object of our analysis in this chapter: treadle loom weaving and brickmaking. Up to this point, we have examined in considerable detail the objective material conditions that give rise to and sustain relations of production between direct producers of commodities and others who underwrite their activity either by supplying critical means of production or by buying-up and marketing what they produce.

The "others," as we have shown, may be owners of places of employment and the necessary means of production, as is the case with proprietors of weaving shops in Teotitlán and Xaagá or of brickyards in Santa Lucía, or they may be intermediaries who either put-out raw materials for finishing or buy-up finished products (usually as a quid pro quo for supplying raw materials, cash or credit), as is the case with intermediaries operating in the woolen products and the cotton products branches of the treadle loom weaving/garment industry. Under both sets of conditions, value created by the labor of direct producers is appropriated by the "others" without compensation. The shop proprietor and putter-out accomplish this by paying a piece wage that is below the value of the labor embodied in the commodity produced (i.e., bricks, cotton cloth, wool blankets, shawls) and selling the commodity for a price that exceeds the wage bill (and other production costs); the intermediary appropriates value by charging high prices for raw materials supplied or high interest on cash advanced, and/or paying low prices (i.e., lower than the market value and lower than the reproduction cost of the labor contained in them) for the commodities acquired.

The social consciousness of artisans, as well as their social relations and the value created by their labor, is also partially penetrated by the division between workers who do not profit and profit-takers who operate enterprises. In this section, our purpose is to put some ideological flesh on the bones of infrastructure, essentially by looking at how concrete relations of production that are part and parcel of people's quotidian experience translate into opinions and attitudes.

Teotitlán del Valle, because of its preeminence in weaving and the large size of its artisan population, was selected for an additional set of questions for each household surveyed, including five open-ended questions designed to elicit attitudes regarding the distribution of income and wealth.[15] Among the answers to the five questions, an average of one-third of the informants disapprovingly cited intermediaries or employers as appropriators of a disproportionate share of the income produced by the weaving industry. The question with the lowest percentage of such responses (16.7 percent) asked the respondents to explain why most artisans were poor. A typical charge of those who blamed intermediaries for artisan poverty was that they "didn't pay what products were worth" or that "they know how to take advantage of the artisans." According to 21.7 percent of the respondents to this question, artisan sloth or poor-quality work was responsible for their poverty; 13.3 percent attributed poverty to the will of God or to bad luck; and 48.3 percent considered it to be a consequence of various structural conditions beyond their control (e.g., lack of sales opportunities, high cost of materials, and cheap prices for their products, lack of capital or means of production, and lack of education).

The question that elicited the highest incidence of anti-intermediary responses (62.3 percent) was one posing a hypothetical situation in which a weaver sold a serape to an intermediary who, on the same day, resold it for a substantial profit. Eighteen percent of the respondents viewed the transaction as a rip-off and were of the opinion that the artisan was grossly underpaid, whereas another 16.4 percent agreed to the rip-off and underpayment interpretations but argued further that the weaver had a right to a higher price because it was his labor, and not the intermediary's, that produced the serape ("The weaver wove the serape and his work ought to be better paid."). Those respondents who felt that the transaction did not reflect badly on the intermediary did so mostly on grounds that a "deal is a deal" or that the intermediary has a right to whatever profit he or she can obtain in a given transaction.

The theme that the direct producers have the right to the whole value of what they produce (and sell) emerged in several answers to a question as to whether the respondents felt that they received what they deserved when they sold their products (cf. Cook 1984a: 113–116). Two notable responses link an emphatic "no" to this question with the above-mentioned theme as well as with specific disapproval of intermediaries, as follows:

> We receive very little of what our products are worth because the intermediary receives a cut. Our work is worth more but the reseller receives the other part.

> The persons who earn are the intermediaries who buy from us. When they don't pay us what our work is worth that is where they are exploiting us. Since we are the producers it is necessary for us to sell directly to clients, and that way we will obtain the total value of our work.

The fact that just over half of the respondents to this question indicated that they did earn what they were due from weaving is not surprising when it is pointed out that 55 percent were self-employed weavers who did not buy yarn on credit. In other words, this response is skewed toward the successful household enterprises in one of the Oaxaca Valley's most lucrative peasant-artisan industries.

The last of the five questions in this series is perhaps the most telling in regard to the extent to which the social consciousness of Teotitlán weavers reflects the class division of their village. When asked whether they believed there were persons (or groups of persons) in their village who had more material advantages and privileges than others, 82.5 percent responded positively. In specifying the identity of these persons or groups, 28.1 percent mentioned intermediaries, whereas the remainder cited merchants (a category that includes intermediaries, store owners, and business operators in general) or those who had capital to invest (e.g., *tienen algún capital para mover,* or literally, "they have capital to move"). Also emphasized in this response was that the persons in this category had more friends, more contacts, sharper wits (*piensan mejor*), or better language skills (*hablan mejor*). One of the most noteworthy responses, not surprisingly, came from a weaver who lived in a rather remote *barrio* in this spectacularly sprawling community. He identified as fortunate "the merchants [*comerciantes*] along the principal streets because they have the advantage that the tourists arrive there." As anyone who has visited Teotitlán periodically over the last twenty-five years can testify, the commercial development along its main street and in the vicinity of its square has been remarkable and presents tangible proof of the capitalist accumulation that is alluded to in this and other informants' statements.

Turning now to the case of Xaagá, similar questions regarding social differentiation and wealth distribution were asked to a subsample of weavers. In contrast to the much larger community of Teotitlán, where there is considerable socioeconomic differentiation, Xaagá informants appropriately downplay the socioeconomic differences between households there and accentuate the differences between themselves and the Mitleños. Internal differences are admitted to exist with regard to ownership of means of production (e.g., number of looms, amount of land, number of cattle); occupation (e.g., weaver, peasant, agricultural laborer); work habits (some work more diligently or more competently than others); and household size (surprisingly enough, large households are typically associated with more poverty, an emic pattern not supported by our survey data). A representative statement was: "We don't all live equally but according to the means of each household. There are households with many family members and the poor head only works as a day laborer [*jornalero*]."

With specific regard to the garment industry, only one informant, a full time pieceworker, came close to characterizing differences among its personnel in class terms. In his words: "The loom owners can earn more than us because without working they still get a week's income and what we get is a week of work—but not any profit. All those who have worked here, even though with one or two looms, seem to be progressing. I, working for a piecewage, don't progress—I just stay put." The other informants characterized intra-industry differences strictly in terms of number of looms, level of earnings, work habits, and product pricing.

When it came to answering the question as to whether there were others who earned profits from their products, however, nine of thirteen informants pointed to the Mitla intermediaries; two piece-workers cited their employers ("The profits stay with him. One is the proprietor and the other works."), but one of them even mentioned the Mitla merchants. One of the two largest workshop owners characterized the Mitla intermediaries in the same terms employed by his colleagues, which stop just short of accusing the Mitleños of exploitation: "Those gentlemen dedicate themselves to selling our products, whether in the beach resorts or in the homes of foreigners. Some of them export to foreign markets. They profit by buying at one price and reselling at another. And they don't sell one hundred pieces like we do but one thousand. That is their advantage." As will be discussed in Chapter 6, the posture of the Xaagá shop owners regarding the Mitleños is that of neophytes to expert role models; they admire and seek to emulate the material success of Mitla entrepreneurs even if it means longer hours and harder work for them and their dependents.

In the case of the brick industry, social relations are conducted through a split-level idiom. At one level, the focus is on the asymmetrical nature of relations between *patrones* (employers) and *mileros* (pieceworkers) and their ongoing struggle over the distribution of income from brick sales. At the other level, the asymmetrical, instrumental, and conflictive nature of their relations is downplayed; rather, work relations are portrayed as being conducted in a spirit of familism and common interest—with the latter subject to harm from impersonal market forces and government meddling.

On the first level, the principal concern is over wages and prices—not only the price of bricks but also, from the standpoint of the brickyard operators, the prices of nonlabor inputs (e.g., fuel for kiln firing, gasoline for the trucks that haul bricks), and from the standpoint of the pieceworkers, the prices of wage goods (e.g., tortillas, bread, sugar, beans, clothing) and basic services (e.g., transportation, medical care, etc.). Two statements, the first by a *milero* and the second by a *patrón*, are illustrative of this level of ideological expression.

> *The milero*: The boss pays me cheap but he doesn't sell the bricks I make cheap. He sells them for double what he pays me. I am losing. The bosses pay us cheap and we go to buy in the city where prices are expensive—starting with corn, beans, clothing—everything is expensive. Yet one works for the same piece rate.

> *The patrón*: The *mileros* are always on top of you. If they hear that you sold bricks for more than the going price they ask for a 50 peso raise. But they forget that sometimes sales are sluggish. If that happens, one sells below the going price in order to do business and to be able to pay the *mileros*. They never take reductions in the piece rate but only increases. But when I see that I have a big inventory of bricks on hand, I have to lower the price of bricks to sell so I can get money to pay my *mileros*.

The second level of ideological expression of brickyard social relations is employer centered and reflects their response to competition—for sales as well as for pieceworkers. The following statement by an employer exemplifies this level:

> If the standard price of bricks goes up, then one should raise the *mileros'* wage accordingly. But if by chance I sell a thousand bricks for 3,000 pesos because the clients liked them and were willing to pay that price, well in that case I don't have to raise the *mileros'* piece rate. On the other hand, if there is a price increase in other brickyards, of course, I have to raise the piece rate. One has to "get along" [*convivir*] with the *mileros*. One should treat them as members of one's own family and help them with their problems. That way they will be content, and will work quietly and do a good job.

This is a statement of an employer strategy to deal with attrition among the pieceworkers, who are not easily replaced. The strategy includes treating employees as though they were equals and allowing them to go about their work with as little direct supervision as possible, as well as making them loans or providing them with assistance in household crises. The *mileros* expect this kind of behavior from an employer but recognize that there are limits to its exercise. They also realize that it does not change the fundamental nature of the relationship between them and their employers. Consequently, they do not hesitate to take advantage of paternalism without allowing it to bind them permanently to one employer. This posture is illustrated in the following statement by a *milero*:

> My boss used to get mad at times when I went to work in another brickyard. He'd scold me and I didn't like to respond to him. We used to argue but we never fought. I think it was last May when I worked for a few days with another boss. My regular boss got angry and insisted that I should work only for him and not for another boss too. I told him that maybe it would be better for me to change bosses, and that I would pay him back the money I owed him, in installments of 500 pesos. I owed him 2,500 pesos.

Underlying brickyard owners' use of paternalism to attempt to bind *mileros* to them, and of opportunism by *mileros* to obtain income from more than one employer, is a pragmatic ideology that recognizes separate class divisions and interest. This is an ideology that is most clearly expressed by *mileros*. It combines a bipolar conception of community social structure (i.e., as split into two strata, defined as rich and poor) with a fundamental class division in the brick industry. As one *milero* expressed it: "The bosses earn, they have the wherewithal, while the poor worker gets only his wage. The bosses own the brickyards. They are the ones who really earn." Although only a minority of informants in our interview sample considered the Santa Lucía population to be divided along lines of role in the production process, income, and standard of living, all who did so were *mileros*. It is significant, however, that this bedrock class ideology has not led to industry-wide organization (see Cook 1984a: 139–148, 162–167; 1984b: 72–77).

Petty Commodity Production and Petty Capitalism: Recapitulation and Conclusions

It is clear from our study that capitalist development is not occurring uniformly in the rural petty industrial sector and that in several industries it is not occurring at all. Petty capitalist enterprises persist intergenerationally or disappear intragenerationally; there is turnover in personnel and differential time involvement (e.g., full-time vs. part-time, seasonal vs. annual) both by capital and labor. It is important, however, not to mistake smallness in scale, improvisation, and irregular performance for the absence of capitalist production relations and forms of enterprise (cf. Schmitz 1982: 6). After all, such dynamism, improvisation, and irregularity are also characteristic of advanced capitalism where competition and declining rates of profit are dealt with through reorganizational strategies and capital redeployments that keep labor divided and on the defensive, profits flowing, and capitalist hegemony intact (e.g., Frobel et al. 1978, 1980; Portes 1983; Nash and Fernández-Kelly [eds.] 1983).

Once it is shown that small enterprises accumulate capital between turnover periods, that they reinvest capital to further production (in a way that raises productive capacity, even if not in a technologically innovative way that raises labor productivity), that they regularly employ wage labor by piece rate, and that the value created by that labor is unequally distributed between wages and profits, then it is logical to assume that these small enterprises represent some form of capitalism rather than petty commodity production. This is confirmed ideologically when the piece-wage nexus divides employers from wage workers in people's social consciousness, when cash shares of the value produced are conceptualized as "profits" or "wages," and when these relative shares are subject to ongoing negotiation.[16]

As we have noted, the key to distinguishing petty commodity production from petty industrial capitalist production in a given household enterprise revolves around the conditions of value-creating labor. Students of petty commodity production have been slow to recognize, and draw out the implications of the fact, that capital is necessarily accumulated for replacement and also, possibly, for investment in household production units dependent exclusively upon unwaged labor. To counter this oversight and to highlight its importance, the process—the dynamics and outcome of which may be significantly influenced by household size, composition, and stage in the life cycle—has been conceptualized as "endofamilial accumulation" and assigned a prominent role in the development of peasant-artisan capitalist enterprise (Cook 1984a, 1984c, and 1985b). This concept strengthens the Leninist analysis of capital accumulation and social differentiation by focusing attention on factors internal to the household (see Schmitz 1982: 164–168 for a stimulating discussion of several such factors as determinants of accumulation).

The Chayanovian model of peasant-artisan production for own-use, in which household labor is either unassisted or predominant and in which simple rather than expanded reproduction is the goal, is deceptive under conditions in which household survival depends upon the purchase and sale of commodities in a capitalist economy. It creates the illusion that demographic and life cycle factors located in the households themselves, rather than socioeconomic factors located in the surrounding capitalist system, intervene as prime movers in the rural social economy. More important, in linking the demographic and life cycle variables to simple reproduction logic, the Chayanovian approach hinders understanding the new role that these variables can play when petty commodity production is operating within a capitalist economy.

Contrary to the Chayanovian emphasis, these variables need not necessarily operate to preclude capitalist development at the level of specific household enterprises. Indeed, as shown above, our Oaxaca Valley findings demonstrate that they may serve as catalysts that propel some household enterprises across the dividing line between simple reproduction and regular capital accumulation. To the degree that this occurs in conjunction with the increasing employment of wage labor and a commitment to profit taking, it is diagnostic of petty capitalist production.

Household demographics, by contributing to high levels of endofamilial accumulation, may help move specific enterprises across the dividing line between noncapitalist and capitalist production; or, alternatively, by contributing to a diminution in levels of capital accumulation, may promote a scaling down into petty commodity production. At the industry level, however, if the structural conditions underlying the possible transformation of individual enterprises remain in place, the reorganization of some as petty commodity producers will be counterbalanced by the reorganization of others as petty capitalist producers. Furthermore, despite the shifting mix of unwaged and hired labor—linked among other things to changing household demographics—a certain proportion of petty capitalist enterprises in a given branch of production is not likely to experience reorganization on a petty commodity basis. Then, the problem of analysis is to explain why petty capitalist accumulation does not lead to more-advanced forms of accumulation. This is a more legitimate problem than the ill-conceived Chayanovian question that asks why capitalist accumulation does not occur at all.

Chapter 5. Gender, Household Reproduction, and Commodity Production

Females, Chores, and Commodity Production: An Overview

The proposition that the condition and performance of labor in peasant-artisan populations is affected by factors both internal and external to the single household unit is accepted by all schools of thought. Disagreements persist, however, regarding the identity and causal role of these factors. As discussed in Chapter 4, Chayanovians focus upon household size, sex-age composition, and stage in the life cycle, whereas Marxists emphasize the relational process between households and the wider economy, especially as it involves commoditization or increasing market involvement. When emphasis upon one of these two sets of factors leads to the exclusion of the other, explanations of rural economy and society will be deficient. In our approach we give greater weight to relations between households and the wider economy but we also reserve a place for the examination of household demographics (also affected by the wider economy) as influences upon socioeconomic process in rural commodity production.

In this chapter, we will investigate some of the implications of this viewpoint for understanding the specific situation of peasant-artisan women under conditions of petty commodity production and capitalism. In taking up this issue, we enter a terrain alien to both classic Marxist and Chayanovian approaches, neither of which addresses the problem of female labor. Engels did establish a connection between women's subordination and their role in the domestic sphere (Harris 1984: 136), but, until recently, Marxists have not concerned themselves with the process of production/reproduction of labor power in which female domestic labor predominates.

Equipped with a recognition of the role of household demographics in peasant production, the Marxist approach is compatible with the assumption that, under conditions of little or no commoditization or market involvement (i.e., among "middle peasants"), the nature and intensity of female labor would, ceteris paribus, vary according to household size, composition, and stage in the household's biosocial cycle. Conflicts would necessarily arise in the scheduling of women's labor time throughout the household life cycle, but these would vary in intensity from one stage to another. These conflicts can be expected to increase, however, as the household becomes more involved in the commodity economy and, especially, as women, already burdened with housekeeping tasks, confront rescheduling decisions occasioned by their insertion into commodity production.

Needless to say, under conditions of capitalist economy—whether women are petty commodity producers or piece-wage workers—there is constant pressure to extend the amount of labor time and to intensify work in commodity production. In these circumstances, which are essentially those confronting peasant-artisan women in the Oaxaca Valley today, we can anticipate the likelihood of changes within the gender division of labor and in the ideology that surrounds it.

Regarding the specific role of female labor in the rural Oaxaca Valley, a preliminary analysis (see Cook 1984a: 167–172) suggested that when peasant-artisan women become more directly involved in wage labor or in independent commodity production their household status will tend to change. The reasoning was that female involvement in commodity production, regardless of its degree of visibility or its prominence in the labor process, created scheduling conflicts in household allocation of labor for domestic own-use production. Accordingly, the importance of the domestic own-use sphere would be highlighted, especially because of its crucial role in the short- and long-term reproduction of labor power (Benería and Sen 1981: 291–93).

Highlighting this performance would have practical as well as ideological repercussions. It would reinforce other factors operating to subvert the rigid stereotyping of sex roles in the regional division of labor by dramatically demonstrating women's capacity for hard, remunerative work in the sphere of commodity production on a level commensurate with that of men and emphasize the importance of domestic use-value production traditionally assigned to women (Cook 1984a: 173). In other words, women's work would become more "visible" and the ideological underpinnings of its "invisibility" would be exposed as contradictory.

Given the absence of a control population (i.e., women whose labor time is not involved in commodity production or exchange), we cannot critically evaluate the validity of this hypothesis against the project's empirical record. What we can do, however, is examine the nature and implications of increasing pressure upon women to extend the amount and intensity of labor in commodity production, as well as compare their participation in petty commodity production with that in capitalist piecework. This will at least move us in the direction of clarifying the relationship between women's involvement in commodity production and their level of gender and/or class consciousness. It is precisely when women combine domestic work with commodity production that it becomes appropriate to conceptualize their situation as involving the strain and conflict of the "double day" (Young 1978: 146). Under conditions of increasing commoditization of female labor it is appropriate to assume that these strains and conflicts intensify.

Prior analysis (Cook 1984a: 173) has provided the basis for framing one specific proposition for critical evaluation, namely, that those peasant-artisan women who are directly remunerated only for labor they expend in petty commodity production generally have lower degrees of gender or class consciousness than women whose "double day" includes the performance of ancillary, detail labor (perhaps unpaid) or outwork (paid according to piece rate) in peasant capitalist industries like treadle loom weaving or brickmaking or in merchant capitalist industries like embroidery. An analysis of interview and case study data from palm plaiters and backstrap loom weavers who independently produce and market their commodities, from independent petty producers and outworkers in embroidery who deal with buying-up and/or putting-out merchants, and from women participating as waged or unwaged workers in the treadle loom weaving and brickmaking industries will be instrumental in evaluating this proposition.

It can be noted at the outset that there are four ways in which women contribute to rural economy in the Oaxaca Valley: (a) as principal decision makers in those households that are not headed by men (about 8 percent of our total sample of 1,008); (b) as domestic workers who prepare food, wash clothes, care for children, and perform other unpaid tasks that are critical to the long-term reproduction of households; (c) as unpaid laborers within domestic commodity-producing enterprises where they carry out specific tasks in a labor process for which the male household head is the sole recipient of cash remuneration; and (d) as income-earning commodity producers (either self-employed or as piece-rate outworkers) or as traders, directly remunerated, whose contribution to household income is therefore overt rather than concealed behind the control which men exercise over production in other circumstances.

We have examined the gender division of labor in sufficient detail in Chapters 3 and 4 to show that rural Oaxaca Valley women, for the most part, are found in lower-paying craft occupations than are men. It has also been observed that many petty commodity enterprises are exclusively household undertakings that involve the coordinated participation of both sexes in production, although household income is generated in a number of industries with a strong component of gender segregation by a male agriculturalist and female domestic worker/craft producer. The predominantly female industries are characterized by the lowest rates of return. After examining the overall status of females in the total sample of households surveyed, we analyze the participation by female workers in five branches of rural industrial commodity production—palm plaiting, backstrap loom weaving, embroidery, treadle loom weaving, and brickmaking—and discuss some broader economic and ideological implications of their participation.

Gender, Household Demographics, and Commodity Production

Overview: All Households

In classifying occupations by gender, occupations of up to two producers for each household were identified. The results for principal occupations are presented in Table 24. Our sample yielded 448 males distributed into thirty-six discrete craft occupations, compared to 485 females distributed among only twelve craft occupations. The predominant male occupation was weaving, which had 232 participants (51.8 percent). Only two other occupations, those of basket maker with 26 male participants (5.8 percent) and wood carver, also with 26 males, accounted for more than 5 percent of the total male craftsmen. For the females, four occupations accounted for almost 90 percent of the craftswomen, led by embroidery with 237 females (48.9 percent). Substantial proportions of palm plaiters (101, or 20.8 percent), thread spinners (50, or 10.3 percent) and backstrap loom weavers (42, or 8.7 percent) were also recorded. Backstrap loom weaving is the only occupation with substantial male-female overlap. With the exception of palm plaiting, the females in our survey were mostly involved in one or another branch of the textile industry—spinning, weaving, and embroidery.

Cooperation between the sexes in particular industries can be

Table 24. *Crafts by Level of Income and Gender Participation*

Craft	Males (N)[a]	%	Females (N)[a]	%	Income[b] (md. pesos)	N
E	19	7.4	237	92.6	1,095.0	236
TS	1	2.0	50	98.0	1,414.4	42
SF	0	0	19	100.0	1,825.0	16
PP	2	1.9	101	98.1	2,737.5	97
BM	19	100.0	0	0.0	3,650.0	17
SMO	4	18.2	18	81.8	4,988.3	15
B	26	100.0	0	0.0	8,668.8	25
BSW	43	55.8	34	44.2	9,550.8	76
WC	26	100.0	0	0.0	12,242.7	24
TLW	189	95.9	8	4.1	18,980.0	155
BK	20	95.2	1	4.8	77,562.5	17

[a] Total number of artisans included in the second part of the survey.

[b] Based on those cases for which adequate data existed to compute annual median producer income.

E = embroidery; TS = thread spinning; SF = shawl finishing; PP = palm plaiting; BM = broom making; SMO = sewing machine operating; B = basketry; BSW = backstrap loom weaving; WC = wood carving; TLW = treadle loom weaving; BK = brickmaking.

overlooked if only household survey data are consulted. For example, from Table 24, basketry appears to be an exclusively male occupation. Observations in San Pedro Mártir, the principal basketry village in our sample, however, disclosed that many women help men in basketry, especially in preparing strips of *carrizo* for plaiting. Their contribution was not recorded in the household census because the villagers think of basketry as a male activity (Littlefield 1979b: 1). The situation is reversed in the case of the Albarradas villages' palm industry, which is an overwhelmingly female industry. In fact, our field work and intensive postcensus interviewing disclosed that palm is cut, sorted, bundled, hauled to the village, dried, and stored by men. In this case, the villagers uniformly define palm plaiting as a female activity—and will not mention male participation unless questioned carefully. Other examples could also be presented to make the same point: the appearance of a rigid gender division of labor in the Oaxaca Valley often dissolves in the reality of cooperation between the sexes.

Over 50 percent of the females learned their craft from one of their parents, compared to only 23 percent of the males. Males were more likely to learn an occupation from a nonrelative (12.2 percent) or through apprenticeship (18 percent) than were females, a finding that indicates that, by and large, females have less freedom of maneuver than males do in Oaxaca Valley society. Nevertheless, a significant proportion of each sex (20.8 percent of males and 15.8 percent of females) learned their craft by self-instruction, often because of the absence of one of their parents (e.g., through death, divorce, or separation) or of older household members.

Female craft producers, by and large, tend to have had shorter careers in craft production than males. Thus, 58.7 percent of females, as compared to 33.8 percent of males in craft work, had less than five years of experience, while 37.6 percent of the males and only 25.6 percent of the females had worked for more than 20 years. To a degree, however, these figures may be an artifact of age, since male artisans were somewhat older than females.

Income data for craft occupations with fifteen or more representatives have been tabulated in Table 24 and ordered by rank, from the occupation that provides the lowest net yearly income per producer (embroidery) to the one that provides the highest (brickmaking). The strong gender division of labor in Oaxaca Valley craft production has already been noted; it merely remains to point out that those crafts most closely associated with females—embroidery, thread spinning, shawl finishing, and palm plaiting—are also those that yield the lowest yearly incomes.

Not only do these occupations pay poorly but they are also highly labor intensive, with little or no investment in instruments of labor. They are generally treated, both practically and ideologically, as part-time occupations and are practiced to supplement household incomes that have their principal sources elsewhere, usually either in farming and/or in a male-dominated craft. Suffice it to note that embroiderers, who account for almost 50 percent of female artisans, earn a median annual income of only 1,095 pesos, barely one-fourteenth that earned by weavers, the occupational category that accounts for over 50 percent of male artisans.

Female-Headed Households

Of the 1,008 households in the sample, 80, or 7.9 percent, are headed by women. The average age of the female household heads is 56 years, 11 years older than that of the male household heads (45 years), accounted for by the fact that a majority of the female household heads are widows. Largely as a consequence of this, female-headed households are on the average smaller in size (mean of 4.8 members) than male-headed households (mean of 5.9 members), although the

number of working household members differs slightly, probably
due to the fact that more of the male-headed households (over 60
percent of which consist of nuclear families) contain children too
young to contribute in any substantial way to household income.
Consequently, the consumer/worker ratio (which conditions labor
intensity—see Chayanov 1966; Chibnik 1984; Cook and Binford
1986; Binford and Cook 1987) is lower for female-headed households
(mean = 2.25 and median = 1.75) than for male-headed households (mean = 2.62 and median = 2.0). Although the ratio of consumers to workers is lower in the female-headed households, per
capita income is only one-third to one-fourth that of the male-
headed households.

Two reasons account for the poor economic performance of female-
headed households. First, female-headed households are less likely
to have land than are male-headed households. When they do, they
tend to have only 70 percent as much land. As a consequence, they
are more dependent upon cash earnings from petty commodity production and mercantile activities to cover their subsistence needs.
Second, when we examine the means at their disposal for obtaining
this cash, we find that women are (with a few exceptions) restricted
by the gender division of labor to rural industrial (craft) activities
that are remunerated at much lower rates than are the activities
available to men.

In what follows we analyze the participation by female workers in
specific craft industries and discuss some broader economic and
ideological implications of their participation.

The Palm Plaiters

Palm plaiting is a predominantly female activity transmitted intergenerationally through matrilines.[1] Most native-born women in the
Albarradas villages (San Lorenzo and Santo Domingo) fully participate in the industry by the time they reach their early teens and continue to do so into old age. Mothers, grandmothers, and aunts teach
daughters, granddaughters, and nieces. Often females representing
at least two generations are found working side by side during the
day or evening in village homesteads. A majority of our twenty informants attributed their involvement in palm plaiting to the fact
that it is their village's traditionally accepted occupation through
which females contribute to household budgets, either through cash
earnings or wage goods acquired in exchange for mats with village
buyers-up/grocers (i.e., the *empleadoras*).[2] The only partial exception is the case of one male informant (a bachelor and the only male

who regularly plaited palm) who took up the craft when he was 19 following an incapacitating accident. Nevertheless, as is the case with the female informants, he viewed his participation as a consequence of a lack of viable employment alternatives, which, for him, was summed up in the saying "When need obliges, one loses his freedom of choice."

In the case of this unique male plaiter, as for all the females, the fact that plaiting is done in the confines of the home gives it an added attraction since it can be conveniently interspersed with household work. In the words of a female informant: "Working palm permits me to be at home and at the same time tend the animals and to do my chores." Indeed, Albarradas women's participation in this branch of commodity production is taken for granted just as is their participation in household duties. One informant expressed it matter-of-factly: "One cooks in order to eat and one plaits *petates* in order to earn a few cents." The widespread pragmatic acceptance of this double work load, however, is not accompanied by a uniform fondness for the craft. Another informant expressed the view, shared by many of her companions, that, "if we could find another occupation, we would stop weaving *petates* since it is a lot of work, is poorly paid, and one gets fed up with it."

The acceptance of the double work load is not accompanied by a single strategy for performing it, although cooperation among females within and between households is clearly the favored strategy. One notable consequence of the relatively high number of offspring per housewife plaiter is the availability of daughters who help ease the burden of work on their mothers. Moreover, all our informants who were either widowed or unmarried lived in households with other females of working age. This is not coincidental but is a demographic consequence of the high demands placed on female labor in these peasant-artisan households. Only in those households with more than one female worker can mat production possibly begin to approach the status of a full-time activity. Even so it is typically described as a "for a little while" (*por ratos*) activity; household tasks are assigned highest priority, even to the extreme that women often say they turn to plaiting when they are "not occupied." ("When one is not busy she makes a *petate*," or "One has to do her chores first, and then when she's not busy she has to make a *petate*.") Informant statements underline the importance of the gender division of tasks within peasant-artisan households and, more specifically, highlight the extent to which the household mix of production for own-use and commodity production requires collective and cooperative female labor, usually involving representatives of two generations.[3]

The fact that one-quarter of our informants reported that they had left their villages for periods of time ranging from less than one year to eleven years to work as domestic servants in Mexico City exposes another cash-earning strategy involving female labor that is widely employed by rural Oaxaca households in lieu of, or to supplement, craft production. Through a family kinship network, young women often find jobs in Mexico City as live-in domestic workers (cooking, washing, cleaning) and send regular cash remittances back to their village households until such time as they resume their status as resident members or, in other cases, set up independent households either in the village or in Mexico City.

While this involvement of rural females in the urban domestic service market in Mexico is well documented, less so is their return to the sending villages and their reintegration into the peasant-artisan household. Against a widespread tendency to view rural-to-urban female labor migration as a one-way route to urbanization or modernization, our data lead us to view this migration as a circulatory process linking rural and urban branches of what has been characterized as an "informal sector" (Portes 1983) in the Mexican economy. Alternatively, it can be said that village household economy is partially reproduced through cash inputs derived from the urban informal sector without necessarily entailing the eventual permanent loss (through rural-urban migration) of the female wage earners. The most striking case illustrating this is that of a 60-year-old informant, Rosa, who grew up as a palm plaiter in Santo Domingo, left as a young woman for a twenty-six-year career in domestic service in Oaxaca City and Mexico City (where she spent eleven years as the cook for a well-known popular songstress), and returned to the village to reside with her niece and resume palm plaiting in her "retirement."

The case of Rosa is especially significant because it provides a graphic illustration of the comparatively low remuneration received by female labor of "peasant-Indian" origin in the urban domestic service and in the rural craft sectors of the Mexican economy. Her twenty-six years of work in domestic service did not generate adequate savings to support her retirement, obliging her to take up palm plaiting, which she had not practiced since her youth. Admitting that she liked life better in the village because she was with her family, and emphasizing that it is sad when one has to leave one's village and family because of need, she nevertheless would have preferred, after her return to the village, to have taken up an occupation other than palm plaiting, which she said tired her out. The theme of "obliging need" is evoked by her explanation of the rationale for having to plait palm: "One tires out sometimes. When one is tired one does not want to plait. Sometimes one stops plaiting for two or three days. Afterward one says to oneself: 'Where is the money?' So, one is obliged to plait."

The palm plaiters' perceptions of the complexities, significance and source of economic differences vary. On one plane, most informants would agree with the generalization that "one spends a lot of time making a mat and earns a few cents," but, on another, there is widespread recognition of differential household productivity and earnings (e.g., "There are people who work more and some who earn more"). Also, it is recognized that there are differences in the quality of plaiting that are associated with differential earnings (e.g., "There are persons who know how to plait really well, and others who plait more simply. Buyers take note and pay accordingly"). Differential productivity is understood to result from either self-exploitation (e.g., "Some plait a lot, others a little. The ones who have time work all day. The ones who don't, leave work for the next day") or from reciprocal joint work arrangements referred to in the mountain Zapotec villages as *golaneche* (e.g., "Some earn more because they sit down with two persons to one *petate*, and if they sit down early, they can finish it in one day," or "One advances more working with another. One mat is plaited between two persons so the work is not so punishing. Working together has no other advantage").[4]

Regarding value and price, a majority of informants considered that they confronted a buyers' market in which the village intermediaries set prices. They recognized the possibility of bargaining for better prices in the extravillage marketplace but rejected this as unrealistic given the need to quickly convert mats into cash or wage goods in the village. One informant stated the dilemma well in the context of her answer to the question of whether she would like to have another kind of employment:

If there was other work here, even to earn five pesos a day, we would do it. Then we would stop plaiting. Since we plait *petates* for short periods over three days—what do we do about the cash that we need daily? Well, if there isn't any during those three days that I plait a *petate*, then I ask for a loan. When I finish the *petate* I have to pay off the loan. Well, I'm back where I started, there is no progress. For that reason I am telling you that if there was other work where I could earn five pesos a day, well it would be good for me.

In other words, the daily need for cash would incline her toward work in which daily earnings were possible. Only in households with more than one plaiter is it possible to earn money daily from plaiting mats (it is possible to do so from plaiting fans or small baskets although the *empleadoras* prefer to buy mats). Households that have only one plaiter are obliged to meet their daily cash needs through credit extended by *empleadoras* in return for a claim on future mat output. An *empleadora* who operates a small grocery store in one room of her house outlined the kind of transactions she habitually engaged in with palm plaiters: "Women come here to buy on credit. They need something and don't have the money to pay for it, so I give it to them on credit and they pay me later with *petates*. That's how I do business." A more established *empleadora*-storekeeper claimed, however, that, although she continued to make cash advances to plaiters, she no longer exchanged inventory in her store for palm products because the practice cost her money. She preferred to conduct her transactions strictly on a cash basis.

Relatively few households build up an inventory of their own palm products for periodic sale in the extravillage marketplace, although such a strategy is recognized as desirable (for those households with the resources to support it) simply because mats or baskets can be sold for higher prices in the extravillage marketplace than in the village.

A common theme in many informant statements is a use value oriented pragmatism that places short-term consumer needs above any possibility of longer-term profits. The plaiters tend to sell in the village as a matter of expediency and need. They are first and foremost producers of commodities to compensate for deficiencies in their capacity to produce for own-use, that is, they are unable to produce directly everything they consume and must enter the market economy to acquire commodities and services necessary to their way of life. As one woman expressed it, "We earn from our craft but we consume what we earn for the household."

When products are taken to extravillage marketplaces some plaiters, like other artisans, express a preference to sell to clients who buy for own-use; this seems to reflect a homespun, quasi-Thomistic bias against profit-oriented resellers (e.g., "I prefer to sell to people who will use *petates* rather than to resellers who only do business with them"). The majority, however, simply express a desire to sell to whomever will buy at a price that is subject to negotiation but that they see as hovering around a "going price" that no single seller can control. Their view is that resellers have a right to whatever profit the market will bear, although this is counterbalanced by a grudging (and, perhaps, envious) recognition that what is for them a craft pursued for subsistence is for the resellers a business pursued for profit.

The palm plaiters do not subject cash returns from mat (or basket) sales to any sort of accounting procedure that would include a summation of costs in terms of labor or raw materials to arrive at a profit estimate. This is consistent with their image of palm plaiting as a nonbusiness that yields cash but not profits (*ganancias*). One informant who rarely goes to an extravillage marketplace with her products expressed it this way: "We make *petates* but we don't account for the days that we spend making them. I get 25 or 30 pesos for a *petate*, that's all, so I sell them because I have to. We don't account for anything." Another informant who regularly travels to the marketplace expressed a similar view with a different emphasis: "Upon arrival in the marketplace to sell, buyers come to look over the *petates* and ask how much, and one quotes a price. Then one haggles until she sells it. I don't take into account hours worked since it's only a matter of short periods [*ratos*]—one hour here, a half hour there. I don't take work time into account."

The discontinuous nature of mat production, which this informant alluded to, also confuses labor accounting, even in the case of our lone male informant, who periodically works as a hired hand (day wage) in agriculture. This is apparent from the following statement: "This year I went to work in Tlacolula since they paid sixty pesos with meals. But one can't calculate this way with *petates*. One can't finish a *petate* in a day, so as to be able to say that he's going to sell it for sixty pesos because that's what my day is worth. It takes two days to plait a *petate*. So one earns thirty pesos a day and has to provide his own meals." This informant is aware of the opportunity cost of allocating his labor to plaiting mats in the village (as opposed to working in agriculture outside the village) but accepts that cost as a necessary trade off for the convenience of working at home. By contrast, the lack of wage-earning opportunities for women in these villages essentially reduces decision making by women to a choice between unpaid domestic chores and plaiting.

With regard to broader questions of social inequality, a majority of the palm plaiters considered the households in their villages divided into relatively better-off and poor strata and generally explained this as reflective of differential work performance. The better-off households were said to work harder or to have more available workers or fewer dependents. Interestingly, a few informants directly linked palm plaiting to poverty (e.g., "The poor do not have jobs, only the poor woman with her *petates*. That's why they are backwards"), and, in one case, the reselling of palm products by *empleadoras* was associated with their relative wealth as follows:

> They are poor because of the family, since they have a lot of children who can't help them. The men go to work elsewhere because here in the village they can earn only 50 pesos daily. Where there is family that's not enough. Then there's the mother with her *petates* and *tenates;* she sells them to the *empleadora.* To store *petates* one must have money. If not, one can't do it. Some people here have money and they begin to buy and store *petates.* That's how their money keeps growing. They sell *petates* in the marketplace and bring back other things to sell, that's where the money is.

In short, the possibility of material progress from a condition of poverty was seen by several informants as realizable only through hard work and saving, though others viewed it as either unrealizable in the village context (e.g., "In this village a poor family cannot become rich—leaving the village, perhaps") or requiring luck (e.g., "If a fortune falls in his lap") or divine intervention ("God decides," or "If God so wills it").

Without exception, the palm plaiters asserted that men earned more than women. Many agreed that this was the case because men worked harder than women, and they also noted that men were customarily paid by the day and often worked outside the village. Female palm plaiters did not express antagonism over differential pay. Nor was the fact that palm plaiters were paid by the piece (which typically is not produced daily), whereas most men's work was paid by the day, cause for lament. In fact, the differential earnings and payment forms between men and women were not described as being unjust; they were accepted uncritically as expressions of the way things were. Indeed, if any tendency exists in their responses, it is for women to belittle the contribution their plaiting makes to the household economy by dismissing it simply as "passing the day." The one reported case of disagreement between a palm plaiter and her husband regarding work, however, serves as an appropriate summing up of the contradictory role of this occupation in the village economy: "He says that I am entertaining myself with the *petate,* nothing more. But I tell him that there are times when the children ask for snacks or things like school supplies and that I pay for them with the *petate.* I tell him that if he alone works there is not enough money. It's just a way of helping out a little." Despite its ideological devaluation by men and women alike, the empirical record consis-

tently shows that female craftwork, like housework, is hardly an un-
productive pastime but is an activity critical to the survival of peasant households in a cash economy.

The Backstrap Loom Weavers

Like palm plaiting, backstrap loom weaving is customarily associated in popular and scientific culture with the female domain in the
rural Mesoamerican gender division of labor (cf. Villanueva 1985:
19). Nevertheless, it is by no means an exclusively female occupation in the villages we surveyed. Indeed, in the Jalieza area of
Ocotlán district, a striking contrast exists between Santo Tomás,
where 71 percent of the weavers in our survey of half its households
were female, and the neighboring villages of Santo Domingo, Santa
Cecilia, and San Pedro, where the percentage of female weavers was
significantly less (10 percent, 17 percent, and 53 percent, respectively). In other words, if backstrap loom weaving was once an exclusively or predominantly female industry in the Oaxaca Valley, it
clearly is not one today.[5]

Before examining these contrasts within the gender division of labor more closely and, particularly, before attempting to explain the
partial defeminization of the labor force in weaving, it is necessary
to present some background information regarding the Jalieza area
villages and the weaving industry. Although smaller than Santo Domingo, Santo Tomás is the head village politically, probably because
of its strategic location on the valley floor near the highway linking
Oaxaca City to the district town of Ocotlán de Morelos. Santo
Tomás is currently the Oaxaca Valley leader in backstrap loom
weaving; it generally produces a wider variety and better quality of
products than its neighbors, which, together with its proximity to
the highway, has made it a favorite stop on the tourist circuit (especially on Friday market day in Ocotlán, which regularly attracts the
tourist trade). The Santo Tomás weavers display their products on
Fridays in a site adjoining the municipal plaza and garden. This activity is organized by a marketing cooperative that has operated in
the village since 1963 and has had considerable impact upon the
craft, despite the fact that it has never had a majority of weavers in
its membership (Bertocci 1964).[6]

By contrast, in the other Jalieza weaving villages, which are off the
highway and essentially inaccessible to the tourist trade, there are
fewer weavers and no formal weavers' organization and products are
sold on an individual basis to intermediaries or to tourist-shop owners in Oaxaca City. The product line of these villages is limited to

sashes and carrying bags of generally poor quality in comparison with those from Santo Tomás. To a degree, this is probably due to the recent diffusion of backstrap loom weaving into these villages from Santo Tomás where it has been practiced continuously for at least 130 years (Clemens 1987b: 2).

The serious entry of Santo Tomás (and other Jalieza area) males into weaving probably occurred in response to their search for ways to compensate for a shortage of good arable land as well as to the growing demand for woven goods, which created unprecedented cash-earning opportunities. In other words, the allocation of male labor to weaving rather than to other cash-earning activities provided a material advantage to Santo Tomás (and the other Jalieza area) households. Males appear to have first entered the industry in Santo Tomás, and later their influence spread to the other Jalieza area villages. Several male weavers in Santo Domingo reported that they learned to weave from a friend or acquaintance in Santo Tomás, whereas most of the others reported that they learned from neighbors or on their own. It is not clear under what conditions Santo Tomás weavers taught the Santo Domingans, but we have no evidence of any employment relationship between them.[7]

Our survey data point to an elaboration of the household division of labor with task and/or product specialization by gender. For example, adult males tend to weave newer products, such as tapestries, which often require wider looms, or belts, which require leatherwork in addition to weaving, whereas women are increasingly associated with weaving smaller or finer products and in operating sewing machines to assemble newly introduced clothing products, such as vests, slipover shawls, and shoulder bags.

Compared to the female weavers, more male weavers (70 percent vs. 50 percent of the females) in Santo Tomás tend to sell their products weekly and earn larger average sales receipts than do the females (median = 690 pesos vs. 270 pesos). This may reflect the greater productiveness of male weavers deriving either from a greater time commitment to weaving (because of fewer competing demands for their labor, especially in land-poor households) or higher productivity per hour worked. The earnings differential may also reflect a further gender division in marketing patterns, since a somewhat higher percentage of males than females reported that they sold their products in Oaxaca City. The data also show that men were more likely to sell their products to resellers instead of to buyers for own-use.

The average age of the female weavers (N = 13), who were selected for postsurvey interviews conducted in 1980, was 40; all were either married or widowed and, with the exception of two who were childless, had an average of 4.6 children. The average age at which these women began to weave was 12 and, at the time they were interviewed, they had been weaving for an average of twenty-eight years each. As might be expected, most of them learned to weave from their mother, grandmother, or aunt. Only four women stated that they had worked in agricultural activities prior to marriage, and all of them had helped with various domestic chores from a young age. One index of the importance of weaving to the household economy is the fact that only two of the women had extravillage work experience, a much lower percentage than for the palm plaiters from the more remote Albarradas villages.

Only five of these thirteen female weavers considered that life was better than it was when they were growing up, a judgment that belies any simplistic assumption that everyone has benefited equally from the apparent increase in weaving business or that benefits have been enduring. On the contrary, per capita income and the living conditions index vary widely among weaving households in Santo Tomás. Accordingly, their explanations as to why they weave reinforce the "obliging need" theme: weaving is the most viable cash-earning activity available to them in the village, and the need for cash income to meet daily household expenses is constant. Under these circumstances, low remuneration is better than none at all.

Despite a nearly universal insistence that they weave because they want to, many female weavers also admitted paradoxically that weaving is the work the village provides for them ("That is our work," or "That is the work for a person from here"). Although many volunteered that they were not obliged to weave by their husbands, others expressed the belief that there is a mutual obligation between husband and wife to help each other out ("It is an obligation for each of us to help out the other") and that their household cannot survive on only their husband's earnings ("I do it because I have an obligation to work as does my husband . . . With the children we can't make it on what my husband earns"). We are reminded of the material urgency of their situation by one informant's statement, "With the sashes that I weave, I buy food for my children."

As was the case with the palm plaiters, these same themes emerged repeatedly in informant responses to the question as to whether or not they would like to withdraw from their occupation. Even though a majority of them reported paltry, if variable, earnings and complained of steadily rising costs of materials (e.g., thread, dyes, etc.) and that the work was tiring (especially hard on the back and knees), they argued unanimously that they would not consider quitting, simply because there was no other convenient or acceptable way to earn cash ("Why would I give up weaving? How else am I going to earn a few cents?"). In short, backstrap weaving is a tiring activity with limited rewards in most cases, but it is the only one available to many women.

The informants expressed widespread agreement that differences within the industry related to the quantity, quality, and value of work performed by weavers representing different households. They explained the sources of this differential productivity by referring to household size, amount of work, and product mix, all factors that our research confirmed to be associated with socioeconomic differentiation.

When asked specifically about the sources of wealth and poverty in the village, however, most informants emphasized the importance of landholdings and, especially, of inheritance as the principal means for acquiring land. The attitude linking relative wealth and poverty of village households to the land situation (the less land the more poverty) was prevalent, as was the notion that, the more households are dependent upon weaving rather than agriculture for their livelihood, the worse off they will be.[8]

Work scheduling and task management among the backstrap weavers are essentially the same as that reported for the palm plaiters. Most women prefer to get up early and complete domestic chores in order to free a block of time for weaving ("One does household chores early and when one finishes she begins to weave. We begin at 1:00 P.M. and work for about five hours"), whereas others intersperse chores with weaving throughout the day. They spend an average of two to five hours daily at weaving (average ca. 3.5 hours), seven days a week.

The marketing of products by the Santo Tomás weavers is more diversified than that of the palm plaiters. In addition to selling to tourists in the village plaza, about one-third of the weaving households surveyed also sold periodically in Oaxaca City or outside the state (e.g., Mexico City). Sales are to buyers for own-use as well as to intermediaries. Probably, proportionally fewer sales of woven products are to intermediaries than in the case of palm products, but the woven products business, dependent as it is on the tourist and export trades, is considerably more lucrative. Given this situation, it is not surprising that all our informants responded to the question as to whether other people earned money from the weavers, by citing the intermediaries. A high percentage of them expressed a clear understanding of the marketing and profit strategies of the intermediaries, and a few expressed veiled resentment against intermediary activities, as the following statement illustrates: "The buyers-up pay cheap. They earn more than those who work. Since I don't agree with this I don't work very much. The buyers-up are together on prices and they are bothered if one asks them to increase prices. They say that they can't. They take advantage of us." Notwithstanding such statements, most of the backstrap loom weavers—as is habitually the case with Oaxaca craft producers—agreed that intermediaries were entitled to their profits.[9]

The Embroiderers

Social relations more closely resembling those of industrial capitalism are established when merchant capitalists relate to peasant-artisan producers, not merely to buy-up their products, but also to put-out their raw materials. Whether the context be the East Anglian textile industry beginning in the fourteenth century (and subsequently in much of the English textile industry—Goody 1982: 12–21), the nineteenth-century lace industry in the Moscow Gubernia of Russia (Lenin 1964: 362–369), or the present-day needlework industry in the Ocotlán district of Oaxaca, when merchant capital penetrates petty industrial commodity production, from outside or inside the ranks of direct producers, it has a contradictory impact upon the household economy (see Chapter 6 for a more extensive discussion of merchant capital).

For example, in the Ocotlán embroidery industry, each new outworker recruited by a rural putting-out merchant is a potential future competitor. Such new employees typically have little or no previous experience in wage labor but their petty commodity background has instilled in them a double-sided familiarity with merchant capital—one side resentfully perceives it as opportunistic profiteering, and the other perceives it as a career model to emulate. Accordingly, the prevalent outworker strategy for increasing earnings—aside from producing more by working harder or longer hours—is to cease to accept materials on a putting-out basis, to purchase materials independently, to enlist the cooperation of household workers, and, when sufficient capital is accumulated, to establish a small buying-up and/or putting-out business. This individualized accumulation strategy is encouraged by the dispersal of outworkers in their separate villages and homesteads and by the piece-rate payment form, which gives each outworker the illusion of being in charge of her or his own economic destiny (cf. Cook 1984a: 124). Together, outworker dispersal and the piece rate assure that embroiderers develop no collective or cooperative organization.

Although the needlework industry is dominated by merchant capital through dispersed mass production on a buying-up and putting-out basis (see Chapter 6), the independent petty commodity producer is by no means absent. Indeed, as long as there is space for independent units with specialized skills and a marketing network that provides a variety of sales opportunities, self-employed producers are unlikely to disappear. It appears, however, that self-employed producers will become increasingly dependent upon buyers-up who extend cash advances (*adelantos*) in order to establish liens on future output.

One interesting feature of the needlework industry is the variation, between and within villages, of the status and role of household enterprises. Most needlework households in several villages (e.g., Santa Cecilia and Santo Domingo Jalieza, Magdalena Ocotlán, San Baltazar Chichicapan, and Santa Lucía Ocotlán) are outworker units for absentee merchants; the outworkers pick up a prepatterned, unassembled set of pieces for one or more garments (with or without the necessary thread) from a merchant in the regional marketplace or from a village commission agent, embroider the separate pieces at home (often with different household members being allocated different pieces within a set), and then turn in the completed work (pieces embroidered but not assembled) to the merchant (or commission agent) for a lump-sum payment.

In some villages (e.g., San Juan Chilateca and San Pedro Mártir), side by side with outworker households of the type just described, some households independently cut, design, embroider, crochet, and assemble by machine sewing the garment (usually a blouse or dress). These self-employed units may or may not have dependent outworkers; if they do, they will distribute various tasks in the production process to outworkers and specialize in assembly and other selected tasks themselves.

Consequently, different levels of skill, task assignment, and piece-rate remuneration are found within the outworker population. Some workers specialize in embroidering intricately designed figures on the pleated front of blouses below the neck (referred to appropriately as *Haz me si puedes,* or "Make me if you can"), whereas others specialize in simpler embroidery, crocheting, or designing and cutting garment sets. It is worth reiterating that our evidence suggests that these self-employed embroiderers are becoming increasingly dependent upon buyers-up through cash advances (*adelantos*) or special order (*encargo*) relationships.

Data from San Pedro Mártir, one of the Ocotlán villages with an interhousehold specialization of tasks in the embroidery industry, show that out of thirty-four women surveyed, three specialized in designing and cutting for an average wage of 90 pesos ($4.00) weekly, eleven did the intricate embroidering of figures on pleated blouse fronts and earned an average of 87 pesos weekly, and five did crocheting for an average wage of 68 pesos ($3.00) weekly. Women who did simpler needlework earned substantially less. The average payment by piece was 10 pesos ($.44) for designing and cutting, 11 pesos ($.49) for intricate figure embroidering, and 9 pesos ($.40) for crocheting. Our data show that the women who specialize in these tasks earn higher weekly incomes than nonspecialists, but that they also work longer hours. As a consequence, the discrepancy in hourly returns between specialized and unspecialized labor is small.

An interesting feature of the needlework industry that parallels backstrap loom weaving is the entry of males into a craft that has traditionally been in the female domain. Cook still recalls his surprise one morning in 1979 upon first visiting San Isidro Zegache where he saw male heads of household seated on chairs, either on their porches or under shade trees, diligently embroidering floral designs on blouses or dresses. These were the first male embroiderers Cook had seen in the Oaxaca Valley. He had thought that embroidery was exclusively a female occupation. As it turned out, only four of the eleven villages with embroidery households had no male embroiderers. San Isidro, with 35 percent of its embroiderers being males, was by far the industry leader in that regard, although nearly 15 percent of the embroiderers in San Jacinto Chilateca and 10 percent in Santa Cecilia Jalieza were also males. Overall, however, the embroidery population surveyed is predominantly female (92.7 percent of 450 embroiderers), and there is no reason to believe that a process of defeminization of the embroidery labor force is underway, as there seems to be in the case of backstrap loom weaving.

Some clues to the structure of the needlework industry can be ascertained by considering what villages without male embroiderers have in common. Three of the four villages without male embroiderers (Santa Lucía Ocotlán, San Baltazar Chichicapan, and San Dionisio Ocotlán) are latecomers to the industry; they have a low percentage of household participation in embroidery and have major occupational involvements in other areas. For example, for historical reasons, a large number of men in Santa Lucía and San Dionisio are employed in highway maintenance and construction jobs, whereas San Baltazar, an important agricultural village, has several mescal distilleries and a thread spinning industry that is the largest employer of women. San Juan Chilateca is a prosperous agricultural and commercial community with a small sugarcane processing industry. Many households in San Juan have members with salaried jobs in the public and private sectors.

By contrast, San Isidro Zegache, which has many male embroiderers, is a newly established, land-poor agrarian reform community
of mestizo former ranch hands, many of whom practice modern hor-
ticulture on small private plots or work as hired hands or sharecroppers in neighboring villages (especially San Antonino). The men of
San Isidro took up embroidery as a cash-earning supplement to hor-
ticulture, agricultural wage labor, or sharecropping. This was the
only village in which the embroidery households (with one exception) were independent petty commodity producers and participated
in just one branch of craft production. Thus the entry of men into
embroidery would appear to be related to land poverty and the absence of nonagricultural cash-generating activities for men.

A general profile of the population of female embroiderers reveals
that one-third are between 10 and 19 years of age and that 46 percent
are equally divided between the 20–29 and 30–39 age categories.[10]
Female participation in embroidery steadily declines with age to
12.2 percent in the 40–49 category, 5.8 percent in the 50–59 category, and 2.4 percent among women over 60. Two factors are probably involved in this decline. First, in many villages, embroidery has
been introduced only recently and is usually learned in school or is
self-taught rather than transmitted through the family structure.
Second, failing eyesight also contributes to the decline of participation of older embroiderers. These same two factors no doubt have a
bearing on the high participation rate of girls between 10 and 19, together with the fact that they are either in their prime as dependent
workers or are new housewives without heavy domestic chore obligations in the initial stages of the independent household cycle. Although female participation in embroidery diminishes as the household biosocial cycle progresses (from stage 1 to stages 2 and 3), it is
significant that participation declines by only about 10 percentage
points and remains steady among women between 20 and 39. This is
possible because embroidery is perfectly suited to the "for a little
while" pattern of work necessitated by the demanding daily regime
of domestic chores that characterizes these years.

Of 265 embroidery households distributed among eleven Ocotlán
villages in our sample, 18 households in two villages, Santa Cecilia
Jalieza and San Jacinto Chilateca, were selected for follow-up interviewing. Prior to their recent involvement in embroidery outwork,
the Santa Cecilia women had not been directly involved in craft
production, whereas most of the San Jacinto women recently had
switched to embroidery from backstrap loom weaving.

The average age of these informants (all females) at the time they were interviewed was 38 (range from 16–57); only two were unmarried, and the fifteen women with children had an average of four children each. Work histories of these two groups of women are different. As noted above, most of the San Jacinto women grew up as weavers (most as household workers, others as outworkers for Santo Tomás weavers) but abandoned weaving for embroidery after they were married. The major reasons cited for the changeover were the steadily rising cost of yarn, sluggish and erratic sales, and low earnings. Since rising costs and low earnings also characterize embroidery, it is more likely that the abandonment of weaving in San Jacinto has to do with marketing difficulties, the main source of which is undoubtedly the market dominance of the Santo Tomás industry. In any case, not a single informant expressed regrets about switching from weaving to embroidery. Even those who were unhappy with embroidery did not want to take up weaving again.[11]

One 38-year-old informant, who was taught to weave when she was 7 years old by her mother, took up embroidery, in addition to weaving, after she married because of her husband's poverty (they are landless and must buy all their food). This is the only case among our informants of a continuing involvement in both weaving and embroidery. Why did this informant choose to pursue both? In her words, "I weave and I embroider because I have to do both to earn enough for food and to help with the children's expenses" (she has five children ranging from 14 to 3 years of age). She spends five to six hours daily, mostly in the afternoon and evening, embroidering and weaves for about four hours once a week. When she needs money quickly she spends more time weaving and less time embroidering.

It is clear that the viability of embroidering independently rather than as an outworker—once the embroiderer has sufficient experience and knowledge of the labor process—hinges on the ability to earn enough cash to cover production costs (e.g., cloth and thread) plus a net income. One informant who alternately does outwork and works on her own account commented on the difference as follows: "When I finish my own shirt, I am going to embroider one for someone else since I have run out of cloth. I deliver a dress every two weeks. They pay me 150 pesos. It is someone else's dress. When it is mine, I sell it for 300 pesos. It doesn't pay much but it helps to buy food for the children."

An embroidered dress that sells for 300 pesos requires 4 meters of cloth at 30 pesos per meter and 35 pesos worth of thread—a total cost of 155 pesos (1979 values, $1.00 = 22.50 pesos). Thus, an outworker presumably earns about the same per dress as she would by buying the raw materials and selling it herself. Our data suggest, however, that successful independent embroiderers either sell their dresses for higher prices or pay outworkers less per dress than the above figures indicate. For example, one informant, who told us that she sells her dresses for 300 pesos each to a merchant from the Zona Rosa in Mexico City, said that she had five outworkers whom she pays only 100 pesos ($4.44) per dress. Incidentally, the Zona Rosa merchant resold these 300 peso ($13.33) dresses for 800 to 1,000 pesos ($33.55 to $44.44), a common level of mark-up.[12]

To the extent that these embroiderers (most of whom are illiterate) keep accounts, they do so only in their heads, but all of them recognize that their work is grossly underpaid. None of them, however, calculates exactly the returns on her labor. In this industry, the system of payment by results neatly circumvents labor-time accounting. Petty merchant and producer alike think only in terms of lump sums—the former, of cost per piece and net earnings per sale, the latter, only of gross income per piece. In some general sense, Lenin's (1964: 363) assertion that "production for sale teaches that time is money" may be true. Petty producers' understandings of the lesson, however, do not necessarily lead to labor-time accounting in production, much less to a strategy for securing just compensation for expended labor.

The Santa Cecilia women began to embroider in the 1970s; some of our younger informants had been embroidering for less than one year at the time we interviewed them. Several of them were participating in a program sponsored by FONART (Fondo Nacional para el Fomento de las Artesanías), which included instruction in design, cutting, embroidery techniques, and machine sewing. FONART helped finance and supply the instructor, the sewing machines, and the cloth and thread and was buying-up the finished garments (discounting cost of cloth and thread).[13] Although the program seemed to be functioning reasonably well, several informants stated that they could make more money by making tortillas for sale in Oaxaca City and that they found tortilla making less tiring. As one of them expressed it: "I prefer to make tortillas for sale because the earnings are better. Embroidery is slow work, it tires out one's brain. I don't see well. But with tortillas, even when I fill up my bucket with dough, nothing happens to me." This same informant said that it took her two days to make one hundred tortillas, which she sold for one peso each in a Oaxaca City marketplace. Working on her embroidery for two or three hours daily, it took her approximately one month to finish embroidering a dress for which she was paid 110 pesos. Clearly, the material incentive would seem to favor tortilla making and discourage embroidery—except of course that tortillas require corn as well as a prolonged stretch of labor time.

The reason women embroider mostly during spare time intervals ("For short periods, when there is time") is clear from the following description by this 33-year-old woman with four small children: "When I finish making tortillas and preparing *tejate* [beverage prepared with ground corn], then, I grab my embroidery. Later the children cry, I nurse them, and I have to stop embroidering. When the children fall asleep, I grab the embroidery again." Another informant described how her first work priority is food preparation and how friction with her husband arises when embroidery interferes with this: "Women don't just embroider. The husband is always asking for his *tejate*. One prepares meals, one hurries up more in preparing meals than with the embroidery. The husband will say, 'Give me some food, stop that work. I go out to work so that we have money. Stop it. First give me something to eat and then you can continue to embroider.'" In Santa Cecilia, women's involvement in commodity production is completely subordinated to domestic provisioning. Both tortilla making and embroidery are undertaken strictly as necessary cash-raising activities. "One's life is poor," one informant lamented. "Hunger itself obliges us to embroider."

Although the embroidery women are poorly educated and functionally illiterate and, in the case of the Santa Cecilians, relatively recent direct participants in commodity production, their experience has taught them that direct producers earn little, resellers earn more, and that the best route to increase cash income is to combine production for sale with putting-out and/or buying-up for resale. Despite the fact that half of the embroiderers rejected the proposition that the poor can successfully escape poverty through hard work and enterprise, they agreed with an outworking colleague (who did not reject the possibility of success) who said, "I work and the owner takes the cents." In other words, regardless of their position in the embroidery industry, producer for own account or outworker, our informants shared the judgment that intermediaries were the biggest earners and that they obtain this condition because they pay low wages (or prices) and sell dear. This was succinctly summed up by a Santa Cecilia informant who said, "The buyer-up earns and the ones who do the work don't."

Brickyard Women

The empirical record of participation by women in the labor process of brick production showed that their contribution is most impor-

tant in the finishing stages of trimming and stacking bricks, although some of them also assist in clay preparation. In this section,
additional data on the role of women in the brickyards are presented
and analyzed, together with women's and men's views of that role.[14]

The mean age of the eight women interviewed was 34 (youngest
25, oldest 50). None was born in Santa Lucía and only two were born
in the Oaxaca Valley. The majority were born and raised in rural
communities in other regions of the state. Most of their fathers were
peasants, and their mothers divided their time between household
duties, agricultural work, and/or the production and sale of tortillas.
Two of these women had relatively uneventful childhoods in which
they performed mainly household duties assisting their mothers.
The others were involved in some form of paid work by the age of 10,
employed either as domestic servants in Oaxaca City or Mexico
City, as artisans, as helpers in small businesses, or as agricultural
workers.

The relatively sheltered upbringing of one woman ended abruptly
after she married. She spent several months in Mexico City as a
seamstress, a newspaper vendor, and a general purpose helper in a
restaurant. Later she ended up in the brickyards as the only woman
(in our sample) who regularly performs all the tasks in brick production in order to support her alcoholic husband and their four children. The mean age at which these women were first married is 16
(two of them have been divorced and remarried); they have an average of 3.5 children each and have lived in the brickyards for an average
of 6 years (range from 6 months to 15 years).

When asked to compare the quality of their lives in the brickyards
with that of their childhoods, half of them felt that life was better in
the brickyards—principally because of the proximity to the city and
a somewhat higher standard of living. Only one respondent, Marcela,
who supports her alcoholic husband through her work in the brickyards, said that she was worse off than she was before her marriage.
This is understandable since her living conditions at the time she
was interviewed were as poor as any that can be found in rural
Oaxaca.

With only one exception, the brickyard women had no prior experience in the brick industry before moving to Santa Lucía. They all
maintain that their contribution to brick production is voluntary and
does not reflect their husbands' coercion or suggestion, yet this dis-
claimer is academic given the constant economic crisis that households confront and the efforts to overcome such crises through work.
The following statement by Marcela describes how she replaced her
husband as the full-time *milero* in their employer's brickyard:

I worked with my husband for a week, and after that I started working alone. The boss showed up one day when I was in the pit with my neighbor Lola who also wanted to learn the work. The boss wouldn't accept her bricks because they were too badly made but he said that mine were okay and he paid me for them. That's how I began. I make bricks because I want to. Sometimes my husband gets mad about it. But I tell him that there's no other way for us to make it. The boss is now in the habit of giving me loans when my husband isn't working, since he knows that I can deliver. But when my husband goes to see him he won't give him money because he knows that he'll waste it on mescal.

Marcela was the only female informant who talked about her brickyard activities as "work" (trabajo) and who was paid directly for them. All the others adhered to the ideology of male dominance, which classifies men's activities as "work" and women's activities as "helping out" (ayuda). None of them received any direct payment, a fact that did not seem to bother most. As one woman succinctly expressed it: "I help out and my husband gets paid." One informant admitted that she would like to be paid but felt that it was up to the boss to make a decision to do so; in the meantime her work was tied to her husband's.[15]

The interview data clearly show that brickyard women are confronted with conflicts in the scheduling of their labor time between household duties and brickyard tasks. Marcela, for example, continued to prepare tortillas while making bricks but found the schedule too demanding. She subsequently reached an accord with her husband that it would be better to buy ready-made tortillas so that she could devote more time to brick production. As she explained it: "I got up early to make tortillas; then I went to the patio, molded, laid out some bricks, and then came back to the house to finish making my tortillas. I bought corn to make dough from scratch. I did it that way for a while but afterward I realized it was better to buy tortillas because, as I told my husband, it was too much of a hassle to mold bricks and then make tortillas from scratch."

Women follow various strategies to enable them to combine household chores with brickyard work. Some women postpone or reschedule domestic chores or leave a block of time for brickyard work. Typically, this entails getting an earlier than usual start on chores in the morning. Other women prefer to alternate between domestic chores and brickyard tasks throughout the day.

Most of the informants said that they preferred housework to brickyard work; they also considered it to be more important, as well as the most appropriate activity for women. Several women, however, said they did not mind doing brickyard work; they noted that their contribution increased their husband's daily brick output and the household's weekly cash income. As one woman expressed it: "It's worthwhile to help him in the brickyard because it earns us more money for our expenses. But domestic chores are more important because I feed and care for the children."

Even though women regularly perform many brickyard tasks that obviously increase daily brick output, most of their men expressed views that seemed to ignore this. The men's views strongly supported a traditional conception of the gender division of labor, stereotyping women as the weaker sex whose proper role is housework. "A woman," said one *milero*, "was not made to work in the brickyard. She's made to be in the home, to do domestic chores. She should always be there at lunchtime, at suppertime, to wash clothes, and so on." Another said, "Women are weaker than men. They help us with our work the little that they can." The last statement is especially ironic since it was made by none other than the husband of Marcela, who had displaced him in the eyes of the employer as the *milero* of their household. Only two *mileros* acknowledged their wives' contributions to brickyard income, and only one considered his wife's housework to be as important and demanding as his work in the brickyard.

Every female informant expressed the view that men work more and that a woman's place is in the home. A typical statement was: "Men do the brickyard work, and women do housework. Men work more. Men earn more than women. Women do nothing more than make some tortillas to sell to make a little cash to help out the men." What is ironic about these women's situation is not so much their contention that work done by men is physically more demanding and more remunerative than that done by women, which is generally true of the brickyards, but that they all (except Marcela) implicitly accept a rigid gender division of labor between housework and brickyard work, even though all of them perform several tasks in the brickyard daily.

On other issues, the views expressed by the *mileros'* wives departed significantly from their husband's views. With regard to their responses to a question about how they would spend a windfall of several thousand pesos, the wives were uniform in saying they would buy a lot and build a house, whereas half of their husbands said they would buy a brickyard. This difference in priorities may reflect men's and women's differing degrees of involvement in the brick industry. It can also be viewed as representing a stronger internalization of the ideology of domesticity among the women. In a similar vein, the women were for the most part less assertive than the men on the issue of whether poor households could become more affluent. Two of them responded negatively and the rest (with one exception) felt that this could be achieved through work and saving. None of the women specified any plausible strategies related to their concrete circumstances for achieving this, though some of the men did.

On the issue of household budget management, husbands and wives were in consensus that all earnings should be pooled and administered either jointly or by the husband alone. This is quite compatible with the cooperative nature of the labor process of brick production. Nevertheless, the fact that men are the payees makes it relatively easy for them to divert earnings from the household pool (e.g., for purchase of mescal in the local cantinas).

Finally, with regard to the issue of social inequality and employer-worker relations, the women's views were compatible with the men's but were expressed with less clarity. Most women recognized that there was inequality between households in their community but only two related it, in very general terms, to differential control over means of production. The majority simply said that some people had better jobs or higher incomes than others. A few associated the condition of wage labor with poverty (e.g., "We are among the poor because we work for a wage") and one attributed it to the fact that they cannot sell the bricks they produce. Several linked wealth to the ownership of land but only a handful specified this in the context of the brick industry. Their position was that wealth was associated with the ownership of brickyards, trucks, or kilns.

Seamstresses and Shawl Knotters

Women are found operating treadle looms in at least two Zapotec villages in the Oaxaca Valley where men have traditionally been loom operators. But in the Xaagá branch of the industry (which specializes in cotton, synthetic fiber, and wool clothing products, including shirts, blouses, shawls, and vests) women work either as shawl finishers or as seamstresses. As pointed out in Chapter 4, Xaagá has a short history of independent craft specialization that is no more than two decades long. Consequently, the women of Xaagá are relative newcomers to the realm of craft commodity production. In this section we will focus on sixteen women from Xaagá (average age 30, two single, and fourteen married with an average of 3.6 children or 1.9 daughters) whose participation in the weaving industry engenders a striking series of contradictions between use-value production and commodity production and between subsistence and accumulation within the household matrix.

Despite the recentness of Xaagá's specialization in craft production, its women have had long experience with commodity and labor markets as a function of their village's historical dependency upon Mitla. Indeed, one-quarter of our informants initiated their extra-household work careers either as servants in Mitla households or as vendors in the Mitla marketplace and one-third were employed as domestic servants for periods ranging from eight months to ten years in Mitla, Tlacolula, Oaxaca City, Mexico City, or some combination of these prior to their participation in the weaving industry. It is likely that this kind of market participation by females has characterized Xaagá across several generations—although its frequency has probably increased in recent decades.

The participation of Xaagá females in craft production dates from the middle 1960s when five young girls were recruited by Mitla weavers to finish shawls on an outwork basis. As one of them described it: "I learned to tie shawls with a girl from Mitla. I had to go to Mitla to deliver and then they would supply me with more. Three or four days would go by, until I finished all of them—depending on how many they gave me." Then, as today, the shawl finishers were paid by piece rate. A standard shawl can be finished in about three hours of continuous work, a task that earned 4 pesos in 1980; the typical shawl-finishing household finished an average of eight standard shawls weekly for an average gross return of 32 pesos (or 1.33 pesos per hour). Standard shawls sold for 30–50 pesos each, depending upon from whom and where they were purchased (i.e., from weaver or intermediary in Xaagá or Mitla).

It is not surprising, given this low remuneration combined with the tedious and tiring nature of the work, that fourteen of our sixteen informants abandoned shawl finishing, after a career spanning several years, for sewing on machines, as the treadle loom weaving industry took root in the Xaagá household. Suffice it to say that the spread of treadle loom weaving—and, especially, the rapid growth in scale experienced by several of its component enterprises—could not have occurred without a pool of employable females to work as seamstresses as well as at other tasks (e.g., washing, dying, and spooling yarn and thread). Most informants who made the transition from shawl finishing to machine sewing would agree with the following statement by one of the most adept seamstresses, an unmarried young woman of 17 who had worked for five years as a shawl finisher prior to getting employment as a seamstress two years before being interviewed: "Because one earns more, I prefer sewing to tying shawls. Tying shawls I can't earn 60–80 pesos daily, and sewing only four hours a day, I can make that much." Aside from earning differentials, half of the housewife-seamstresses in our sample cited the direct involvement of their weaver husbands in their entry into machine sewing.[16]

In several cases, the formation of a successful household weaving enterprise occurred at the initiative of the male weaver and required the recruitment of wives, together with other available female household members, in a joint or cooperative labor process. As was detailed in Chapter 4, successful capital accumulation in the Mitla branch of the treadle loom weaving industry requires the combination of treadle loom and sewing machine so that the thread woven into cloth on the loom can be further transformed into finished commodities (e.g., *camisas deshiladas*, or loose-weave cotton polo shirts). In other words, higher profits can be realized by selling finished commodities like shirts than by selling semi-finished commodities (bolts of cloth). In Xaagá, the preferred mode of organizing weaving enterprises to promote capital accumulation has been along gender lines, that is, to occupy males on the looms and females on the cutting boards and sewing machines, with most subsidiary tasks (e.g., washing and bleaching or dying thread, winding thread on spools) assigned on an ad hoc basis without regard to gender. Obviously, the most accessible and capital-saving labor pool is that provided by the weaver's own household.

One of the immediate implications of the recruitment of working-age females into household commodity-producing activities is that it forces rescheduling of essential use-value producing activities like food preparation, cleaning, and washing that draw predominantly on female labor. One informant candidly described her rescheduling of tasks when she entered as a young girl into the weaving industry as a shawl-finishing outworker: "There were times when I helped my mother make tortillas, but, once I learned to tie shawls, I no longer helped her out. I told her: Now you can make tortillas and I'm going to tie shawls." This same informant also described the specific impact on her household routines of her switch to sewing after marriage: "Now that my mother-in-law is with us, she makes tortillas and helps out in the kitchen. I cut cloth and sew shirts." In addition to cooperation in carrying out household tasks, some informants indicated that they dealt with the "double day" essentially by extending their daily work time. For example, one informant stated that she did all her domestic tasks during the morning and into the afternoon and did her sewing from late afternoon until 11:00 in the evening—a work schedule made possible by the installation of electric lighting.

Some of our informants manifested signs of discontent with their new roles in the division of labor with regard to the issues of household budget and, more particularly, income or payment form. It also became clear from responses to questions in this area that Xaagá household enterprises do not deal with the problem of "payment" for family workers in any uniform way. The piece rate is the prevailing payment form in the weaving industry and, as explained above, all the seamstresses became accustomed to payment by piece rate in their careers as shawl finishers. Also, from the beginning, those seamstresses who were employed by household enterprises other than their own were paid by piece rate (the prevailing rate in 1980 was 2 pesos per shirt). Most of our housewife informants who worked as seamstresses in their own household's enterprise said that they did not receive a wage or other direct compensation for their work. As one informant expressed it: "I help out my husband but he doesn't pay me. I just help him out. The help that I give him is for him." The following statement by another informant reflects the thinking of the majority of unpaid homeworking seamstresses about this situation: "When they bring me shirts from outside, I sew them and they pay me. But here in the house I don't charge to sew them. It's 'helping out' my husband. I agree with this because, since he doesn't have to pay for the sewing I do, we are able to buy a few other things." In other words, like the first informant, her work is considered to be "helping out" in the household enterprise run by her husband (note the similarity in views with the brickyard women); but unlike the first woman, who viewed unpaid wages as her husband's income, the wages not paid to her are viewed as an addition to the operating income of the household—to be spent for domestic provisioning or enterprise purposes. That not all women in this situation were as happy as this informant appeared to be can be inferred from such statements as, "I don't earn anything but I would like to earn something because I need the money."

Other households, however, had another sort of arrangement where the wife-seamstress is not paid a wage as such but does expect and receives a cash allowance from her husband. One woman in this situation said, "I don't earn anything because the work is within the family," yet she admitted that she did not have to earn a salary because her husband gave her an allowance.

At the other extreme from households that paid no wages were those in which the wife-seamstress was paid a piece wage by her husband-employer just as if she were an employed nonhousehold member. The following statement illustrates this kind of arrangement: "When I make ten shirts I earn 20 pesos. He pays me for them. He pays me according to the number of shirts made. Then I take my share and pay off the other seamstresses. My husband tells me: 'Now that you finished sewing, well, take your share of the money and spend it as you wish.' Then I take my share and spend it on candy or clothes for the kids." This informant's husband operates a large workshop with several paid employees. The informant, as the chief cloth cutter and seamstress, serves as the boss of the employed seamstresses. It is clear from her statement that she spends her salary to meet household consumption needs. In a smaller workshop with only household workers, the wife-seamstress told us that she was paid by her husband according to the number of shirts she sewed. She specified, "I sew from 15 to 25 shirts a week. He gives me 30 to 50 pesos [$1.33 to $2.22] a week. That is for me and it's up to me how I spend the money."

Regardless of their particular payment situation, the wife-seamstresses were nearly unanimous in viewing their role pragmatically. They worked willingly and in accord with their husbands to avoid having to put-out their cloth to outworkers for sewing. They considered this of mutual material benefit to themselves and to their husbands. It was also clear, however, that most of them have their husband's consent to take in outside work and do so when possible to supplement household income. Not a single informant suggested that her husband took a hard line regarding her work schedule or habits: "He says, 'Whatever you want, if you want to work on the sewing machine, well, there it is, if you don't want to, then you don't have to.' He doesn't really obligate me." In short, our impression is that the following statement, by a seamstress whose husband operates one of the village's largest workshops, would find little dissent among the other seamstresses: "The men of this village see the work of us women as 'helping out,' not like we are sharing the work with them. They encourage their wives to help them more." The only qualification that we would add is that we are also of the impression that seamstresses who are not paid a wage for "helping out" their husbands would prefer to be. At least such payment, which has already proven in several households to represent no threat to conjugal solidarity, is likely to become more common in the future.

It is appropriate here to reiterate the importance of a conjugal division of labor in the development of a weaving enterprise by considering the case of the first and most successful enterprise in Xaagá. Javier, the enterprise founder (who was 30 years old when interviewed in 1979), had worked long hours as a loom operator for eight years in Mitla workshops prior to acquiring a loom in 1976 for weaving in his home. In the following narrative his wife, Ruperta, explains how she improvised the tactic of "unsewing" (*descoser*) to cut cloth for shirts:

> We got a sample shirt in Mitla and I "unsewed" it and took it apart. That's how we learned to make them. The Mitla weavers didn't want to give us a sample because they know that my husband is a weaver. To get around this my husband made friends with a Mitleño and asked him to get hold of a shirt for us. The friend managed to get hold of one and my husband bought it from him. Then my husband brought it to me and I unsewed it, took it apart, and then began to cut pieces from our cloth to match those that I had unsewed. I made pattern cutouts on paper, then I put them on the whole cloth and began to cut—I improved with practice. My husband asked me: "How's it going? You know we're weaving cloth for the shirts." I did the unsewing and the cutouts in one afternoon. The first shirt I cut out didn't turn out so good but the second one turned out all right.

This account is of interest not only because it exemplifies conjugal economic cooperation, as well as improvisational ingenuity on the part of Javier and Ruperta, but also because it shows how industrial techniques—even in the context of small-scale village enterprises—are diffused through a combination of stealth and imitation. It is amusing to consider that the ultrasophisticated high tech industry of the Silicon Valley has apparently achieved no more success in recent years in preventing the diffusion of technical information to potential competitors than have the treadle loom weavers of Mitla.

With few exceptions seamstresses voiced approval of the level of income generated from their household's participation in the weaving industry and, given the qualifications noted above, with the returns to their own labor. This is no doubt the case because the prevailing piece rate for sewing allows for a substantially higher daily wage (reflecting the higher productivity of labor) for a comparable period of expended labor time than does the piece rate for shawl finishing. Indeed, several informants admitted that by working as seamstresses for a day they could earn a wage equal to or greater than that earned by male loom operators—a fact that our data support. By contrast, those informants who have not switched to sewing and continue to work as shawl finishers voiced unanimous disapproval of their income.

The informants approached consensus in identifying Mitla merchants as the group that profits most from weaving through their dominant role in marketing. One shawl finisher, for example, referred to the Mitla putting-out merchant for whom she works as "the owner of the work" who "pays cheaply" for the work done by shawl finishers. Several seamstress outworkers were quite articulate about the exploitative nature of their relationship with putters-out and speculated that collective bargaining would be a strategy to improve their earnings.[17] Although there is an awareness of exploitation, as well as of the possibility that it might be reduced through an organization of the exploited created to negotiate a higher piece rate, this awareness never crosses the threshold from incipient reformism to organized radicalism. The exploiters are exclusively identified as Mitla merchants; no Xaagá workshop operator is identified in these terms by any of the outworkers, who work mostly for Xaagá employers. The informants' preferred strategy to deal with the merchants is to organize a producer's cooperative (including outworkers and wives of independent proprietors—both of whom perceive themselves as subject to exploitation by Mitla merchants) that would facilitate collective bargaining over either piece rates or prices.

The informants gave contradictory responses to a question designed to elicit their views on social inequality in the village. Some denied that inequality existed, asserting categorically that "here there are only poor people" or "all of us are poor." Most recognized that inequality existed among households in the village's weaving industry but had different ideas about its causes; these ranged from inheritance ("There are fathers who leave an inheritance to their sons") to type of employment ("There are some who work for a wage and others who work at home"). There was wide agreement that those households that work more (because they have either more workers or more industrious workers) produce more cloth and cloth products and, consequently, generate more income. This reflects the pervasiveness of a small-producer ideology of progress through hard work, enterprise, thrift, investment, and, perhaps, a bit of luck (or divine intervention). The response by one informant to a question as to whether she thought it possible for a poor household to progress in the weaving industry represents this ideology well: "With God's help. Working and saving pennies. Supposing one has a thousand pesos saved—if one invests those thousand pesos in, for example, the purchase of thread and makes cloth and shirts, then afterward the returns will be more than a thousand pesos."

In summary, the treadle loom weaving industry women manifest higher, if still inchoate, degrees of gender and class consciousness than other women as a function of their more direct involvement in capitalist relations of production. This generalization and its implications require further elaboration in the concluding section.

Conclusions: Females as Helpers or Workers?

This chapter examined some of the contradictory organizational and ideological aspects of the gender division of labor in household-based commodity production in contemporary peasant-artisan communities. We know enough about the evolution, structure, and functioning of commodity production in Mesoamerica to be certain that, in the complex tributary economies of the late prehispanic and colonial periods, women in the peasant household economy were pressured to produce tributary craft commodities (see Villanueva 1985). It is unclear whether the Oaxaca Valley had anything comparable to the *repartimiento de hilazos* (the distribution of thread) that operated in the Guatemalan highlands until the end of the colonial period. There Spanish officials put out raw cotton for peasant-Indian women of highland Maya towns to spin into thread for token or no payment (Bossen 1984: 324–325) in an arrangement similar to that which binds today's urban merchants to peasant-artisan women in the embroidery industry.

In any case, it is untenable to argue that the "double day" or the "segmented labor market" are twentieth-century capitalist innovations in the Oaxaca Valley. This is especially true when we consider the fact that household craft production was important as a source not only of tributary commodities but also of market commodities, which have been essential to the material reproduction of peasant-artisan households and communities in Mesoamerica for centuries (Taylor 1971, 1972; Cook and Diskin (eds.) 1976; Blanton et al. 1981; Blanton and Kowalewski 1981; Kowalewski and Finsten 1983). In other words, the labor of peasant-artisan women in the Oaxaca Valley today is no stranger to the stresses and strains of the double burden of household production for use and for exchange.

When women experience direct proletarianization, however, these strains appear to become more severe. For example, several seamstresses in the treadle loom weaving industry and at least one woman pieceworker in the brickyards have begun to question the traditional view of women's work. When a woman becomes a full-time brickyard pieceworker, as Marcela did, then a significant portion of her labor power enters the direct remuneration circuit. Even if this involvement in wage labor is temporary, it still could have an impact on her status in the household, resulting for example in more control over how household income is spent. In Marcela's case, her labor appeared to be accompanied by a higher degree of class consciousness than was manifested by brickyard women who were not pieceworkers. She no longer referred to her work as "helping out" and developed a clearer understanding of the proposition that exploitation is a relationship of production rather than of exchange. Similarly, the increasing subordination of women's labor by merchant putting-out capital in industries like embroidery seems to be accompanied by inchoate but empirically demonstrable changes in women's consciousness of exploitation. This incipient consciousness should provoke changes in the undervalued status of women's labor.

It remains the case that most of the female pieceworkers continue to view their work as "helping out" and as a "for a while" adjunct to householding. Like petty commodity producers, they practice self-exploitation but begin to recognize that their failure to earn more income has to do with production and market relationships rather than with themselves. One difference is that, to petty commodity producers, market relationships are personified by the buyers-up, whereas in their own situation these are personified by the putters-out. Another difference, perhaps more important, is that some outworkers begin to view their employers (or the buyers of their labor power and the owners of the raw materials they work with) as unjustly depriving them of a portion of the fruits of their labor by, in essence, paying them less than their labor is worth. They reject the idea, so common among the petty commodity producers, that merchants, whose modus operandi is to buy cheap and sell dear, are entitled to whatever the market returns to them for their haggling prowess or luck.

One important issue that this study has shed some light on is the extent to which discernible differences in female labor participation arise from differences in the marketing structures of the industries in which they participate. It was shown, for example, that the palm plaiting industry exclusively produces utilitarian commodities that are purchased and used regionally by the rural population, whereas both backstrap loom weaving and embroidery are almost entirely dedicated to production for the urban tourist market. One result of this is an increase in the scale of these industries vis-à-vis palm plaiting as well as in the intensification of production under the aegis of a nested merchant hierarchy of buyers-up and putters-out. For purposes of this chapter the important question becomes: Is there a discernible difference between the quantity and quality of commodity production involvement and its ideological implications between palm plaiters and weavers or embroiderers?

Unfortunately, the data analyzed above do not permit a definitive answer to this difficult question. They do encourage us to conclude that the rise and spread of a putting-out system in embroidery is associated with an expanding tourist market where substantial profits can be made by selling at prices much higher than the cost of production (cf. Goody 1982: 33). In this sense, the Oaxaca embroidery industry seems to be following more closely the trajectory of English cotton textile production in previous centuries.

Embroidery in Oaxaca is located in the countryside essentially because *the labor comes from women who have no other source of employment; anything they are able to earn makes at least a marginal improvement to the household's standard of living. The men bring in something from agriculture or other work, so the women's work does not have to meet all the household's subsistence costs.* We have taken the liberty of slightly rephrasing these statements in italics from a discussion of cotton-textile production in premodern (early Ch'ing) China (cf. Goody 1982: 33). These statements were intended to explain why this production remained a cottage industry *not* organized by the putting-out system. In present-day Oaxaca, however, these same conditions exist in an embroidery industry organized by the putting-out system. In any case, we are dealing with self-exploiting, and superexploited peasant-artisan women who are working diligently for paltry wages, paid and abetted by a nested hierarchy of merchant capitalists.

What is undeniable is that in today's multitiered political economy the process of commoditization is more advanced than ever before and that, to an unprecedented degree, capitalist accumulation has become a pervasive, integrative force. Without considering questions of comparison with situations in past centuries, this imposes a heavy burden on today's peasant-artisan women. It requires their participation in household production for own-use as well as in commodity production. Both types of production are essential to the short-term reproduction of labor power and to childbearing and childcare, which are essential to the long-run reproduction of labor power (cf. Benería and Sen 1981: 291–293; Young 1978).

Among the Oaxaca Valley peasantry, women's work in the domestic sphere of mothering and household chores, if not invisible, tends to be ideologically separated from and devalued vis-à-vis men's work. Petty commodity production by women has traditionally been viewed as an extension of their household activities and has suffered the same fate (as mothering and chores) of ideological segregation and devaluation; it has, in effect, not been perceived as "work" (*trabajo*) by either men or women but rather as "helping out" (*ayuda*) (cf. Deere and León de Leal 1981: 349; Lynch and Fahmy 1984: 4; Cook 1984a: 169). With some exceptions, such separation and devaluation continue to be present in those cases in which women participate as petty commodity producers in industries where buying-up merchants are prominent but where capital accumulation potential is low, such as palm plaiting. It is even present in those petty capitalist industries, like treadle loom weaving and brickmaking, where women are engaged as unpaid pieceworkers' assistants or are household workers in petty capitalist enterprises run by men (Cook and Binford 1986). In all these situations, the ideological devaluation of women obfuscates their real contribution to household subsistence and capital accumulation. It creates the false impression that most household industries do not involve a necessary cooperation between the sexes; in industries like brickmaking and treadle loom weaving, women's tasks are relatively invisible but, in fact, are just as critical as those performed by men to the overall production process. Here the androcentric image of females as helpers collapses in the reality of their devalued role as workers.

Chapter 6. Intermediary Capital and Petty Industry in the City and the Countryside

Introduction

The concept of a monetized commodity economy, reduced to its minimal content, encompasses two separate yet necessarily interrelated processes: production and circulation. This separation, in turn, implies the possibility of two sets of subjects, direct producers and intermediaries, whose respective activities revolve around either commodity fabrication, on the one hand, or commodity exchange, on the other. In such an economy, the circuit of direct producers, $C-M-C'$, implies the circuit of merchant-intermediaries, $M-C-M'$. Or, expressed differently, "selling in order to buy, both logically and in practice, implies its reverse: buying in order to sell" (Kay 1975: 64). Logically, of course, there is no reason why both types of activity cannot be performed by a single set of subjects or, more specifically, why direct producers cannot also be sellers or marketers of the commodities they produce.

As the empirical record shows, however, the development of commodity economy and the division of labor entails, among other things, the specialization of economic subjects in either production or circulation. While there is disagreement among scholars as to the antiquity of specialized commodity trade, they express little doubt that such trade was present long before the appearance of capitalism in Europe (e.g., Bucher 1901: 177–119 et passim; Polanyi et al. (eds.), 1957; Weber 1961: 57 et passim; Adams 1966: 154–157, 163–164; Mandel 1968: 102–106; Sabloff and Lamberg-Karlovsky (eds.), 1975). A large corpus of recent scholarship (Adams 1973; Wright 1974; Wallerstein 1974: 19 et passim; Goody 1982: 25–28; Kriedte et al (eds.), 1981: 98–101 et passim; Berdan 1982: 31–35) substantiates White's (1959: 346) thesis that "paralleling the distinction between money, on the one hand, and commodities, on the other, is a social differentiation within the commercial process. Just as money evolves as a special economic mechanism of commerce, so do merchants evolve as a special class within society."

Perhaps the best theoretical explanation as to why this occurs has been provided by Kay (1975: 65) who argues that in the process of facilitating the social distribution of commodities as use-values, allowing producers to exchange commodities for which they have no direct use for others that they can use, trading "becomes indispensable to the whole structure of commodity production itself." Kay (ibid.) uses the following circuit to illustrate how trading (i.e., the activity of merchant-intermediaries) mediates between the direct producers and links the two poles of the circuit of social reproduction in a commodity economy:

$$P \ldots C-(M-C-M')-C' \ldots Cn$$

This circuit starts with production (P) and ends with consumption (Cn). Direct producers carry their product to market ($C-M$) and buy the commodities they want ($M-C'$). But neither transaction involves producer-sellers dealing directly with producer-buyers but, rather, with merchants uninvolved in production. Merchants buy commodities from producer-sellers ($M-C$) and sell them to producer-buyers ($C-M'$). All but the pettiest and most impoverished of merchants engage in these transactions to make a profit, i.e., to maximize the difference, in monetary terms, between M and M'. The upshot of this is that merchants, engaging in the quest for exchange-value as a means of survival and profit, come to occupy a separate social location, alongside direct producers (who produce and exchange use-values for other use- and/or exchange-values) in commodity economies (cf. Kay 1975: 66; Cook and Diskin 1976: 271–272).

Although merchants are distinguished by their interest in appropriating surplus value from petty direct producers by buying-up their commodities cheap and selling them dear, it is clear that certain conjunctural conditions (e.g., heightened competition, labor problems) compel them to insert their circulationist strategy into the capital-absorbing and capital-fixating realm of production by establishing dispersed (i.e., putting-out) or congregated manufactories. The empirical record of today's developing economies is replete with such insertions, which resemble prior developments in the evolution of European capitalism (e.g., Geertz 1963: 50–58; Littlefield 1976: 108–138; Hopkins 1978: 475–477; Swallow 1982; Lynch and Fahmy 1984: 25–31). The point is not to support fallacious notions of replication in the Third World of a lineal trajectory of prior European capitalist development but to promote careful comparative analysis in the study of capitalist industrialization whenever and wherever it occurs (Cook 1984a: 30–31).

It must also be noted that, wherever merchant capital thrives, it does not do so parasitically without also serving economically positive functions. For example, it can be argued that intermediaries like those who operate in the Oaxaca Valley craft sector render specific services for which they merit remuneration. In a more general Latin American context, Sidney Mintz (1964: 4) expressed this argument as follows: "The services are not imposed on customers; they are salable because buyers and sellers require them. Intermediaries transport, process, accumulate stock, break stock, grant credit to agricultural producers and to urban consumers, pay taxes, keep truckers employed, and contribute much else to the ready functioning of the economy." Insufficient emphasis is placed on the fact that merchant capital facilitates the circulation of commodities produced by petty producers through specializing in marketing. In this sense, it promotes petty commodity production (by maintaining or speeding up commodity circulation) even as it appropriates a portion of the value that direct producers create (cf. Cook 1985a: 254). Impoverishment of petty commodity producers through appropriation of absolute surplus value (when merchant capital extends itself into production, as with, the embroidery merchants) does act as something of a barrier upon technological development. Impoverishment itself, however, may also act as a stimulus to increase the supply of peasant-artisan products, since the peasant-artisan units must intensify their labor in all areas in order to generate a minimal income.

Intermediary Capital in the Oaxaca Valley Today: An Overview

In the Oaxaca Valley a basic distinction in everyday rural parlance exists betwen *propio* (producer-seller) and *revendedor* (reseller), with the latter being the closest thing to a cover term for merchant-intermediary (i.e., anyone who buys and sells commodities for a profit, cf. Beals 1975: 286)—although the term *regatón* often is used synonymously with *revendedor*. Perhaps the first question raised by this distinction is the relative importance of resellers in the circulation of commodities in the Oaxaca economy. On the basis of a field survey conducted in eight principal marketplaces in the Oaxaca Valley in 1965, it was estimated that "approximately half of all participants are primary producers of the goods they sell" (Diskin 1976: 64). Although we have no quantitative basis for making a comparable estimate for 1979–1980, our impression is that while direct producers continue to sell their products in the marketplace system, they do so on a reduced scale, and that the role of intermediaries has expanded since 1965.

Indeed, the regional commodity economy long ago evolved to a point where it became impossible to return to a situation in which producer-mediated commodity exchange sufficed to keep the economy functioning (cf. Cook and Diskin (eds.), 1976: 260). For example, industries like *metate* making and palm plaiting, which entered the twentieth century with *propios* predominant in marketing, will leave the century with *regatones* predominant. While we have no comprehensive explanation for this apparent trend (not an irreversible lineal progression), it most likely reflects responses to conjunctural conditions (e.g., price levels, wage levels, opportunity costs, transportation) associated with capitalist development.

It would be a mistake to infer from the distinction between *propio* and *revendedor* any opposition between the village and the outside world. Just as the marketing of commodities may be conducted by the households that produce them, it is also an activity that may be taken up as a specialized occupation to supplement own-household direct production or by other village households that do not produce the commodity in question. As described in Chapters 3 and 5, such intermediaries are found in nearly every branch of industrial commodity production included in our study. It would not be a mistake to read into the *propio-revendedor* distinction a possible opposition between direct producer and reseller. Direct producers forego marketing themselves more often as a matter of necessity than of convenience or expediency; their need for cash obliges them to sell their products to intermediaries for prices that they recognize to be below prevailing market prices. This element of compulsion evokes ambivalence among direct producers regarding the role of intermediaries: on the one hand, they resent the low prices the intermediaries pay; on the other, they tend to view profits derived from reselling as representative of just compensation for the initiative, costs, and risks entailed in marketing. Indeed, many aspire to become resellers themselves.

Merchant capital in Oaxaca today has two broad categories of agents: (*a*) the middlemen, or *regatones* (literally, "hagglers" or "bargainers"), whose principal arena is the *plaza* or marketplace, and (*b*) site-focussed vendors, often referred to by the cover term *comerciantes*, whose activities are conducted mostly in formal business locales or as agents for commercial enterprises ranging from marketplace stalls to stores (cf. Beals 1975: 146–185). Within each of these two broad categories several specific types (and subtypes) of merchants can be isolated on the basis of the specific way in which they conduct their trading operations.

In the most comprehensive classification, Beals (1975: 286–287) posited three types of middlemen (*regatones*) and eight types of site-focussed vendors. He failed to mention, however, two important types of merchants—the putters-out and those who operate craft shops or manufactories (cf. Malinowski and de La Fuente 1982: 185). A more significant shortcoming of Beals' heavily descriptive analysis of trading activities and roles is that it obscures a crucial difference between two types of intermediary capital: the type that earns profit by reselling commodities acquired from small-scale household production units (peasants, peasant-artisans, or artisans) and the type that earns profit by reselling commodities produced by capitalist factories.

The first type may be designated as merchant capital; it also (as in treadle loom weaving and embroidery) traffics in commodities produced with wage labor employed by piece rate as home-based outworkers or shopworkers. Marx (1967, III: 325) referred to it as being "older than the capitalist mode of production . . . historically the oldest free state of existence of capital" and as requiring "no other conditions for its existence . . . outside those necessary for the simple circulation of commodities and money."

The second type, which Marx and many subsequent Marxists also call merchant capital (presumably since it is viewed as an evolved form of the first type), we prefer to designate as commercial capital. Marx (1967, III: 336) refers to this type as the "servant of industrial production" because its principal role is to facilitate the realization of surplus embodied in capitalist commodities. This type, as an adjunct of industrial capital, profits from unequal exchange conducted in the process of realizing surplus value originating as the unrewarded product of labor in capitalist production (cf. Kay 1975: 88); in effect, it is the marketing branch of industrial capital. According to this distinction, then, intermediaries who deal in factory products—regardless of the scale of their businesses or whether they are ambulatory or site confined in their activities—are representatives of commercial capital.

It must be emphasized that this, too, is mainly a descriptive distinction rather than a theoretical one. Both merchant and commercial capital function in the same way according to the formula $M-C-M'$. The principal difference has to do with their insertion as intermediaries of commodities deriving from petty commodity production or from industrial capitalist production. Hence, merchant capital, as indicated above, was an earlier form of circulation capital than was commercial capital; its persistence into an era that is dominated by industrial capital is, however, no more and no less a result of the persistence of petty commodity production itself.

As might be expected in a case like the Oaxaca Valley, many intermediaries straddle these two types of capital and assume the role of "double dealers." Rural and urban storekeepers often combine operations like buying-up and reselling craft products from peasant-artisans with reselling factory products. For example, in the palm plaiting villages storekeepers buy-up palm products on a cash, credit, or in-kind basis; and in treadle loom weaving villages storekeepers buy-up woven products and resell factory-made yarn from their store inventories. As described in Chapter 3, most of the weavers in Santa Ana del Valle weave at home on their own looms with yarn that is taken on credit from local buyers-up. The Santa Ana buyers-up resell these products in Tlacolula or Oaxaca City markets and to merchants in Teotitlán del Valle, many of whom own shops located near the areas most frequented by tourists, the main street and the central square of the village. For all practical purposes, these weaving intermediaries are as much putters-out as they are buyers-up since they use their control over the local yarn supply as a means for stipulating the kind and quality of products that they wish to buy back from the weavers they supply. The weavers who participate in this arrangement, however, do not consider themselves to be outworkers but insist that they are self-employed.

By contrast, in the needlework industry some village storekeepers sell factory-made cloth, thread, and needles to embroiderers and may also buy-up embroidered garments for resale purposes. We encountered no evidence, however, that this pattern was as widespread in embroidery as it was in treadle loom weaving in Teotitlán del Valle—and no informants identified it as a credit (fiado) system. As pointed out in Chapter 5, the predominant pattern in the embroidery industry was putting-out, with most embroiderers being outworkers, who like the weavers a fiado in Santa Ana (though to a lesser extent), tended to identify themselves as self-employed despite their ties to the putters-out.

Given this empirical complexity, why do we insist on the importance of making an analytical distinction between two subtypes of intermediary capital, which we designate as "merchant" and "commercial"? For our purposes we would consider it to be analytically unrewarding to insist upon the relevance of historicist formulas or "tendential laws" that would prescribe discrete economic, social, and political tendencies for each of these two types of capital. Indeed, in our judgment they do not represent two different accumulation strategies so much as they do the application of a similar strategy (common to all subtypes of intermediary capital) in two separate spheres of circulation that have different consequences for accumulation, enterprise operations, and, possibly, the entire economy.

Merchant capitalists invest accumulated capital primarily to maintain or expand their buying-up and reselling operations, although, under certain conditions (see Young 1978: 127; Schlumbohm 1981), they do invest in production. They do so, however, without committing their enterprises to the capital intensification of technology as a means to increase labor productivity.[1] Even when merchant capital enters production, it tends to focus on reorganizing the technology presented to it by the petty production regime it exploits; thus the dispersed or congregated manufactories it establishes utilize or replicate, rather than revolutionize, existing technology (cf. Schlumbohm 1981: 107–111). In short, merchant capital in production adheres to accumulation strategies that focus upon the appropriation of absolute surplus value from labor (i.e., by lengthening the working day or intensifying work performed in a given period of time) rather than relative surplus value (i.e., curtailing necessary labor time and increasing surplus labor time during the course of the working day or securing a fall in the value of labor power) (Marx 1967, I: 315; Himmelweit 1983: 474).

Commercial capital, however, intervenes on behalf of industrial capital in areas where industrial capital does not intervene directly. It then proceeds to undermine domestic manufacture and to encourage the production of raw materials for capitalist industry and foodstuffs for the urban proletariat—resulting in radical social transformation (Young 1978: 128). Young (130–131) posits three dimensions of this transformation: (a) by restructuring local economies away from self-provisioning, the linkage between local resources and human population may be severed (i.e., the community or local area is no longer the unit of reproduction and structural constraints on rapid population growth may be removed); (b) by destroying some branches of production and fostering others, social differentiation within the local community is encouraged; such differentiation is permanent because there is unequal access to means of earning a living (e.g., land, marketing, employment); and (c) it promotes the twin process of depeasantization and proletarianization. We essentially agree with Young's scenario, with the proviso that merchant capital (and petty industrial capital) that moves into manufacturing can also have an impact on local and regional economies—though clearly not of the same transformative character as commercial and big industrial capital.

Young documents a profound transformation between 1870 and 1970 for the northern sierra of Oaxaca. The initial stage witnessed the demise of independent petty craft commodity production (backstrap loom weaving by females) and the rise of a merchant-controlled coffee economy based on small farm production. Later, as coffee production underwent capitalist rationalization and coffee prices rose, merchants and producers alike became increasingly involved in money-mediated transactions. As the economy was monetized, the production regime differentiated socially, wage labor became predominant, and the merchants-qua-commercial agents began to resell increasing quantities of factory-made commodities locally. In Young's words (1978: 135), "the initial response to the intervention of commercial capital brought mobility and an apparent diversification of economic activity. This expansion was, however, accompanied by the increasing privatisation of land, the undermining of local small-scale domestic manufacturing, and the setting free of labour." Near the end of the one-hundred-year period, restructuring of the local economy by commercial capital had proceeded even further. To quote Young again: "the creation of a relative surplus population leads to the redistribution of that population through out-migration and the sharpening of economic differentiation." Among other things, Young (149–153 et passim) documents important changes in women's economic roles. From relatively independent, household-based petty commodity producers, women were reduced to seasonal wage laborers or unpaid household workers in coffee.

Unquestionably, the process of commercialization documented by Young has been more intense in the central valleys than it has in the northern sierra. But, unlike the scenario she depicts, commercial capital has not displaced merchant capital nor has it destroyed rural industrial commodity production in the central valleys. To the contrary, the proliferation of the hybrid type of merchant (who straddles the two subtypes of intermediary capital) referred to earlier is evidence of their insertion in the marketing of factory-produced tools, raw materials, and wage goods to petty producers. This mostly hybrid, indigenous type of merchant capital has expanded in industries like embroidery, treadle loom weaving, and other crafts geared to the tourist (or export) market; and rural industrial commodity production has either held its own or expanded in many industries where women are skilled artisans and where petty merchant capital operates (e.g., backstrap loom weaving, palm plaiting, pottery). Not only has commercialization failed to destroy local small-scale manufacturing but it has also either stimulated or accompanied indigenous small-scale industrialization in several branches of production (e.g., brickmaking, treadle loom weaving, mescal distilling) in which petty industrial capital has emerged from a petty commodity matrix. In the remainder of this chapter we will describe the background and activities of various types of intermediaries operating in urban and rural branches of the craft sector of the Oaxaca Valley economy.

The Craft Business Population: A General Profile

Table 25 provides information on ninety-nine businesses whose proprietors were interviewed during the course of the study.[2] The sample can be classified into four groups according to the location of their businesses, as follows: (a) operators of separate extramarketplace establishments in Oaxaca City—a very heterogeneous group ranging from large stores/manufactories to small family shops (N = 38); (b) sellers in the open-air street market for craft products in Oaxaca City (N = 10); (c) operators (known as *caseteros* or *locatarios*) of permanent stalls in two large Oaxaca City marketplaces, 20 de Noviembre and Central de Abastos (N = 21); and (d) town- and village-based merchant-embroiderers in the district of Ocotlán (N = 30).

The survey coverage was essentially complete for the Oaxaca City extramarketplace and wholesale businesses that deal exclusively in craft commodities (groups a and b), and it also approached completeness for the stall operators in the two major Oaxaca City marketplaces who deal in *ropa típica* (e.g., embroidered blouses and *huipiles*) (group c). While it was incomplete for the Ocotlán district embroidery merchants (group d), it did cover most of the principal "puttersout" residing in five different communities in the district.

The average business owner is about 47 years old with six years of schooling. Proprietorship is divided more or less equally between males and females, although most of the owners of extramarketplace businesses are male.[3] Three-quarters of our sample purchased their businesses with capital either inherited or acquired through other business earnings or saved from a current or previous employment. Only about one-quarter employ a bookkeeper or accountant to aid in record keeping and accounting; a slightly greater percentage owns agricultural land.[4]

Such summary statements would be misleading, however, if applied to all (or even the majority) of the craft businesses in the

Table 25. *Selected Variables for Material Means of Production for Four Groups of Oaxaca Valley Merchants*

	Tools	Facilities (sales and/or production)	Equipment (sales)	Assets
Business Proprietors (extramarket place) (N=38)	25,000 200,457 344,375 (N=14)	625,000 211,125 410,882 (N=8)	125,000 61,833 183,971 (N=22)	60,000 371,156 828,891 (N=32)
Open-air sellers (N=10)	1,050 662 544 (N=6)	0	0	300 (N=3)
Stall operators (N=21)	20,000 (N=1)	0	1,000 1,384 865 (N=13)	10,500 22,100 22,583 (N=20)
Embroidery merchants (N=30)	3,100 5,382 6,442 (N=27)	75,000 (N=20)	0	3,000 27,257 61,472 (N=9)

Note: Values are listed in the following order: medians, means, and standard deviations. Single-value listings are medians. All values are given in pesos. The peso-to-dollar exchange rate in 1979 was approximately 22.50 to 1.

sample, for there is substantial inter- and intragroup variation, as Table 25 makes clear. Not only do the proprietors vary in education, years in the business, control over land, and so on from one group to another, but the size, scale, and mode of operation of the businesses in the different groups vary substantially as well. Major differences exist with respect to the value of fixed assets, number of employees, degree of specialization, and relationship with direct producers. Some urban businesses, for instance, have associated workshops in which labor and means of production are combined under the eye of the merchant. The majority of the merchants appropriate surplus value solely in the sphere of circulation. The embroidery merchants in Ocotlán district, however, have developed control over female outworkers, who are dispersed in peasant-artisan households, by putting-out raw materials and buying-up the semifinished products. Given these variations, it makes sense to examine in more detail the four business groups that were identified above.

Group A: Extramarketplace Establishments

The operators of extramarketplace establishments most closely approximate the contemporary Western stereotype of the "businessman" involved in wholesale/retail activities. The proprietors of these businesses are substantially older and better educated than those of other groups, and they have more years of business experience as well. They operate shops or stores that in many cases represent sizable investments. They have nondomestic employees and hire the services of professional bookkeepers or accountants more frequently than do other business persons. Apart from buying and selling, many are heavily involved in production, a characteristic that they share with the Ocotlán embroidery merchants. But while the majority of the embroidery merchants are engaged both as members of household production units and as managers of extensive putting-out networks, the extramarketplace business people are engaged in production primarily through workshops (42 percent) and only secondarily through own-household or outworker units (32 percent). Most of those that do have outworkers operate small businesses, with only one of eight employing more than nine outworkers—this being the case of an American expatriate who employs thirty-eight outworkers and exports high-quality hand-spun yarn and hand-woven textile products to the United States. These businesses sell both retail and wholesale, locally and for export, although most depend heavily on local retail sales, usually at fixed prices.

Group B: Open Air Vendors

The members of this group most closely resemble the bazaar-type street hawkers found in peasant marketplaces throughout the Third World. They are all of peasant-artisan background and combine sales of products made in their own household workshops with products purchased from producers in their home villages or from other producers for resale. Most members of this group represented a sort of village-artisan elite who, because of their prominence in artisan cooperatives in their home communities and their dues-paying membership in the National Confederation of Popular Organizations (CNOP), which operates as their conduit to the *PRI-Gobierno*, were granted permission to sell their wares in the Plazuela Labastida, a small park in a prime Oaxaca City tourist zone.[5] Included in this group were sellers of woven goods from Teotitlán del Valle, Santa Ana del Valle, and Mitla; and three city natives who had prior histories as street vendors of assorted textile products, one of whom was also the head of a union representing members of her trade. All the sellers in this group sell retail on a cash basis only, but prices are haggled rather than fixed.

Group C: Permanent Stall Operators

The marketplace stall operators have the least direct involvement in production of all four business groups. Except for three who have putting-out operations in embroidery and employ household labor in pattern design and finishing activities, the members of this group limit themselves to the purchase of finished products from either direct producers or village-to-marketplace intermediaries. Transactions are on a cash basis and goods are not taken on consignment, as they sometimes are by village-to-marketplace intermediaries (Beals 1975: 147–148)—a pattern that probably reflects seller preference and the general lack of relationships of confidence between villagers and their urban clients.

Group D: Embroidery Intermediaries

The embroidery merchants of Ocotlán district occasionally purchase small quantities of embroidered products from independent producers, but most of their income derives from their role as suppliers of thread and precut cloth to outworking embroiderers and the purchase and assembly of the embroidered pieces, which are then sold to merchants in Oaxaca City. The outworkers are remunerated by the piece (payment by results), and the vast majority are female (wives or dependent daughters) members of peasant-artisan households. As an enterprise, embroidery is characterized by very low capital intensity and high labor intensity; partly as a consequence of this, wages are very low and unit profits are small. The putter-out attempts to increase the volume of output in order to compensate for low unit profits; this volume is dependent upon the number of outworkers which he or she supplies. Nineteen of the twenty-four Ocotlán merchants interviewed employ between 1 and 12 outworkers (median = 4); however, five of them employ between 150 and 400 outworkers each and, as we shall discuss below, generate incomes that approach those of the wealthiest Oaxaca extramarketplace merchants.

The embroidery merchants stand out from all others because 60 percent initiated their careers as putters-out with capital accumulated solely from work as embroiderers (and embroidery was a partial contributor in another 13.3 percent of the cases). Nonetheless, most of the embroidery merchants remain small scale, as noted above, and 30 percent of them work part-time at occupations ranging from peasant cultivator, livestock breeder, tailor, and baker to grocer, agricultural products trader, and mason. This dual occupational involvement is, to a large extent, associated with the relatively low income generated from their craft businesses and is found only among the embroidery businessmen.

Capital Accumulation and Differentiation in the Craft Business Sector

Clearly, craft businesses are differentiated in terms of objective measures of size and performance between and within the four groups. In this section the sources and nature of this differentiation will be examined in greater detail.

Two categories of variables can be constructed that have a direct bearing on differentiation: one includes variables that measure the value of material means of production (e.g., tools, equipment, facilities, motor vehicles, raw materials on hand); another includes variables that measure the value of finished products (e.g., value of products produced or purchased for resale, finished product inventories, sales estimates). An examination of frequency distributions for the variables in these two categories discloses, with some exceptions, a similar intergroup rank order of median values per business unit, as follows (from highest to lowest): (a) extramarketplace proprietors in Oaxaca City; (b) marketplace stall operators in Oaxaca City; (c) embroidery merchants in the district of Ocotlán; and (d) sellers in the open-air craft market in Oaxaca City. Table 26 presents median and mean values for selected variables in the four categories.[6]

Although the median values for the variables in this table essentially support the order that ranks the extramarketplace businesses as the most prosperous and the open-air sellers as the least prosperous, it should be emphasized that the range of values is wide for most of these variables so that, with regard to any one variable, the values for one or more, say, embroidery units, may exceed those for several Oaxaca City extramarketplace or marketplace stall units.

For example, two embroidery enterprises reported gross annual sales exceeding one million pesos ($44,444), which is higher than the reported sales of 80 percent of the extramarketplace businesses

Table 26. Selected Variables for Value of Products Bought, Produced, and Sold by Oaxaca Valley Merchants

	Value/Month of Products Bought	Value/Month of Products Produced	Total Value/ Month of all Products (sum of columns 1, 2 medians only)
Business proprietors (extramarketplace) (N = 38)	10,150 17,068 25,693 N=16)	30,000 97,173 252,160 (N=15)	40,150 (N=31)
Open-air sellers (N = 10)	1,600 (N=3)	3,150 2,612 3,064 (N=6)	4,750 (N=9)
Stall operators (N = 21)	7,000 6,216 3,066 (N=6)	22,500 (N=2)	29,500 (N=8)
Embroidery merchants (N = 30)	2,050 (N=2)	3,100 10,073 18,737 (N=6)	5,150 (N=31)

Note: Values are listed in the following order: medians, means, and standard deviations. Single-value listings are medians. All values are given in pesos.

and of all of the marketplace stall enterprises. Likewise, three of the open-air market sellers reported gross annual sales ranging from 104,000 to 245,000 pesos ($4,622 to $10,889), which are higher than figures reported by 23 percent of the extramarketplace businesses and 77 percent of the embroidery units. In short, intergroup ranking does exist as a central tendency but individual units within each group may deviate significantly from the central tendencies for one or more variable and, consequently, be statistically unrepresentative of their group.

When these businesses are disaggregated and placed in a rank order according to reported values for selected variables measuring scale and business performance, the extent to which patterns derived from aggregate analysis are violated becomes even more clear. For example, in a rank ordering of the top twenty-five businesses for two separate estimates of the value of total annual sales, 72 percent of the businesses on both lists are extramarketplace businesses in Oaxaca City, underlining their predominance in the craft sector (these businesses represent only 38 percent of those in the sample). The Ocotlán embroidery businesses come out a distant second with 24 percent of the top twenty-five cases in aggregate yearly sales and 20 percent of the top twenty-five in gross yearly sales (compared to their 30 percent representation in the sample of craft businesses). It is also noteworthy, however, that of the eight businesses that appear in the top ten in both rank orders, two are operated by rural embroidery merchants.

Six Oaxaca City extramarketplace businesses appear in the top ten in two separate rank orders of businesses by total annual sales. Four of these are directly engaged in production: one is a cotton products manufactory (mantelería), one is a pottery manufactory, one is owned by a treadle loom weaver who operates a weaving manufactory in his village (Teotitlán del Valle), and the fourth has an extensive putting-out/buying-up operation in basketry. In addition, one of the remaining two top-10 businesses consisted of a cutlery workshop that was closed down shortly before our survey was conducted. This demonstrates once again the importance that direct involvement in production has as a capital-generating activity in these businesses. The median annual value of products produced by the fifty businesses that are directly engaged in production is $3,466.

To summarize the data presented and analyzed in this section, it can be said that craft product businesses in the Oaxaca Valley are quite heterogeneous with respect to the location, size, organization, and conduct of their operations. With some exceptions the most successful businesses are those in which capital directly engages labor power in either dispersed or congregated manufacturing—*but does so in conjunction with, rather than as an alternative to, intermediary operations.* While rank orderings for selected variables measuring size and performance of these businesses demonstrate the overall predominance of city-based over village-based capital, several important exceptions can be shown, especially in the embroidery industry.

Craft Businesses and the Distribution of Value

Aggregate statistics on fifteen city manufactories and thirty rural embroidery units serve as a basis for comparing the volume and distribution of value in these two groups of businesses. Aggregate monthly profits for the fifteen Oaxaca city manufactories are just under $20,000, which averages out to $1,217 monthly per manufactory. This compares with aggregate monthly profits for the thirty Ocotlán embroidery merchants of $2,700, which averages out to only $88 monthly per merchant.

Due to the higher organic composition of capital (i.e., cost of means of production/wage bill, or C/V) in the Oaxaca city manufactories (7.83 vs. 1.67), the aggregate wage bill in embroidery represents a much higher proportion of the value of the total product (44 percent) than it does in the city manufactories (27 percent), despite the fact that the per capita monthly wage is three times higher for the city manufactory pieceworker ($32) than it is for the embroidery outworker ($10). Even so, the manufactory pieceworker earns substantially less than the official monthly minimum wage for Oaxaca City, equivalent to $80 (Murphy and Selby 1981: 251). In sum, the city manufactory appropriates a larger share of the total social product than the Ocotlán embroidery unit, which means that the rate of exploitation (S/V) of the urban pieceworker (notwithstanding his or her higher absolute average wage) is above that of the poorly remunerated Ocotlán embroidery outworker.[7]

The mean wage for the city manufactory pieceworker must be interpreted in the context of an urban economy in which the median monthly household income in 1979 was 2,518 pesos or $112 (1,966 pesos or $87 for "poor" households) (Murphy and Selby 1981: 253); and in which the median monthly household per adult equivalent income was 667 pesos or $30 (400 pesos or $18 for the "marginally poor") (Higgins 1983: 173). Although the pieceworker mean wage is in line with these other figures, our impression is that it is nonetheless skewed to the low side because an undetermined percentage of the total workforce is casual or part-time. In the words of one weaving workshop proprietor: "When they want to work, they work all day; and when they don't want to work they don't come. We are short of workers but we have to manage. We lack human material. All of them want to be clerks. There are no longer many who want to be artisans."

Among other things, this pattern of irregular work is associated with an urban situation in which "the majority of households have as many teenage and adult members working as possible" and where "there is a lack of unemployment because the majority of people are underemployed" (Higgins 1983: 7). It is also possible that low-wage jobs in the service sector are more attractive to members of these households than are piecework jobs in archaic manufactories.

By contrast, the low mean per capita wage for rural embroidery outworkers is a reflection of the sex and age composition of that population: a significant proportion of embroidery outwork is done by young, dependent, unmarried, and childless females (38 percent), although a majority (51.5 percent) of the embroidery outworkers are married and have dependent children. Regardless of who performs it, embroidery work is tedious and poorly remunerated. Out of fifteen outworker households for which detailed budget data are available, the highest hourly return was just under 6 pesos (25 cents) and the lowest a paltry 60 centavos (3 cents)!

As was documented in Chapter 5, from the perspective of the female embroidery outworkers, the critical issue is not so much *low* remuneration as it is *no* remuneration. They have relatively few cash-earning alternatives that are easily adaptable to daily household routines (Cook 1982: 64). In other words, the Oaxaca Valley countryside provides a fertile recruiting ground for outworkers—a fact that is borne out by the remarkable proliferation of the embroidery industry in the district of Ocotlán and elsewhere in the Valley over the last decade.

As was also documented in Chapter 5, women who do receive wages are paid much less than men. Littlefield (1978: 504) observed as much in her study of Yucatán hammock weavers and noted—in an argument that is as valid for the Oaxaca Valley as it is for Yucatán—that "this differential in the average wages of men and of women . . . allows labor in weaving [and embroidery] to be paid less than its value in terms of the conventional necessities of life." This conclusion takes on added significance in light of the fact that the average price of male labor power in Oaxaca, as indicated above, is itself undervalued. Thus, if men in Oaxaca can be said to suffer *su-perexploitation*, women, such as embroiderers and thread spinners, suffer *hyperexploitation*.

Production and Value Distribution in Oaxaca City Craft Industries

A comparison of rural and urban craft production units in the Oaxaca Valley division of labor discloses differences and similarities. In those branches of production (e.g., treadle loom weaving, pottery making, basketry) where both urban and rural units participate, the former are likely to be more highly capitalized, larger-scale enterprises with their production operations concentrated in one locale rather than dispersed. Also, it is often the case in urban enterprises (less so in rural ones) that production operations are extensions of retail or wholesale selling operations with the proprietors themselves not being artisans. The results of a survey of sixty-five craft businesses in Oaxaca City, however, show that there are many petty commodity-producing shops in the "informal" sector in Oaxaca City, just as there are several examples of retail and wholesale businesses that have been developed by artisan-entrepreneurs as extensions of craft shops (Cook 1984a: 194–198; 1985a).

Table 27 presents data on ten Oaxaca City craft businesses, a representative cross-section of those in which wage laborers (remunerated by piece rate in all but two cases) regularly participate in production, in some cases in combination with, but in most cases in lieu of, household laborers. Of a total of thirty-eight craft-producing and/or craft vending businesses (located outside formal marketplaces) surveyed in Oaxaca City, 86 percent were found to be significantly involved in production operations—principally through workshops (42 percent) and secondarily through proprietor's own household or hired-outworker units (32 percent). As a rule these businesses undertake direct involvement in production in combination with intermediary operations.

In addition to pottery making, shirt making, leatherworking, and treadle loom weaving (represented in the sub-sample), their production operations include jewelry making, cutlery making, tin working, and basketry. Seven of the ten proprietors of the businesses in the subsample are working artisans (this is true of 45 percent of the total sample); five of them learned the craft from their fathers, and four inherited their businesses. This indicates that the origin and viability of urban craft businesses owe nearly as much to capital

Table 27. Production Data for 10 Oaxaca City Craft Shops (all values in U.S. dollars)

I.D.	Number of workers family	Number of workers hired	Means of Production (MP)	Raw Materials	Wages (W)	Value of Output	Profit (P)	P/W	P/ (RM+W)
1A	0	8	667	407	1,067	1,955	481	.45	.33
2B	1	5	1,333	90	355	667	222	.63	.50
3A	0	13	66,665	191	1,733	3,700	1,776	1.02	.92
4T	1	3	4,444	888	533	1,777	356	.67	.25
5G	2	5	8,000	900	580	2,286	806	1.39	.54
6M+A	0	72	32,753	13,333	12,230	51,111	25,548	2.09	1.00
7M	0	5	8,200	444	800	1,422	178	.22	.12
8M	0	2	890	444	427	933	62	.15	.07
9M	3	3	445	822	284	2,133	1,027	3.6	.93
10M	0	8	3,300	1,100	540	1,790	150	.28	.09
Total	7	124	126,697	18,619	18,549	67,774	30,606	—	.48
Mean	.7	12.4	12,670	1,862	1,855	6,777	3,061	1.05	.48
Median	0	5.0	3,872	633	560	1,873	419	.65	.42

Note: A = alfarería, or pottery; T = talabartería, or leatherwork; G = guayabera, or shirtmaking; M = mantelería, or weaving; B = basketry.

accumulated through household labor in a petty industrial commodity-producing context as they do to capital that has penetrated craft production from mercantile or other sources. In other words, behind a present-generation business proprietor-artisan there is often a past-generation artisan-household head.

It is apparent that these businesses range from petty to medium in scale of operations as measured by the estimates in Table 27 for the value of means of production, number of workers, and monthly expenditures on raw materials and wages, as well as for the value of monthly output and profit. Despite this variability in scale, all these enterprises—including those that continue to engage household labor—depend on the regular employment of wage labor, are profit-oriented, and, in essence, are completely immersed in the provincial capitalist market economy. They are divided between the "formal" and "informal" sectors (Portes 1983; Moser 1978). For example, several of them rely on professional bookkeeping and cost accounting procedures, pay a full range of taxes, and comply with federal social security and labor laws, whereas others rely on unsophisticated bookkeeping and accounting methods, pay taxes selectively, and do not comply with federal social security and labor laws. Significantly, even the largest and most professionally managed of these enterprises (no. 6M + A) has in recent years relocated some of its weaving operations to rural areas (including the employment of incarcerated workers) to evade formal sector labor requirements and lower its labor costs.

Indeed, it appears that the urban craft business sector's direct involvement in production is either undergoing a relocation to the countryside (e.g., in treadle loom weaving) or surrendering this sphere to worker control (e.g., a tin workshop employing 45 workers, operated as part of a large merchant enterprise, was sold outright to the employees in 1980). This is occurring primarily because it appears to be the best way these businesses can adapt to the changing structure of the regional and national state-capitalist economy with its proliferating bureaucracy, corporatist legalism, and corruption. This retreat from production by urban merchants is matched by an expansion of intermediary operations in handicrafts, by abandonment of the craft sector altogether (often because of increasing competition from government enterprises), or by a diversification of business interests—primarily in the burgeoning service sector (e.g., tourist agencies, restaurants, real estate, insurance). Thus in contemporary Oaxaca City, the "union of a sale shop with the work-shop" (Bucher 1901: 206) may be anachronistic and not so much indicative of future trends as it is of conjunctural expediencies of the past and present (see Cook 1985a for a further discussion of craft businesses in Oaxaca City).

Production and Value Distribution in Embroidery

A comparison of aggregate measures of economic scale in Tables 27 and 28 shows that the typical urban enterprise is substantially larger than the typical rural enterprise. For example, the median value of means of production for the city enterprise is 16 times that for the rural enterprise, its average monthly output is worth 7 times more, and its average monthly profit is about 3.3 times more. Although the city enterprise is more profitable in the aggregate, its degree of profitability, relative to the rural enterprise, is not so impressive considering its much heavier investment in fixed capital and in wages (4 times more monthly). Overall the median rate of profit of ten Oaxaca City craft shops was 42 percent compared to 35 percent for fifteen Ocotlán embroidery units.[8]

As pointed out in Chapter 5, there is good evidence that capital accumulation and associated social differentiation are occurring within the rural petty commodity sector. This can be illustrated through a consideration of the embroidery industry where 60 percent of the proprietors of the units surveyed in five different communities in the Ocotlán district initiated their careers as putters-out with capital accumulated from previous employment as outworkers. This industry, in fact, provides a good example of a rapid-growth labor-intensive industry based upon the proliferation of dependent, direct producers (i.e., outworkers), from among whom have developed independent employer units. Some of these units have become comparable in scale and volume of business with the industry's largest and longest-established putting-out units.

Whereas the typical embroidery enterprise (like the typical weaving enterprise) nets about one-third of the monthly profit of the typical brickmaking enterprise, it is significant to note that two of the fifteen enterprises in the subsample (nos. 9 and 15) reported gross monthly products higher than those reported for any weaving or brickmaking unit and, in fact, were exceeded by only one urban business (6M+A). We do not have detailed case study data on these and other successful embroidery units, but the survey data suggest that unwaged household labor—especially female—is one key to their economic success. In most of these units, the assembly by sewing machine of garments distributed and collected in unassembled

Table 28. Production Data, 15 Rural Putting-Out Units in Ocotlán Embroidery (all values in U.S. dollars)

(1) Case Number	(2) family	(3) hired	(4) Instruments of Production	(5) Raw Materials	(6) Wages (W)	(7) Value of Output	(8) Profit (P)	(9) P/W	(10) P/ (RM+W)
		Number of workers							
1.	2	6	155	96	9	133	28	3.11	.27
2.	3	6	410	58	40	373	275	6.87	2.81
3.	3	3	355	23	23	173	127	5.52	2.76
4.	1	3	265	11	32	80	37	1.16	.86
5.	1	6	90	23	28	90	39	1.39	.76
6.	4	400	1,065	355	470	1,022	197	.42	.24
7.	3	200	890	622	711	1,991	658	.93	.49
8.	4	12	200	20	68	222	134	1.97	1.52
9.	2	180	1,044	1,415	1,918	4,078	745	.39	.22
10.	1	5	300	55	142	330	133	.94	.68
11.	1	4	120	355	384	750	11	.03	.01
12.	4	3	170	62	50	138	26	.52	.23
13.	2	10	130	89	112	235	34	.30	.17
14.	3	5	200	132	57	256	67	1.17	.35
15.	4	100+	244	2,311	2,667	5,333	355	.13	.07
Total	38	940	5,638	5,627	6,711	15,204	2,866	—	—
Mean	2.5	63	376	375	447	1,014	191	1.66	.76
Median	3.0	6.0	244	89	68	256	127	.94	.35

Note: Values in columns 5–10 have been computed for periods of one month.

sets from embroidery outworkers, as well as the washing, ironing, folding, and packaging of the assembled garment, is done primarily by unwaged females in the putting-out household.

Intermediary Capital and Provincial Development

It is safe to infer from the empirical record that the textile industry in the city of Oaxaca today is only a pale shadow of what it was in the past. Despite the fact that the city was apparently never the site of large-scale textile manufactories (or *obrajes*) as, at least, one scholar has implied (Semo 1973: 161–187; cf. Chance 1978: 111, Salvucci 1987: 55), there is evidence from both the eighteenth (Chance 1978: 148) and nineteenth (Esparza 1983: x) centuries that attests to the dominance of the textile industry in the urban economy. Also, it is probably true that the social, political, and economic importance of today's merchant class (not to be confused with commercial businesses that represent large industrial capitalist firms) is less than that of seventeenth and eighteenth (and, perhaps, nineteenth and early twentieth) century merchant classes (Hamnett 1971; Chance 1978; Nolasco 1981; Chassen 1986). Those classes—and the artisan-proletariats that they exploited—were dominant forces in the regional development of mercantile capitalism, whereas today's counterparts are subsumed players in a provincial capitalism that is even more statized and bureaucratized than it was under the Spanish or, for that matter, the postcolonial dictatorship of Porfirio Díaz. With a few exceptions, all the businesses we have dealt with are adjuncts of the Oaxaca economy's tourist sector, which has experienced an accelerated development since 1940. They produce and/or traffick in essentially luxury commodities, the social demand for which originates among urban middle classes outside Oaxaca and, in a majority of cases, outside Mexico. Like any other enclave sector, this one processes raw materials that are, for the most part, not produced locally or regionally and injects its finished commodities into marketing channels that lead to destinations outside the state of Oaxaca.

It is not our intention here to create a scenario that precludes a role for labor-intensive industrialization in the future of capitalist development in Oaxaca. What we are suggesting is that this role—in the tourist crafts line of production, at least—will be increasingly played out in the countryside. A significant role may exist, however, in the city, as well as in the countryside, for a new type of labor-intensive feeder industry—either of the assembly shop (*maquiladora*) variety or of rejuvenated or newly established manufactories or factories producing or assembling new lines of commodities for absentee mass merchandising and/or production enterprises.

Industrial capitalist development is nascent in the Oaxaca Valley; it is developing from within simple commodity forms in the country-side in industries like weaving, mescal distilling, and brickmaking. It has been successfully introduced in modern capital-intensive forms in a handful of industries like plywood production, hydrated lime quarrying and processing, and tractor-trailer assembly but unsuccessfully introduced in milk pasteurizing, brickmaking, and, it appears, mescal distilling. Consequently, the well-documented "underdevelopment" of the Oaxaca Valley political economy is associated with a relative absence of modern industrial capitalist enterprise.

This statement puts us in the company of Marx and Lenin—and in opposition to most contemporary Marxists—regarding the potential of industrial capitalism for generating economic development in poor nations and regions. It is our contention, along with that of some political economists (Mandle 1980; Warren 1980), that a "reluctance to acknowledge the growth-promoting nature of capitalism has unnecessarily handicapped" Marxist analysis (Mandle 1980: 871). Indeed, before Marxists can make an effective case against the inequities and irrationalities endemic to capitalism, they must first acknowledge "that capitalism is capable of promoting a significant revolution in productive capacity" (872).

Even though regional capitalist development in today's Third World usually means dependence upon big national and/or transnational capital, it seems to us that there is a correlation between the relative presence of industrial capital and the material well-being of the general population in various regions of Mexico: namely, that the areas of highest concentration of capitalist industry are those with the highest percentages of households with greater than minimum adequate income. Such a correlation has at least been made in one recent study comparing Oaxaca City with three northern Mexican cities (Murphy and Selby 1981).

Whether or not this correlation is suggestive rather than definitive, one thing is certain: underdevelopment in Oaxaca cannot be eliminated by the triumvirate of simple commodity production, merchant capital, and commercial capital. The significant out-migration of population from the Oaxaca Valley and its hinterland over the years—and the flow of migrants to more highly capitalized regions— is diagnostic of the failures of this triumvirate to generate the quantity and quality of employment opportunities required and expected by the migrating masses.

The relative underdevelopment of industrial capital in Oaxaca does not necessarily mean that Oaxaca's working people will be unable to find ways to negotiate a more equitable share of the social product created by their participation in the Mexican commodity economy. As we will discuss in the concluding chapter, Oaxacans do achieve consciousness of their material interests and sometimes organize or take individual action in defense of them, as petty commodity producers, petty industrial capitalists, and pieceworkers. Despite their relative lack of direct exposure to modern industrial capital, which has traditionally been a crucible of working-class consciousness, the contradictions of their location in Mexican commodity production become apparent to them either at the point of production, in their roles as buyers of capital or wage goods, as borrowers of capital, as payers of taxes, or, finally, as citizens in an authoritarian polity. Recognition of these contradictions and how they impact their own material interests can and does generate political responses. This is especially true during a period of crisis, such as that of the 1980s.

Chapter 7. Petty Industry, Class Maneuvers, and the Crisis of Mexican Capitalism

Contours of the Economic Crisis

From 1976 to early 1982, the Mexican economy enjoyed six years of rapid, though sectorally uneven, growth fueled by the burgeoning petroleum sector and a massive inflow of short-term loans that contributed to an unprecedented escalation in public sector debt. When oil prices declined in 1981, many of the loans came due and confidence in the overvalued peso (sustained previously by the central bank) collapsed. With the peso devaluation of February 1982 (followed by additional devaluations in August and December), the Mexican economy entered into its worst crisis of the postwar period (Ros 1985).[1]

Led by President Miguel de la Madrid Hurtado, who succeeded the discredited José López Portillo in December 1982, government efforts to deal with the crisis have been extensive—if of limited effectiveness. Following discussions with representatives from the International Monetary Fund, the de la Madrid administration instituted a series of tough fiscal measures (e.g., tax reforms) designed to reduce the federal budget deficit (Ramírez 1988). In addition, it put over two hundred unprofitable public sector enterprises on the market, cut subsidies to consumers (mainly in public transportation and basic food staples) and to industry (e.g., energy, imported raw materials, land, and water), and eliminated almost 100,000 positions from the government bureaucracy. Finally, and perhaps most significantly, the de la Madrid administration began to ease restrictions on foreign direct investment, thus seeking new sources of foreign exchange, technology, and employment (Hamilton 1984: 23–24; Durán 1985: 97–98; Levy and Szekely 1986: 17). After signs of recovery in 1984, when the GNP improved by 3.5 percent over 1983, the economy entered another slide in 1985, which was exacerbated by the disastrous September earthquakes.[2]

Little firsthand, systematic social scientific investigation of the impact of the crisis upon the Mexican populace can be found. Economists and journalists (drawing mostly on official statistics) reported an increase in the rate of open unemployment from 5 percent in 1982 to an estimated 12 percent by mid-1983. By mid-1987 4.5 million heads of household were unemployed, or 1 in every 6 eligible workers—the largest number of unemployed recorded in over half of a century and a level of unemployment four times larger than that reported for 1982. Worse still, if the figures for underemployment are considered, 1 of every 2 Mexican workers was either underemployed or unemployed as of mid-1987 (Orozco 1987). Also on record are severe increases in inflation rates, which averaged over 80 percent annually from 1982 to the end of 1986—with the annual rate for the latter year officially reported to be 105.7 percent, the highest ever recorded in the nation's history (Acosta 1987: 30). During 1987, the annual inflation rate hovered between 132 and 136 percent and by February 1988 the Bank of Mexico reported that the Consumer Price Index was increasing at an annual rate of 176.9 percent (Orozco 1987; Calzada and Hernández 1987; Acosta and Monge 1988: 20). Moreover, the government's IMF-imposed obligation to reduce budgetary outlays led it to adopt a tough negotiating stance with public sector unions and to restrict increases in minimum wages. For instance, during the first four months of 1987, the minimum wage was raised by 20 percent whereas prices increased by 35 percent. Urban wages, then, have not kept pace with inflation so that real wages have declined steadily and substantially since 1982, as has labor's share of the national income. As one commentator expressed it, "the dramatic collapse of wages as a part of GDP . . . simply reflects a dramatic increase in the rate of exploitation, the system's natural response to restore profits" (Bortz 1986: 44).[3]

The dramatic deterioration in real minimum wages—earned by approximately 67 percent of Mexico's 25 million workers (Ramírez 1988: 13)—has necessitated changes in the composition and size of the basic consumption basket. "Cheaper items have been substituted for more expensive ones, or when this is not possible, they have reduced altogether their consumption of protein-rich foods such as meat, eggs, and milk" (Ramírez 1988: 16). Finally, given the continuing devaluation of the peso (which has been allowed to freely float against the dollar), imported goods have become too expensive for the shrinking incomes of most Mexicans. All this translates into a progressively severe reduction in the standard of living for the working class.

The above statistics refer primarily to the urban, formal sector of the economy. Much less is known about the effects of the crisis in the countryside, but it is reasonable to assume that, for example, rural landed households, given their capacity to produce basic food stuffs and raise animals for their own consumption, will experience and respond to inflation and other crisis-related processes differently than urban households. Grindle (1987: 8–9), for instance, stated unequivocally that, "for peasants who had access to land and especially those who produced an agricultural surplus, the impact of the crisis was . . . muted." This chapter addresses these issues through the analysis and presentation of material from an exploratory study conducted by Cook in 1985 among Oaxaca Valley peasant-artisan households. The exploratory study involved a series of interviews with 25 informants residing in seven different communities and representing the following craft industries: *metate* fabrication, palm plaiting, treadle loom weaving, wood carving, embroidery, backstrap loom weaving, and brickmaking. Three of these industries—namely, treadle loom weaving, embroidery, and brickmaking—are organized predominantly by capitalist piecework relations; the remainder are organized around relations among self-employed petty commodity producers (some of whom have varying degrees of dependency upon buyers-up).

The Exploratory Study and the Issue of Peasant versus Proletarian Households within Capitalism

Although the sample was small, an effort was made to be as representative as possible—not only of the different industries but also of other factors that operate to differentiate PAHs, such as job position (self-employed, employer, employee), degree of involvement in agriculture, income, and level of material well-being. The informants include men and women, self-employed and employees, landed and landless, poor and relatively affluent.

The interview was not restricted exclusively to the economic impact of inflation but included questions dealing with its ideological and political impacts. For example, it was designed to find out how these informants defined the crisis, how they understood its causes, how they compared or evaluated the performance of the *PRI*-government (Partido Revolucionario Institutional, or the Institutional Revolutionary Party) and of the two major opposition parties, PAN (Partido de Acción Nacional, or the National Action Party) and PSUM (Partido Socialista Unificado de México, or the Unified Socialist Party, since 1988 incorporated, along with the Mexican Workers Party and other parties, into the PMS, the Mexican Socialist Party), with regard to the crisis, and how they viewed the future of their work and of the economic situation in general.

Most informants identified the crisis with a marked decline in their purchasing power that they attributed to price increases unmatched by increases in their income. Whereas this identification is undoubtedly shared by urban working-class and middle-class Mexicans, the specific efforts undertaken by urban and rural (or employee vs. self-employed) households to deal with the crisis can be expected to differ. Full-time salaried workers, for instance, really have only two alternative strategies (short of violent struggle). They can look for ways to increase monetary income or they can economize (i.e., buy less or buy more selectively). Only the first strategy presents the possibility of an appropriate defense of their living standards; the second is bound to result in an erosion of those standards and, if sustained and severe, may lead to health and/or nutritional problems that threaten the short- and long-term reproduction of labor power (e.g., via elevated incidence of disease, malnutrition, mortality rates, premature death). This limited room for maneuver in times of inflationary crisis by urban employee households is a consequence of the fact that practically all the material goods they consume must be purchased with wages in the capitalist market. By and large, such households do not have access to the means of production of their own subsistence; those means and the production of most wage goods are controlled by capitalist enterprises.[4]

Peasant-artisan households, by contrast, are in a relatively advantageous position because their dual involvement in commodity production (agriculture and crafts), together with subsistence food production, provides a basis for pursuing several different strategies that can be modified to take best advantage of current (or anticipated) market conditions. For example, it has been documented (e.g., Warman 1980: 215−216) that, during periods of high inflation in Mexico, peasants intensify home consumption and sell less of their produce; or that they increase the cultivation of subsistence crops on marginal lands (Lewis 1960: 33−34).

Moreover, to the extent that they produce commodities, PAHs earn money through the sale of commodities in markets that are often more flexible, more open, and more competitive than the labor market in which urban "formal sector" employees earn their incomes. Consequently, PAHs are frequently able to adjust the selling prices of their commodities upward to offset increases in the prices of producer's goods and wage goods, as well as services, that they buy.

This means that they can often avoid the situation of the fictitious peasant "Juan Garabato" who regularly finds himself confronted with the necessity of "selling cheap and buying dear." According to a popular saying in the rural Oaxaca Valley: "*Juan Garabato vende barato y compra caro.*" For example, even in the *metate* industry where buying-up merchants do exercise some price-setting power in the market, Cook found that individual *metate* producers were still able to compensate for inflation by raising *metate* prices to individual buyers and buyers-up. Their ability to do this, however, hinged upon the fact that there is a relatively inelastic demand for *metates* combined with a supply situation approximating conditions of natural monopoly.[5]

Raising prices is a particularly realistic counterinflationary strategy for those households in industries like weaving and wood carving that produce for the tourist market. Many tourists have relatively high incomes and/or are non-Mexicans and, therefore, tend to find that the impact of inflation upon their purchasing power is offset by continuous peso devaluation vis-à-vis the dollar and other strong currencies; as a result, the tourist market is less susceptible than domestic markets to reductions in purchasing power (and demand) attributable to inflation in the national economy.

Even pieceworkers in certain rural industries, for example, the piece-rate brick molders known as *mileros,* enjoy apparent advantages over urban formal-sector workers with regard to the ability to negotiate increases in piece rates or in seeking to match increases in their expenditures with increases in their incomes in inflationary times. The situation in the brickyards is such that the demand for skilled, reliable labor power regularly exceeds supply; moreover, intense competition among the brickyard owner-operators usually favors the workers in periodic, informal wage negotiations (Cook 1984a). A comparable situation also exists in the treadle loom weaving industry.

It is not our intention to convey the impression that inflation has no negative impact upon rural petty commodity producers. Of course it does; the majority of them would enjoy better living and working conditions if there was no inflationary crisis. Our contention is simply that many peasant-artisans, and even some members of the rural pieceworking proletariat, can (when conditions permit) mitigate the worst effects of inflation, either by producing for own use, by intensifying labor in their craft, or by negotiating upward adjustments in the prices of the products or labor power they sell.

The existence of extensive social differentiation and economic inequality within and between Oaxaca Valley village populations, as extensively documented in Chapter 4, suggests the differential capacity of PAHs to adjust to conditions of economic crisis. Informant statements lend support to the thesis that some households suffer more than others from the ongoing inflationary crisis. For example, a *metate* maker replied as follows when asked about the impact of the crisis on his village: "The crisis has affected us in the sense that the prices of everything have gone up. As peasants we feel something, but not so much, I think, as other people. That is, there are people who don't have any means of earning money, who don't have a craft or land to cultivate. From what are they going to live? When I need money I can sell a *metate* and with regard to food, well we grow our own." Other informants expressed similar opinions regarding the relative advantage, in times of economic crisis, of peasant-artisan petty commodity producers vis-à-vis groups without land or craft occupations.

The Crisis, Its Causes, and Its Material Consequences: The Informants' Views

The 1985 interview was initiated by asking informants what they understood by the term "crisis" and how their lives had been affected by it. As is usually the case with open-ended interviews, the quality of answers was variable.

Informants tended, however, not to answer this question merely with generalities lacking substance; on the contrary, their answers typically included specific examples of the impact of the inflationary crisis on their daily lives. The following answers are illustrative:

Woman who finishes shawls (her husband is a peasant-weaver): "Everyone is suffering. One buys more expensive than one sells. For example, let's suppose that we are going to sell a woven product . . . we take account of how much it cost us and we make very little when we sell. When one goes to buy sugar or soap, well, it's very expensive. One has to sell a goat or a turkey or a chicken."

Weaver (backstrap loom, male): "The crisis means misery, little money. Things have gotten worse in many ways. With regard to food, clothing, everything. High prices across the board. One must buy expensive. One's income no longer stretches to buy what one needs."

Wood carver: "Now one cannot buy anything at last year's prices. The stores no longer have fixed prices, they sell at any price they want. A half-kilo bag of soap detergent sold for 80 pesos last year, now it sells for 160. Everything is more expensive. The bus fare to town was 80 pesos, now it is 150—almost double. There isn't anything that can be bought for 100 pesos."

Answers to another question, namely, "How do you feel your life this year has been, easier or more difficult in comparison with previous years?," were overwhelmingly indicative of a decline in the quality of life as a result of inflation. Only one informant said that life was better in 1985; four responded that it was the same; and the rest, 80 percent of the informants, indicated that their life had worsened during 1985.[6]

The interview included the following two questions designed to elicit the opinions of the informants concerning the causes of inflation: "To what can price increases be attributed?" and "In your opinion who is responsible?" About 70 percent of those who answered either blamed the government or said that the government was probably responsible. Businessmen or intermediaries were blamed by 30 percent of the respondents, mostly by self-employed weavers and embroiderers (who buy cloth, thread, and other materials from merchants) who feel that the merchants engage in arbitrary price gouging. A few of these informants, however, traced the source of the problem beyond the middlemen to the factories. For example, one of them said: "It's a question of the factories . . . Like two or three months ago I bought 200 kilos of thread. A week later the store was charging 125 pesos more per kilo than they had charged me a week earlier. I said to them: 'It's impossible that prices are increasing daily by 10 percent.' 'That's the way it is,' they told me, and they showed me the factory invoice. What could I say?" Another informant said: "We are suffering the repercussions of what's happening in the large cities—inflation, so the worker needs to earn more, and in the factories they go on strike because they want to earn more. The bosses give them raises and then turn around and increase the selling prices of their products. That's what's happening."

Several informants who blamed the government for inflation referred specifically to the government's policy of increasing prices in the sector of nationalized or parastate enterprises—especially petroleum. For example, one informant said, "The price of gasoline increases and then everything goes up. That liquid makes everything else move." Another opined that, "The government has nationalized petroleum, sugar, electricity—well it shouldn't increase prices in these industries. But it is the first to raise prices and then the cost of transportation goes up, everything else goes up. What can we do? How are we going to pay?"

Many "middle-strata" peasant-artisans expressed a general senti-
ment of anguish, frustration, and indignation toward *both* the government and the private business sector. According to one informant:
"They say that because of the government everything happens. It
never helps peasants. What it tries to do is screw-over the peasant.
All the store owners sell at the price they want, and day by day
prices go higher. On the other hand, what we sell or our work almost
is worth nothing." The inflationary crisis impacts especially hard on
those petty commodity producers (like this informant who is a self-
employed embroiderer heavily dependent on buyers-up) who find it
difficult to make compensatory adjustments in the prices of the
commodities they sell.

The Variable Effects of Inflation on the Conduct of
Specific Household Enterprises: Some Examples

A content analysis of informant statements discloses two categories
of effects: first, those that impact upon the process of reproduction
of labor power at the interior of the PAH; and, second, those that impact upon the process of (*a*) valorization of capital within petty capitalist units or (*b*) the process of the realization of exchange value
within units of petty commodity production (i.e., the self-employed).
In the ensuing discussion we will emphasize the differences in these
effects upon piecework units (employee and employer) and units
that are not involved in piecework.

PAHs employ three strategies to counter the negative impact of
inflation upon the reproduction of labor power: (*a*) increase subsistence crop production (maize, beans, squash); (*b*) initiate a process of
substituting wage goods purchased in the capitalist market with
goods produced for autoconsumption through a combination of own
agriculture and collection of wild plant foods; and (*c*) reduce consumption of wage goods without substituting goods produced for
own use.

The results of these measures, which are not mutually exclusive,
are identical, that is they reduce (or avoid the increase of) the cost of
reproduction of labor power. A fourth strategy consists of selling
crops destined for autoconsumption (for example, corn) but this alternative ultimately has negative repercussions on the PAH since
the sold crop will later have to be replaced, usually at elevated prices.
The effect of this strategy, which is applied only as an emergency
measure, is to increase the PAH's cost of labor power reproduction.

In the second category of effects of inflation upon petty enterprises (i.e., those that impact upon the valorization of capital or the

realization of exchange value), strategies employed by PAHs include the following: (a) intensification (or diminishment) of nonagricultural production; (b) intensification of the production of cash crops; (c) compensatory increases in selling prices of commodities produced by the enterprise or in the price of labor power (i.e., in piece rates in households that sell labor power); (d) sale of fattened animals; (e) rationalization/diversification of commodity production (or other income-earning activities); (f) marketing innovations; (g) entrance into the migratory labor stream; and (h) reduction of production costs by reducing the scale of the enterprise (fire employees) or by substituting household workers for paid workers.

The result of these measures, which usually are applied in combination, is to check, minimize, or mitigate declines in the process of realization of exchange value within petty commodity units or declines in the process of valorizing capital within petty capitalist piecework units.

The first strategy includes two mutually exclusive alternatives— intensification or diminution of nonagricultural production; which alternative, if either, is employed depends upon the concrete situation of the PAH. For example, one of the industries that appears to be most affected by the crisis is embroidery. Even though it produces exclusively for the tourist or export market, it has experienced in recent years a crisis either of oversupply or of underconsumption. In one village, where the majority of households in 1980 embroidered (several of them as petty merchant capitalists with outworkers), the 1985 interviews disclosed that several households withdrew from embroidery and took up garden cropping (the second strategy), whereas others reduced the scale of embroidery operations.

The strategy of diversifying/intensifying cash crop production also occurs among the most affluent petty capitalist units in our sample, as exemplified in the following case of a proprietor of a weaving workshop. In 1980 this individual had distributed most of his land to sharecroppers and was considering withdrawing completely from agriculture to devote all of his time, effort, and capital to weaving. Nevertheless, in 1985 he told Cook the following:

> We changed our system. Now I don't give out so much land to sharecroppers. We have animals and I don't get enough harvest through sharecropping. I am cultivating the land on my own account now. I spend more time in agriculture than before. We do everything. I plan to plant tomatoes on a share basis with another person. We are working more seriously in agriculture now. Last year I sold five tons of corn. With the earnings I bought

thread. That's the reason that I haven't gone bankrupt because I saw others who began with me and now they are bankrupt. Also I bought another piece of land last year and planted garlic. That earned me some 150,000 pesos in profits over four months (that is a 50 percent profit on my investment).

There were indications from the 1985 study that a partial reorganization of production was underway in some pieceworker households in the brick industry. More specifically, women and children were replacing men in brick molding so that the men could take advantage of other types of wage labor that are available in the brickyards, especially loading and unloading kilns and trucks. In this way, the total income of the household was increased. If this process becomes widespread it will represent a significant change in the structure of brick production because it violates traditional concepts of the division of labor by gender and age in this industry. In 1980, only one woman molded bricks in the large brickyard area studied; and, at that time, everyone was openly critical and disparaging of the woman's husband for allowing her to work at a "man's job" (molding bricks). To the degree that this crossover continues and shows signs of persisting, the brick industry will provide an interesting case study of change in the gender division of labor.

The third strategy, according to which PAHs seek compensatory increases in the selling prices of commodities that they produce (or in prices of labor power, that is, in piece rates) is pursued as often as possible. The frequency and the size of such increases vary by industry and according to the economic situation of the PAH, although, given the competitiveness of most of these markets, it is difficult for single producers to increase prices arbitrarily. Relevant examples of the exercise of this strategy can be found in all of the industries surveyed. A good example is provided by the previously quoted weaving workshop operator: "I buy thread by the kilo. When I make a piece I do some figuring—so much material, so much wage labor. Then on that basis I have to continue raising the price of that piece so that my capital, which is a small capital, won't decrease. It may not increase but at least it won't decrease. If it decreases then I know that the business is going bankrupt and we can't continue working."

In 1985 in this same industry, the *operarios,* or the weavers, were paid by piece rate (by meter of cloth woven). According to this same informant they "were asking for increases each month. Just a month ago the rate was sixty pesos per meter. I increase the rate voluntarily by ten pesos each month. That way I am compensated and they are compensated." The same situation exists among the seamstresses (costureras) in this industry. Again, quoting the same workshop operator: "The seamstresses are also saying that for the coming month they want 20 pesos per piece. Right now I am paying 15 pesos. They provide the sewing machine and their labor; I provide the thread and the cloth."

It is important to remember that within the petty capitalist industries, treadle loom weaving and brickmaking, the pieceworkers are reasonably well positioned regarding piece-rate negotiations with their employers. The combination of competition among the enterprises and a relative shortage of qualified, reliable workers seems to favor the latter vis-à-vis their requests for piece-rate increases. During the eight years that these industries have been monitored, piece rates have steadily increased without a single decrease. Under such volatile conditions, however, the relative value shares of employer and employee fluctuate capriciously and complicate accounting. Another weaving shop operator put the situation in perspective: "When one of my seamstresses says, 'You know in Mitla they are paying more,' well I tell her, 'I'm going to pay you the same so that you don't have to go to work for them.' Here the labor of every person is solicited. In Mitla, a weaving proprietor who has a big order and is under pressure will come here and offer the workers an extra ten pesos so that they will leave and go to work for him. That's the worst." With regard to his weavers, it is necessary for this employer to anticipate their petitions for piece-rate increases. As he expressed it: "I have to give them two or three pesos more than they are paying in Mitla . . . because, aside from the fact that I want them to work, I also don't want them to change employers or to be motivated to move to another employer."

Three examples illustrate the strategy of rationalizing or diversifying commodity production (or other income-earning activities). The first is from the *metate* industry where the direct producers have found that it pays them to sell their products in unfinished or semifinished form. In recent years, several intermediaries, who buy unfinished or semifinished products and perform the finishing themselves, have entered the *metate* market. The second example is from the treadle loom weaving industry where the shop operators experiment with new designs or, at times, with new styles of clothing. The third is from the brick industry where one brickyard operator, who is also a trucker, decided to reduce his own production of bricks until the market improved, and in the interim resell and/or haul bricks from other brickyards. With the income he earned from these activities he was able to keep one employee at work making bricks, though he found it necessary to dismiss another.

Finally, marketing innovations and the reduction of production costs by employee layoffs, the sixth and eighth strategies, respectively, were both employed by informants in treadle loom weaving. Marketing innovations included traveling outside Oaxaca to resort areas like Cancún to attempt to sell products—a strategy that was less successful than product innovations. Employee layoffs have apparently been widespread in the Xaagá branch of this industry, even to the extent that several smaller enterprises have either failed or been temporarily shut down. The other side of the coin is that a few better-run, more highly capitalized enterprises have been able to expand operations as a result of these failures and shutdowns. By contrast, at least one village branch of the embroidery industry (i.e., San Isidro Zegache) has experienced layoffs, failures, or shutdowns without any compensatory expansion by a few enterprises. What is noteworthy is that putting-out operations among the surviving enterprises were eliminated and production was maintained strictly on a household labor basis.

In short, these examples sustain the survivability thesis regarding rural petty industrial enterprises in times of inflationary crisis; however, they also show that survival by specific enterprises in particular branches of production is not guaranteed.

It seems appropriate in concluding this exploratory discussion of crisis impact to propose four likely crisis-related effects for future study that were not touched upon in the 1985 exploratory study: (a) decline in government transfer payments through reductions in the availability of low-interest agricultural loans, reduction in price supports (precios de garantía) in the purchase and sale of basic consumer goods, and reduction or elimination of government subsidies in the sale of electricity or petroleum products; (b) alteration in market demand for the products of PAHs due to a general decline in consumer purchasing power; (c) absorption by rural areas of returning urban migrants or an increase or diminution in the rate of migration; and (d) possible alteration in PAHs dependency on external private sources of cash (including wage labor), credit, means of production or wage goods (e.g., moneylenders, merchants), and the overall impact of the inflationary crisis on indebtedness.

Not only can future research be expected to uncover additional strategies employed by rural household enterprises to defend themselves against increases in the costs of commodities and services they must acquire in the market from capitalists (or from other PAHs) but it must also be directed at other possible direct and indirect effects of inflation or other crisis-related processes upon rural households/enterprises (cf. Binford 1989).

Clearly rural Oaxaca is by no means immune to the general trend throughout rural Mexico toward less exclusive dependency on tilling the soil and increased diversification of household income-earning activities to include petty commerce and manufacturing and various kinds of wage labor employment, which may involve migration (cf. Grindle 1987: 19). The typical rural Oaxaca Valley household is quite diversified in this sense, and such diversification—which is by no means new or unprecedented—is certainly structural rather than conjunctural in nature; it is there to stay. One implication of this diversified household economic structure, which involves households in commodity relations and transactions beyond the confines of localities, is to definitively shatter the straitjacket of "peasant economy," which has been so widely and persistently fitted to them by researchers.

Petty Production, Politics, and the Crisis

Petty Producers, Commodity Production, and Politics

Before considering the impact of the crisis on political attitudes, it is appropriate to consider some fundamental aspects of the politics of petty producers within capitalism. All petty commodity producers are proprietors of or control means of production, and in capitalist societies this inclines them politically toward support of the hegemonic ideology that worships at the altar of private property and private enterprise. Defense of this property, or frustrated aspirations to acquire more, however, may conjuncturally enhance the appeal of anticapitalist political discourse or, at the very least, encourage the formation of organizations and alliances with reformist and populist, if not anticapitalist, forces. The material interests of petty commodity producers must be contested daily against those of other petty (and often capitalist) competitors and are squeezed by various transactions and commitments (ranging from acquisition of wage goods and raw materials or producers' goods to the payment of fees or taxes to the government). As a consequence, the political tendencies of petty commodity producers are very much linked to their material circumstances and to the material results of their economic performance. As Wolf (1969: 292) points out, many peasant (and, by extension, artisan) struggles are attempts to "reverse the action" of capitalism. We would add, however, that they are equally likely to be attempts to support or extend capitalist development.

This political ambivalence of petty producers within capitalism reflects the contradictions of their class location as worker-owners.

They are employers of their own labor as well as of unpaid household labor and, perhaps, of hired labor in addition to or in lieu of unpaid household labor. As employers and enterprise operators they may be successful or unsuccessful in meeting the requirements of simple reproduction with or without capital accumulation. If successful, their politics are much more likely to be subdued or follow lines of compatibility with hegemonic capitalist politics; if not, they may well have one foot in the semiproletariat and be on a possible trajectory to full proletarianization, which will not only activate them politically but also may incline their politics in counterhegemonic directions.

In pre-1982 Mexico, peasant political movements occurred most often among land-poor households with limited access to credit and technical assistance. Their demands included land, higher rural minimum wages, social insurance, medical benefits, and subsidized prices for food staples (Paré 1985; Carr 1986; Prieto 1986; Grindle 1987: 2). This dovetails with the situation in Central America, where many political activists are partially involved in wage labor or are becoming fully involved. Most combatants in both the Salvadorean (FMLN) and Guatemalan (URNG) revolutionary movements are either semiproletarianized peasants or relatively new members of the rural proletariat, created by the expansion of capitalist agriculture in the highlands and the coastal plains—the latter opened to cattle raising and cotton production by road construction and increased use of pesticides. Rural migration in search of supplementary income opened up communities and increased contacts among rural direct producers who, although participating in wage labor, retained some access to land. Concomitantly, during the 1960s and early 1970s, producer cooperatives and peasant unions grew rapidly (Handy 1984; Williams 1985; Pearce 1986). Repression of these organizations contributed to the subsequent emergence of politico-military movements.[7]

This is not to claim that the subjection of petty commodity producers to exploitation by capital inevitably leads to their politicization, much less to revolution, or that those not subjected to such exploitation are necessarily politically quiescent. Social relations of production, so readily distilled into classes by the social scientist, are lived concretely, often ambiguously, through complex vertical and horizontal ties of kinship, patronage, and dependency and encompassed by discourses that develop around such factors as locality, kinship, and ethnicity along with class. Their distillation in the consciousness of petty producers, in a form that promotes political action of whatever stripe, cannot be guaranteed. This is what

Marx presumably had in mind when he characterized the peasantry, because of its ambiguous location in the class structure and its contradictory relations with other classes (or class fractions), as potentially either revolutionary or conservative, with its actual posture depending on the presence or absence of connections that could promote a "feeling of community, national links, or a political organization" (quoted in Roseberry 1982: 116).

Such connections tend to be enhanced to the degree that others, tying the producer to particular sites and patrons, are dissolved from above, broken from below, or become sites of a more-or-less public struggle over the distribution of resources. As many field investigators know, and as Scott (1985) has recently highlighted, antagonistic relations between poor and rich peasants, rent payers and rent receivers, wage earners and wage payers, petty commodity producers and merchants, interest payers and money lenders, and so on—all of which belie notions of village homogeneity and reciprocity-based solidarity or communalism and are natural loci for class struggle— are rife among rural populations in Third World capitalism. The ubiquitousness of such relations, combined with the relatively few cases in which they give rise to full-blown and overt class struggle, implies that they remain, for the most part, local in scope, piecemeal in character, and moderate in intensity ("small arms in the class war," to borrow Scott's Gramscian phraseology).

A host of social ties and cultural practices or understandings— often the precipitates of historically deep communal and regional traditions—operate to diffuse tendencies toward the distillation of economic interest into class consciousness. Among these are institutions of kinship and fictive kinship, ethnicity, reciprocity, paternalism, and religiously motivated, ritualized redistribution that operate simultaneously to mitigate the impact of economic inequality and to counterbalance economic differentiation. Equally important, however, is the impact of ideas about economic relations and conduct associated with privatized commodity economy. Concepts of private property, monetary remuneration for hard work and enterprise, capital accumulation, material progress, labor time, and so on serve to justify, legitimize, and, therefore, mask the multiple forms of exploitation of labor by capital. These concepts, which are part and parcel of petty commodity economy, meld into the hegemonic ideology of capitalism and reinforce the orthodox neoclassical view of income distribution (i.e., that capital and labor are cooperating factors in production that are justly rewarded according to their respective contributions—see Cook 1984a: 113–114).

We should add to the factors discussed above the social separation of petty enterprises and the accompanying ideologies of independence and control. Because all petty commodity producers have, at least, a modicum of control over processes of production and/or commercialization, the belief that hard work and enterprise are the keys to material progress and upward mobility is strongly adhered to. In branches of production where capitalist development is underway, the small percentage of enterprises that have crossed the capitalist threshold serve as examples of business success and, thus, reinforce the aforementioned petty bourgeois credo. This "demonstration effect" has been documented in the cases of embroidery, treadle loom weaving, and brickmaking—and illustrates the ideological compatibility of petty commodity and capitalist forms of industry.

Self-organization by producers, where it occurs, is apt to be in reaction to price gouging by suppliers of raw materials or to unjust tax policies or other abuses by governments. In Oaxaca, active public protests have been carried out by producer organizations of urban bakers, periurban brick producers, and rural mescal distillers. In the first case, the protest was against mercantile monopolies in the distribution of yeast, sugar, and flour (Cook 1982: 371); in the second, the focus of protest has been government taxation and labor relations policies, which were perceived by the producers to be unfair (Cook 1984a); and, in the third, the protest was directed against abuses by revenue agents in the collection of the liquor tax (Díaz Móntes 1979: 119–126; Cook 1982: 367). Only in the case of the urban bakery operators, however, is there a single, permanent industry-wide organization.[8] In the case of the mescal industry, several competing organizations claim to represent the interests of distillers (Díaz Móntes 1979: 153; Nieman and Miller 1987: 28–29), and in the brick industry, the producers have never formed a formal, permanent organization but rather organize themselves periodically on an informal, ad hoc basis (Cook 1984a: 173–186). In neither of the last two cases are matters internal to the industry, such as raw material and product prices, and wages, addressed at the level of the producers' organization; rather, these are handled strictly at the level of the discrete production unit.

The piece-wage system is often an overlooked nexus between petty forms of industrial commodity production that employ only household labor and those that regularly employ wage labor. Under both of these petty production forms, labor is structurally inclined toward self-exploitation and the individual worker is encouraged to believe that he or she is the master of his or her own economic destiny and will earn in direct proportion to what he or she produces

(Cook 1984a: 124; cf. 199). This, at least, partly explains why piece-workers in petty industries in Oaxaca fail to organize for collective bargaining over piece rates with their employers, and why antiunion sentiments exist among industrial outworkers and contract workers in such diverse settings as Mexico City and Cali, Colombia (Birk-beck 1979; Roldán 1985).

Some evidence suggests that, since the onset of the 1982 crisis in Mexico, political mobilization among rural direct producers has emerged, not over access to land or their status as producers, "but over issues that affect them as consumers, wage earners, and citi-zens"—a tendency that seems to be linked to the diversified commodity economy involvement of their households (Grindle 1987: 3). This tendency can be inferred, for example, from the participation of *campesino* groups in "popular fronts" since 1982 and, in particular, from the National Front in Defense of Wages and against Austerity (FNDSCAC), which "demanded protection for wages and employment, improved standards of living, democratic freedoms, an end to repression, and the resolution of *campesino* demands" (Prieto 1986: 89). Nevertheless, the latter demands included land distribution and regularization of tenure and titles, which are, of course, issues of traditional concern to *campesinos*. Rather than shifting their focus away from land-related issues, peasant movements are showing signs of pursuing more sophisticated agendas dealing with making the land more productive (Prieto 1986: 87; Fox 1987: 16). It is probably premature to pronounce a trend away from land- or production-centered agendas in *campesino* movements, just as it is premature to downplay the continuing importance of land-based household strategies among Mexico's rural direct producers, regardless of the diversification of their income-earning activities or increasing vulnerability to wage goods inflation as government subsidies to rural consumers are reduced (cf. Fox 1987).

Attitudes Toward the Crisis Programs of the PRI-Government and the Opposition Parties

In order to clarify to what extent the tendency to blame the government for the crisis affected political attitudes of the informants interviewed in 1985, a question was asked that evoked a comparison between the three major parties—PRI, PAN, PSUM—with regard to the informant's estimate of a particular party's capacity to resolve the crisis. On the one hand, the answers were not surprising: the informants were divided between those who expressed a realistic, if unenthusiastic, acceptance of the hegemony of PRI (and who considered that it had over the years partially fulfilled promises made to help their villages), and those who expressed either cynicism or indifference with regard to all the parties, lumping them together in a category of "promising a lot prior to elections but not following through on promises afterward."

Several informants in both groups also expressed fears about the possibility of conflict or division in their villages if the opposition parties began to actively recruit members, or they expressed the opinion that perhaps a change in the government party would make conditions worse. The following response was typical:

> With regard to that party stuff, I don't vote. I was a political officeholder here. I realize that they make promises, they tell you that they are going to do something and they sit down and expect you to make an arrangement—well if you bribe them they'll do something, if you don't the whole thing dies right there. What we've dealt with most here is the PRI. We're totally for the PRI. People don't bother to vote. There are difficult problems at times because one is for the PRI, another is for PAN. That's where trouble begins among themselves. One must be independent. Not long ago some PAN representatives showed up with a deal if we would join them. We don't want divisions in our village. When people get involved in parties . . . then come the problems.

On the other hand, it was surprising—in view of the fact that, nationwide, the economic crisis has apparently intensified the opposition to PRI from the left and the right—that many informants in more than half of the villages where interviews were conducted said that they were unfamiliar with the programs of the opposition parties, especially of the PSUM. Nevertheless, our impression is that the idea of a government not controlled by the PRI is definitely present in the social consciousness of many Oaxaca Valley villagers, and it is plausible to assume that, if the crisis worsens, this subversive idea will spread.

By contrast, the responses to another question that was asked, namely, "Do you think that there is more wealth or more poverty in the village today in comparison with previous years?," indicate that, with the exception of 1985, things were not so bad. Perhaps this judgment explains why there were so many contradictions and ambiguities in informant attitudes toward the opposition parties and toward the PRI-government itself. More than 60 percent (versus 40 percent who felt things were the same or worse) said that there was more wealth (despite the post-1982 crisis) and, in general, a higher standard of living in recent years than in previous years. In other words, the majority believe that there has been long-run progress and—even though they tended to attribute this to popular effort or to the initiative and work of each household—they implicitly recognized that, to some extent, this progress reflected the success of the policies of PRI.

Petty Producers and the Changing Political Landscape in Mexico

To a degree, the government is able to use short-term or piecemeal concessions to mitigate the worst effects of the economic crisis. More difficult to respond to is the growing consensus that politics, in general, and economic policy making, in particular, must be democratized. As the candidate for the major leftist opposition party, the Partido Mexicano Socialista, said during the 1988 presidential campaign (Castillo 1988): "The key problem for us is 'who decides, when, and how.' There are economic measures that are positive when taken on time but when applied at the wrong time only aggravate the crisis. But all measures ought to be taken with the consensus of the population, with the direct participation of the workers, the peasants, and the small and medium business people."

What remains an open question, however, is the degree to which petty producers will pursue their desire for change by supporting the opposition to the government party and, if they do, whether that support will be given to the left or to the right opposition.

If the case of the community supply councils is a pacesetter for future trends, there would appear to be some hope for local-level participatory democratization of central government policy making and improvement in its role in meeting the needs of those sectors of the rural population most vulnerable to inflation. Beginning in 1982, the central government—through its National Basic Foods Company (CONASUPO, or Compañía Nacional de Subsistencias Populares) and DICONSA, CONASUPO's retail subsidiary—organized a program of distribution of basic foodstuffs (e.g., corn, beans, cooking oil, salt, sugar) to rural communities. Rural supply committees and community supply councils were established as a combined result of a social promotion program undertaken by CONASUPO and autonomous grassroots initiatives by nonpartisan community activists (Fox 1987: 9–10) as a means for assuring that regional CONASUPO warehouses adequately supplied their village retail outlets, a process that was easily subverted by the operation of various local and regional special interests through the gigantic CONASUPO bureaucracy. By 1985, the Oaxaca Supply Council Coordinating Network claimed to represent 856 communities with over 1.4 million low-income rural consumers (Fox 1987: 16). This network functioned in the interest of peasants as both consumers and producers and by late 1986 had spun off several autonomous regional producers' organizations (ibid.)—a trend that bodes well for populist reform movements that seek to work within the PRI governmental structure.

If recent state-level election results are to be taken as indicative of future trends, the outlook for the opposition, whether of the left or right, is not especially heartening, since the drop in popular support for the government party does not directly translate into support for opposition parties (Martínez Assad 1987: 41–42). The results of Oaxaca municipal elections of November 1983 reflect not only the continuing dominance of PRI but also, despite several antidemocratic abuses and conditions operating on its behalf, a relative consensus favoring it (Martínez and Arellanes 1985: 227). Only two *municipios* included in Cook's 1979–1980 household survey with significant populations of petty industrialists have been involved in anti-PRI currents to the extent that municipal elections have recently been won by an opposition party. These two *municipios*, however, are among only 93 (out of 570) in which opposition parties were on the ballots and among only 11 in which opposition parties won (225–226).

As it turns out, both of these *municipios* are located in the Ocotlán district: Magdalena has many households involved in *metate* making and/or embroidery and San Antonino del Castillo is a major embroidery center. It appears that the political trajectory of San Antonino, which went to the right with the Partido de Acción Nacional, is probably more diagnostic of future trends among rural industrialists in the Valley than is that of Magdalena, which went to the left with the Partido Socialista Unificado de México but which has a history of agrarian struggle and leftist partisanship linked to its establishment as an ejido in the early 1920s by the Obregón regime (Cook 1984b: 74).

On the other hand, regarding San Antonino, a plausible case can be made for a direct linkage between the relatively successful economic performance of its two major industries, embroidery and truck gardening, which have produced a significant petty bourgeoisie, and the growth of a support base for the right-wing PAN. A similar linkage, though not yet resulting in a takeover of the municipal government, also exists in Santa Lucía del Camino between certain segments of the brick industry bourgeoisie and support for PAN. While it seems reasonable to argue that industries with pieceworking proletariats, such as brickmaking, embroidery, basketry, and treadle loom weaving, could provide a fertile recruiting ground for the socialist opposition, up to this point there is no evidence that this has been the case (Cook 1984b: 74–75).

A dynamic operating within each of these industries diffuses and dampens class consciousness. Pieceworkers do have varying degrees of awareness of exploitation but are inclined to view their employers as constrained by competition or capricious demand with regard to their ability to grant wage increases; they also tend to consider profits as a legitimate reward for proprietorship or entrepreneurship. They do, nevertheless, seek wage increases but also develop strategies for achieving independence and, if possible, employer or merchant (buyer-up/putter-out) status themselves. Most of them have seen this transition realized by household enterprises in their own and in other communities, and they—however unrealistically—aspire to experience it personally. In other words, they seem likely to support political programs that they perceive to be most compatible with their goals for achieving material progress through hard work and enterprise.

Postscript

In these last few pages, we would like to sum up what we think are the major points of this study. It is our hope that this will clarify our contribution to setting the agenda for future research designed to extend and deepen the understanding of petty commodity production in Third World countries like Mexico. The dynamics of petty industrial production among countryfolk in the Oaxaca Valley revolve around small-scale household enterprises using technologies energized primarily by human labor power and relying heavily on unwaged household workers. Appearances to the contrary, and against the grain of neopopulist thought, some of these enterprises in particular branches of production accumulate capital, enlarge their stock of instruments of labor and raw materials, and even hire additional nonhousehold workers in order to expand output. When enterprises take the latter step, it is our contention that they are functioning in a partially capitalist fashion even if they are operated by worker-owners and employ unwaged household workers in addition to wage workers. Evidence from the weaving/garment industry and the brick industry in the Oaxaca Valley shows that some enterprises, which initiate development along a capitalist trajectory, complete the transition from petty commodity production to petty capitalist production. The precise point at which this transition occurs is certainly subject to debate, but we have defined it as the point at which more than half of the value of enterprise output is created by wage laborers.

We have also argued that development of petty capitalism out of petty commodity production is potentially reversible at the levels of enterprise, industry, and branch of production. Such reverses are likely to occur with greater frequency among individual enterprises since it is at this level that competition is most severe and economic performance is most directly influenced by social and cultural variables. This is not to deny that industry and branch structures are subject to change regarding the conditions that nurture or subvert petty enterprise. After all, within a capitalist social formation, dependent, endogenous petty capitalist development occurs through relations of production and exchange that in all likelihood are dominated by larger enterprises with substantial concentrations of capital. In such a framework it is logical to assume that the operating space for petty enterprises of all types is ultimately contingent upon the performance and interests of large enterprises—with the proviso that the latter's influence and interests vary from one branch and industry to another.

This monograph has also mustered considerable support for the thesis that simple material reproduction without capital accumulation is a condition imposed upon Oaxaca Valley petty producers by the wider process of uneven capitalist development. We have also presented evidence, however, that this is not a condition that embodies their expectations, their goals, or their aspirations. On the contrary, independent peasant-artisan producers tend to measure their own economic performance against those enterprises in their industry that appear to enjoy the most business success, that is, enterprises that have embarked upon a trajectory involving capital accumulation and expanded productivity. This tendency is rooted neither in naïveté regarding the vicissitudes of petty commodity production in a capitalist market economy nor in blind faith in a hegemonic free enterprise ideology according to which everyone can achieve upward mobility and material gain through hard work and shrewd calculation. Notwithstanding the fact that such naïveté and blind faith are present to some degree in Oaxaca today, the tendency to emulate successful enterprises is rooted in daily experience in a commodity economy that, by its very nature, generates differential economic performance and unequal distribution of material rewards.

While we believe in its general applicability, this thesis is far too abstract to represent a satisfying conclusion. Our intention from the outset has been to avoid unduly sacrificing cogency of explanation and concern with issues of global political economy and theory to analytical precision and empirical detail. The arguments presented in the foregoing paragraph, therefore, cannot be allowed to stand without some additional elaboration. It is correct that simple material reproduction is "imposed" upon petty commodity-producing units by the dominant forces of modern capitalism but more needs to be said about how these forces operate unevenly.

First, in some industries, the development of petty capitalism itself tends to create obstacles blocking further transition from petty commodity production to capitalism. For example, the brick industry has a finite material base. The more land that is controlled by capitalist brickyard operators the less that is available for noncapitalist producers; moreover, the costs of entering the industry rise as the land is eaten away to extract clay for bricks.

Second, simple material reproduction is not so much *imposed* in some industries (e.g., palm weaving) as it is a consequence of low productivity and the maintenance of control by producers over raw material supply. Social differentiation in the palm-plaiting villages is unaccompanied by endogenous capitalist development due to low entry costs, competitive markets, *and* the articulation of palm weaving with agriculture, which drives down the price of palm products (further reduced because they are produced by undervalued female labor power) to a point that makes capital accumulation almost impossible. Also, in San Lorenzo Albarradas the stands of palm are located on ejidal lands and harvest rights to them are allocated more or less equitably to each household. Thus, unlike weaving or brickmaking, the principal raw material is equally available to all would-be producers in the industry's main village.

Third, progressing beyond petty commodity production is precluded for most direct producers by the appropriative role of intermediary capital. Even though such industries as embroidery are essentially organized by capitalist relations of production, with most of the embroiderers being piece-rate outworkers, we still have to address the reasons why its enterprises are apparently limited to a putting-out level of development and why functional specialization by production units in the countryside does not result in the development of rural workshops and manufactories (see Cooper 1980). One reason would be the downward pressure on piece rates associated with the integration of embroidery and agriculture (i.e., embroidery as a supplement to the consumption fund) or embroidery and housework. Another would be the specific product, a handmade product that competes in a luxury market with other such products and by the very nature of its market situation *cannot* be subjected (at least in the embroidery stage) to mechanization.

Petty intermediaries, therefore, must be content to appropriate small amounts of surplus from large numbers of people. Capital accumulated in petty mercantile enterprises can be productively invested in branches, such as embroidery, only if the market expands. Otherwise, it must be spent to raise the household's level of material reproduction above the community norm or invested elsewhere (e.g., store, purchases of a truck). Of course, if petty capitalists in garment industries like embroidery and treadle loom weaving (cotton products branch) were to seek product diversification and target consumers outside the tourist or handicraft market, they would then enter the very competitive arena of the ready-made clothing industry dominated by highly capitalized and experienced urban firms.

In provincial areas of Mexico like the rural Oaxaca Valley, village-dwelling peasant-artisans are often portrayed as subjects in their own economy or mode of production. This reified "peasant economy" is endowed with an identity separate from the capitalist economy yet subsumed by it. As the analysis in Chapter 7 made clear, however, the impact of the post-1982 inflationary crisis underlines the fact that there is only one Mexican economy that is both commodity producing and dominated by capital, despite its variegated, regionalized nature. Confronted with data collected from Oaxaca Valley peasant-artisan households coping with the crisis conditions of the 1980s, the paradoxical notion of a separate but subsumed peasant economy or petty commodity mode of production dissolves.

What emerges in its place is the notion of a single, complex, regionally and locally segmented commodity economy encompassing a variety of production units in various socioeconomic circumstances, including those of household producers for own consumption, of petty commodity producers, of petty capitalists, and of wage laborers typically paid by piece rate. It is obvious that all these subjects act within the same economy and that there are differences in their modes of involvement in that economy, as well as in the material results of their participation. Nevertheless, there is little empirical basis for interpreting such differences as evidence for an "economy within an economy."

It is our belief that a failure to understand petty producers as subjects in a unitarian commodity economy will perpetuate the legacy of (a) misconceived policy proposals intended to promote their role or improve the terms of their participation in national development and (b) abortive political projects intended to encourage their direct participation or address their interests and concerns.

Technocratic interventions in rural development programs are customarily undertaken without regard for preexisting regional and local social differentiation. Consequently, infusions of capital, credit, and technology tend to reinforce or exacerbate socioeconomic inequality; the largest and wealthiest production units are further enlarged and enriched while formerly self-employed small- to medium-sized producers become further entrenched in the ranks of the rural proletariat. The technocrats become confused, angered, and baffled when evidence is presented showing that the living standards of most of the client population are not improving as planned. And the clients themselves are provided with yet another pretext for viewing that government as ineffective in eliminating the sources of their impoverishment, if not directly responsible for it.

These critical statements should not be construed as an indictment of all rural development initiatives or to suggest that the countryfolk of the Third World are better left to their own devices. As the case of the palm/ixtle villages suggests, there is no particular merit in participation in a low-productivity, low-income-generating rural industry. As one of our informants stated, "If there was other work here, even to earn five pesos a day, we would stop plaiting and do it." Equally important is the fact that with or without the intervention of the State, international development agencies, such as the World Bank, and private voluntary organizations, socioeconomic inequality will continue to worsen as a natural fallout from population growth in a capitalist-dominated commodity economy. The challenge, it seems to us, for those concerned with the fates of countryfolk in the Third World, is to develop strategies and programs that simultaneously raise the productivity of rural agriculture and rural industry (through cost-effective, appropriate technological inputs), retain most of the enhanced fund of surplus value in the countryside, and distribute its fruits equitably among the direct producers themselves. We are not optimistic about the possibility of such projects on more than a small scale since, particularly under current conditions, they appear to run counter to capitalist interests.

At least in Mexico, rural development on a more egalitarian basis is not likely to occur unless a fundamental shift in State development policy takes place. The incumbent president, Carlos Salinas de Gortari, orchestrated the austerity policies of the previous de la Madrid regime and is committed to continuing a strategy of privatizing parastate enterprises and further loosening the restrictions on foreign investment. In the Salinas administration, rural development means further promotion of agrarian capitalism and perhaps capitalist industrialization through the ruralization of some *maquiladoras* and the relocation/decentralization of industry from the northern triad of Mexico City, Monterrey, and Guadalajara. This will take place at the cost of more belt tightening among the middle-class and working-class majority to meet the demands for austerity imposed by the IMF and Mexico's other international creditors.

It is on the basis of such policies that the left and right oppositions have been able to mount important challenges to the PRI in recent years. Rural inhabitants are destined to be subjected to an increasing barrage of rhetoric urging them to affiliate with one side or the other. From our perspective, petty producers are vulnerable to different political discourses; as both proprietors and workers they are ideologically susceptible to either capitalist-class or working-class agendas. The Oaxaca Valley, however, has a variegated socioeconomic and political terrain, as is illustrated by the development of petty merchant and petty industrial capital that has generated an overt and a covert proletariat and semiproletariat. Many of these workers exhibit views that, in an embryonic way, reflect their class location even if they also believe in the sanctity of private property (associated with access to land and the capacity to produce directly for own consumption). For many of these rural inhabitants, demands for more and better land continue to be important because direct agricultural production provides the most secure hedge against inflation and crisis in the commodity economy; such demands have to be taken seriously by any political party that seeks their support.

Despite its importance, agriculture generated a smaller proportion (33 percent) of the total income of peasant-artisans than did craft production (56 percent), making the latter equally critical. In other parts of the Oaxaca Valley and in other areas of rural Mexico it is wage labor that supplements agriculture or, perhaps better stated, it is agriculture that supplements wage labor (cf. Grindle 1987, 1988). In short, rural petty producers have a plethora of economic interests that impact upon their political views. Opposition to the PRI will have to address issues of wages, employment, and the market as well as those pertaining to land, credit, and support prices. They will have to do so in relation not only to large-scale capital-intensive industry but also to small-scale labor-intensive industry, which is widespread in rural areas and helps alleviate unemployment and underemployment, albeit with jobs that are often part-time and low paying.

Perhaps the only issue that unites the differentiated rural population is an ambivalent and contradictory relationship with *la ciudad*, and this too is probably changing as rural poverty enforces higher rates of rural-urban migration. Political projects designed to appeal singularly to *los campesinos* are likely to fail. Today, *los campesinos*, in addition to an involvement in agriculture, often have dual involvements as wage workers and craft producers; some of them accumulate capital through endofamilial accumulation and others have already become petty capitalists, even if further growth is precluded by their position at the bottom of a hierarchy of different-sized capitals. Political mobilization in rural Mexico must take account of class and economic pluralism; it must devise programs to attract the support of a majority of direct producers through an appeal to their multiple needs for land, credit, jobs, health insurance, and, most important, equitable remuneration for their labor and greater rewards for their enterprise.

Appendix. Review of the Oaxaca Valley Small Industries Project

The primary machine-readable data set for the project was derived from a survey of 952 households in twenty villages located in the districts of Ocotlán, Tlacolula, and Centro. The data were collected directly by project staff through the use of pretested census forms/ interview schedules and cover economic, social, and cultural aspects of production and exchange in the selected localities. The content of the questionnaire is described in greater detail below.

Apart from information from the twenty-village sample, the project's data base also includes data coded from a 1977 pilot survey in Tlacolula de Matamoros and from a special survey of artisans in Ocotlán de Morelos, Mitla, and Oaxaca City conducted in 1978–1979. Each of these surveys used a version of the questionnaire employed in the twenty-village survey. All told, then, the project data base contains information for 1,008 household production units in twenty-four localities.

A separate interview schedule, designed to focus on intermediaries as well as sales shops (with or without direct involvement in production), was also administered to a sample of 69 informants in Oaxaca City and to a sample of 31 merchant-embroiderers in various localities in the district of Ocotlán. This information was coded separately and was processed as a separate machine-readable data set. This component of the project is described in greater detail in items 2 and 3 below.

Let us say a few words about the rationale and the comparative analytical possibilities of the household survey component of the project. The survey-generated data make possible comparative analyses between several localities within a particular branch of production (e.g., weaving and brickmaking) based in one or more localities. It was decided early in the project to concentrate on the districts of Ocotlán, Tlacolula, and Centro (Oaxaca City and a series of rural satellite communities including Santa Lucía del Camino) because these are the districts that have the highest incidence of craft production in the "Central Valleys" region (see Cook 1978 and Chapter 2 above).

While some important rural industries were not included in the survey (e.g., pottery), most of them were; and the data collected for local branches of these industries are, in most cases, representative of the entire regional industry. This is especially true where the project surveyed leading or other important localities in a particular regional industry, as was the case with backstrap loom weaving (Santo Tomás Jalieza and three other localities), treadle loom weaving (Teotitlán del Valle and three other localities), embroidery (San Juan Chilateca and nine other communities), palm plaiting (San Lorenzo Albarradas and Santo Domingo Albarradas), and brickmaking (Santa Lucía del Camino).

No localities were surveyed that did not have households participating in a regional craft industry. However, the survey covered a random sample of households in each locality and, as it turned out, about one-quarter of these were not involved in craft production. While these households may not be statistically representative of noncraft households in districts or localities not covered by the project, we think that something can be learned about them by making a separate analysis of these data. Moreover, a comparative analysis of the noncraft and the craft-producing households in the localities surveyed should make an important contribution to our knowledge about the regional division of labor (without assuming that the localities surveyed comprise a microcosm of the regional population).

The survey instrument was administered to a random sample of the total population of household heads in each community. The procedure for drawing a sample of household heads for survey purposes was uniform: a table of random numbers was employed to select the first household to be interviewed on each complete list of households (compiled from lists supplied by community officials), and then other households were chosen in accordance with the predetermined interval. Uncooperative or "not-at-home" households were replaced by selecting the next name on the master list. The percentage of households surveyed varied. During the early weeks of the survey a 50 percent sample was surveyed but, subsequently, this percentage was reduced; in several large communities a 10 percent sample was judged to be adequate. The following general guidelines for determining the percentage of household heads to be included in the survey in any given community were adhered to:

Number of Households in Community	Sampling Interval
150 and below	33% (every third case)
151–300	20% (every fifth case)
301 and above	10% (every tenth case)

Table A lists by community the total number of household heads, the number of household heads sampled, the percentage of household heads sampled, and the starting and completion dates of the survey.

As a perusal of the remaining parts of this Appendix shows, the household survey represents only one component of the primary data corpus. In the qualitative sense, the most important data were collected through a combination of observation, structured and unstructured interviewing, and archival work. Unfortunately, it was not possible to collect these kinds of data in every community surveyed but we were able to do so for each major industry. Those industries in which the best integration of various kinds of primary data was achieved are the brick industry, the treadle loom weaving industry, and the palm weaving industry. A less complete yet adequate integration was achieved in the wooden utensils industry, the backstrap loom weaving industry, and the embroidery industry.

The main data-gathering instrument in the twenty-village household survey was a pretested, structured census form, which was organized into the following sections: resident members of the household (name, relation, sex, age, birthplace, civil status, languages, schooling); socioeconomic data on resident household members (occupation, position in occupation, type of work, time dedicated to occupation, form of payment, income); housing (8 questions); family budget (5 questions); agricultural data (6 questions); instruments of labor (7 questions); animal raising (7 questions); relations of production in agriculture (7 questions); nonagricultural commodity production (both principal and secondary occupations—50 questions on details of means of production, labor process, circulation of products, relations of production and exchange).

In addition to the data collected by administering the household census form, which was subsequently coded into more than 250 variables for computer processing, the project data base consists of the following components:

1. Transcribed texts of tape-recorded, structured interviews with 160 craft producers (74 men, 82 women) from eight different villages

Table A. Oaxaca Small Industries Project Village Survey Data

Locality and District	No. of Household Heads	No. of Household Heads Sampled	% of Household in Sample	Dates of Survey
Ocotlán				
Santo Tomás Jalieza	100	54	50	10/18/78–11/15/78
Santa Cecilia Jalieza	57	34	50	10/27/78–11/25/78
Santo Domingo Jalieza	140	69	50	11/27/78–12/5/78
San Pedro Guegorexe	75	42	56	12/12/78–12/20/78
San Juan Chilateca	200	40	20	1/23/79–2/4/79
San Isidro Zegache	55	24	40	3/6/79–3/11/79
Magdalena Ocotlán	168	37	22	2/20/79–3/1/79
San Dionisio Ocotlán	118	27	23	2/28/79–3/3/79
San Pedro Mártir	392	38	10	3/15/79–3/24/79
San Baltazar Chichicapán	640	64	10	4/2/79–4/16/79
Santa Lucía Ocotlán	179	51	28	8/23/79–8/30/79
San Jacinto Chilateca	107	35	33	8/6/79–8/14/79

Tlacolula				
Santa Ana del Valle	390	42	10	1/26/79–4/20/79
Teotitlán del Valle	797	79	10	5/7/79–5/31/79
Díaz Ordaz	664	68	10	5/27/79–6/8/79
San Miguel[a] del Valle	—	25	—	6/11/79–6/22/79
Xaagá[b]	189	55	28	10/3/79–11/7/79
San Lorenzo Albarradas	387	74	20	1/30/80–3/30/80
Santo Domingo Albarradas	170	38	23	4/29/80–5/6/80
Centro				
Santa Lucía del Camino[c]	370	56	15	2/26/80–10/21/80

[a] In San Miguel, because we were unable to obtain a list of household heads, the survey simply proceeded by locating households with weavers. Only weaving households were surveyed; it was impossible to estimate what percentage they represented of the total number of households in the village or of the total number of weaving households.

[b] The household survey was conducted in two phases. Phase 1 was begun on October 3 and completed on October 17; a random sample of 38 households were surveyed representing 20 percent of the total of 189 households. It was decided to expand the survey to include a higher percentage of weavers so 16 additional weaving households were surveyed by November 7, bringing the total number of households surveyed to 54.

[c] This survey presented the most difficult problems in determining the universe from which a random sample could be drawn. A two-phase survey was also conducted here. The first phase proceeded according to a 10 percent random sample of 370 households on a composite list and resulted in 32 completed forms. The second phase entailed a survey of households in the brickyards, together with surveying several brick industry households that did not reside in the brickyards; it yielded 24 completed forms (see Cook 1984a: 211–212).

and towns in three districts (Ocotlán, Tlacolula, and Centro) and representing the following occupations: backstrap loom weaving, treadle loom weaving, embroidery, wood carving, palm weaving, broom making, rope making, brickmaking, mescal distilling, basket making, fireworks making, sandal making, blacksmithing, and carpentry. The basic format for these tape-recorded interviews includes 48 questions (mostly open-ended) organized into seven sections as follows: occupational history and current occupational situation (14 questions); occupational ideology (8 questions); product valuation (2 questions); civil-religious hierarchy participation/attitudes (4 questions); economic ideology (12 questions); class consciousness (8 questions). In addition to this basic interview schedule (which includes several optional questions for respondents who were females and/or employees and/or self-employed producers), special versions were designed and used, taking into account industry-specific conditions, in interviews with mescal distillers, brickmakers, and brickmakers' wives.

2. A specially designed interview schedule was administered to 31 intermediaries in the embroidery industry in five localities in the district of Ocotlán as follows: San Antonino del Castillo (11), Ocotlán de Morelos (8), San Juan Chilateca (7), San Martín Tilcajete (4), and San Pedro Guegorexe (1). This schedule has a total of fifty questions distributed under the following headings: biographical data (15 questions); products sold (listed by place of origin and mode of acquisition); products bought (7 questions); products manufactured (4 questions); means of production (listed by type, quantity, where and when acquired, cost); employees (5 questions); sales (3 questions); wholesale operations (4 questions); retail operations (2 questions); capitalization and organization of business (5 questions); attitudes (4 questions).

3. The interview schedule described above was also administered to 69 craft business proprietors in Oaxaca City; 47 of these interviews were tape-recorded and have been transcribed. The respondents can be categorized by type and/or location of their business as follows: pottery workshops—6 interviews (4 recorded); weaving workshops or *mantelerías*—11 interviews (7 recorded); miscellaneous workshops—7 interviews (all recorded as follows: 2 tinsmiths, 1 leatherworker, 1 knife maker, 1 rope maker, 1 sandal maker, 1 shirt maker); stall keepers in the artisans' market—11 interviews; stall keepers in the main market (Central de Abastos)—7 interviews; stall keepers in the 20 de Noviembre market—14 interviews; store proprietors—21 interviews (all recorded).

4. Fifteen detailed household budget studies in four different vil-

lages (Santo Tomás Jalieza, San Pedro Guegorexe, Xaagá, and Santa Lucía del Camino), ranging from four to ten weeks each using a form requiring daily itemizing by the informant of income and expenditures together with tasks performed.

5. Observational studies, field notes, and preliminary field reports for each of the localities and industries surveyed. The field notes and observational studies are most important in the case of treadle loom weaving in Xaagá, palm harvesting and weaving in San Lorenzo Albarradas, ixtle fiber production in Santo Domingo Albarradas, and brickmaking in Santa Lucía.

Notes

1. Petty Production in Third World Capitalism Today

1. Throughout this monograph and for purposes of our Oaxaca research (data collection, coding, analysis), the term "household" is used interchangeably with "domestic group" to refer to those persons residing on a common residence lot who eat together and have a common budget; however, it also includes nonresident or absent members who regularly contribute cash remittances to the unit's income. The unit is assumed to have a dual nature: (a) as a kinship/demographic unit of society and (b) as a labor/enterprise unit of economy (see Galeski 1972). It is important to keep in mind the objective empirical variability of the household locally and regionally. This variability is evidenced not only in terms of size, composition, and stage in the life cycle but also in terms of the class location, occupational mix of its members, and differential impact of economic roles on household members according to age and gender. According to Redclift and Mingione (1985: 6): "Empirical studies of the household reveal a very wide range of different forms of an often contradictory nature. Patterns of incorporation in the wider economy are multiple, and the ideology of household unity may conceal a diverse set of internal interests" (cf. Harris 1984; Roldán 1985; Stolcke 1984).

In the Oaxaca Valley, some production and, perhaps, even more consumption occur at interhousehold and, in some cases, village-wide levels of organization. Much of this activity in production is linked to reciprocal labor arrangements between households (guelaguetzas) or to village labor drafts (tequíos) on communal fields or public works projects and in consumption is linked to the ceremonial/festive cycle, which includes celebrations of saints' cults festivals (mayordomías), wedding celebrations (fandangos), and celebrations related to certain offices (cargos) in the civil-religious hierarchy.

2. A good deal of documentation suggests that poverty is on the rise, not only in Third World countries like Mexico but also in First World countries like the United States (Kloby 1987). But this trend requires continuing empirical scrutiny. It must be kept in mind—as one of the most sophisticated recent analyses (Reyes Héroles 1983) of the Mexican economy demon-

strates—that the gap between the poorest and the middle social sectors has been increasing since the 1960s; therefore, the distributive effects of macroeconomic policies are not uniform but vary in impact according to labor market segment or population category (Bortz 1987). It is precisely according to such a formula that the periodic crises of capitalism are ameliorated.

3. See Mingione (1985: 15) who makes a similar point regarding southern Italy.

4. According to Portes (1983: 163), many types of informal sector employment in contemporary world capitalism help to "alleviate, from the point of view of firms, consequences of the proletarianization process." Despite the trenchant criticisms that have been leveled at the "formal" versus "informal" sector dichotomy for its obvious dualism, theoretical sterility, and lack of operationalizability (e.g., Bremen 1976; Moser 1978; Redclift and Mingione 1985; Connolly 1985) and, more particularly, against the "greatly reified" (Worsley 1984: 213) concept of "informal sector" (Bromley 1978), we continue to use the terms here essentially because of a pragmatic recognition of the fact that the distinction seems to have become permanently implanted in the literature—both in empirical studies and in policy-oriented work (Trager 1985: 260–263). Also, it cannot be denied that the distinction has generated theoretically provocative research and debate. The employment categories invariably labeled as informal are those characterized by less than minimum wages, part-time or self-employed work, unpaid household labor, and women's employment (Connolly 1985: 82). However, we agree with Connolly that "proving the existence of a subgroup of employment situations which show a reasonably high proportion of shared characteristics does not . . . overcome the theoretical muddle which inspired the selection of these characteristics" (74). We share her assessment of the informal sector concept as follows (86): "As far as the analysis of employment structures is concerned, very little is gained by grouping a whole series of economic activities under one conceptual category, and a great deal is lost. Undervaluation of wage labour is confused with small enterprise and noncommodity production or with illegal *modus vivendi;* the specific nature of gender exploitation is lost as women's work is associated with unskilled manual labor; any badly paid job is disguised as unemployment and, lastly, no distinction is admitted between brutal, alienating labour relations and potentially autonomous, creative forms of production."

5. Throughout this monograph we use the term "Oaxaca City" for expository convenience to refer to the capital and largest urban center of the state of Oaxaca which since 1877 has been officially known as "Oaxaca de Júarez." In colloquial Oaxaca Spanish, and paralleling the usage in Mexican parlance with regard to *la ciudad de México* (which is referred to simply as "México"), the city of Oaxaca (*la ciudad de Oaxaca*) is referred to as "Oaxaca" (as in *"Me voy a Oaxaca"* or "I'm going to Oaxaca"). Accordingly, just as *la ciudad de México* is customarily translated as "Mexico City" we have elected to translate *"la ciudad de Oaxaca"* as "Oaxaca City."

6. During their long precapitalist history, production for own use and for exchange were essential to the reproduction of labor. In this role it was inti-

mately related to the "production of people: not merely the bearing of children (which might be called biological reproduction) but also their care and socialization, and the maintenance of adult individuals through their lives, processes which create individuals to fit more or less into the social structure of society and so assure the continuation of that society in the next generation" (Mackintosh 1984: 11). Aside from the issue of the division of labor by gender and age, with all the implications this has for human social life, at least two other critical issues arise, in the broad context of world historical development, to complicate our understanding of the nature and role of petty production: (a) how the emergence of large-scale production—either privatized or statized—alters the labor-reproduction function of petty production and (b) how the increasing commoditization (and monetization) of economic life alters the mix between production for autoconsumption and commodity production at the interior of petty production (i.e., household) units.

7. We also assume that, in the development of the economy, commodity production appeared prior to petty commodity production and that the latter appeared prior to the capitalist form of commodity production. The appearance of petty commodity production is predicated upon a level of development of the productive forces adequate to sustain a separation of agriculture and industry and, thus, occupational specialization through the development of the social division of labor, which, in turn, developed hand in hand with market exchange. Mandel (1968: 66) dates petty commodity production from the sixth century B.C. in Greece, about the eighth century B.C. in the Islamic world, and the eleventh century A.D. in Western Europe, and he notes that "it reached its most characteristic development in the southern Netherlands and in Italy in the thirteenth to fifteenth centuries."

Contemporary scholars generally agree that petty commodity production "never has constituted the dominant or total production of a society but has always been articulated within another social formation, whether this be dominated by feudalism or capitalism" (Moser 1978: 1,057; cf. Gerry and Birkbeck 1981: 128–129; Long and Richardson 1978: 185; G. Smith 1985: 100).

8. According to Hart (1982: 39), the definition and study of petty commodity production "must be set firmly within an understanding of human social evolution as a totality." Although Hart assumes a global tendency toward the progressively wider role of privatized commodity production and market-driven economic behavior, this should not be construed to imply the inevitability of unilinear, unidirectional stepwise trajectories for specific social economies. It is compatible with an emphasis on the conjunctural, fluctuating, and cyclical nature of commodity production and market-driven economic behavior. From our perspective, then, any laws of motion that may operate in commodity economy across time and space are strictly tendential and contingent.

9. Of course, peasant-artisans may exchange products of their labor by other than money-mediated market mechanisms. To the extent that they do so, they are not "petty commodity producers," according to our definition,

but are participating in some other form of commodity production that, for want of a better term, Cook (1976: 399) has labeled " 'undeveloped' or 'primitive' commodity production."

10. Thus, with regard to Keith Hart's (1982: 40−41) scheme of historical/logical stages in the abstraction of human labor, we would argue that generic peasants/peasant-artisans should be conceived as having passed through the first five, or one less than required to sustain generic petty commodity production. This simply means that, unlike petty commodity production, peasant-artisan production can be sustained in a given precapitalist social formation without general purpose money; reciprocity, direct barter, or indirect barter mediated by special purpose monies suffice to facilitate commodity circulation. Our attempt to generalize about this type of production should not be construed as an effort to construct a theoretical concept of a separate production form or mode. We reject any such effort since it contradicts our search for a way around dualistic and reificatory thinking. Our effort to generalize about the peasant-artisan category is analytically justified by virtue of the fact that in the rural Third World rural direct producers of this type comprise a numerically significant population component—even though regularly undercounted in censuses by being lumped within the general category of "agricultural producer."

11. In other words, the economic situation of the PAH, within capitalism, is much more complex than a simplified scheme involving only three variables—production for autoconsumption (PA), commodity production (CP), and wage labor (WL)—leads one to believe (e.g., Palerm 1980: 216 et passim). Logically, five situations for PAHs within capitalism, regarding the mix of these three variables, may be posited as follows: (1) $PA > CP + WL$; (2) $PA + CP > WL$; (3) $PA < CP + WL$; (4) $CP > PA + WL$; (5) $PA + CP < WL$. It may be heuristically suggestive to link changes in these mixes at the interior of PAH enterprises to changes in PAHs as household units (e.g., size, sex-age composition, stage in developmental cycle) or to changes in relations to capital and the direction of the accumulation process as Palerm has done (ibid.). In our judgment, however, there are too few variables in his scheme to permit us to deal adequately with the complex empirical reality that confronts the analysis of PAHs within capitalism.

The most critical of the missing variables in Palerm's scheme are those that would provide the basis for the analysis of social differentiation, for example, the level of stocks of means of production at time "t" and at time "$t + 1$" (cf. Deere and de Janvry 1979: 603).

12. We must note here substantial confusion in the English translation of Chayanov's principal works—and in the subsequent Chayanovian literature—regarding the precise nature of the rural production unit that was the focus of Chayanov's theorization of peasant economy. Three types of household-based units are encountered in Chayanov's works and have been translated into English as (a) "family farm," which normally operates without wage labor but might engage in petty commodity production; (b) "peasant family labor farm," which employs no wage labor and is not commodity producing; and (c) "peasant farm," which is commodity producing, may em-

ploy wage labor, and may even be capitalist (Chayanov 1966: 273–274). Chayanov's principal theoretical contribution was focused on the "peasant family labor farm," not on either of the commodity-producing or wage labor employing units. The household development cycle, together with a series of demographic factors, was identified by Chayanov as crucial to understanding the internal dynamics of his idealized "natural economy." He posited peasant households as exclusively dedicated to production for their own use with unwaged household labor to achieve a culturally standard level of consumption, as well as a balanced budget. However, he (e.g., Chayanov 1966: 108–109) drew on this theory to analyze peasant-artisan household enterprises participating in the national market economy through commodity production and wage labor. In doing so he violated the natural economy limits of his theory and contradicted his admission (e.g., 244–245) that the Marxist approach was valid under conditions of commodity economy where peasant households experienced class differentiation.

13. This doctrine had its first theoretical expression in peasant studies in the United States in essays by Thorner (1966) and Kerblay (1966), accompanying the publication in English of Chayanov's (1966) major treatise, and in Eric Wolf's book (1966). In Latin America and Mexico, the Spanish edition of Chayanov's treatise was published in 1974 and his ideas were presented in works by Archetti and Stolen (1975), Bartra (1974, 1975), and Palerm (1976), among others (cf. Hewitt de Alcántara 1984: 135).

14. Among those Marxists so attracted are Amin 1977: 37–72; Bartra 1975; Palerm 1976: 138–149, 1980: 209–211; Banaji 1976a; and Worsley 1984: 131–132. See de Janvry 1981: 95–106 for a discussion of these views.

One of the most influential recent applications of Chayanov's ideas is by James Scott (1976), who imbues southeast Asian peasants with a Chayanovian "safety-first subsistence ethic" in an effort to explain rebellions during that region's colonial period. According to Scott, in an argument anthropologists will find quite reminiscent of Eric Wolf's (1966: 17) "funds" approach to the "peasant dilemma," these peasants acknowledge claims to surplus product by landlords and the state, but only in so far as such claims do not cut into the culturally defined standard of living, which is sacrosanct (Scott 1976: 6–7, 29). In typical Chayanovian fashion, Scott (25) recognized the reality of social differentiation among peasants but chose to analyze variables like land distribution, household demographics, psychology, decision making, and propensity for risk taking, which enabled him to address the question of why a preexisting pattern of social differentiation persists but not how it came to be or how it changes. It is no coincidence, then, that he found the Marxist notion of exploitation inadequate because it did not accord with "peasant perceptions" (31).

15. We wish to put on record here our reservations about accepting Feder's bifurcation of the protagonists in this polemic. He himself recognizes that within the *campesinista* approach alone "there are more elements than implied by first impressions," including a "wide spectrum of political tendencies" (1977: 1,443). Hewitt de Alcántara's (1984: Ch. 5) analysis of the debate under the rubric of "Historical Structuralism and the Fate of

the Peasantry, 1970–1980" is, at once, more sensitive to the intellectual differences between individual scholars and more comprehensive in its coverage of the issues. Her major division is between Marxists of what can be characterized as "articulationist" (i.e., Roger Bartra and his French structuralist or "modes-of-production" school) tendencies and others (e.g., Luisa Paré and Armando Bartra) of "circulationist" tendencies, and with considerable acumen and objectivity she examines the split between *campesinistas* and *descampesinistas* in this larger theoretical context (Hewitt de Alcántara 1984: 156–158).

16. Not surprisingly, there tends to be a different political project associated with each current: the *campesinistas* are more prone to favor the possibility of a nonsocialist alternative to capitalism in Mexico. This, of course, could be organized around the persisting peasantry, which, according to them, is undifferentiated by capitalist relations (Redclift 1980; see Hewitt de Alcántara 1984: 158 on political differences among *campesinistas*). The *proletaristas*, who presumably favor the establishment of a socialist regime in Mexico, think that the advance of capitalist development in agriculture can only serve to strengthen the worker-peasant alliance, which must be the sustaining force of the movement toward socialism (cf. Foladori 1981: 7). Thus, according to Hewitt de Alcántara (1984: 141), the potential for political activity was "the heart of the argument for the progressive nature of the proletarianization of the peasantry, and underlay the convinced optimism with which Marxists like [Roger] Bartra greeted the absorption of ever-increasing numbers of peasants and their families into the wage labor sector of rural and urban Mexico. To be exploited as a peasant offered no political future; to be exploited as a proletarian laid the groundwork for socialism."

17. Paré (1977) argued that the process of proletarianization, as distinct from the process of depeasantization, is relatively slow in some Mexican regions (54–55) and has led to a situation of prolonged *partial* proletarianization of the peasantry—a condition in which wage labor provides the peasant household with the material means to produce for autoconsumption (56). This is essentially the position taken by de la Peña (1981: 89) in his interpretation of research conducted in four rural communities and expressed by him as follows: "the sector of autoconsumption—that is no longer self-sufficient—persists fundamentally because the household has the support of income from wage labor or commodity production." Incidentally, Paré (1977: 54–55) defines proletarianization as the "process by which the salary of the seller of labor power becomes the principal basis for his or her reproduction" and depeasantization as the "separation of the peasantry from exclusive dependence upon the land for their subsistence."

De la Peña considers household agricultural production for own-use to be an element of traditional peasant economy and views the cash earnings of its members, in effect, as enabling the rural semiproletarian household to function as a vehicle for reproducing the "formal appearance of a peasant economy" within Mexican capitalism (80–91).

18. Impoverishment, though falling short of complete depeasantization

in many cases, is undeniably one major consequence of capitalist development in the rural Third World, but, then again, so is enrichment, though falling short of complete embourgeoisement in many cases. The contradictory impact of capitalist development, however, must be addressed at two separate levels or in two separate contexts. First, at the macrolevel of the international economy where the focus is on the relations between the industrialized core countries (or multinational corporations) and the so-called peripheral, industrializing countries. Second, at the level of the developing national economy where the focus is on the internal, indigenous development and impact of national, regional, and local capitals. Unfortunately, the literature that addresses capitalist development in the first context habitually implies (quite wrongly) that there is no other locus of capitalist dynamics, and, therefore, that capitalism always must originate externally from "underdeveloped" countries. It also implies (again quite wrongly) that all capital is big capital (especially of the transnational corporate type) and that small capital either doesn't exist (i.e., it is petty commodity production and not capitalism) or is inconsequential (cf. Cook 1984b: 77–81).

19. In terms of global analysis Marx was perhaps right in his concern with the transformation from formal to real subsumption. Where he erred was in assuming that the transformation would take place uniformly throughout the capitalist system, failing to acknowledge that the real subsumption of labor preserves (or creates) spaces within the capitalist economy for enterprises (and even entire branches of production) based on the formal subsumption of labor.

2. Agriculture and Craft Production: An Expedient Relationship

1. The most authoritative summary statement we have found on the commoditization/privatization of land in the Oaxaca Valley, which is corroborated by Cassidy's (1981) more detailed study, is by Whitecotton (1977: 222) as follows: "it appears that communal lands generally were small in size and existing data suggest that private ownership already had become the most important type of land tenure in Indian communities before La Reforma." He continues: "During 1856 and 1857, after the initial disamortization of lands brought about by the Juárez reforms, Indian communities surrounding the city of Oaxaca in the central district, those in the Etla district, and perhaps those in other districts of the Valley, sold most of their remaining communal lands to conform to the new laws. These lands seem to have been purchased mostly in small parcels by nuclear families already residing within the Indian community; in rare cases, some lands were bought by outsiders."

The complexity of the contemporary land tenure situation in the Oaxaca Valley makes it necessary to be cautious in generalizing about property matters. This is because privatized landed property may be held through allotted control over usufruct rights or through ownership that is legally titled or untitled. Although the agricultural land tenure system is mostly privatized, there is still some communal or municipal tenure (i.e., plots held and sometimes worked in common). Moreover, the ejidal or federal agrarian reform type of tenure in the Oaxaca Valley involves land that is legally national patrimony but that is possessed in allotments by individual peasants through their elected village ejidal authorities who serve as stewards of the federal land. Most of the arable ejidal land is held in private usufruct with possession/use rights being inheritable between generations of family members. About 90 percent of the farm units in the Oaxaca Valley are less than 5 hectares in size with the land privately owned (Cook 1978: 322). Private ownership usually, but not always, implies that the owner has a legal written property title (Dennis 1976: 42–48).

2. This measure of "seasonal land units" was based upon Kirkby's (1973) study of the ecology and agriculture of the Oaxaca Valley and was obtained by assigning each hectare of watered land twice the value of a hectare of seasonal (rainfall-dependent) land. The implicit assumption is that watered land produces two crops yearly with an average harvest yield double that of the single crop produced from seasonal land.

3. As Martin Diskin, on the basis of field work in San Sebastian Teitipac (Tlacolula district), expresses it: "The agricultural year has two important phases. The first consists in the preparation of the soil and planting, operations that require an oxteam, a plow, and labor power. The second, the harvest, requires an oxteam, a cart, and labor power" (1986: 278).

4. There are twenty households with a cart but no oxen. Many in this group may have had to sell one or more of their oxen in order to meet medical or other sorts of household emergencies (or, possibly, to meet expenses related to service in the civil-religious hierarchy, cult of the saints, or other ceremonial obligations—see Diskin 1986). Also, there are twelve oxteams and three oxcarts distributed among the 243 landless households. Probably some of these are owned by persons who practiced agriculture in the past and/or plan to pursue it in the future. Yet even for nonagriculturalists in rural areas, oxteams and oxcarts can serve as sources of additional income; the former rented out for plowing, the combination of oxteam and cart rented for the hauling of crops, firewood, and construction materials, such as, bricks, sand, and cement.

5. Apart from the initial cost of purchasing plow animals, the peasant must have access to fodder for their upkeep. Whereas cattle may graze on communal pasture or forage in uncultivated communal land during the rainy season, they are fed during the dry season on cornstalks and leaves from previously harvested fields and are also fed degrained corncobs. There is obviously a relationship between amount of cultivated land and the availability of these fodder resources.

6. Our estimate of the proportion of household corn needs met by corn production was obtained by multiplying informants' estimates of average daily household corn consumption by 365 to obtain yearly corn need; this figure was then divided into their estimate of the last (1979) corn harvest. The closer the resulting figure is to 1.0, the less corn the household must purchase in the form of grain or tortillas (i.e., the more self-sufficient it is in corn production). Beals (1975: 93) estimated the minimal annual maize con-

sumption for a Oaxaca household of two adults and two children 6 and 8 years of age, based on a daily consumption of 0.5 kilograms per person, to be 730 kilograms, with the maximum consumption for such a family probably not exceeding 950 kilograms annually. Kirkby (1973: 89) estimated that "an average family of five persons eats about one metric ton of corn a year at an absolute minimum." The difficulties in obtaining accurate data on household corn consumption are discussed in Beals 1975: 92−94. See also Cook 1982: 122−123, 125—126.

Corn is the staple, but by no means is it the only crop grown for autoconsumption by Oaxaca Valley households. Typically, corn is planted together with beans and squash. Moreover, many additional crops may be grown, even on seasonal land, for autoconsumption or sale. For example, castor beans (higuerilla) and maguey are two cash crops, and chickpeas (garbanzos) a crop for autoconsumption, that are widely cultivated on seasonal land. For this reason, the size of a household's corn crop is only an approximate indicator of its overall agricultural viability.

7. Chayanov (1966: 54) was aware of the existence of cultural variations in family composition and that these had effects upon the size and thus the economic activity of the household: "In many agricultural districts . . . you may frequently encounter living together several married couples of two or even three generations, united in a single complex patriarchal family." However, he also maintained that, "however varied the everyday features of the family, its basis remains the purely biological concept of the married couple, living together with their descendants and the aged representatives of the older generation" (ibid.).

8. His basic definition of the family labor farm included a place for trades and crafts (1966: 51). In addressing himself to the economic activity of the peasant family, he spoke of "a family that does not hire outside labor, has a certain amount of land available to it, has its own means of production, *and is sometimes obliged to expend some of its labor force on non-agricultural crafts and trades*" (our emphasis).

9. Support for this view also comes from the Cajamarca region of northern Peru, where artisan production is most frequently observed among near-landless households that otherwise would be compelled to expel family workers who cannot be employed upon infrasubsistence-sized holdings (Deere and de Janvry 1981: 356).

10. The consumer/worker ratio has been calculated in two ways, each of which has particular advantages and disadvantages. The lower figures (column labeled "Ratio" in Table 5) derive from the Deere and de Janvry (1981) method in which persons of different ages within the household are assigned work values in proportion to the degree to which they are estimated to carry out the labor of a full-time worker (value of 1.0). The figures are calculated, however, from demographic information and make no allowance for actual variations in labor intensity of persons of different ages and sexes. The measure perhaps more closely approximates the potential labor that "might" be marshalled by the household as opposed to the actual labor that is performed by its members. It does assume that members of the household who are not

normally viewed as workers (especially the young dependent members between the ages of 6 and 15) may yet contribute to social reproduction through the unpaid labor they perform (although in many cases they may also contribute to social production of value). Like the Deere and de Janvry measure (column labeled "CW" in Table 5), an alternative measure uses household size as the numerator, but in calculating the denominator it counts as a worker only those members who are engaged in productive labor (with the exception of the female spouse), with the information coming from interviews. Here, the active domestic labor force is probably underestimated and the labor intensity of available workers (number of consumers that each worker is responsible for reproducing) appears much higher than it actually is, especially for the Stage II and Stage III households, which tend to be large and have many children. By contrast the Deere and de Janvry method probably leads to the underestimation of labor intensity because it fails to differentiate between productive and reproductive labor—that dedicated to the production of subsistence goods or cash and that engaged in exchange/conversion of goods into consumable form. For these reasons we include both sets of calculations.

11. The variable "paid jobs" refers to the number of people employed in remunerated work whatever its form (i.e., payment for agricultural day labor, sale of domestically produced agricultural or craft goods, or transfers from within the household, as when a weaver pays his wife for her labor in the manufacture of shirts from the cloth which he has produced on his loom). On the other hand, "unpaid jobs" refers to the number of workers whose sole remuneration takes the form of a share of the consumption goods directly produced or purchased by the enterprise. The sum of these two figures results in "total jobs."

12. Likewise, Novelo (1976: 103–104, 166 et passim) presented examples of "potters [and carpenters] with land" in Michoacán where this also occurred. In addition, she observed cases in which agricultural means of production were sold to raise cash for the purpose of expanding craft production through mechanization (168).

3. Obliging Need: Craft Production and Simple Reproduction

1. It should be clarified that campesino (literally meaning "countryperson" but loosely translated as "peasant") is the cover term for countryfolk in the Oaxaca vernacular. Our hyphenated term "peasant-artisan" is not present in the Oaxaca vernacular. We employ it to refer to that segment of the rural population which practices agriculture in combination with craft production as a regular strategy of subsistence and/or accumulation. The term "countryfolk" is borrowed from Polly Hill (1986: 8) and implies our agreement with her that the use of the generic term "peasants" distorts analysis by (a) glossing over the reality of social differentiation and economic inequality, which "always exists within any rural community in which cash circulates" (16), and (b) enhancing the "belief in the appropriateness of the notion of an average [typical or modal] household" (70).

2. As Schmitz (1982: 193) noted: "the issue is not *whether* small enterprises have growth and employment potential but *under what conditions.*" To a degree it is the confusion of the "whether" and the "what conditions" that has attracted some anthropologists to the Chayanovian perspective.

3. The 765 artisan and peasant-artisan households (574 peasant-artisans) contain more than 933 artisan occupations. Although we inquired as to the number and specific occupation of all workers, remunerated and nonremunerated, in each household surveyed, we gathered detailed occupational information on a maximum of two artisans per household. This formed the basis for the computer analysis. In the sample, there are, of course, some very large households with five and even six artisans, many of which are found in the embroidery and treadle loom industries.

4. The "mixed-craft" category includes villages like Santa Cecilia Jalieza, where wood carving, embroidery, and some backstrap loom weaving are practiced; Santo Domingo Jalieza, where embroidery, broom making, basketry, and backstrap loom weaving are practiced; San Baltazar Chichicapán, where mezcal distilling, thread spinning, and embroidery are practiced; and San Pedro Guegorexe, where lime production, backstrap loom weaving, and embroidery are practiced.

5. Artisans' income was calculated by multiplying net income for the last production cycle (gross value of marketed commodities less expenses) times the number of turnover cycles per year. To this was added estimated income from the sale of sheep and goats and cash income from agricultural wage labor at 75 pesos daily, the standard wage rate during the study period. Peasant-artisans' income calculations included the estimated value of agricultural products (beans valued at 6 pesos/kg and corn at 3.5 pesos/kg), regardless of whether these were directly consumed by the household or sold for cash. Remittances, not included in these income calculations, have been analyzed separately. It is probable that some income sources, such as the sale of domestic animals, were overlooked, and that others were over- (or under-) estimated. For instance, artisan income may fluctuate seasonally, as Cook (1982) demonstrated in an earlier study of the *metate* industry, placing into question yearly estimates of craft income projected on the basis of the study of a single turnover period. Inquiries directed toward the last production cycle, however, are more likely to yield reliable information than those that ask informants (many of whom are illiterate and have little record-keeping experience) to estimate their yearly income and expenses from given sources. We do not contend that our income estimates are complete and error free; we do believe, though, that they provide an adequate basis for comparing levels of remuneration of different demographic, occupational and socioeconomic categories.

6. It is sobering for U.S. readers to consider the income data in terms of dollars. The 1979 peso-to-dollar exchange rate was 22.50 to 1 which, when applied to the weekly household income figures, yields the following dollar equivalents (from the top of the column to the bottom): $16.53, $30.62, $13.11, $17.87, $9.38, $20.58, and $64.13. This drives home the fact that we are dealing with economic realities of a quite different order and magni-

tude than those presented by life within metropolitan urban-industrial capitalism.

7. One informant described the situation in his grandfather's days as follows: "One can live from this occupation if one goes into the mountains and leaves the village. That's how they lived in my grandfather's time. After the Day of the Dead festival they left with a basket for the mountains, they slept there for a week, and then came down to the Oaxaca City market. Next they came to the village to load up on tortillas and left again for the mountains. That's how our people sustained themselves before we got the ejido allotments. They planted crops but didn't harvest anything. Not until 1924 when they got some land nearby—but when they had food to eat they were invaded. And, then how did they eat? That's been the history of this village. Because of poverty they take your land away."

8. An example of their shrewdness and aggressiveness in marketing and in identifying new markets (and uses) for their products is provided by Cook's chance encounter with several Santa Cecilians peddling their "letter openers" (which they also realized could be used as book markers) in March 1989 among the multitudes attending the annual Book Fair (Fería de Libros) in Mexico City (held in the Palacio de Minería).

9. Ixtle is derived from the Nahuatl word *ichtli* and is used in contemporary Mexico to refer to the filament extracted from processing the leaf of the maguey (*agave*) plant. By extension the term is applied with reference to all kinds of fibers extracted from all members of the agave family (Cabrera 1974: 84).

10. This sketch of the modern history of the cloth industry in Oaxaca City is derived from a brief preliminary report entitled *La industria textil mantelera de Oaxaca y el desarrollo capitalista dependiente* written by Ana Emma Jaillet for the Oaxaca Small Industries Project in 1979. The topic obviously requires more rigorous and thorough investigation.

11. This section on Teotitlán del Valle and Santa Ana del Valle draws heavily on field reports written by Jim Schillinger for the Oaxaca Small Industries Project in June 1979. As a project employee and for purposes of doctoral dissertation research, Schillinger resided in Teotitlán for an extended period in 1978–1979.

12. A 1965 study of Santa Ana weaving by Stuart Plattner (1965: 18–19) reported that every adult male in the village knew how to weave blankets (*cobijas*) and that more than half of the houses had working looms. He also noted that Teotitlán blankets had a better quality of weave and design than those woven in Santa Ana—but was shown samples of old blankets from Santa Ana, which were much more finely woven than contemporary ones. In 1965, according to Plattner (19–21), all Santa Ana blankets were woven of pure wool—most of which was bought at the Sunday *plaza* (market) in Tlacolula and then cleaned, washed, carded, and spun into yarn (by both men and women) in Santa Ana.

13. The significant presence of women in Santa Ana weaving in 1979 did represent a substantial change from 1965 when Plattner reported that some Santa Ana "women may know how to weave, but they never do so" (1965:

23). Our explanation of the difference between the 1979 situation in Teotitlán and Santa Ana would seem to apply as well to the apparent movement of women into weaving between 1965 and 1979. Plattner reported a much higher degree of wool processing and thread spinning, as well as dyeing (activities that would have absorbed available female labor) than we found in 1979.

14. Plattner (1965: 26) reported that in 1965 most of the blankets produced in Santa Ana were sold in the Tlacolula Sunday *plaza*, either by *propios* (i.e., the weavers themselves) or by *regatones* (intermediaries). There were four buyers-up in Santa Ana in 1965 who either bought finished blankets or gave cash advances on blankets to be delivered at some stipulated future date. He also reported that, among friends and relatives, money was lent on the understanding that the loan would be repaid in blankets. Also, blankets were directly convertible into goods at two stores in Santa Ana— usually to repay goods taken on credit.

15. The Hacienda Xaagá began as a *sitio de ganado menor* in 1564 and became an important agricultural and livestock-raising enterprise. It is classified by Taylor (1972: 123) as one of eight estates in the Oaxaca Valley that "approached the larger definition of hacienda" and, by the late eighteenth century, encompassed 7 *estancias* (135).

In their 1936 petition for an ejido grant, the peasants of the Xaagá Hacienda stated that, "lacking our own land to meet our needs, we find ourselves obligated to sell our work at a low price, to hand over the greater part of the products of our annual harvest, to serve without pay at the hacendado's command and to neglect the education of our children and our selves" (*Archivo de la Secretaría de Reforma Agraria, Expediente* No. 955). Their petition was successful and they were granted 2,147 hectares in 1937. All told, the Hacienda lost 8,368 hectares in the expropriation—a grant of 4,436 going to the mountain community of San Lorenzo Albarradas, which had waged guerrilla warfare with the Hacienda from the turn of the century.

The historical origin of the exclusively Spanish-speaking Xaagá population, surrounded on all sides by Zapotec-speaking populations, is disputed in the literature. Responsibility for its origin and that of other Spanish-speaking populations in this region likely rests with the Hacienda and the Spanish colonial regime (see Cook 1983).

16. As Wolf (1982), Mandel (1975), and others have noted, capitalism tends to generate differentiation globally, nationally, regionally, and within industries and classes at the same time that it leads to class polarization.

17. Perhaps the most comprehensive treatment of the whole question of "growth constraints of small enterprises," based on a literature survey as well as empirical case studies, is by Schmitz (1982). Although most of the studies cited by Schmitz, as well as his own Brazilian study, deal with urban petty enterprises, we feel that his findings are still relevant to our analysis of the rural Oaxaca Valley situation—especially to those household enterprises that are regular capital accumulators. With regard to the issue of the growth of petty enterprises being braked by the lack of entrepreneurial or managerial skills, Schmitz (14) emphasizes that his and other studies have

found such enterprises to "reveal great initiative, inventiveness, responsiveness and readiness to jump at opportunities . . ." On the question of technical skills, Schmitz cites approvingly studies that downplay a consideration of the internal technical dimension as an obstacle to petty enterprise growth and, instead, treat as major obstacles structural or external factors like availability of credit and a lack of a favorable government technology policy (14−15). Finally, in his conclusion Schmitz (164) emphasizes that his case studies show that his petty producing respondents display "dedication, initiative, hard work, readiness to jump at opportunities, [and] preparedness to take risks."

18. Among other reasons, it is because of his failure to take this into account that we are unconvinced by Annis' (1987: esp. Ch. 5) claim that net saving and investment automatically result when Catholic peasant-Indians, who undergo conversion to evangelical Protestantism in Guatemala, withdraw from the cargo system and cult of the saints.

Martin Diskin (1986) has studied the impact on household budgets of participation in the cult of the saints (i.e., *mayordomía*) and other ceremonial activities in a village in Tlacolula district and makes contradictory interpretations (285); however, his broader conclusion, namely, that "there are still ethnic communities where what is reproduced are not capitalist relations," is fully supportive of "ethnopopulism," a perspective that we reject (see Chapter 1).

4. Beyond Simple Reproduction: The Dynamics of Peasant-Artisan Differentiation

1. It should be noted that Marx's discussion of peasant differentiation, in Vol. I of *Capital*, takes as a starting point the abolition of feudal restrictions on private property. Similarly, it was only after the official elimination of serfdom in Russia that Lenin and Chayanov could address the differentiating tendencies of petty commodity producing peasant agriculture. It should be noted that socioeconomic stratification was not uncommon in European feudal villages but, as Hilton (1974: 210) emphasized, it approached class dimensions especially among "free families holding in free tenure."

2. Deere and de Janvry (1981: 335) have concisely summed up the differences in the Lenin and Chayanov approaches to the differentiation issue as follows: "For Lenin, inequality in the concentration of means of production among Russian peasants at the turn of the century was evidence of capitalist class formation. Social differentiation increasingly forced the mass of direct producers into selling their labor power, whereas a minority was able to capitalize the productive process on the basis of its use of wage labor. In contrast, for Chayanov, inequality in farm size and in the distribution of income among Russian peasant households was explained by demographic differentiation. Over the household life cycle, increasing household size spurred the acquisition of additional land and other means of production. Inequality in farm size reflected a purely demographic process of household

evolution over time which was repeated in a stable fashion from generation to generation."

3. Chayanov's theoretical model assumed that the typical peasant-artisan domestic unit was the "fully natural family farm" (or "family labor unit," cf., 1966: 10–13) in which noncommodity activities, value forms (1966: 27), and relations prevailed; while he did not consider all rural households in early twentieth-century Russia to fit into this category (e.g., 1966: 222–223, 244–249), much of his analysis proceeds as if they did. He agreed with Lenin's (1946) analysis of American farming, which he summarized as arguing that "bringing agriculture into the general capitalist system" may involve drawing "masses of scattered peasant farms into its sphere of influence and, having bound these small scale commodity producers to the market, economically subordinates them to its influence" (1966: 257). Also, Chayanov (1966: 258) accepted the Marxist view that this process was the "first path for the penetration of capitalist relations into the countryside," which would result in integrating small peasant undertakings into the world economy.

In the last analysis, however, Chayanov's agreements with Marxism were outweighed by his reliance on Neoclassical economics and household demographic/life cycle factors in elaborating his theory of peasant economy; therefore, it is not coincidental that his reputation and the application of his theory in later-twentieth-century social science has been sustained mostly by those students of rural social economy who, for whatever reasons, comfortably embrace his peasant household economism in their quest for a non- (or anti-) Marxist approach (e.g., see Durrenberger (ed.), 1984 for several examples), which downplays the material bases of class differentiation and struggle.

4. For example, when Carol Smith (1984) writing about Western Guatemalan highland weavers or Joel Kahn (1975; 1980) writing about West Sumatran blacksmiths encounter production units that are apparently founded on capitalist relations of production but fail to modernize and expand their means of production, they interpret this to be diagnostic of petty commodity production. Kahn (1980: 99–100, 110–111, 118) repeatedly points to the "low level of technology," the "low level of forces of production," or the "low organic composition of capital" as indicative of the absence of capitalist organization (which he clearly associates exclusively with large-scale entrepreneurial units having higher compositions of capital) in West Sumatran smithing; for him capitalism is defined by the "productive organization in the West," which "has produced a continuous revolution at the level of the productive forces" (1975: 144).

Smith (1984: 89–91 et passim), in addition to accepting Kahn's thesis, goes on to insist that capitalism operates only through a permanent, free proletariat. Her argument not only ignores capitalism's early European history of exploitation of a rural semiproletariat but also contradicts findings from a growing body of research on the "informal sector," which shows that many advanced capitalist firms "deproletarianize" labor in order to reduce its cost (e.g., avoiding minimum wages and fringe benefits through sub-contracting household labor) (Portes 1983: 163). This more recent development parallels the earlier tendency of "protoindustrial" capital to employ rural or semirural household labor (e.g., Goody 1982; Kriedte et al. 1981; Medick 1976, 1981).

5. It could be argued that the dynamic of the four household groupings is fundamentally different with, for instance, the peasant households embedded in a "peasant or domestic mode of production" and the artisan households inserted in a "petty commodity mode of production"—each with separate and different tendential laws of motion. Such a position loses its rationale when it is acknowledged that the variable insertion of all rural households in the Oaxaca Valley into noncapitalist circuits, such as home production for own use, nonprofit-oriented commodity production, barter, and reciprocity, is clearly influenced by their insertion into capitalist circuits (e.g., profit-oriented commodity production, wage labor, acquisition of wage goods, money rent for use of means of production). In other words, not only is peasant and peasant-artisan household involvement in noncapitalist circuits conditioned by their involvement in capitalist circuits but the latter must be considered as dominant and subsumptive with regard to those households' activities.

6. The third axis included only peasant-artisan and artisan households categorized by activity and craft location. That is, communities were assigned to one of seven locations according to the dominant craft practiced. Thus, a household practicing embroidery but residing in a predominantly backstrap loom weaving community was eliminated from the sample at this stage. The "town artisan" and "mixed-craft" categories incorporated communities lacking a single predominant craft industry. The fact that this exercise only reduced combined artisan and peasant-artisan households from 765 to 709 testifies to the degree to which most communities are characterized by a single, dominant craft occupation.

7. For each of the three measures of economic performance included in Table 17, the standard deviation is several times larger than the mean. This is due to the fact that a small percentage of very high values result in a rightward skewing of the distribution. The median values, much lower in every case, become a more acceptable measure of central tendency here. Income distributions skewed in this manner are particularly characteristic of under-developed capitalist social formations in which most of the households are poor, the middle stratum is small, and a small upper stratum (comprising the various fractions of the bourgeoisie) attracts to itself a disproportionate (compared to the bourgeoisie in developed capitalist nations) share of the national income.

8. As indicated in Chapter 2, the consumer/worker ratio was calculated by two methods. In the first (CWRATIO), all informants with paid or unpaid jobs were treated as adult worker equivalents; by this method the labor contributions of adolescents (and especially children under 12) tended to be ignored or underrepresented, except in those cases in which they were actively involved in craft production, wage labor, and so on. Informants tended

to interpret questions about "work" or "employment" as referring exclusively to productive work, overlooking domestic work or chores. According to the second method (RATIO), labor contributions were prorated by age (from 0, no labor contribution, to 1.0, an adult equivalent), using a scale employed by Deere and de Janvry (1981) in their study of the Cajamarca (Peru) peasantry. This scale accords well with other evaluations of the labor contribution of pre-adults in rural Third World areas (Cain 1977; Nag, White, and Peet, 1978: 295-296), as well as with our ethnographic observations in rural Oaxaca.

In the discussion focused on Tables 19 and 20, the correlations involving the C/W ratio use the first method; correlations based on the second method tend to be lower but are of the same order of magnitude. The two consumer/worker ratio measures correlate with each other at a .49 level of significance. Due to the skewed character of the distribution of most of the variables in these two tables, Spearman rank order correlation coefficients were employed instead of Pearson product moment correlation coefficients.

9. A great deal of recent evidence (Caldwell 1982; Nardi 1983; Harris and Ross 1987: esp. 171-175) suggests that the rate at which the parental generation has children is largely determined by the extent to which having each additional child results in a net gain of benefits over costs for the average couple (cf. Harris 1987: 92). Harris (93) puts this in world-historical perspective as follows: "With the advent of agriculture and domesticated animals, the balance of reproductive costs and benefits shifted in favor of having more children." After reviewing the literature on the costs and benefits of raising children in contemporary peasant communities, including studies by White (1976, 1982) in Java and Cain (1977) in Bangladesh, Harris (94) draws the following conclusions: "contrary to the popular perception that people in less developed countries have large numbers of children simply because they do not know how to avoid conception, there is much evidence that more children and larger households mean a higher, not a lower, standard of living in the short run."

10. The "housescale index" was formulated by assigning different numerical values to contrasting house types, ranging from low to high cost (i.e., thatch, adobe, or masonry construction), types of house flooring (dirt, tile, concrete), number of rooms, tenure status of the residence and residence lot (owned, rented, borrowed), and ownership of a television set. The assigned values were then summed up to arrive at an overall index value.

11. The values for production variables in Table 23 have been computed on the basis of figures given during interviews with direct producers. The values for means of production represent the aggregate of actual (and in some cases imputed) costs of all tools and equipment; the cost of land is excluded in the computation of these values in the case of the brick industry but the cost of kilns, storage sheds, and flat-bed trucks is included. The values for the variables in columns 5-10 are computed, for the sake of exposition, on a monthly basis.

If we take Marx's definition of the "turnover time" of capital (1967, II: Chapter VII) as the "time taken for the value of a given capital to be realized through production and exchange" (i.e., the sum of the production period and the circulation or marketing time) (Harvey 1982: 62), it is very difficult to arrive at anything other than a rough estimate of it for those petty industries in the Oaxaca Valley (like embroidery, treadle loom weaving, and brickmaking) that are not integrated into the periodic marketplace system and, consequently, market their commodities either on random buyer demand, on order, or when a particular target inventory is on hand.

Ideally, the producer would like to be able to sell commodities immediately upon the completion of a production cycle but this is often not possible. In treadle loom weaving, for instance, the wide diversity of woven products, not to mention the differential productivities of different weavers, guarantee that there will be considerable variation in duration of production cycles per loom both within and between communities. In a multiloom workshop in which loom capacities, weaver productivity, and products are similar, it is likely that production cycles are staggered between looms. In other words, one loom may be completing a cycle on the same day that another is beginning (or still another has half completed) a cycle of transforming a given quantity of thread entered on the loom into a given quantity of cloth.

Under these circumstances, the workshop operator pursues various strategies to keep looms supplied with thread; he may arbitrarily identify a "turnover period" (though, in contrast to Smith, we did not find any particular word like *turno* used in the Oaxaca Valley to express this) and replenish his supply either through the expenditure of "saved earnings" (preferably) or through credit (which is quite typical). In short, the only way to get at the actual dynamics of value production and accounting in these petty enterprises is through case studies, which can then provide a basis for making accurate extrapolations from survey data. For example, detailed data from case 9 in the embroidery industry suggest that employer units will spend one-third of the value of their output per production cycle on raw materials and three-fifths on wages. Such formulas as this, derived from case studies judged to be highly reliable, can be used to overcome the variations in estimates derived from one-time interviews; such estimates are always subject to the limitations of informant lying, poor recall, or mistakes.

12. The figures for the three- and four-weaver households are less reliable than the rest for two reasons: (a) they are based upon a small number of cases and (b) the "cash" calculation incorporates the output of only two artisan workers in each household. In most industries, the value contributions of additional household workers would be included in the figures due to the fact that the production process is social and devoted to the fabrication of a single product. Treadle loom weaving is a social process as well, but the raw material worked up by nonweaving household workers is then parceled out among different weavers (or to different looms). When we focus upon the weaver as the complete subunit of production and limit our analysis to a maximum of two weavers per household, a portion of the labor product of nonweavers (i.e., that which was parceled out to third and fourth weavers) and all of the labor product of additional weavers (for whom data by production cycles were not gathered, much less coded) is lost. If we, in

fact, had these missing data it is likely that, in household enterprises with more than two weavers, per capita income would continue to increase. Its rate of increase would be dependent (considering only factors internal to the production unit) upon the age and skill of the weavers and the number of nonweaving workers. Only detailed case study material of the type that we have from Xaagá can clarify the reasons why particular production units hire nonhousehold members. It may be to expand output (either by adding more looms or by operating a loom already in place for a longer period per day) or maintain output (i.e., to replace household workers who withdraw from the enterprise). At least three of the sixty-nine households surveyed in Teotitlán have taken this step; and the figures presented above pertaining to number of weavers (and looms), despite the limitations just explained, illustrate the basis upon which the capital necessary for enterprise expansion might be appropriated from the unpaid labor of household workers.

Finally, it should be noted that of the 130 weaving households in the three major weaving villages, only 18 (13.8 percent) contain three or more weavers and/or three or more looms. The number of weavers outnumber the number of looms in seven cases (meaning that looms are generally shared) and looms outnumber weavers in eight cases (most of which are employer households). In the remaining three cases the number of weavers and the number of looms are the same.

13. This means that the petty capitalist unit is continuously under external pressures to operate as effectively as possible within the limited space it occupies in the wider capitalist division of labor. These pressures and the unit's responses to them, at any given conjuncture, may result in either its insolvency, its reorganization as a petty commodity enterprise, or, conceivably, its metamorphosis into a larger-scale, more mechanized type of capitalist enterprise.

This series of operational criteria for a petty capitalist enterprise is designed to embrace both a dispersed and a nucleated form of manufactory. In other words, an enterprise so designated may operate on a putting-out or outworker basis or, alternatively, it may operate on a shop or site-confined, inworker basis.

14. The material in this and the following section on the brick industry is based on Cook (1984a).

15. The five questions selected for analysis here are as follows: (1) Regarding your and your household's work, do you obtain the income or the earnings that you have coming to you? Why? (2) Do you think that there are persons or groups of persons in this village that have more advantages, possibilities, or privileges than others? Who? Why? (3) Do you think that when serape sales are good everyone in the weaving industry here benefits equally? Why? (4) Do you believe that most artisans are poor because they don't want to work? Why? (5) [Hypothetical situation] Juan sold a serape to Pancho for 400 pesos. Pancho resold that serape the same day for 700 pesos. Do you think that Pancho should have paid more to Juan? Why?

16. In her Tontonicapán study, Carol Smith (1984: 83, 86) attributes the noncapitalist nature of weaving partially to the fact that high wage levels

(i.e., high relative to profits) discourage employers from investing capital in technology, which would increase labor productivity and act as an incentive for wage workers to independently engage in production (i.e., because of low initial start-up costs and the possibility of saving earnings from wage work). She tells us that weavers are hired on a piece-rate basis (71) but fails to appreciate the implications of the piece wage system for capital and labor in the Tontonicapán weaving industry. A substantial body of evidence (e.g., ILO 1951; Hopkins 1978; Cook 1984a: esp. 124–129, 194–199) reinforces Marx's (1967: 556 et passim) original thesis that the piece wage is the predominant form of labor remuneration in petty, incipient, or competitively squeezed capitalist enterprises. The piece wage is well adapted to situations in which capitalization of the labor process is neither feasible nor desirable and in which labor-intensive forms prevail because its linkage of payment to results, under conditions in which workers are more or less free to schedule and pace their work, serves to intensify productivity without employer coercion.

Likewise, Joel Kahn (1980: 90–91) notes incidentally that work in the West Sumatra blacksmithing industry is paid on a piece-rate basis but, paradoxically, his analysis of value distribution assumes a constant wage and does not consider the implications of a system of payment by results.

Smith (1984) focused exclusively on the concept of "relative surplus value" in a situation where "absolute surplus value" is more relevant. Under conditions of incipient capitalist enterprise the type of surplus value created by labor and appropriated by small capital is absolute, that is, it derives from the "prolongation of the working day beyond the point at which the laborer would have produced just an equivalent for the value of his labour-power" (Marx 1967, I: 509) or from an action functionally equivalent to this. According to Marx, it is absolute surplus value that "forms the general groundwork of the capitalist system, and the starting point for the production of relative surplus-value" (ibid.). Whereas Marx emphasized that the production of relative surplus value implies the real, not merely the formal, subjection of labor to capital, he (1967, I: 510) acknowledged the possible emergence of "intermediate forms" as illustrated by "modern 'domestic industry'" or by transitional (to modern industry) forms—incidentally, forms in which the piece-wage system is likely to prevail (cf. Marx 1967, I: 553–554). Absolute surplus value is created either by a prolongation of the working day, by speeding up or increasing the intensity of work, or by underpayment of workers—conditions that are promoted under the piece-wage regime, especially in the underdeveloped economies like that of Guatemala. Of course, labor intensification also may impact on the production of relative surplus value (e.g., "When the majority of workers begin to work intensively, socially necessary labor time becomes shorter" [Ryndina et al. 1980: 53; cf. Eaton 1966: 87–91]).

In her discussion "Sectoral Articulation and Wage Rates," Smith (1984: 84–89) repeatedly refers to "wage rates" without distinguishing between time and piece rates and assumes intersectoral uniformity of these rates (e.g., 88)—an assumption that is invalid for industrial subsectors where the system of payment by results prevails. Reed (1984: 114) in his analysis of agricultural piecework in nineteenth-century England criticizes Hobsbawm and Rude for downplaying the differing consequences of piece- and time-rate payment forms and shows how the piece-rate form generated differential performance and earnings by workers.

5. Gender, Household Reproduction, and Commodity Production

1. For reasons of expository clarity we have chosen to gloss the Spanish word *tejer*, which means both "to weave" and "to braid" (and is used by the palm workers to denote their craft) as "to plait."

2. The average age of these informants was 46; thirteen were married with an average of four children each. Three were single, and four were widowed.

3. The following responses to a question as to how the informant managed to combine household tasks with mat plaiting are illustrative: (a) "First I do the household chores and then I grab the *petate*. My daughter helps me make tortillas before she goes to school. When she comes home from school she helps me plait." (b) "In the morning after one prepares the meal one begins plaiting a *petate*. Afterward, when it is mealtime again, one stops plaiting. My daughter helps me haul water and make tortillas. Daily we spend about two hours plaiting." (c) "When I finish making tortillas, and after caring for the children, I plait a little. For short periods only. To sit down and plait all day long is not possible." (d) "I do all the household chores: the tortillas, wash dishes, prepare meals, make the beds. Then I sit down to plait a *petate*, if only for a little while."

4. Reciprocity is institutionalized in the rural Zapotec Oaxaca Valley as *guelaguetza*. It is operative both in the ceremonial-ritual context and in nonceremonial-economic life. It involves formal and informal exchanges of cash, commodities, and labor services between households. See Cook 1982: 65–67, 109–114, 213–216; Beals 1970; and Martínez Ríos 1964.

5. Backstrap loom weaving of "traditional" woolen sashes and wrap-around skirts remains a female occupation in Mitla where, however, it has largely been displaced by male treadle loom weaving. See Beals 1975: 257–260.

6. San Tomás Jalieza's weavers produce sashes (*fajas*), belts (*cinturones*), shoulder bags (*bolsas* or *morrales*), slipover shawls (*cotorinas*), wall hangings and throw cloths (*tapetes*), and place mats from cotton and/or wool and/or acrylic yarn. Six of our thirteen female informants belonged to the weaver's cooperative at the time they were interviewed, and three others had been members previously but had quit. The main reasons cited for quitting were high membership fees or assessments and too few concrete benefits. Those who remained active saw the principal benefit in doing so to be wholesale purchases made by special orders from Mexico City and foreign clients.

7. The average age of the male weavers in our Santo Tomás sample, fif-

teen of whom are household heads, is 34. They weave for an average of 35 hours weekly with most reporting that they did so on a permanent year-round basis—although those with arable land wove fewer hours per week during the agricultural season. These male informants, at the time they were interviewed in 1978, reported that they had been weaving for an average of 8.5 years; the longest that any of them had been weaving was 23 years and only six others had been weaving for more than 10 years (all between 11 and 15 years). These results support a 1964 study of weaving in Santo Tomás (Bertocci) that characterized it as a female industry and made no mention of male participation. The fact that all our male informants were taught to weave by females, more than half of them by their wives, suggests that a process of defeminization of labor in the industry may have begun during our informants' lifetimes—probably not much before 1955 (assuming that the informant in our sample with 23 years as a weaver was accurate when he claimed to be a pioneer among male weavers). Interestingly enough, recent archival research uncovered official censuses showing that some men practiced weaving in Santo Tomás in 1857 and in 1890 (Clemens 1987: 3–4; 1988).

Even though men now comprise almost one-third of the weaving labor force in Santo Tomás, they have taken up weaving largely to supplement female labor. What appears to have happened after 1963, probably as a result of the establishment of the cooperative, which rationalized production and marketing in ways that diversified the product line and improved quality, thus stimulating sales (Bertocci 1964), is a village-wide increase in the weaving population. This, in turn, led to an increase in the household labor force and/or an intensification of work.

8. As one informant expressed it: "One-third of the village is in difficult circumstances but others go to the fields and don't bother with weaving, they have land. They don't suffer much. Those who weave are the only ones that find things more difficult. We don't have land and we dedicate ourselves to weaving. If we had land we would stop weaving." Among other things this statement reminds us once again that the ideology that portrays (accurately in some cases, less so in others) rural industry as the handmaiden of agriculture is espoused by carriers as well as by students of peasant culture.

9. There were, nonetheless, two notable exceptions that merit quotation here since they are genuine expressions of awareness of exploitation by intermediaries: (a) "The one who does all the work is the one who ought to earn. The buyers-up buy a product and sell it for a profit later; the one who spent two days to make it doesn't profit. Only because we have a need to make it do the buyers-up earn their money from one day to another." (b) "The buyer-up earns but the weaver who did the work doesn't share the earnings. The buyer-up wants to enrich himself with the sweat of the weaver."

It is precisely through expressions such as these by producers themselves that the idea that petty commodity production contains the wage labor/capital relation (Gibbon and Neocosmos 1985) assumes credibility as something other than a logical construct.

10. This age structure must be evaluated against the number of women (total) in those categories. There are more younger women so they will account for a larger proportion of embroiderers.

11. Illustrative statements are as follows: (a) "Embroidery no longer pays. I like weaving better because it was the work of my childhood. I have wanted to quit embroidery because I earn so little. If I had a place to deliver what I produced where they paid a good price it would be different. But right now one earns nothing. I want to quit. I don't want to take up weaving again because my lungs are too weak." (A common complaint of the weavers is that weaving damages their lungs.) (b) "I don't like to embroider but I don't want to work in weaving again. Weaving tires you out more than embroidery."

12. The difficulties faced by these women in dealing with costs, prices, and earnings emerge clearly in the following statements: (a) "I don't know how much it costs. The people who buy it say how much it's worth—well embroidered 350, in pieces, but if it's poorly done, only 250. The buyer says, 'That's all I'll give you. If you don't want to sell it, keep it, go and find another buyer who'll pay you more.' With luck another buyer will pay 10 pesos more. They no longer want to pay. The buyers-up do our accounting. I don't do it because I don't know how to read. What am I going to do? Sometimes when I buy cloth I earn a little for each meter but, at times, there are no earnings." (b) "One figures her accounts but one is obliged to sell even though she realizes that she's losing. One takes into account so much for the cloth, so much for the thread—and if she takes her work into account— it doesn't come out. One realizes how much she lost but it doesn't matter. What can we do? No one pays more. Prices are the same everywhere." (c) "We don't figure our accounts with a pencil and paper but we do make an accounting in our heads of the cloth and the thread. It figures out to be a gift. There are no earnings. Our work is given as a gift."

13. The role of FONART among Mexico's artisans is controversial (see Novelo 1976; Cook 1981). Cook's experience has been that the effectiveness of its often well-planned and well-intentioned programs for artisan assistance/development founder because of sometimes larcenous or incompetent personnel who staff its regional offices, budgetary problems, and lack of program continuity within and between *sexenios* (six-year presidential terms).

Cook's 1985 visit to Santa Cecilia confirmed that the embroidery program that was functioning reasonably well in 1979 had disappeared, together with the sewing machines that had belonged to the program. Presumably, these have been privatized—a common fate of cooperative ventures in Oaxaca Valley villages.

14. It is informative to compare the situation of women in the Oaxaca Valley brickyards with that of women in the brickyards of Kerala, India. The main difference is that in Kerala women participate full-time exclusively as brick haulers on a piece-rate basis; men and boys perform all other tasks. Brick hauling is classified as unskilled work, whereas tasks performed by boys and men are classified as semiskilled and skilled, respectively. Women's daily earnings average out to about one-half those of boys and men—which

reflects the lower piece rates assigned to unskilled labor rather than actual number of hours worked (Gulati 1982).

15. Deere and León de Leal (1981: 349) make a similar observation regarding attitudes toward women's tasks in the Peruvian Andes: "A typical aspect of this technical division of labor is that both men and women consider the tasks carried out by women to be much less important than the tasks carried out by men. This is reflected in the way that both sexes often refer to women's participation in agricultural production as simply 'helping out.' But women's tasks in such a technical division of labor are certainly important to the production process. If these weren't carried out by women, they would have to be carried out by men, and often are."

16. Two informant statements illustrative of this are (a) "My husband began to weave and then asked me: 'Who is going to make the shirts?' I replied: 'I will make the shirts, let's buy a sewing machine.' He said: 'You can't do it.' I told him: 'Yes I can do it.' Then he bought the sewing machine and when cloth came off the loom I made shirts. I learned because my husband needed someone to do it." (b) "He began to work on the loom and to make cloth for shirts. Then he told me: 'Let's make shirts. I will weave the cloth and you can sew them up.' And that's how we did it—I started to sew on a machine that belonged to my mother. On that machine I sewed shirts and he wove the cloth on the loom."

17. A representative statement by a seamstress outworker is as follows: "The owners of the shirts benefit because they sell the shirts at high prices and pay low wages for the sewing. We make shirts in order to have low earnings. We could resolve the situation if all of us who have sewing machines could get together and agree to raise the piece rate we charge to the putting-out weavers. I think they would pay higher piece rates for sewing shirts. I was talking the other day with another seamstress about the fact that we need to come to an agreement among ourselves to propose to the putters-out that because they deliver the cloth and don't do any work to cut-out and sew-up shirts, we work more than they do. I can't do anything about this until the other seamstresses agree to charge more for our work—even one peso per shirt. If we all agree on a piece rate then the putters-out won't be able to hire anyone for less."

6. Intermediary Capital and Petty Industry in the City and the Countryside

1. Kay (1975: 95) has asserted that "merchant capital is trading capital and the surplus value it seizes is used to expand trade not the forces of production."

2. We wish to acknowledge the valuable contribution of Alice Littlefield and Ana Emma Jaillet in collecting the data on craft businesses.

3. Given the importance of women in craft industries in Oaxaca documented in Chapter 5, it should come as no surprise that half of these craft business proprietors are women, or that the embroidery group has the highest proportion of females (83 percent). The overrepresentation of females as

proprietors of embroidery businesses is offset by their underrepresentation as proprietors of the extramarketplace businesses. Still, it is noteworthy that women are proprietors of three of the top ten (i.e., in terms of annual gross sales) businesses in this group.

4. Only 29 percent of the business operators indicated that they currently had agricultural land. Relatively few of the permanent Oaxaca City dwellers among them had any agricultural landholdings; 11 percent of the extramarketplace merchants reported that they held such land but only 5 percent of the marketplace stall operators did. By contrast, 60 percent of the open-air market sellers and embroidery merchants, all of whom are rural dwellers, reported having agricultural land. The average reported landholding was nonirrigated and measured 2.8 hectares.

5. In the Mexican literature the Party-State apparatus is identified as *PRI-Gobierno*. This is a shorthand reference to the ruling Partido Revolucionario Institucional (Institutional Revolutionary Party) as inseparable from the government that it has controlled for more than half of a century of unbroken rule.

The role of CNOP in Oaxaca, especially as a vehicle through which upwardly mobile village-based artisans and traders gain entry to urban markets, needs further study. At the national level it has been referred to as the "organized middle class on the march" and it occupies a position vis-à-vis the PRI-government apparatus that may overshadow that of the mass peasant and labor organizations with their "long-established claims upon the Revolution" (Padgett 1966: 123). Interestingly enough, the statutes of the CNOP specifically target small agriculturists, small industrialists, small merchants, artisans, and members of cooperative enterprises as likely constituencies (cited in Padgett 124).

6. The great disparity between the means and the medians in these tables, as well as the exceptionally large standard deviations, derives from distributions skewed by the presence of a few cases with abnormally high values. Because the data do not fit the normal curve, the best measure of central tendency is the median. The variations in "N" throughout the tables result from the fact that, for many of the units surveyed in all groups, the relevant data were incomplete or not reported.

7. Marx elaborated his theory of exploitation in Volume 1 of *Capital* where he argued that the worker's day is bifurcated into "necessary labor time" (that period during which the magnitude of the value that he or she creates is equal to the value of the commodities he or she indirectly receives from the wage paid to him or her by the capitalist—i.e., "wage goods") and "surplus labor time" (that period during which the worker creates value in excess of that received in wages). Thus, the rate of exploitation is the ratio of surplus to necessary labor time, or S/V (Howard and King 1975: 42).

8. The profit rate was estimated without regard to costs of means of production, which, with a few exceptions, are higher in the Oaxaca City craft shops (Table 25) than in the Ocotlán embroidery industry (Table 26). Expenditures for means of production are generally low and periods of amortization are long (5–20 years or more), resulting in the small contribution that

costs of means of production makes to overall costs of doing business. It should be stated that our estimates of profit rates are just that—estimates. If we factored in the costs of means of production, business taxes, transport costs, and treated household workers as though they were waged (for accounting purposes), it is highly unlikely that our estimates of enterprise profitability would show such enormous variation (from 1 to 281 percent).

7. Petty Industry, Class Maneuvers, and the Crisis of Mexican Capitalism

1. Major oil price declines in 1986 were continuing causes of crisis conditions in the Mexican economy (Orozco 1987).

2. See *Revista Mexicana de Ciencias Políticas y Sociales* 32 (1986) for a discussion of the effects of the earthquake and reconstruction efforts. The 1986 entry of Mexico into GATT is yet another crisis-induced move that should have the effect of opening up the Mexican market to more and cheaper foreign (especially U.S.) imports—but will probably force the shutdown of even more Mexican manufacturing enterprises (see Acosta 1986; Corro and Ortega 1986; González 1986).

3. In their seminal study, Barkin and Esteva (1979: 14) define inflation as "a continual rise in the level of market prices."

4. The recent literature (e.g., Mingione 1985 and Smith et al. 1984) dealing with the problem of economic restructuring and informalization tendencies within the world capitalist system with a special focus on household activities suggests, among other things, that urban working-class and "surplus" working-class households engage in many "informal" cash-generating productive activities to achieve reproductive viability under crisis conditions. The fact that they don't have the same means of defense as do landed peasant-artisans does not mean that they are without defenses against crisis. Pahl (1984), however, provides evidence from the Isle of Sheppy in Kent, England, that self-provisioning (i.e., home improvement, vegetable gardening, home auto repair) is a more frequent response of working- and middle-class households to economic crisis.

5. See Cook (1982) for a detailed study of the *metate* industry.

6. Since answers to both these questions emphasize the negative impact of the inflationary crisis, they downplay the variable capacity of peasant-artisan households to adjust or adapt to inflation. Despite the fact that all PAHs experience the negative impact of constant increases in consumers' and producers' goods that they customarily buy, there are factors, as specified in the previous section, that can intervene in any given case to mitigate inflation-driven damage to a PAH's standard of living.

7. In these cases, proletarianization was largely imposed from without through the forceful and often illegal expropriation of land and as a consequence of the declining terms of trade between city and countryside. One wonders whether the peasantry, left more to its own resources, would have received (and reinterpreted) liberation theology in quite the same way as it did. The Nicaraguan Revolution, which completed its first phase in July 1979 when the FSLN marched into Managua, was largely urban in origin

with students and tradespeople the primary forces (Vilas 1986: 113), despite the fact that proletarianization of the labor force had advanced farther in the rural areas than in the cities. Vilas suggested that semiproletarian farmers used their salaries to re-create the peasant economy, thus reinforcing their attachment to the land (66). He did point out, however, that 62 percent of the proletarian participants were offspring of the self-employed and merchants, traders, and small entrepreneurs: "In a certain sense, this permits one to see a concrete moment in the process of proletarianization of these 'intermediate' or petty-bourgeois fractions in two generations of each household; they are consistent with what we pointed out . . . about the progressive reduction of the artisan sector and in general of urban petty production through the process of industrial expansion" (116).

8. Bertaux and Bertaux-Wiame (1981) have made an interesting case study of French artisan bakers who have for decades successfully resisted encroachment by agro-industrial baking firms. There are over 50,000 bakeries in France, about one for every 1,000 inhabitants, employing 80,000 workers, 40 percent of whom are apprentices (1981: 156). Most of these are petty commodity enterprises that compete successfully with a small number of petty capitalist bakeries (averaging 10–15 employees each). The artisan baker's survival depends upon the persistence of small grain mills (to supply flour) and the extended services and low prices they can offer the consumer because of the high level of self-exploitation of the owners (and household workers) and their exploitation of apprentices, who one day hope to take over the business. The bakers have a national union, the Syndicat de la Boulangerie (Baker's Professional Union), which represents their interests before the government and the public. It appears, however, that the crux of their struggle involves the day-to-day circumvention of the laws that limit the hours of labor of the apprentices, a largely clandestine struggle carried out on an independent basis (162–163).

Bibliography

Acosta, C.
1986 "La reconversión, síntesis de planes fracasados, que no hay con que realizar." *Proceso,* September 22.
1987 "Logró el gobierno, en 1986, la tasa de inflación más alta de la historia." *Proceso,* January 12.

Acosta, C., and R. Monge
1988 "Los contribuyentes empobrecen ante la oleada de impuestos." *Proceso,* February 15: 20–23.

Adams, R. McC.
1966 *The Evolution of Urban Society.* Chicago: Aldine.
1973 "Anthropological Perspectives on Ancient Trade." Paper presented at International Congress of Ethnological Sciences, Chicago.

Aguilar Medina, José I.
1980 *El hombre y la urbe: La ciudad de Oaxaca.* Mexico City: SEP-INAH.

Alba, C., and J. Cisterna
1949 "Las industrias zapotecas." In Mendieta y Nuñez et al. 1949.

Alonso, J.
1983 "The Domestic Clothing Workers in the Mexican Metropolis and Their Relation to Dependent Capitalism." In Nash and Fernández Kelly, eds., 1983: 161–172.

Alonso, J., ed.
1980 *Lucha urbana y acumulación de capital.* Ediciones de la Casa Chata, No. 12. Mexico City: CIS-INAH.

Alvarado, A., ed.
1987 *Electoral Patterns and Perspectives in Mexico.* Monograph Series 22. Center for U.S.-Mexican Studies, University of California, San Diego.

Amin, S.
1976 *Unequal Development.* New York: Monthly Review Press.

Annis, S.
1987 *God and Production in a Guatemalan Town.* Austin: University of Texas Press.

Archetti, E., and K. Stolen
1975 *Explotación familiar y acumulación de capital en el campo argentino*. Buenos Aires: Siglo Veintiuno.
Arizpe, L.
1978 *Migración, etnicismo, y cambio económico*. Mexico City: Colegio de México.
Athreya, V., et al.
1987 "Indentification of Agrarian Classes: A Methodological Essay with Empirical Material from South India." *Journal of Peasant Studies* 14 (2): 147–190.
Banaji, J.
1976a "Chayanov, Kautsky, Lenin: Considerations Towards a Synthesis." *Economic and Political Weekly*, October 2: 1594–1607.
1976b "Summary of Selected Parts of Kautsky's *The Agrarian Question*." *Economy and Society* 5 (1): 1–49.
Barabas, A., and M. Bartolomé, eds.
1986 *Etnicidad y pluralismo cultural: La dinámica en Oaxaca*. Mexico City: INAH.
Barkin, D., and G. Esteva
1979 *Inflación y democracia: El caso de México*. Mexico City: Siglo Veintiuno.
Bartolomé, M., and A. Barabas
1986 "La pluralidad desigual en Oaxaca." In Barabas and Bartolomé, eds., 1986: 15–95.
Bartra, R.
1974 *Estructura agraria y clases sociales en México*. Mexico City: Ediciones Era.
1975 "La teoría del valor y la economía campesina: Invitación a la lectura de Chayanov." *Comercio Exterior* 25 (5): 517–524.
1978 *El poder despótico burgués*. Mexico City: Ediciones Era.
Bartra, R., and G. Otero
1987 "Agrarian Crisis and Social Differentiation in Mexico." *Journal of Peasant Studies* 14 (3): 334–362.
Beals, R.
1970 "Gifting, Reciprocity, Savings, and Credit in Peasant Oaxaca." *Southwestern Journal of Anthropology* 26: 231–241.
1975 *The Peasant Marketing System of Oaxaca, Mexico*. Berkeley and Los Angeles: University of California Press.
Beckhofer, F., and B. Elliot, eds.
1981 *The Petite Bourgeosie*. London: Macmillan.
Benería, L., and M. Roldán
1987 *The Crossroads of Class and Gender: Industrial Homework, Subcontracting, and Household Dynamics in Mexico City*. Chicago and London: University of Chicago Press.
Benería, L., and G. Sen
1981 "Accumulation, Reproduction, and Women's Role in Economic Development: Boserup Revisited." *Signs* 7: 279–298.

Benítez Zenteno, R., ed.
  1980 *Sociedad y política en Oaxaca, 1980: 15 estudios del caso.* Oaxaca: Universidad Benito Juárez.
Berdan, F.
  1982 *The Aztecs of Central Mexico: An Imperial Society.* New York: Holt, Rinehart and Winston.
Bernstein, H.
  1979 "African Peasantries: A Theoretical Framework." *Journal of Peasant Studies* 6: 421–443.
  1986 "Capitalism and Petty Commodity Production." *Social Analysis,* no. 20 (December): 11–28.
  1988 "Capitalism and Petty-Bourgeois Production." *Journal of Peasant Studies* 15 (2): 258–271.
Bernstein, H., and B. K. Cambell, eds.
  1985 *Contradictions of Accumulation in Africa: Studies in Economy and State.* Beverly Hills: Sage Publications.
Bernstein, H., and A. Thomas
  1983 *The "Third World" and "Development."* Manchester: Open University Press.
Bertaux, D. and I. Bertaux-Wiame
  1981 "Artisanal Bakery in France: How It Lives and Why it Survives." In Beckhofer and Elliot, eds., 1981: 155–182.
Bertocci, P.
  1964 "An Artisans' Cooperative." Summer Field Training Program in Anthropology (Oaxaca, Mexico). Department of Anthropology, Stanford University. Oaxaca Archives, Mimeograph.
Binford, L.
  1989 "Economic Crisis and Peasant Defense in Rural Mexico." Occasional Papers in Latin American Studies. Center for Latin American and Caribbean Studies, University of Connecticut, Storrs.
Binford, L., and S. Cook
  1987 "Toward a Marxist Rethinking of Third World Rural Industrialization." In England, ed., 1987: 61–88.
Birbeck, C.
  1979 "The Vultures of Cali." In Bromley and Gerry, eds., 1979: 161–183.
Blanton, R., and S. A. Kowalewski
  1981 "Monte Albán and After in the Valley of Oaxaca." In Sabloff, ed., 1981.
Blanton, R., S. A. Kowalewski, G. Feinman, and J. Appel
  1981 *Ancient Mesoamerica: A Comparison of Three Regions.* Cambridge: Cambridge University Press.
Boege, E., ed.
  1977 *Desarrollo del capitalismo y transformación de la estructura de poder en la región de Tuxtepec, Oaxaca.* Cuaderno 1 (Serie investigaciones de la especialidad de antropología social). Mexico City: Escuela Nacional de Antropología e Historia.

Bortz, J.
1986 "Wages and Economic Crisis in Mexico." In Carr and Anzaldua, eds., 1986: 33–46.
1987 "The Postwar Mexican Economy." *Mexican Studies/Estudios Mexicanos* 3 (1): 151–162.
Bossen, L.
1984 *The Redivision of Labor.* Albany: SUNY Press.
Bottomore, T., L. Harris, V. Kiernan, and R. Miliband, eds.
1983 *A Dictionary of Marxist Thought.* Cambridge, Mass.: Harvard University Press.
Breman, J.
1976 "A Dualistic Labour System? A Critique of the 'Informal Sector' Concept." *Economic and Political Weekly,* 2: 48–50.
1977 "Labour Relations in the 'Formal' and 'Informal' Sectors: Report of a Case Study in South Gujarat, India." *Journal of Peasant Studies* 4: 171–205 and 337–359.
1985 "A Dualistic Labour System? A Critique of the 'Informal Sector' Concept." In Bromley, ed., 1985: 43–64.
Bromley, R.
1978 "Introduction—The Urban Informal Sector: Why Is It Worth Discussing?" *World Development* 6 (9/10): 1033–1040.
Bromley, R., ed.
1985 *Planning for Small Enterprises in Third World Cities.* Oxford: Pergamon Press.
Bromley, R., and C. Gerry, eds.
1979 *Casual Work and Poverty in Third World Cities.* Chichester: Wiley.
Bucher, C.
1901 *Industrial Evolution.* New York: Henry Holt.
Cabrera, L.
1974 *Diccionario de aztecquismos.* Mexico City: Ediciones Oasis.
Cain, M.
1977 "The Economic Activities of Children in a Village in Bangladesh." *Population and Development Review* 3: 201–227.
Caldwell, J.
1982 *Theory of Fertility Decline.* New York: Academic Press.
Calzada, F., and F. Hernández y Puente
1987 "Ineficacia antiinflacionaria." *La Jornada,* May 25: 14.
Carr, B.
1986 "The Mexican Left, the Popular Movements, and the Politics of Austerity, 1982–1985." In Carr and Anzaldua, eds., 1986: 1–18.
Carr, B., and R. Anzaldua, eds.
1986 *The Mexican Left, the Popular Movements, and the Politics of Austerity.* Center for U.S.-Mexican Studies. University of California, San Diego. Monograph Series, 18.
Cassidy, T.
1981 "Haciendas and Pueblos in Nineteenth Century Oaxaca." Ph.D. dissertation. Christ's College, Cambridge University.

Castillo, H.
  1988 "Una economía para vivir mejor." *Proceso*, February 29: 15.
CEPAL
  1982 *Economía campesina y agricultura empresarial.* Mexico City: Siglo Veintiuno.
Chance, J.
  1978 *Race and Class in Colonial Oaxaca.* Stanford: Stanford University Press.
Chassen, F.
  1986 "Oaxaca: Del Porfiriato a la revolución, 1902–1911." Ph.D. thesis. Facultad de Filosofía y Letras, Universidad Nacional Autónoma de México.
Chattopadhyay, P.
  1972 "On the Question of the Mode of Production in Indian Agriculture: A Preliminary Note." *Economic and Political Weekly* 7 (13) (Review of Agriculture, March 25): A39–A46.
Chayanov, A. V.
  1966 *The Theory of Peasant Economy.* D. Thorner, B. Kerblay, and R. E. F. Smith (eds.). Homewood, Ill.: Irwin. Reprint, Madison: University of Wisconsin Press, 1986.
Chevalier, J.
  1982 *Civilization and the Stolen Gift.* Toronto: University of Toronto Press.
  1983 "There is Nothing Simple about Simple Commodity Production." *Journal of Peasant Studies* 10 (4): 153–186.
Chibnik, M.
  1984 "A Cross-Cultural Examination of Chayanov's Theory." *Current Anthropology* 25 (3): 335–340.
  1987 "The Economic Effects of Household Demography: A Cross-Cultural Assessment of Chayanov's Theory." In Maclachlan, ed., 1987: 74–106.
Clammer, J., ed.
  1978 *The New Economic Anthropology.* New York: St. Martin's.
Clarke, C.
  1986 *Livelihood Systems, Settlements, and Levels of Living in Los Valles Centrales de Oaxaca, Mexico.* Research Paper no. 37. School of Geography, Oxford University.
Clemens, H.
  1987a *Santo Tomás Jalieza: Esbozo de la historia de una comunidad artesana.* Forthcoming in *Historia de Oaxaca,* series, ed. Angeles Romero. Centro Regional de INAH.
  1987b "Weaving in Two Oaxaca Communities: An Historical Perspective." Paper presented at the 47th Annual Meeting, the Society for Applied Anthropology. Oaxaca, Mexico, April 8-12.
  1988 "Buscando la Forma: Self-Reorganization in Craft Commercialization." Paper presented at the 46th International Congress of Americanists, July 4-8. Amsterdam, The Netherlands.

Cockcroft, J.
  1983 "Immiseration, Not Marginalization: The Case of Mexico." *Latin American Perspectives* 10 (Spring): 86–107.
Connolly, P.
  1985 "The Politics of the Informal Sector: A Critique." In Redclift and Mingione, eds., 1985: 55–91.
Cook, S.
  1969 *Teitipac and Its Metateros: An Economic Anthropological Study of Production and Exchange in a Peasant-Artisan Economy in the Valley of Oaxaca, Mexico.* Ann Arbor: University Microfilms.
  1976 "Value, Price, and Simple Commodity Production: The Case of the Zapotec Stoneworkers." *Journal of Peasant Studies* 3 (4): 395–427.
  1977 "Beyond the Formen: Towards a Revised Marxist Theory of Precapitalist Formations and the Transition to Capitalism." *Journal of Peasant Studies* 4 (4): 360–389.
  1978 "Petty Commodity Production and Capitalist Development in the 'Central Valleys' Region of Oaxaca, Mexico." *Nova Americana* 1: 285–332.
  1981 "Crafts, Capitalist Development, and Cultural Property in Oaxaca, Mexico." *Inter-American Economic Affairs* 35 (3): 53–68.
  1982 *Zapotec Stoneworkers.* Lanham, Md.: University Press of America.
  1983a "Comment on 'The Economic Systems of Ancient Oaxaca' by S. Kowalewski and L. Finsten." *Current Anthropology* 24 (4): 427–428.
  1983b "Mestizo Palm Weavers among the Zapotecs: A Critical Reexamination of the 'Albarradas Enigma.'" *Notas Mesoamericanas,* no. 9: 39–46.
  1984a *Peasant Capitalist Industry.* Lanham, Md.: University Press of America.
  1984b "Rural Industry, Social Differentiation, and the Contradictions of Provincial Mexican Capitalism." *Latin American Perspectives,* Issue 43, Vol. 11 (4): 60–85.
  1984c "Peasant Economy, Rural Industry, and Capitalist Development in the Oaxaca Valley, Mexico." *Journal of Peasant Studies* 12 (1): 3–40.
  1985a "Craft Business, Piece Work, and Value Distribution in the Oaxaca Valley, Mexico." In Plattner, ed., 1985: 235–258.
  1985b Review of E. P. Durrenberger (ed.), *Chayanov, Peasants, and Economic Anthropology. American Ethnologist* 12 (1): 157–158.
  1986 "Entrepreneurship, Capital Accumulation, and the Dynamics of Simple Commodity Production in Rural Oaxaca, Mexico." In Greenfield and Strickon, eds., 1986: 54–95.
  1988 "Inflation and Rural Livelihood in a Mexican Province: An Exploratory Analysis." *Mexican Studies/Estudios Mexicanos* 4 (1): 55–77.
Cook, S., and L. Binford
  1986 "Petty Commodity Production, Capital Accumulation, and Peasant Differentiation: Lenin vs. Chayanov in Rural Mexico." *Review of Radical Political Economics* 18 (4): 1–31.

Cook, S., and M. Diskin, eds.
  1976 *Markets in Oaxaca.* Austin: University of Texas Press.
Cooper, E.
  1980 *The Wood-Carvers of Hong Kong.* Cambridge: Cambridge University Press.
Cornelius, W., and F. Trueblood, eds.
  1975 *Urbanization and Inequality: The Political Economy of Urban and Rural Development in Latin America.* Beverly Hills: Sage Publications.
Corro, S., and F. Ortega
  1986 "Para los trabajadores, el desastre; para los empresarios, espejismo." *Proceso,* September 22.
Cox, T.
  1979 "Awkward Class or Awkward Classes? Class Relations in the Russian Peasantry before Collectivization." *Journal of Peasant Studies* 7 (1): 70–85.
  1984 "Class Analysis of the Russian Peasantry: The Research of Kritsman and His School." *Journal of Peasant Studies* 11 (2): 11–60.
  1986 *Peasants, Class, and Capitalism.* Oxford: Clarendon Press.
Cox, T., and G. Littlejohn, eds.
  1984 *Kritsman and the Agrarian Marxists. Journal of Peasant Studies* 11 (2).
Crow, B., and A. Thomas
  1983 *Third World Atlas.* Milton Keynes and Philadelphia: Open University Press.
Davies, R.
  1979 "Informal Sector or Subordinate Mode of Production? A Model." In Bromley and Gerry, eds., 1979: 87–104.
de Appendini, K., and V. Almeida
  1976 "Agricultura capitalista y agricultura campesina en México: Diferencias regionales en base al análisis de datos censuales." In Stavenhagen et al., 1976: 29–68.
Deere, C. D., and A. de Janvry
  1979 "A Conceptual Framework for the Empirical Analysis of Peasants." *American Journal of Agricultural Economics* 61: 601–611.
Deere, C. D., and A. de Janvry
  1981 "Demographic and Social Differentiation among Northern Peruvian Peasants." *Journal of Peasant Studies* 8 (3): 335–366.
Deere, C. D., and M. León de Leal
  1981 "Peasant Production, Proletarianization, and the Sexual Division of Labor in the Andes." *Signs* 7 (2): 338–360.
de Janvry, A.
  1981 *The Agrarian Question and Reformism in Latin America.* Baltimore and London: Johns Hopkins University Press.
de la Peña, S.
  1981 *Capitalismo en cuatro comunidades rurales.* Mexico City: Siglo Veintiuno.

Dennis, P.
　1976　*Conflictos por tierras en el Valle de Oaxaca, México.* Mexico City: SEP-INAH.
de Rouffignac, A.
　1985　*The Contemporary Peasantry in Mexico: A Class Analysis.* New York: Praeger.
de Teresa, A. P., and M. W. Rees
　1989　"Transformation of the Conditions of Work Force Reproduction in Yucatan, Mexico, 1930–1983." Paper presented at the Annual Meetings of the Society for Economic Anthropology. Central Michigan University, Mt. Pleasant, Michigan, April.
Díaz Montes, F.
　1979　"El impacto de la agroindustria del mezcal en la estructura social de una comunidad." Licenciatura thesis. Centro para la Formación de Profesores e Investigadores en Ciencias Sociales, Universidad Autónoma "Benito Juárez" de Oaxaca, México.
Diskin, M.
　1976　"The Structure of a Peasant Market System in Oaxaca." In Cook and Diskin, eds., 1976: 49–66.
　1986　"La economía de la comunidad étnica en Oaxaca." In Barabas and Bartolomé, eds., 1986: 257–298.
Dobb, M.
　1963　*Studies in the Development of Capitalism.* New York: Monthly Review Press.
Downing, T.
　1971　"Field Fragmentation in Zapotec Land Inheritance." Paper presented at the 1971 Annual Meeting of the Southwestern Anthropological Association. Tucson, Arizona.
Druijven, P.
　1988　"El cuento de las canastas: Cestería en miseria? Basketry as Component Part of Livelihood Strategies of Rural Households in the Tlacolula Valley, Oaxaca, Mexico." Paper presented in the symposium "Artesanías y Sociedad." Organized by D. Papousek and E. Cuellar for the 46th International Congress of Americanists, July 4–8. Amsterdam, The Netherlands.
Durán, E.
　1985　"Mexico: Economic Realism and Political Efficiency." *World Today* 41 (5): 96–99.
Durrenberger, E. P., ed.
　1984　*Chayanov, Peasants, and Economic Anthropology.* Orlando, Fla.: Academic Press.
Eaton, J.
　1966　*Political Economy.* New York: International Publishers.
Emmanuel, A.
　1972　*Unequal Exchange.* New York: Monthly Review Press.

Engels, F.
1967 "Supplement to Capital, Volume Three." In Marx, *Capital* Vol. 3: 889–910. New York: International Publishers, 1967.

England, R., ed.
1987 *Economic Processes and Political Conflicts.* New York: Praeger.

Ennew, J., P. Hirst, and K. Tribe
1977 "Peasantry as an Economic Category." *Journal of Peasant Studies* 4 (4): 295–322.

Esparza, M.
1983 "Introduction" to *Padrón de capitación de la ciudad de Oaxaca, 1875.* Documentos del Archivo, Gobierno del Estado de Oaxaca, Oaxaca, México.

Esteva, G.
1983 *The Struggle for Rural Mexico.* South Hadley, Mass.: Bergin and Garvey.

Feder, E.
1977 "Campesinistas y descampesinistas: Tres enfoques divergentes (no incompatibles) sobre la destrucción del campesinado." *Comercio Exterior* 27 (12): 1439–1446.

Feinman, G.
1986 "The Emergence of Specialized Ceramic Production in Formative Oaxaca." *Research in Economic Anthropology,* Supp. 2: 347–373.

Foladori, G.
1981 *Polémica en torno a las teorías del campesinado.* Mexico City: ENAH-INAH.

Fox, J.
1987 "Popular Participation and Access to Food: Mexico's Community Supply Councils, 1979–1985." Forthcoming in Scott Whiteford and Ann Ferguson, eds., *Food Security and Hunger in Central America and Mexico.* Boulder: Westview Press.

Friedman, H.
1980 "Household Production and the National Economy: Concepts for the Analysis of Agrarian Formations." *Journal of Peasant Studies* 7 (2): 158–184.

Frobel, F., J. Heinrichs, and O. Kreye
1978 "The New International Division of Labor." *Social Science Information* 17 (1): 123–142.
1980 *The New International Division of Labor.* Cambridge: Cambridge University Press.

Galeski, B.
1972 *Basic Concepts in Rural Sociology.* Manchester: Manchester University Press.

Geertz, C.
1963 *Peddlers and Princes.* Chicago: University of Chicago Press.

Gerry, C.
1979 "Small-Scale Manufacturing and Repairs in Dakar: A Survey of

Market Relations within the Urban Economy." In Bromley and Gerry, eds., 1979: 229–250.

Gerry, C., and C. Birkbeck

1981 "The Petty Commodity Producer in Third World Cities: Petit-Bourgeois or 'Disguised' Proletarian?." In Beckhofer and Elliot, eds., 1981: 121–154.

Gibbon, P., and M. Neocosmos

1985 "Some Problems in the Political Economy of 'African Socialism.'" In Bernstein and Campbell, eds., 1985: 153–206.

González, R.

1986 "México llegó al GATT cuando las mercancías que ofrecen pierden mercado." *Proceso*, September 22.

González Casanova, P., and H. Aguilar Camín, eds.

1985 *México ante la crisis*. Vol. 1. Mexico City: Siglo Veintiuno.

Goodman, D., and M. Redclift

1982 *From Peasant to Proletarian*. New York: St. Martin's Press.

Goody, E., ed.

1982 *From Craft to Industry*. Cambridge: Cambridge University Press.

Greenfield, S., and A. Strickon, eds.

1986 *Entrepreneurship*. Lanham, Md.: University Press of America.

Grindle, M.

1987 "The Response to Austerity: Political and Economic Strategies of Mexico's Rural Poor." Harvard Institute for International Development, Cambridge, Mass.

Gulati, L.

1982 *Profiles in Female Poverty*. Oxford: Pergamon Press.

Hamilton, N.

1984 "State-Class Alliances and Conflicts: Issues and Actors in the Mexican Economic Crisis." *Latin American Perspectives*, Issue 43, Vol. 11.

Hamnett, B.

1971 *Politics and Trade in Southern Mexico, 1750–1821*. Cambridge: Cambridge University Press.

Handy, J.

1984 *Gift of the Devil*. Boston: South End Press.

Harris, M.

1987 *Cultural Anthropology*. New York: Harper and Row.

Harris, M., and E. Ross

1987 *Death, Sex, and Fertility: Population Regulation in Preindustrial and Developing Societies*. New York: Columbia University Press.

Harris, O.

1984 "Households as Natural Units." In Young et al., eds., 1984: 136–156.

Harrison, M.

1975 "Chayanov and the Economics of the Russian Peasantry." *Journal of Peasant Studies* 2 (4): 389–417.

1977 "The Peasant Mode of Production in the Work of A. V. Chayanov." *Journal of Peasant Studies* 4 (4): 323–336.

Hart, K.
1973 "Informal Income Opportunities and Urban Employment in Ghana." *Journal of Modern African Studies* 11 (1): 61–89.
1982 "On Commoditization." In Goody, ed., 1982: 38–49.

Harvey, D.
1982 *The Limits to Capital.* Chicago: University of Chicago Press.

Herman, T.
1957 "Cottage Industries: A Reply." *Economic Development and Cultural Change* 6: 374–375.

Hernández, E., and J. Córdoba
1982 *La distribución del ingreso en México.* Mexico City: Centro de Investigación para la Integración Social.

Herring, R.
1984 "Chayanovian versus Neoclassical Perspectives on Land Tenure and Productivity Interactions." In Durrenberger, ed., 1984: 133–150.

Hewitt de Alcántara, C.
1984 *Anthropological Perspectives on Rural Mexico.* London: Routledge and Kegan Paul.

Higgins, M.
1983 *Somos Tocayos.* Lanham, Md.: University Press of America.

Hill, P.
1986 *Development Economics on Trial.* Cambridge: Cambridge University Press.

Hilton, R.
1974 "Medieval Peasants—Any Lessons?." *Journal of Peasant Studies* 1 (2): 207–219.

Himmelweit, S.
1983 "Surplus Value." In Bottomore, et al., eds., 1983: 472–475.

Hoogvelt, A.
1982 *Third World in Global Development.* London: Macmillan.

Hopkins, T.
1978 "The Articulation of the Modes of Production: Tailoring in Tunisia." *American Ethnologist* 5 (3): 468–483.

Howard, M., and J. King
1975 *The Political Economy of Marx.* London: Longman.

Hunt, D.
1979 "Chayanov's Model of Peasant Household Resource Allocations." *Journal of Peasant Studies* 6 (3): 247–285.

International Labor Office
1951 *Payment by Results.* Geneva: International Labor Office.

Jaillet, A. E.
1979 "La industria textil mantelera de Oaxaca y el desarrollo capitalista dependiente." Oaxaca Small Industries Project. Unpublished.

Kahn, J.
1975 "Economic Scale and the Cycle of Petty Commodity Production."

In M. Bloch, ed., *Marxist Analyses and Social Anthropology*. 1975: 137–158. New York: Wiley.

1978   "Ideology and Social Structure in Indonesia." *Comparative Studies in Society and History* 20 (1): 103–122.

1980   *Minangkabau Social Formations*. Cambridge: Cambridge University Press.

Kautsky, K.

1974   *La cuestión agraria*. Mexico City: Siglo Veintiuno.

Kay, G.

1975   *Development and Underdevelopment: A Marxist Analysis*. New York: St. Martin's Press.

Kemper, R., and G. Foster

1975   "Urbanization in Mexico: The View from Tzintzuntzan." In Cornelius and Trueblood, eds., 1975: 53–75.

Kerblay, B.

1966   "A. V. Chayanov: Life, Career, Works." In Chayanov, 1966: xxv–lxxv.

Kingston-Mann, E.

1980   "A Strategy for Marxist Bourgeois Evolution: Lenin and the Peasantry." *Journal of Peasant Studies* 7 (2): 131–157.

Kirkby, A.

1973   *The Use of Land and Water Resources in the Past and Present Valley of Oaxaca, Mexico*. Memoirs of the Museum of Anthropology, no. 5. Ann Arbor: University of Michigan.

Kitching, G.

1982   *Development and Underdevelopment in Historical Perspective*. London and New York: Methuen.

Kloby, J.

1987   "The Growing Divide: Class Polarization in the 1980s." *Monthly Review* 39 (4): 1–8.

Kowalewski, S., and L. Finsten

1983   "The Economic Systems of Ancient Oaxaca: A Regional Perspective." *Current Anthropology* 24 (4): 413–442.

Kriedte, P., H. Medick, and J. Schlumbohm

1981   *Industrialization before Industrialization*. Cambridge: Cambridge University Press.

Kritsman, L. N.

1984   "Class Stratification of the Soviet Countryside." Ed. and trans. G. Littlejohn. In Cox and Littlejohn, 1984: 85–143.

Kuhn, A., and A. Wolpe, eds.

1978   *Feminism and Materialism*. London: Routledge and Kegan Paul.

Larmer, B.

1988   "Village Hopes Rest on Long Trek North." *Christian Science Monitor*, February 11: 1 and 27.

Leacock, E., H. Safa, et al.

1986   *Women's Work*. South Hadley, Mass.: Bergin and Garvey.

LeBrun, O., and C. Gerry
1975 "Petty Producers and Capitalism." *Review of African Political Economy*, no. 3.
Lenin, V. I.
1946 *Capitalism and Agriculture*. New York: International Publishers.
1963 "The Handicraft Census of 1894–95 in Perm Gubernia and General Problems of Handicraft Industry." In *Collected Works of V. I. Lenin, Vol. 2, 1895–1897:* 358–400. London: Lawrence and Wishart.
1964 *The Development of Capitalism in Russia*. Moscow: Progress Publishers.
Levy, D., and G. Szekely
1986 "Mexico: Challenge and Responses." *Current History* 85 (January): 16–20.
Lewin, A. C.
1985 "The Dialectic of Dominance: Petty Production and Peripheral Capitalism." In Bromley, ed., 1985: 107–135.
Lewin, M.
1975 *Russian Peasants and Soviet Power*. New York: Norton.
Lewis, O.
1960 *Tepoztlán, Village in Mexico*. New York: Holt, Rinehart and Winston.
Littlefield, A.
1976 *La industria de las hamacas en Yucatán, México*. Mexico City: SEP-INI.
1978 "Exploitation and the Expansion of Capitalism: The Case of the Hammock Industry of Yucatan." *American Ethnologist* 5: 495–508.
1979a "The Expansion of Capitalist Relations of Production in Mexican Crafts." *Journal of Peasant Studies* 6 (4): 471–488.
1979b *Informe preliminar, San Pedro Mártir, Ocotlán*. Archives of the Proyecto de Estudios Socioeconómicos sobre las Pequeñas Industrias de Oaxaca (PESPIDEO). Unpublished internal report.
Long, N., and P. Richardson
1978 "Informal Sector, Petty Commodity Production, and the Social Relations of Small-Scale Enterprise." In Clammer, ed., 1978: 176–209.
Lynch, P., and H. Fahmy
1984 *Craftswomen in Kerdassa, Egypt: Household Production and Reproduction*. Geneva: ILO.
MacEwen Scott, A.
1979 "Who Are the Self-Employed?." In Bromley and Gerry, eds., 1979: 105–129.
MacEwen Scott, A., ed.
1986 *Rethinking Petty Commodity Production. Social Analysis*, no. 20.
Mackintosh, M.
1984 "Gender and Economics: The Sexual Division of Labor and the Subordination of Women." In Young et al., eds., 1984: 3–17.

Maclachlan, M., ed.
  1987 *Household Economies and Their Transformation.* Lanham, Md.:
         University Press of America.
Malinowski, B., and J. de la Fuente
  1982 *The Economics of a Mexican Market System.* London: Routledge
         and Kegan Paul.
Mandel, E.
  1968 *Marxist Economic Theory, Vol. 1.* New York: Monthly Review
         Press.
  1975 *Late Capitalism.* London: New Left Books.
Mandle, J.
  1980 "Marxist Analyses and Capitalist Development in the Third
         World." *Theory and Society* 9: 865–876.
Martínez, V. V., and A. Arellanes M.
  1985 "Negociación y conflicto en Oaxaca." In Martínez Assad, ed., 1985:
         203–227.
Martínez Assad, C.
  1987 "State Elections in Mexico." In Alvarado, ed., 1987: 33–42.
Martínez Assad, C., ed.
  1985 *Municipios en conflicto.* Mexico City: GV Editores, Instituto de In-
         vestigaciones Sociales (UNAM).
Martínez Ríos, J.
  1964 "Análisis funcional de la 'Guelaguetza Agrícola.'" *Revista Mexi-
         cana de Sociología* 26 (1): 79–125.
Marx, K.
  1963 *Theories of Surplus Value, Part I.* Moscow: Progress Publishers.
  1967 *Capital, Vol. 1.* New York: International Publishers.
  1977 "Results of the Immediate Process of Production." Appendix to
         Marx, *Capital, Vol. 1:* 943–1084. New York: Random House.
Medick, H.
  1976 "The Proto-Industrial Family Economy: The Structural Function of
         Household and Family during the Transition from Peasant Society
         to Industrial Capitalism." *Social History* 1 (3): 291–315.
  1981 "The Proto-Industrial Family Economy." In Kriedte et al., 1981:
         38–73.
Méndez y Mercado, L.
  1985 *Migración: Decisión involuntaria.* Mexico City: INI.
Mendieta y Nuñez, L., et al.
  1949 *Los Zapotecos.* Instituto de Investigaciones Sociales, UNAM. Mex-
         ico City: Imprenta Universitaria.
Miller, S.
  1986 "Industrial Restructuring and Manufacturing Homework: Immi-
         grant Women in the U.K. Clothing Industry." *Capital and Class* 27
         (Winter): 37–80.
Mingione, E.
  1985 "Social Reproduction of the Surplus Labor Force: The Case of
         Southern Italy." In Redclift and Mingione, eds., 1985: 14–54.

Mintz, S.
1964 "Peasant Marketplaces and Economic Development in Latin America." The Graduate Center for Latin American Studies, Vanderbilt University. Occasional Paper 4.

Moser, C.
1978 "Informal Sector or Petty Commodity Production: Dualism or Dependency in Urban Development?." *World Development* 6 (9/10): 1041–1064.

Murphy, A., and H. Selby
1981 "A Comparison of Household Income and Budgetary Patterns in Four Mexican Cities." *Urban Anthropology* 10 (3): 247–267.

Nag, M., B. White, and R. Peet
1978 "An Anthropological Approach to the Study of the Economic Value of Children in Java and Nepal." *Current Anthropology* 19: 293–306.

Nardi, B.
1983 "Reply to Harbison's Comments on Nardi's Modes of Explanation in Anthropological Population Theory." *American Anthropologist* 85: 662–664.

Nash, J., and M. P. Fernández-Kelly, eds.
1983 *Women, Men, and the International Division of Labor.* Albany: SUNY Press.

Nieman, E., and E. Miller
1987 *La disminución del número de Palenqueros en Matatlán desde fines de los años setenta.* University of Amsterdam, Institute of Human Geography.

Nolasco Armas, M.
1981 Cuatro ciudades: El proceso de urbanización dependiente. Mexico City: INAH.

Novelo, V.
1976 *Artesanías y capitalismo en México.* Mexico City: SEP-INAH.

Ornelas, J.
1980 "La migración en Santo Domingo del Valle, Tlacolula." In Benítez, ed., 1980: 143–165.

Orozco, M.
1987 "El poder adquisitivo en la crísis." *Uno Más Uno (Página Uno, Suplemento Político),* May 24: iv.

Ortíz, G.
1980 "Economía y migración en una comunidad Mixteca: El caso de San Juan Mixtepec." In Benítez, ed., 1980: 11–142.

Padgett, L. V.
1966 *The Mexican Political System.* Boston: Houghton Mifflin.

Pahl, R.
1984 *Divisions of Labour.* London: Blackwell.

Palerm, A.
1976 *Modos de producción y formaciones socioeconómicas.* Mexico City: Editorial Edicol.
1980 *Antropología y marxismo.* Mexico City: Editorial Nueva Imagen.

Paré, L.
1977 *El proletariado agrícola en México.* Mexico City: Siglo Veintiuno.
1985 "Movimiento campesino y política agraria en México, 1976–1982."
Revista Mexicana de Sociología 47 (4): 85–111.
Paré, L., ed.
1979 *Polémica sobre las clases sociales en el campo mexicano.* Mexico
City: Editorial Machual.
Parsons, E.
1936 *Mitla, Town of Souls.* Chicago: University of Chicago Press.
Patnaik, U.
1971a "Capitalist Development in Agriculture." *Economic and Political
Weekly,* September 25: A123–A130.
1971b "Capitalist Development in Agriculture." *Economic and Political
Weekly,* December 25: A190–A194.
1972 "On the Mode of Production in Indian Agriculture." *Economic and
Political Weekly,* September 30: A145–A151.
1979 "Neo-Populism and Marxism: The Chayanovian View of the Agrarian Question and Its Fundamental Fallacy." *Journal of Peasant
Studies* 6 (4): 375–420.
Pearce, J.
1986 *Promised Land: Peasant Rebellion in Chalatenango, El Salvador.*
London: Latin American Bureau.
Plattner, S.
1965 "The Economic Structure of Santa Ana del Valle." The Oaxaca Archives, Stanford University. Summer Field Training Program in
Anthropology. Mimeograph.
Plattner, S., ed.
1985 *Markets and Marketing.* Lanham, Md.: University Press of Amer-
ica.
Polyanyi, K., et al.
1957 *Trade and Market in the Early Empires.* Glencoe, Ill.: Free Press.
Portes, A.
1983 "The Informal Sector: Definition, Controversy, and Relations to
National Development." *Review* 7 (1): 151–174.
Prieto, Ana Maria
1986 "Mexico's National *Coordinadoras* in a Context of Economic Cri-
sis." In Carr and Anzaldua, eds., 1986: 75–94.
Quinn, N.
1964 "Study of Variations in the Division of Inheritance." The Oaxaca
Archives, Stanford University. Summer Field Training Program in
Anthropology. Mimeograph.
Ramírez, M.
1988 "The IMF Austerity Program, 1983–87: Miguel de la Madríd's Leg-
acy." University of Connecticut/Brown University Occasional
Papers in Latin American Studies.

Redclift, M.
1980 "Agrarian Populism in Mexico—The 'Via Campesina.'" *Journal of Peasant Studies* 7 (4): 492–502.
Redclift, N., and E. Mingione, eds.
1985 *Beyond Employment: Household, Gender, and Subsistence.* Oxford: Blackwell.
Reed, M.
1984 "Social Change and Social Conflict in Nineteenth Century England: A Comment." *Journal of Peasant Studies* 12 (1): 109–123.
Reinhardt, N.
1988 *Our Daily Bread: The Peasant Question and Family Farming in the Colombian Andes.* Berkeley and Los Angeles: University of California Press.
Rello, F.
1976 "Modo de producción y clases sociales." *Cuadernos Políticos,* no. 8.
Reyes Héroles, J.
1983 *Política macroeconómica y bienestar en México.* Mexico City: Fondo de Cultura Económica.
Reyes Osorio, S., R. Stavenhagen, S. Eckstein, and J. Ballesteros
1974 *Estructura agraria y desarrollo agrícola en México.* Mexico City: Fondo de Cultura Económica.
Rivermar Pérez, L., and J. Tellez Ortega
1984 "Aspectos económicos y culturales de los textiles del distrito de Ocotlán, Oaxaca." Licenciatura thesis. Escuela Nacional de Antropología e Historia, Mexico City.
Roldán, M.
1985 "Industrial Outworking, Struggles for the Reproduction of the Working Class Families and Gender Subordination." In Redclift and Mingione, eds., 1985: 248–285.
Ros, J.
1985 "La crisis económica: Un análisis general." In González Casanova and Aguilar Camín, eds., 1985: 135–154.
Roseberry, W.
1982 "Peasants, Proletarians, and Politics in Venezuela, 1875–1975." In Weller and Guggenheim, eds., 1982: 106–131.
1983 *Coffee and Capitalism in the Venezuelan Andes.* Austin: University of Texas Press.
Rostow, W. W.
1960 *The Stages of Economic Growth.* Cambridge: Cambridge University Press.
Roxborough, I.
1979 *Theories of Underdevelopment.* Atlantic Highlands, N.J.: Humanities.
Rydina, M., G. Chernikov, and G. Khudokormov
1980 *Fundamentals of Political Economy.* Moscow: Progress Publishers.

Sabloff, J., ed.
  1981 *Supplement to the Handbook of Middle American Indians.* Vol. 1
        Archaeology. Austin: University of Texas Press.
Sabloff, J., and C. Lamberg-Karlovsky, eds.
  1975 *Ancient Civilization and Trade.* Albuquerque: University of New
        Mexico Press.
Sahlins, M.
  1972 *Stone Age Economics.* Chicago: Aldine.
Salvucci, R.
  1987 *Textiles and Capitalism in Mexico.* Princeton, N.J.: Princeton Uni-
        versity Press.
Schejtman, A.
  1983 Oaxaca y Sinaloa: Campesinos y empresarios en dos polos contras-
        tantes de estructura agraria." In G. Bodaigosz G., ed., 1983, *Eco-
        nomía mexicana.* Mexico City: CIDE.
Schlumbohn, J.
  1981 "Relations of Production-Productive Forces Crises in Proto-Indus-
        trialization." In Kriedte et al., 1981: 94–125.
Schmitz, H.
  1982 *Manufacturing in the Backyard.* London: Frances Pinter.
Schneider, J., and A. Weiner, eds.
  1989 *Cloth and Human Experience.* Washington, D.C.: Smithsonian In-
        stitution Press.
Scott, J. C.
  1976 *The Moral Economy of the Peasant.* New Haven: Yale University
        Press.
  1985 *Weapons of the Weak.* New Haven: Yale University Press.
Semo, E.
  1973 *Historia del capitalismo en México: Los orígenes, 1521–1763.*
        Mexico City: Ediciones Era.
Shanin, T.
  1971 "The Nature and Logic of Peasant Economy." In Shanin, ed., 1976,
        Peasants and Peasant Societies. London: Penguin.
  1972 *The Awkward Class.* Oxford: Oxford University Press.
  1980 "Measuring Peasant Capitalism." In E. J. Hobsbawn et al., 1980,
        Peasants in History: 83–104. Oxford: Oxford University Press.
  1986 "Chayanov's Message: Illuminations, Miscomprehension, and the
        Contemporary 'Development Theory.'" In D. Thorner, B. Kerblay,
        and R. E. F. Smith, eds., 1986: *A. V. Chayanov on the Theory of
        Peasant Economy,* 1–24. Madison: University of Wisconsin Press.
Shashahani, S.
  1986 "Mamasani Women: Changes in the Division of Labor among a
        Sedentarized Pastoral People of Iran." In Leacock, Safa, et al., 1986:
        111–121.
Silva, G.
  1980 *Exámen de una economía en Oaxaca estudio de un caso: Teo-*

titlán del Valle. Estudios de Antropología e Historia 21, Centro Regional de Oaxaca, Instituto Nacional de Antropología e Historia.

Smith, C.
1984 "Does a Commodity Economy Enrich the Few While Ruining the Masses? Differentiation among Petty Commodity Producers in Guatemala." *Journal of Peasant Studies* 11 (3): 60–95.

Smith, G.
1979 "Socio-Economic Differentiation and Relations of Production among Petty Producers in Central Peru, 1880–1970." *Journal of Peasant Studies* 6 (3): 286–307.
1985 "Reflections on the Social Relations of Simple Commodity Production." *Journal of Peasant Studies* 13 (1): 99–108.

Smith, J., et al., eds.
1984 *Household and the World Economy.* Beverly Hills: Sage Publications.

Smith, W.
1977 *The Fiesta System and Economic Change.* New York: Columbia University Press.

Solomon, S.
1977 *The Soviet Agrarian Debate: A Controversy in Social Science, 1923–1929.* Boulder: Westview Press.

Spengler, J.
1957 "Cottage Industries: A Comment." *Economic Development and Cultural Change* 6 (July): 371–373.

Stavenhagen, R.
1978 "Capitalism and Peasantry in Mexico." *Latin American Perspectives* 5 (3): 27–37.

Stavenhagen, R., et al.
1976 *Capitalismo y campesinado en México: Estudios de la realidad campesina.* Mexico City: SEP-INAH.

Stolcke, V.
1984 "Women's Labours: The Naturalization of Social Inequality and Women's Subordination." In Young et al., 1984: 159–177.

Swallow, D.
1982 "Production and Control in the Indian Garment Export Industry." In Goody, ed., 1982: 133–165.

Tax, S.
1953 *Penny Capitalism.* Smithsonian Institution, Institute of Social Anthropology Publication 16. Washington D.C.: U.S. Government Printing Office.

Taylor, W.
1971 "The Colonial Background to Peasant Economy in the Valley of Oaxaca." Unpublished manuscript. Personal collection.
1972 *Landlord and Peasant in Colonial Oaxaca.* Stanford: Stanford University Press.

Thorner, D.
　1966 "Chayanov's Concept of Peasant Economy." In Chayanov, 1966: xi–xxiii.
Trager, L.
　1985 "From Yams to Beer in a Nigerian City: Expansion and Change in Informal Sector Trade Activity." In Plattner, ed., 1986: 259–286.
Vásquez, H.
　1980 "Migración zapoteca: Algunos aspectos económicos, demográficos, y culturales." In Benítez, ed., 1980: 167–183.
Vilas, C.
　1986 *The Sandinista Revolution.* New York: Monthly Review Press.
Villanueva, M.
　1985 "From Calpixqui to Corregidor: Appropriation of Women's Cotton Textile Production in Early Colonial Mexico." *Latin American Perspectives* 12 (1): 17–40.
Walicki, A.
　1969 *The Controversy over Capitalism.* Oxford: Oxford University Press.
Wallerstein, I.
　1974 *The Modern World System.* New York: Academic Press.
　1983 *Historical Capitalism.* London: Verso Editions.
Warman, A.
　1974 *Los campesinos, hijos predilectos del régimen.* Mexico City: Editorial Nuestro Tiempo.
　1980 *"We Come to Object"; The Peasants of Morelos and the National State.* Baltimore: Johns Hopkins University Press.
Warren, B.
　1980 *Imperialism, Pioneer of Capitalism.* London: New Left Books.
Wassertrom, R.
　1975 "Revolution in Guatemala: Peasants and Politics under the Arbenz Government." *Comparative Studies in Society and History* 17: 443–478.
　1976 "La investigación regional en ciencias sociales: Una perspectiva chiapaneca." *Historia y Sociedad* 9: 58–73.
　1983 *Class and Society in Central Chiapas.* Berkeley and Los Angeles: University of California Press.
Waterbury, R.
　1989 "Embroidery for Tourists." In Schneider and Weiner, eds., 1989: 243–271.
Weber, M.
　1961 *General Economic History.* New York: Collier Books.
Weller, R., and S. Guggenheim, eds.
　1982 *Power and Protest in the Countryside.* Durham, N.C.: Duke University Policy Studies.
White, B.
　1976 "Production and Reproduction in a Javanese Village." Ph.D. dissertation, Columbia University.

1982 "Child Labor and Population Growth in Rural Asia." *Development and Change* 13: 587–610.

White, L.
1959 *The Evolution of Culture.* New York: McGraw-Hill.

Whitecotton, J.
1977 *The Zapotecs.* Norman: University of Oklahoma Press.

Williams, R.
1986 *Export Agriculture and the Crisis in Central America.* Chapel Hill: University of North Carolina Press.

Wolf, E.
1955 "Types of Latin American Peasantry: A Preliminary Discussion." *American Anthropologist* 57: 452–471.

1966 *Peasants.* Englewood Cliffs, N.J.: Prentice-Hall.

1969 *Peasant Wars of the Twentieth Century.* New York: Prentice Hall.

1982 *Europe and the People without History.* Berkeley and Los Angeles: University of California Press.

Worsley, P.
1984 *The Three Worlds.* Chicago: University of Chicago Press.

Wright, G.
1974 *Archaeology and Trade.* Addison-Wesley Module in Anthropology. Reading, Mass.: Addison-Wesley Publishing.

Young, K.
1976 "The Social Setting of Migration: Factors Affecting Migration from a Sierra Zapotec Village in Oaxaca, Mexico." Ph.D. Thesis, University of London.

1978 "Modes of Appropriation and the Sexual Division of Labour: A Case Study from Oaxaca, Mexico." In Kuhn and Wolpe, eds., 1978: 124–154.

Young, K., C. Wolkowitz, and R. McCullagh, eds.
1984 *Of Marriage and the Market.* 2d ed. London: Routledge and Kegan Paul.

Index

cumulation in, 236; and class consciousness, 154; and commoditization, 10–11; contradictory forces in, 20–21; defined, 10; and division of labor, 253 n.7; and domestic work, 271 n.3; and gender consciousness, 154; historical context of, 252–253 n.6; and informal sector, 9; and petty capitalism, 115, 149–151; preconditions for, 254 n.10; relation to merchant capital, 169, 192; rethinking the concept of, 8–11; scale of related to market structures, 187; survival and expansion in Oaxaca Valley, 197–198; and transition to petty capitalism, 236

Piece rate, Piece wage: in brick industry, 137, 142; and disguised exploitation, 24; and economic crises, 224–225; in embroidery industry, 201; and employee status, 111; and ideology among seamstresses, 274 n.17; in Kerela, India brickyards, 273–274 n.14; and labor time accounting in embroidery, 174; measurement of in shawl finishing, 180; and merchant capital, 194; and politics, 230–231; related to skill in embroidery industry, 170–171; and self-exploitation, 230–231; in treadle loom industry, 91, 93, 95, 97–99, 130, 219, 224–225; under capitalism, 270 n.16

Pieceworker(s): in brick making industry, 5, 137, 140–141, 143; factors limiting class consciousness of, 235; politics of, 234–235; potential for upward mobility of, 140–141, 143; in small and medium workshops, 26

Plattner, S., 93, 262–263 nn.12–14

Plaza. See Marketplace

PMS, 218, 233

Political, Politics: movements, demands of, 228; attitudes of petty commodity producers, 227–235; material interests and views of petty commodity producers within capitalism, 227; and political mobilization, 231, 239, 241–242

Popular fronts, 231

Population(s): control, on absence of in study of female labor, 153–154; of embroidery outworkers, 170; of female embroiderers, 172, 206; impact of government policies on inflation-vulnerable sectors, 233; impact of macroeconomic policies on different segments of, 252 n.2; land poor, craft production among, 56; local and regional, demand for crafts among, 60, 187; local and regional, social differentiation among, 109, 219; in Oaxaca City, 37, 137; in Oaxaca Valley, 37–38, 40–41, 213, 234; rapid growth of as cause of *minifundismo*, 43–44; regional, identification of commodity specialization in, 69–72; relative surplus in northern sierra of Oaxaca, 197; of rural communities, 106–107; in rural Mexico, 18, 20, 213; in rural Oaxaca, 21–22, 240, 260 n.1; in Santa Lucía, 141, 149; in Santo Tomás Jalieza, 272 n.7; in Third World, 3, 229, 240, 254 n.10; in Xaagá, 94, 263 n.15

Portes, A., 252 n.4

Poverty: dimensions of, 261–262 n.6; and dual craft participation, 173; in female-headed households, 158–159; in land, 47; and land in backstrap loom weaving industry, 168; obfuscation of concept of, 101; peasant-artisan views of, 175, 232–233; producer explanations for, 145; unevenness of in Oaxaca Valley,

Lightning Source UK Ltd.
Milton Keynes UK
UKOW05f0748180714

235352UK00001B/19/P